AF539302

THE GARDEN AND THE CROSS

THE GARDEN AND THE CROSS
A Materialist Interpretation of the Bible

V. M. Mohanraj

The Garden and the Cross: A Materialist Interpretation of the Bible
V. M. Mohanraj

Second Edition, Revised and Augmented
Aakar Books, 2012

First Published in 2009
by Publish America, Baltimore, USA

Published by
AAKAR BOOKS
28 E Pocket IV, Mayur Vihar Phase I, Delhi 110 091
Phone : 011 2279 5505 Telefax : 011 2279 5641
aakarbooks@gmail.com; www.aakarbooks.com

Printed at
Mudrak, 30 A, Patparganj, Delhi 110 091

DEDICATION

To

My Grandchildren

Orma, Rekil, Twisha, Nilaav and Deeksha

CONTENTS

Acknowledgements

I am indebted to

Kregel Publications, Grand Rapids, to quote from *The Complete Works of Flavius Josephus*, tr. by William Whiston;

Lawrence and Wishart, London, for permission to quote from the book *The Origins of Christianity*;

Leigh Andersen for permission to quote from the *Journal of Biblical Literature*;

Michael McGraw-Herdeg for permission to quote from the translation of the *Annals* of Tacitus;

Simcha Jacobocici and Charles Pellegrino for permission to quote from their book *The Jesus Family Tomb*.

My thanks are due in no small measure to

Thaliyadath Ravindranath, principal engineer, Energy North West, Richland, USA, and for buying some reference books that I badly wanted;

Rashmi Ravindranath, speech language pathologist, Kennewick, USA, for the facilities provided to enable me to research this book;

Nisha Surendra, head of the Department of English, Vibgyor High, Mumbai for patiently going through the typescript, not once but several times and for giving many invaluable suggestions;

Easau Joseph John, who retired as senior lecturer of English, United Nations Institute of Namibia, Lusaka, for clearing several of my doubts;

Nitya Cherian Mathai, Master, The Lawrence School, Lovedale, Ootacamund, India for giving me some valuable resource material;

Prashanth Mohanraj principal scientist, Indian Council of Agricultural Research, for providing me with some valuable literature pertaining to the Bible from his personal library and buying some books that I wanted to refer to;

Orma Ravindranath, a high school sophmore, for her help;

Kathy Criddle and Corrine M. Johnson, librarians, the Kennewick Public Library, Washington, USA, for all the trouble they have taken to get books for me on inter-library loan;

Sandhya Vasanthkumar, librarian, Nilgiri Library, for scanning and e-mailing to me the references I wanted from the Nilgiri Library, Ootacamund, India;

Mondi Murugan, librarian, The Lawrence School, Library, Lovedale, India, for e-mailing to me some references that I asked for from the school library;

Sulu, my late wife, who planted in my mind the seed of the idea of writing this book; I wish she were here today to see that the seed she planted has sprouted and is growing!

I cannot but place on record my deep debt of gratitude to Kaushal Kumar Saxena, Aakar Books, Delhi for taking up the publication of the second edition of this work.

Preface

Seven years ago, in August 2004, I completed writing my previous book, *The Warrior and the Charioteer*[1] - *A Materialist Interpretation of the Bhagavadgita*, which is a Hindu scripture. And I was giving final touches to the typescript when my wife [now deceased] mooted the idea of writing a materialist interpretation of the Bible and suggested that I should follow it up with interpretations of the scriptures of other major religions also from the same perspective. She was quite conversant with the Scripture, as she had had her entire college education in Christian institutions and could recite many verses from memory. I too had read the Bible through and through several times – not less than four or five times at least – but I had not learnt any verse by heart. Although each time I read the book I found something new in it, I never thought of writing a materialist interpretation of it till that day. Anyway, the very same day, I began to research the Bible.

The title, 'The Garden and the Cross,' that I have chosen out of the four or five that I had in mind for this book, is intended to indicate that my interpretation covers the Bible, both the Old and the New Testaments, from the beginning to the end, and the subtitle of the book, 'A Materialist Interpretation of the Bible,' proclaims the perspective. I have to clarify that the 'Garden' in this context denotes the Garden of Eden and not the garden of Gethsemane[2] on the Mount of Olives, which was Jesus' favourite mountain retreat for prayer and from which he was arrested; nor is it Machpelah[3] where Sarah, *et alii* were buried or any other garden mentioned in the Bible as for example that of Uzza in which Manasseh and Amon were buried.[4] The

Apocrypha, a book included in the Catholic Bible, being a controversial document, does not come within the purview of this study.

An interpretation of a scripture from a materialist angle may seem to be a contradiction in terms but it is not illogical or irrational. It is an attempt to analyse the Scripture free from religious constraints. Materialism, no doubt, implies atheism and atheists contradicting the theistic arguments prove quite convincingly that god does not exist. Belief in god is a superstition and is the mother of all superstitions. Being an atheistic philosophy, materialism also rejects the existence of god or a supernatural being and supra-sensory phenomena like miracles. It is a positive philosophy based on science and as such is not dogmatic. A materialist sees god as a concept that man developed out of necessity and sees concepts or ideas as actual or distorted reflections of the external world in the mind of man. We shall discuss this in detail in Chapter 2, 'The Universe and God.'

The adjective "materialist" in the subtitle thus denotes that in interpreting the scripture, I have totally discounted supernaturalism and god is treated as one of the biblical characters, not an individual but a type as for example the landlord, the messenger (prophet) or an army and in certain cases as a symbol, depending on the context. Inasmuch as god is not the name of a person, it is not a proper noun but a common noun and hence it is written with a lowercase "g" (god). The uppercase "G" for the word is used only in quotes. There are several episodes described in the book under study, like the miracles which Moses, Elisha, Jesus and other protagonists are believed to have performed, that are manifestly irrational and inconsistent with science and materialism. All such stories are meant to attribute supernatural powers to and mythicise the characters concerned. This is a technique resorted to in the scriptures of all religions in order to create an aura of supernaturalism around those characters to mystify the believers who would then look upon them with awe and reverence. That would help keep their faith intact. The Bible being a scripture, this is a necessary technique used by the authors in order to keep up or bolster the faith of the faithful.

The readers may expect the interpreter to take up each verse in the Scripture and elucidate it. But it must be understood that an interpretation is not a paraphrase. A paraphraser expresses the meaning of every verse in the scripture in simpler terms in order to help the reader understand the apparent meaning of the verses in the scripture. An interpreter, on the other hand, looks beyond what is evident and tries to read between the lines for which he does not have to elucidate every verse in the Bible. The reader will find that I have skipped over not just a few sentences and verses but even some chapters and books and have picked out only those verses that are absolutely essential to bring home to the readers the hidden meanings as I see them from a materialist angle. So instead of merely expressing the passages in simpler terms as a paraphraser does, I have placed them against the then socio-economic background and taking the context into cognizance, brought to the notice of the reader what I think is implied therein.

I think it is imperative that I explain the methodology of materialist interpretation. Let me take four typical examples, which will show how I have interpreted them materialistically. I am choosing two from Exodus, one from I Kings and another from II Chronicles. The two from Exodus are the dialogue between god and Moses in which god persuades Moses to go to Egypt to liberate the Hebrews and one of the miracles that god wanted Moses to perform to pressure the Pharaoh to permit the Hebrews to leave Egypt. From I Kings, I have selected the courtiers telling the king of Syria that the Hebrew gods are gods of the hills and hence they prove superior in a war that is waged on the hills. The one from II Chronicles is about god inflicting leprosy on Azariah and his confinement. In the text, the relevant quotes are given in the footnote, but here I shall give the quote before the interpretation to make it convenient for the readers to connect the interpretation with the relevant biblical verse.

Being a materialist interpretation, the idea of "God" conversing with Moses and miracles, the "God of the mountains" helping the Hebrews or "the Lord" making Azariah (Uzziah) a leper are not acceptable because as already stated, materialism is fundamentally an atheistic philosophy rooted in science. A materialist, therefore, is not simply incredulous about but rejects the possibility of such supersensory or extrasensory phenomena.

The "dialogue" between god and Moses during which god urged Moses to go to Egypt and bring his tribe out of the country is interpreted as Moses debating in his mind, how he could help his tribe liberate itself. ***(i) "Come now, therefore, and I shall send you to the Pharaoh, that you may liberate the children of Israel."*** [5] ***(ii) "And Moses said to God, Who am I, that I should go to the Pharaoh, and that I should liberate the children of Israel from Egypt?"*** [6] This is interpreted thus: "Ever since he heard of the death of the Pharaoh who wanted to kill him, Moses had been toying with the idea of going back to Egypt and confronting the new Pharaoh. He wanted to ask the Pharaoh to let him take the enslaved Hebrews out of Egypt. But he asked himself what right or authority he, an insignificant person, had, to do that." (See Chapter 4.)

All "miracles" that Moses and Aaron performed to force the Pharaoh to permit the Hebrews to leave Egypt are explained as the Hebrews' struggle for freedom that turned violent. It is said, ***"Moses stretched forth his rod...and the Lord sent thunder and hail and the fire spread all over the land. And the Lord rained hail on the land of Egypt."*** [7] This is interpreted as follows: "At last, Moses and Aaron brought out swords and spears that they had secretly collected and kept hidden in a cache and distributed to the partisans of freedom. Armed with those weapons, they fought desperately inflicting heavy casualties on the Pharaoh's army and also attacked the Egyptian people at large." (See Chapter 4.)

Similarly, in I Kings, we read: ***"And the servants of the king of Syria said unto him, Their gods are gods of the hills; therefore they are stronger than we, but let us fight against them in the plain, and surely we shall be stronger than they."*** [8] Materialistically interpreting, this would mean "Benhadad chose to draw the Hebrews down to the plains because his strategists advised him to do so. They thought that the Israelite army was good at mountain warfare ["Their gods are gods of the hill"] but it would be at a disadvantage in the plains, where the Syrian soldiers were better trained to fight." (See Chapter 7.)

It is said in II Chronicles, Azariah (Uzziah) the king of Judah was triumphant in two or three wars against the neighbouring kingdoms, which made him proud and he "transgressed against the Lord his God" by burning incense upon the altar, a rite that only priests were entitled to perform. So god punished him by inflicting him with leprosy. ***"...Uzziah the king was a leper until the day of his death and he dwelt in an isolated house because he was a leper...and Jotham the***

king's son was in the palace, judging the people of the land."[9] Leaving aside god, which is a concept not consistent with materialist thought, this verse states that as the king is afflicted with leprosy, his son Jotham succeeds him smoothly and the deposed king is confined in an isolated house. All this suggests a political dimension to the whole episode. It was, so to say, a palace revolution. Hence it is interpreted as follows: "So the Chauvinists[10] conspired with his son, Jotham, who with the tacit support of the Chauvinists deposed his father, Azariah, and placing him under house arrest, acted as regent. Azariah was completely isolated as they would a leper in those days,[11] for no one was allowed to meet him, nor was he allowed to meet anyone. Jotham must have got intelligence that the Liberals were conspiring to liberate Azariah and restore him to the throne. He, therefore, took care to keep his father all alone in a house in a secluded area, incommunicado and no one except a few of his trusted officials knew where exactly he was imprisoned. So the Liberals were not able to contact him. They could not, therefore, rescue him from confinement and unleash a rebellion against Jotham by projecting him as the legitimate king." (See Chapter 7)

I cannot but take note of the presence of a large section of society – the slaves – that surprisingly no commentator appears to notice. We come across several slaves in the Bible, which reveals the developmental stage of the biblical society. But biblical scholars have ignored them because all those commentators look at biblical characters divorced from the society. Most of those commentaries focus on theology, and even those that deal with the secular aspects describe the exploits of kings turning a blind eye to the slaves constituting a large section of the population. Although the slaves do not come into focus in the Bible, the Hebrew society from the period of Abraham to that of Jesus as we shall see was based on slavery. The slaves were naturally suppressed and the rhapsodists who composed the biblical episodes were all freemen and slave owners, who considered the slaves an insignificant segment of society that did not have any role in the unfolding events described in the Bible.

In the extant works of the historians of the Hellenistic and Roman periods, for example, we find little information on the Helot rebellion of the seventh century BCE and the Spartacist uprising under the leadership of Spartacus against the Roman Empire in the second century BCE respectively.[12] Those historians were slave owners and noblemen and in their eyes slaves were of little consequence and their struggles did not deserve to be chronicled. Later historians of all countries also glossed over the liberation struggles of the slaves of their times. In fact, there had been many slave rebellions in all countries, both in the Old and the New Worlds that practised slavery almost till the end of the nineteenth century. But contemporary historians who were all from the upper strata of society busied themselves in recording the activities of the ruling class and did not consider the insurgencies of slaves important enough to be taken note of. Seldom do we find, for example, even a passing reference to, let alone a detailed account of, the New York Slave Rebellion of 1741 or the Black Seminole Slave Rebellion of the 1830s in any of the books written by reputed historians of the period. It is true that those slave insurgencies did not bring about any immediate changes in the society. However as conflict of interest of the slaves and slave owners intensified thanks to the changes in the productive forces of the society, the resolution of social dimorphism became a historical necessity. This did have an effect on the social consciousness or the attitude of the slave owners towards the slaves, thus creating a public opinion against the slave system. And so in course of time the governments concerned were forced to yield to the necessity by enacting laws abolishing slavery.

In the Bible we see only passing references to slaves. In the English version of the Bible the word "slave" appears only in two places, in the Book of the Prophet Jeremiah[13] and the Revelation of St. John the Divine.[14] In all other verses, in which the Hebrew and Greek versions use the words equivalent to "slave" in those languages, the words used in the English translation (KJV) are "servant," "bond servant," "hired servant" or "handmaid" instead, as for example, Hagar who was a slave is referred to as "handmaid." And the word "slavery" is not found at all. That the word "servant" is used to denote "slave" is clear when the Mosaic Law states, "If you buy a Hebrew servant..."[15] It is only slaves that are bought and not servants; servants are hired.

In the Revelation, slaves are clubbed with beasts, sheep, horses and chariots, after which the composer speaks of "souls of men" as if slaves do not fall in the category of souls of men! Some of the revised editions of the King James Version (KJV) have even replaced the word "slaves" with the word "bodies" in the Revelation! The word "body" is generally used to denote the "dead body" of a person and it is beyond one's comprehension why the word "slaves" is substituted by "bodies." Probably, it is a metaphorical way of saying that the slaves, though living, are as good as dead. If the editors have really meant it so, it is commendable but I don't think that was the intention of the editors. When the KJV was being brought out, slavery had become anathema to mankind and the editors were trying to cover up a historical fact.

As I said above, no sooner had I completed the book on the Bhagavadgita, than I began research for this project. When I say I had been researching, it does not mean that I was trying to unearth some information hitherto unknown to biblical scholars. I must, therefore, warn the readers not to expect me to throw some new light on controversial matters like the authorship of the Pentateuch and the historicity of Exodus. But I dare say, my approach is unique and I have not read any commentary of the Bible written from this viewpoint – I mean from a materialist angle. Well, my research has been confined to perusing as many as required, the documents, books and journals that have a bearing on the history of the biblical period and that of the Scripture itself. I wanted to get a wider and clearer picture than what I already had of the backdrop against which the biblical episodes are set as well as the sources of the episodes. I also wanted to find out about the composers and the hands that culled their compositions to bring forth this magnificent Book of Books, as the Bible is otherwise called.

Apart from the collateral literature, including the Qur'an that has drawn profusely from the Bible, I read several commentaries on it. I know there are hundreds of commentaries on the Book of Books, totally and severally. But all those that I could lay my hands on are written from a theistic or theological point of view catering to the faithful with the specific objective of reinforcing their faith. Naturally, the scholars who authored the commentaries seem to be wary of deviating from the beaten track or questioning the traditional interpretation. It is understandable that none of those authors who are Judaists or Christians attempted to break out of the religious barriers. They have discreetly avoided analysing the myths and episodes in the Bible with a critical eye, lest they invite the wrath of the priesthood and social ostracisation. There are also paraphrases, guides and annotated editions of the Bible. Besides, several dictionaries, encyclopedias and concordances are at hand and those have been of immense help to me as ready references. I did find a few commentaries by rationalists and atheists but they were not of any help to me because my approach, which is materialistic, is basically different from theirs; similarities, if any, are little.

Being a materialist, I am not constrained by hermeneutics, which in simple terms, is the science of interpretation of the Bible – to be precise, the branch of theology dealing with the principles of Scriptural interpretation. As a methodology, therefore, hermeneutics demands strict adherence to certain theological principles and rigid rules. This implies that the interpretation is necessarily and firmly anchored in theology, which is inevitably bereft of human touch. But this is an attempt to interpret the Bible from a non-theological standpoint, focusing on the human face of the Scripture.

A scripture is usually believed to be the word of god or god's disclosure of himself and it is infallible and unalterable. The more I pondered on the Bible the more I felt that the Bible was not just a scripture and that it was not the revelation of some non-existent god. No doubt, it is a revelation, but not that of god. The Bible symbolically reveals the prehistory of mankind. It also reveals a broad but blurred picture, exaggerated in certain areas, distorted in others and not always veracious, of the protohistory of the West Asian tribes, particularly the Hebrews. Nevertheless, the history of the kingdoms and empires that were contemporaneous with those tribes is to a great extent presented accurately. The Bible thus stands revealed as a human document rather than the word of an imaginary supernatural being, making it more comprehensible and interesting to the readers whatever be the religions they espouse.

Nevertheless, the Bible is not a book of history. Most commentators of the Bible who look at the episodes and characters in the book through religious spectacles consider almost all the protagonists in the Bible historical personalities and treat the Bible as a reliable source book on the ancient history of the Hebrews. No doubt, it has all the trappings of a chronicle of the events of those times and apparently reads like a series of historical episodes, but most of these are of doubtful authenticity. There is no gainsaying the fact that the myths and allegories with which the Bible (Old Testament) abounds are blended with a dash of history, but the early part of the Old Testament is pure mythology, presenting as stated above, the prehistory of mankind symbolically.

I have interpreted the biblical episodes without taking into cognizance the historical veracity of either the episodes or the protagonists, except pointing out a few anachronisms. The patriarchs and several other protagonists including Moses and Joshua are mythological characters, and in the absence of any external evidence of their historicity I have dealt with them as fictitious and fictional characters only. But Jesus, and characters like Pontius Pilate as well as some kings and emperors that we meet in the Bible, are indubitably historical personalities. On the problem of the historicity of Jesus, I am inclined to accept the view of Archibald Robertson, a distinguished rationalist, progressive thinker and scholar. He says 'the origins of Christianity may have been mainly mythical, and yet there may have been a real Jesus who contributed certain features to the final form of the myth.' In other words, there could have been a historical Jesus and in dealing with this problem, I have leaned heavily on his famous book, *The Origins of Christianity*, the early chapters of which were critically perused by progressive thinkers like Gordon Childe, Maurice Cornforth, Christopher Hill, Jack Lindsay, et al.

I have dealt with the problem of the historicity of Jesus separately in Chapter 9, "The Son of Man." The readers may wonder why I have given this special treatment to Jesus. This is because in the minds of the people at large, the Bible is synonymous with Jesus; he towers over all the other characters, fictitious and historical, in the book. There is another reason too; a personal one. Let me quote what I said in the Preface of my previous publication mentioned above. "My parents, who were devout Hindus, had in their prayer room, along with the pictures of Hindu gods, a picture of Jesus Christ and they had as much faith in Christ as they had in Krishna." I think this had a profound effect on me. But I do not look upon Jesus as a god; I consider him a human being – a great revolutionary leader who roused the Jews to fight for their liberation from Roman imperialism.

In the process of investigating his historicity, I could not but deal with the historicity of Apostles Thomas and Peter. The historicity of Jesus and that of his twelve Apostles are inter-linked. Had Jesus not existed and led a religio-political movement, there would have been no Apostles. Hence, conversely, if the Apostles were historical individuals, Jesus too must have been a historical figure. It is, no doubt, an indirect way of proving Jesus' historicity, but it is a proof that helps corroborate the abundant literary evidence about the historical Jesus. The archaeological finds that testify his historicity are yet to be accepted by the Church, Catholic as well as Protestant. However, I shall discuss it when dealing with Jesus' historicity, for those archaeological evidence cannot be simply brushed aside.

A discussion of the historicity of all the twelve Apostles would have needed not one or two paragraphs or even a chapter but a whole volume. I, therefore, decided to take only two of them, Thomas and Peter, as examples and deal with them briefly in a couple of paragraphs. There is a reason for choosing these two Apostles as examples. I hail from Kerala (India), where it is believed Christianity was introduced by Apostle Thomas in the middle of the first century CE. Besides, I have seen some of the sites connected with the story of his life in Kerala as well as what is said to be his tomb at Mylapore in Chennai (formerly Madras). As far as Peter is concerned, he was the only Apostle who had the courage to follow Jesus to the high priest's court, though he disowned Jesus, saying "I don't know that man" when a girl pointing at him said, "This fellow also was with Jesus of Nazareth."[16] And in discussing the paternity of Jesus, I have drawn on the Infancy Gospel of James, also called the Protoevangelion, which is an apocryphal work of the second century CE. This work is not a part of the King James Version; nor is it a part of the Catholic Bible. I have, however, given a materialistic interpretation to those episodes that I have referred to, to substantiate my arguments, and putting two and two together, I have tried to deduce the secret of Jesus' paternity.

It is not an exaggeration to say that there are myriads of characters in the Bible, but I have not delved into the historicity of any of the other characters. I must warn the readers that when I narrate the episodes in the Bible it should not be misunderstood that I regard as historical figures all the characters that I deal with because it may seem to be so. I am aware that the Bible is not a true chronicle of events of the biblical period; if anything, it is a concoction of symbols, myths, legends, sagas and allegories blended with a little history. However, whether these biblical characters are symbolic, mythical, fictional or historical, it would not make any difference to my interpretation of the events connected with them as presented in the Scripture because I treat the Bible as a work of literature par excellence. As such I have interpreted the Bible primarily to unravel the social developments of the biblical period as seen through the characters, fictional and historical, in a literary work like this. It is, for example, just as Ralph Fox looks at the development of English society of the Victorian era in the trilogies of John Galsworthy which I have referred to in Chapter 1, "The Book of Books." It does not mean Ralph Fox regarded the characters in those novels as historical personalities. As he rightly points out, the characters in realistic fiction "are all types, but they are types in whom the social characteristics constantly reveal the individual ... (who) in turn light up the social background."[17] That is exactly what we find in all the fictional and historical characters like Adam, Abraham, Moses, John the Baptist, Jesus and a host of others that we meet in the Bible.

I remember to have read somewhere that Shakespeare would not have dreamt of all that Bradley had attributed to the dramatist in his critical work, *Shakespearean Tragedy*. Maybe it is true; rather it must be true, for it is true of critical writings of all literary works. It must be understood that a critic finds in the works of a poet, a playwright or a novelist ideas that the writer had not intended but expressed or implied unconsciously. It is left to the critic, interpreter or commentator to bring it to the notice of the readers; otherwise it is not a critique, interpretation or commentary but merely a paraphrase. The scriptures also are no exceptions; and needless to say, being a scripture, the Bible too is no exception. In the final analysis the Bible is also a literary work with a theological thrust. I am sure, the composers would not have dreamt of, even in their wildest of dreams, for example the interpretation I have given to the story of Adam and Eve. Or, when the bard composed, for example, the story of the forbidden fruit, he would, most probably have thought how a preacher, a theist or a theologist, would interpret it but certainly not how a Freudian psychologist, a structuralist or a materialist would interpret it. The bards, who composed the various stories constituting the Bible, narrated what they had heard or/and seen, flavoured with their imagination, and probably the scribes who put them in black and white added some more spice to them.

I have devoted the first chapter to introduce the reader to the book called the Bible. There may be many who have read it or who regard it as scripture but would not have cared to think of what kind of a book it is, who wrote it or when it was written. Those who regard it as scripture would naturally consider it 'word of god' and would not attribute its authorship to a human being. Of course, I have only very briefly dealt with these issues. I have also drawn attention to the controversy regarding the authorship of the Bible and the reactions of the priesthood of the two religions, Judaism and Christianity, to scholarly attempts at probing those particulars.

Chapter 2, "The Universe and God," has been necessitated by the biblical theory of creation presented in the first and second chapters of the book of Genesis, which is the first book of the Pentateuch in the Old Testament. I recognise the fact that the biblical myth of creation, like the myths of creation that are found in practically the scriptures of all religions and mythologies, has an important place in the history of human thought. God is the pivot on which all those creation myths revolve and so it became necessary to deal with the concept of god in detail, which inevitably led to brief discussions on topics like magic, religion and mythology that stem from it. Similarly, I have been constrained to go briefly into the scientific theories of the origin of the universe, the Earth and the evolution of man. I know it does seem out of place in a book that purports to interpret a scripture, but I have purposely dealt with the scientific theories as a touchstone for the readers to judge the tenability of the biblical theory and to provoke the readers to ponder. Ergo, the readers will please bear with me when I outline the relevant scientific theories.

In Chapter 3, "A Virtual Tower of Babel," I have introduced to the readers the various tribes that we see in the Bible. However, I have dealt with the Hebrew tribes in great detail but have devoted only a paragraph or two for each of the other tribes. There is a justification for it. As I have mentioned in Chapter 1, "The Book of Books," the

Bible is a book dealing primarily with the Hebrew tribes (later called Israel[18] and now known as the Jews). All the other tribes come into the picture only when they cross the path of the Hebrews. The Old Testament, which is primarily about the Hebrews, presents a mythologised version of their social and political developments, their civil and criminal laws, their ethics as well as their religion and rituals. The laws that Moses is believed to have proclaimed and codified as the Torah (also known as the Mosaic Law) became the laws of the Hebrews ever since. Although we meet several other tribes that had often clashed with the Hebrews, the Bible does not give any detailed information about them. We only know that they were either barbaric or civilised tribes. The few tribes, of which we get only a glimpse in the Bible and some others the impact of which was minimal on the history of the Hebrews as revealed in the Bible, have not found a place in the chapter and that I think does not call for an explanation.

A critical stage in the social evolution of the Hebrew tribes is dealt with in the next chapter, "Consolidation of Slavery." The subsequent four chapters are interpretations (an example of which is given above) of the biblical version of the history of the region, which the biblical scholars classify as "historical books." In interpreting these books, I have stripped the episodes of the supernaturalism in which they are cloaked and exposed the earthly core, viewing them strictly through a secular lens as the example given above shows. I have not found it necessary to go into the doctrinal and prophetic books of both the Old and the New Testaments, for the purpose of this study is not to analyse the doctrinal theories of the Bible.

A few readers may, perhaps, take exception to my total reliance on the theories of Lewis Henry Morgan, the celebrated American anthropologist of the nineteenth century, in relation to the evolution of society and family. It is true, not all anthropologists have accepted his theory. Apart from Morgan, several anthropologists have put forward their own theories about primitive society and its culture but none of the theories has found favour with all anthropologists. In fact, no anthropologist's theory of pre-civilisation society has found universal acceptance. It is understandable because anthropological studies are, to a great extent, based on deduction and imagination and so the conclusions of each person from what he or she has observed, could be different. Seldom do the conclusions reached by two persons or a group of persons from the same set of premises concur. In the case of anthropology, the situation is worse because the premises themselves are quite inadequate. Even those anthropologists like Morgan, Malinovsky, et al. who lived with and observed the aborigines would not have got the correct idea of the social life and culture, for example, of the Palaeolithic ancestors of those tribes. The impact of the civilised society must have changed the physiognomy of those tribes considerably and so what they saw would have been a pale reflection of their primitive ancestors.

Morgan, an evolutionary anthropologist, had undertaken his study in the early nineteenth century when the tribes would not have been corrupted as much as it is in the twentieth century, although even at that time they would not have retained their pristine purity in all its details. Nevertheless, Morgan had seen exemplifications of those indigenous peoples that he studied in a much less corrupt form than any tribes that anthropologists of the twentieth century had seen unless the tribes had remained ferociously hostile like, perhaps, the Sentinelese of the Andaman and Nicobar Islands. There are several schools of anthropology—evolutionary, functionalist, structuralist and postmodernist, et cetera. Of all these, I am inclined to accept Morgan's evolutionary approach which, I think, is the one that is most compatible with materialist philosophy. That is my justification for leaning totally on his monumental work, *Ancient Society* first published in 1877.

That the Bible can be interpreted in many ways is implicit in the words of Paul when he says, "Be diligent to show yourself approved to God, a workman who does not need to be ashamed rightly dividing the word of truth." And he hastens to add, "But shun profane and idle babblings for they will increase to more ungodliness."[19] It is true, the Bible can be viewed from various angles like sociological, literary, structuralist and materialist, some of which may or may not seem sacrilegious or blasphemous. For a religious fanatic who is intolerant of a different point of view, however, this interpretation may seem sacrilegious or blasphemous and vilifying as it were, all that the Abrahamic religions hold sacrosanct. Nonetheless, I wish the readers, especially those who profess those religions, would go through this book with an open mind, without any preconceived notions or prejudices. The reader has the liberty to accept or reject my views.

I do not espouse any religion but let me stress I am not anti-religion. I respect all religions. I am of the view that religion had doubtless served a purpose (like preventing counter-revolution) long back in biblical times as you will see in Chapter 4, "Consolidation of Slavery" but now it has absolutely lost its relevance. In fact, it has been the cause for not only blatant human rights violations but also bloodbaths since mediaeval times and has been the bane of mankind ever since. I believe religion and god are purely personal matters to be confined to one's heart or places of worship. They pose a danger to humanity when they are brought out of them and when religious identities of persons are mixed with their political or/and national identities. All I ask for is to give me also as much liberty to express my views as the theists have – not more, nor less. I agree with what Tom Paine said in his book, *Age of Reason*: "You will do me the justice to remember, that I have always strenuously supported the right of every man to his opinion, however different that opinion might be to mine." It is not consistent with democratic principles to restrict the freedom of thought and expression, for such intolerance of dissent nurtures authoritarianism, which in the realm of religion takes the diabolic form of religious fundamentalism.

Be that as it may, this interpretation of the Bible is mainly based on the King James Version of the Protestant Bible, comprising the Old and the New Testaments, although I have drawn from the Apocrypha a little historical information that was not in the Protestant Bible. Hence, wherever in this book I say "the Bible," please remember that I am referring to the Protestant Bible (KJV). All quotes from the Scripture given in this book are from the KJV or New KJV, as far as possible avoiding archaic expressions, like "thee," "unto," "killeth," which modern readers may not relish.

Note: The first edition was sold out in about a year and the continuing demand for the book has compelled me to bring out the second edition. I did not find the need to write a separate preface to this edition of the book, an exercise that most authors feel constrained to do for the second edition. However, I want to say this is not just a reprint of the first edition. I have revised the earlier edition clarifying some points in response to the feedbacks

I got from the readers and to be in conformity with it, I have revised the preface to the first edition, as given above.

NOTES

1. Published by LeftWord Books, New Delhi, 2005.
2. Mt.26:36; Jn.18:1, 2. [Mt.26:36 "Then cometh Jesus with them to a place called Gethsamane..." Mt.26:36]
3. Gen.23:19/25:8-9/49:31/50:13. ["...Abraham buried Sarah his wife in the cave of the field of Machpelah... Gen.23:19]
4. II Kgs.21:18, 26. ["...Manasseh slept...and was buried...in the garden of Uzza..." II Kgs.21:18]
5. Ex.3:10.
6. Ex.3:11.
7. Ex.3:11.
8. I Kgs.20:23.
9. II Chr.26:21.
10. The Chauvinists comprised the affluent and the Hebrew upper middle class religio-purist freemen, led by the clergy. The lower middle class freemen, both of the Hebrews and non-Hebrews as well as those of mixed blood, and the workers, excluding slaves, constituted the Liberals.
11. Lev.13:2-59.
12. The Helots were enslaved serfs or state slaves of Sparta. They were owned not by individuals but by the state. The Spartacists were slaves and were so called because a gladiator by name Spartacus led their rebellion which ended with the defeat of the insurgents in the Third Servile War.
13. Jer.2:14
14. Rev. 18:13
15. Ex. 21:2
16. Mt.26:71-72
17. R. Fox, *The Novel and the People*, Moscow, 1956, p.66.
18. Israel in the Bible refers to an individual, the son of Isaac; his descendants, the twelve tribes of the Hebrews; the ten northern tribes led by Ephraim. Today it is the name of a country carved out of Palestine in November 1947.
19. II Tim. 2:15-16.

Part One
PROLOGUE

1

The Book of Books

There are different versions of the Bible. The King James Version of the Protestant Bible, on which this interpretation is based, is a garland of sixty-six books – thirty-nine books of the Old Testament and twenty-seven books of the New Testament. The New Testament, comprising twenty-seven books as can be seen, is much shorter than – to be precise, in terms of its size (not the number of books), less than one third of – the Old Testament. The Roman Catholic version of the Bible has seven books in addition and if these too are taken into account, the Bible would contain seventy-three books. The Bible, therefore, gets the sobriquet the Book of Books. These books are not independent of one another; nor are they sequels or volumes. Although the Bible consists of sixty-six (in the case of the Roman Catholic Bible, seventy-three) books, it must be treated as a single-volume book. In this respect alone, the Bible is comparable to the famous Sanskrit epic, the Mahabharata,[1] which is also a chain of eighteen books called *parvas*, strung together to make a tome of a hundred thousand *slokas* or iambic verses of four lines each.

There is a common thread running through each of these books, and it is this peculiar continuity of the content that makes them single-volume books. In the Bible, Jesus, the central character of the New Testament, is believed to be the sixtieth descendant of the fictitious character of Adam[2] that we meet first in the Bible. Jesus, who is said to have flourished during the apparently halcyon days of *Pax Romana*, is considered the sixtieth descendant of this fictitious character and his historicity is neither authenticated incontrovertibly nor denied totally. Hence, Jesus cannot be regarded as a fictitious character and his historicity deserves to be investigated further, which we shall do briefly in Chapter 9, "The Son of Man."

The Bible is associated with three religions – Judaism, Christianity and Islam. The Bible sans the New Testament – that is, the Old Testament – is the Judaist scripture, while both the Old and the New Testaments together constitute the scripture of Christianity. Although Islam does not consider the Bible on a par with the Qur'an, it enjoins Muslims to regard the Bible as the scripture that Allah had sent to the prophets who preceded Muhammad. The Qur'an says, "O you who believe! Believe in Allah, and His Messenger (Muhammad), and the Book (the Qur'an) which He has sent down to His Messenger, and *the Scripture which He sent down to those before (him)*; and whosoever disbelieves in Allah, His Angels, His Books, His Messengers, and the Last Day, then indeed he has strayed far away."[3] Those predecessors of Muhammad are the biblical prophets like Abraham, Moses, Elijah, Ezra, Jesus and others who appear in the Qur'an in the Arabic forms of their names Ibrahim, Musa, Ilyas, Uzyr and Isa respectively. The Qur'an calls upon the Muslims to believe in "His Books," one of which is the "scripture that He sent down to those before him" and that is the Bible. If we look at the scriptures as literary works, it may not be wrong to say that in the eyes of the Muslims, the Bible is a prequel as it were, to the Qur'an. So interestingly, the Bible is a unique book, because three religions, Judaism, Christianity and Islam, consider it holy while the first two of them as well as their breakaway groups revere it as scripture.

The word "bible" is derived from the Greek word *biblia*, meaning "book," but has been used in English to denote a particular book, and the word is written with the capital letter *B* (Bible). That book is what is today referred to as *The Holy Bible*. It is holy because it is regarded as a scripture, by which it is meant that it is the revelation of god or "God's disclosures of himself and of his will to his creations" and being so, it is the word of god, which as such is sacred, infallible and unalterable. However, Matthew Arnold rightly says that "to understand that the language of the Bible is fluid, passing, and literary, not rigid, fixed and scientific is the first step towards a right understanding of the Bible."[4] When he says that the language is not rigid and fixed but fluid, he implies that it is not a dogmatic document and so not infallible or unalterable. And for the "right understanding" of the Bible, it is imperative that the related circumstances are taken into consideration. In other words, the Bible must be viewed against the background of the period in which the episodes constituting the Scripture were composed.

The Bible, deemed a scripture, is a mélange as it were, of sociology and history, law and ethics, religion and philosophy, biography and essays, theology and apothegms, sermons and hymns, architecture and dietetics,[5] besides myths, legends, stories, essays, songs, drama[6] and poetry. In these we espy the Hebrews and their contemporary tribes as well as the various classes of people like the oppressed slaves and the rich freemen, the autocratic kings and the priests – why, even the prostitutes of the distant past. As such, the Bible throws light, quite dim and dispersed though, on the prehistory of mankind in general and the proto-history of the Hebrews in particular, giving a close-up of their economic, political, social, and cultural life in biblical times. In the process, it gives a peep-hole view of the peoples and empires that the Hebrews came in contact or crossed swords with during that period.

The earliest extant manuscripts of the Bible were two small strips of silver scrolls, about 7.5 cm (3 inches) and 5 cm (2 inches) long respectively, on which were inscribed three verses from Numbers,[7] which is the fourth book of the Pentateuch, and a few verses from the other books of the Pentateuch. Judging by the Hebrew script used on them, these had been dated back to the seventh century BCE. These silver strips were recovered from a tomb by archaeologists in 1979 while excavating near Jerusalem. Its importance lies in the fact that this is the first archaeological find to have been unearthed with the inscription of the name of the Hebrew God, YHWH (Yahweh or Jehovah). A more exciting discovery of leather and parchment scrolls, however, was made in 1947 – interestingly, not by archaeologists but by shepherds! It was exciting because those were the oldest manuscripts of the Bible discovered till then and it was the first time that an archaeological discovery that proved the authenticity of the biblical text had been made, notwithstanding the minor variations found therein.

These are popularly known as the Dead Sea Scrolls because they were retrieved from caves located near the ancient ruins of Wadi Qumran, on the West Bank of the Dead Sea. A substantial part of these scrolls dating from *circa* 250 BCE to about 68 CE contains biblical text, the oldest record of the Hebrew Bible (Old Testament) written in Greek, Hebrew and Aramaic scripts. Among these finds, there was a copper scroll that some scholars believe is a map showing the spot of a hidden treasure. These scrolls had been kept in the Palestinian Archaeological Museum since their discovery and were not allowed to be taken out of the museum precincts, lest they got lost. In fact, no one except a few select scholars were allowed to even see them until 1991when for the first time photographs of these scrolls and a book, *A Preliminary Edition of the Unpublished Dead Sea Scrolls*, were brought out. Since then many books and articles have been published describing the story of the discovery of the scrolls as well as interpreting and analysing them. Recently, however, in cooperation with Israel Antiquities Authority and The Dead Sea Scrolls Foundation, ten of those scrolls, of which four scrolls had never before been seen by the public, had been taken round the Western world and exhibited in several cities.[8]

The Dead Sea Scrolls were chanced upon by three shepherds, Jum'a Muhammad Khalil and his two cousins, Khalil Musa and Muhammad Ahmed el-Hameed, of the Bedouin tribe, the Ta'Amireh. It was in the winter of 1946, while tending his sheep and goats, that Jum'a happened to notice a few crevices in a rock face which aroused his curiosity. On closer examination, he and his companions found, those were openings to caves. The next day, the three of them explored one of the caves and found two mud jars tightly sealed at the mouth in the midst of a few empty ones, carefully deposited in the cave. They hurried out of the cave carrying the two sealed mud jars, perhaps thinking that those jars contained some valuable treasure. They broke open the jars only to be disappointed, for instead of the treasure that they had expected they saw one leather scroll and two parchment scrolls in one of those jars. Not realising the value of these finds, they carelessly threw away a few of the scrolls which were damaged and took with them those that were in a fairly good condition. They tried to sell them to antique dealers but none of them thought it worthwhile to invest upon.

A friend of these Bedouins, however, took these scrolls to someone in the Syrian Orthodox Church, who, thinking that the language was Syriac, promised to get it examined. The then Archbishop of the Church, on examination, believing them to be authentic, decided to purchase them. It was a wise decision because when they were later deciphered, they were found to be the *Isaiah Scroll*, the *Commentary on Habakkuk* and the *Manual of Discipline*. Assured of the sale, the Bedouins went back to the caves, collected the damaged ones that they had thrown away the previous day and retrieved four more scrolls, which they sold to an antique dealer. Eventually, Eleazer Sukenik, an archaeologist of the Hebrew University, happened to see these scrolls and bought two of them, the *War Scroll* and the *Thanksgiving Hymns*.

The news of these discoveries thrilled archaeologists and biblical scholars; and many of them made a beeline to those caves hoping to find more of such scrolls. As a result of their painstaking search, eleven caves were discovered in the area in 1949 and many fragments of scrolls and other artefacts recovered from those caves. To be precise, they retrieved from those caves six hundred tiny scraps of leather and papyrus containing Hebrew transcriptions from the books of Genesis, Deuteronomy and the Book of Judges. Besides these, the Book of Isaiah in its entirety and parts of all other books, except that of Esther, were also found in the scrolls. However, a little less than one-third of the scrolls only contain biblical texts; the rest of the scrolls are manuscripts of commentaries on the texts and the ethics of the period that throw light on the thought and life of the Hebrew community of those times. Although not directly connected with the Bible, it is believed that these commentaries too were then considered part of the Bible and regarded as sacred texts. Among these, there was a manuscript called *Pseudo-Ezekiel Scroll*, which is a copy of a previously unknown composition, in which is given a non-biblical vision of future events in Egypt relating to the Hebrew tribes as revealed to prophet Ezekiel.

A few scholars claimed to have found some connection between those scrolls and Christianity, one of whom, for example, suggesting that these documents proved Christianity must have originated as a fertility cult. Meanwhile another scholar asserted that he described some of the verses of Mark, The Acts, Romans, James and Peter in the scrolls. No other biblical scholar agreed with either of these observations; nor did the Catholic Church. In fact, most scholars were of the view that there was no mention of, not even a passing reference to Christianity or Jesus in any of those scrolls.

However, the carbon test had confirmed beyond doubt that the scribes wrote down those compositions that had come down to them by word of mouth through generations, during the time of Jesus. Yet there was no mention of Jesus in any of those scrolls. That prompted some scholars to raise doubts about the historicity of Jesus. Had Jesus been alive when the scrolls were produced, they said there should have been derogatory, if not objurgatory – or at least some sarcastic – comments about Jesus, whom the Judaist priesthood had feared and hated and whom the priesthood had been plotting to capture and kill.

That nothing is mentioned about Jesus in these scrolls is, however, explicable. These verses, as we know, had been composed by rhapsodists long ago, when Jesus was not even born. The scribes must have merely put in black and white the verses that had come down to them orally, the authorship of which remains and will continue to remain shrouded in mystery. They did not, perhaps, want to interpolate and mar the poetic beauty of the verses or being devout Yahwists, they decided to black out information about Jesus' life and work, from future generations of Hebrews (Jews). Most probably they were afraid of being excommunicated or socially ostracised and even killed if they wrote about Jesus who was spearheading a movement against corruption among the rabbis and the misuse of the synagogue by the priesthood as well as the affluent freemen. Anyway, these scrolls have no bearing on the problem of the historicity or otherwise of Jesus and it cannot be concluded that Jesus was not a historical personality just because nothing about him is found in these scrolls. In fact, the historicity of several of the events and characters recorded in these scrolls is not just questionable but is known to be fictitious.

Before the discovery of these scrolls, the oldest known manuscript of the Bible (Old Testament) was the Masoretic text, which was compiled and edited with diacritical marks by a team of Jews called the Masoretes between the seventh and the tenth centuries CE. Those Jews who compiled the text called it the Masoretic text because they claimed themselves to be Masoretes, meaning "transmitters." By this they implied that they were not the authors of it but were only transmitters of the Hebrew tradition, for the word *mesorah* in the Hebrew language means "transmission of a tradition." In order to prepare this text, the Masoretes had collected all the then available oral traditions and manuscripts that they could get hold of and after they completed the copying work, they destroyed all those earlier manuscripts that they had collected. Why they did so remains a mystery.

This collection of sixty-six (or seventy-three) books called the Bible, strung together by a strong ethnic string dipped in theology and knotted from end to end with mundane matters, is, incontrovertibly, an extraordinary piece of religious literature! The Old Testament is, so to say, the theological basis of Judaism, and the New Testament is the theological foundation of Christianity. Interestingly, Islam traces its origin to Ishmael, the son of Abraham and Hagar. Muhammad the prophet, the founder of Islam, claimed descent from this biblical character. And so do the Arabs. The twelve sons of Ishmael born to his Egyptian wife are said to be the progenitors of the twelve desert tribes of Arabia. In short, Abraham (or Ibrahim as he is called in the Qur'an[9]) is regarded as the Patriarch by all the three religions. However, Islam does not accept the theology of the Bible nor does it derive its theology from the Bible, although as stated already the Bible is considered a scripture by the Muslims but next only to the Qur'an. Anyway, religions and the related theologies are not the focus of this study, although we may touch upon them inasmuch as it has a bearing on the social history of those times. We are concerned, broadly speaking, with the history of the peoples and the period to the extent that the Bible mirrors. There is no gainsaying the fact that both the Old Testament and the New Testament are equally inadequate sources of history, yet glimpses of fragments of history of the tribes and kingdoms of West Asia in ancient times can be had from these two documents.

All imaginary and historical events described in the Bible had taken place mostly in the region lying between the river Euphrates-Tigris and the mouth of the river Nile. This was popularly known as the "Fertile Crescent," which incidentally, constituted "the world" in the eyes of the composers of the Bible (Old Testament). Inhabited by various tribes including the Hebrews, this crescent-shaped area consisting of three distinct geographical features was the scene of intermittent inter-tribal wars as well as the rise and fall of many kingdoms and empires in biblical times. Sandwiched as it were, between the mountainous tablelands in the north and the sandy waste in the south, lay the low-lying arable land stretching from the mouth of the river Nile to the Persian Gulf. The riparian civilisations of Egypt and those of Mesopotamia flourished in this region which, in those times, encompassed Assyria, Babylon, Phoenicia, Egypt and the Euphrates-Tigris valley. Looking at the geopolitical map of today, you will see Iran, Iraq, Syria, Lebanon, Jordan, Israel, Palestine and Upper Egypt constituting what was once called the Fertile Crescent. Watered by the river Nile in the west and the Euphrates-Tigris in the east, this roughly parabolic, low-lying and comparatively more fertile belt had been attracting the tribes from the unfriendly mountainous region of Armenia in the north and the vast stretch of dry, barren land of the peninsular Arabia in the south.

Each of the two parts of the Bible, the Old and the New Testaments that dimly reflects those happenings in the Fertile Crescent, is traditionally classified into three types: historical, doctrinal and prophetical. The historical books of the Old Testament are the Pentateuch, Joshua, Judges, Ruth, I and II Samuel, I and II Kings, I and II Chronicles, Ezra, Nehemiah and Esther. The doctrinal books include the Job, Psalms, Proverbs, Ecclesiastes and Song of Solomon. The Isaiah, Jeremiah, Lamentations, Ezekiel, Daniel, Hosea, Joel, Amos, Obadiah, Jonah, Micah, Nahum, Habakkuk, Zephaniah, Haggai, Zechariah and Malachi constitute the prophetical books. In the New Testament, the historical books are the Matthew, Mark, Luke, John and Acts (of the Apostles). The Romans, I and II Corinthians, Galatians, Ephesians, Philippians, Colossians, I & II Thessalonians, I & II Timothy, Titus, Philemon, Hebrews, James, I & II Peter, I, II & III John and Jude are classified as doctrinal books. The Revelation or Apocalypse is the only prophetical book in the New Testament. Although the traditionalists have classified the Pentateuch and Joshua as historical books, those two cannot be regarded as historical inasmuch as there is no evidence of the historicity of either the protagonists or the events described therein. They are more mythical and fictitious than historical, although the myths allegorise the prehistory of mankind and the social history of the Hebrew tribes. These may, therefore, be categorised as mythico-historical books. The Roman Catholic canon which was fixed at the synod of Hippo in CE 393 and subsequently confirmed by two synods at Carthage in CE 397 and 419, included in the Old Testament what is known as the Deuterocanonical books, which they consider as sacred as the other books of the Bible. There are seven Deuterocanonical books, which are Tobit, Judith, I and II Maccabees, The Wisdom of Solomon, Sirach (Ecclesiasticus) and Baruch. The Protestants and the Jews, however, regard these seven Deuterocanonical books of the Catholic Bible as apocryphal. The word *apocrypha* means "spurious" or "writings of doubtful authority," but the Catholic Church uses the word to mean "hidden or concealed."

The Apocrypha consists of books and chapters found interspersed among the canonical books of the Old Testament in the Vulgate[10] but not in the Hebrew Old Testament. In 1546, at the Council of Trent the Roman Catholic Church received as canonical, all these books, except the two books of Esdras and the Prayer of Manasseh. Like the rest of the Bible, the Apocrypha also is a collection of books. They are I and II Esdras, Additions to the book of Esther, Epistle of Jeremiah, The Prayer of Azariah, The Song of the Three Young Men, Susanna, Bel and Dragon, The Prayer of Manasseh, and the Seven Deuterocanonical books mentioned above. Of these, barring the seven Deuterocanonical books, the rest are today considered part of the Catholic Apocrypha. Although the Deuterocanonical books do not come within the purview of this study, we shall have to draw on the book of the Maccabees for some historical information that the Protestant Bible does not give.

Of the books that constitute the Bible, there are seventeen prophetical books in the Old Testament and one in the New Testament, and these are attributed to different prophets who are considered spokespersons for god. Today a person who prophesies or tells what is going to happen in the future is known as a prophet as for example, the biblical character Elisha or Isaiah. The word "prophet" is derived from Latin *propheta* or Greek *prophetes* meaning "to speak before," that is, to proclaim or announce what god is supposed to have communicated to him when he was in a state of trance. Asimov states, "the very word 'prophet' is from Greek words meaning 'to speak forth;' that is, to relate and interpret the will of god as made manifest to the prophet during his trance or ecstasy."[11] The two aspects of their work were "speaking forth" and "foretelling." The Bible regards as prophets those who preached or prophesied what they claimed had been revealed to them by god or angels. The prophets of the Old Testament were not interpreters of god's will; they, it is believed, merely repeated the actual words, which god is said to have told them. Every religion has its prophet or prophets.

Incidentally, in olden days, a prophet was not looked upon as one who conveyed what he claimed had been revealed to him by god or one who prophesied. The Arabic equivalent of the English word "prophet" is *nabi*, and to those who espouse Islam, *nabi* is a person to whom Allah or god has revealed himself and given the scripture, the Qur'an. In the Hebrew language, however, the word *nabi* or *navi* denotes an announcer, but what he announces need not be prophecy. In biblical times, the prophets went around in groups, singing and announcing what they claimed to be prophecies, and they were looked down upon by the people in general. They "were an order very like the dervishes[12] of modern Islam," that usually belonged to the lower strata of society, and wealthy middle-class men considered them a nuisance. "They go about in organised bands prophesying to the accompaniment of music and are reckoned rather disreputable people...We gather the prophets were usually of the poorer classes and disliked by the great families as mob orators and trouble-makers," writes Robertson.[13] When Saul returned after being anointed by Samuel and the "spirit of God came upon him" he began to prophesy and those who knew him earlier wondered what had gone wrong with him. One of them asked, "What is this that has happened to the son of Kish? (And someone derisively asked), Is Saul also among the prophets? And one of the same place, answered and said, But who is their father?"[14] Therefore it became a proverb: "Is Saul also among the prophets?" This shows the contempt with which the people in general held the prophets in those times, and the story of the sons of Eli[15] and the sons of Samuel[16] "who took bribes and perverted judgment" exemplify the character of the prophets and priests of those days.

Coming back to the history of the Bible, the first Greek version of the Old Testament, the original of which was in Hebrew, dates back to the third century BCE. This, known as the Septuagint, is believed to be the work of about seventy-two scholars, six scholars from each of the twelve tribes of Israel. There is a story of doubtful authenticity about the origin of the Septuagint, as told in the *Letter of Aristeas* written in the second century BCE, which is said to be a pseudepigraphical work. Anyway, according to it, Ptolemy II called Philadelphus, the king of Egypt (283-246 BCE) wanted a Greek translation of the Jewish Law for the library at Alexandria. At his request Eleazer, the high priest of Jerusalem, detailed seventy-two men, six from each of the twelve Hebrew tribes, for the work. Carrying a scroll of the law, they went to Egypt and completed the work in seventy-two days, each of them translating one section. So this version was called "Septuagint,"[17] meaning the translation of the seventy or the LXX. Interestingly, in the Islamic tradition, god is said to have revealed his scripture to seventy *nabis* or prophets in the seventy languages of mankind.

It may be historically true that the translation of the book into Greek was done in the third century BCE, during the reign of Ptolemy II, but not at the request of the king as Aristeas claims in the *Letter*. A large Hebrew community had been dwelling in Egypt for generations. There was a much larger population of the Hebrews in Egypt than in any other part of the Fertile Crescent at that time. It is on record that there were one hundred and twenty-five Jews in Egypt for a population of every one thousand, around the Christian Era.[18] Cut off from the mainstream Hebrew society, those Hebrew tribes had naturally lost touch with the Hebrew language which was, in fact, totally alien to them. They had imbibed the Greek and Hellenistic culture, and so the Jewish scholars in Alexandria decided to translate the Old Testament into Greek for the benefit of the Greek-speaking Hebrew community in Egypt that was incapable of reading the scripture in the original Hebrew language.

The story of seventy-two scholars from the twelve tribes of Israel working at it and completing the work simultaneously in seventy-two days, producing identical translations, seems rather fictitious. Nevertheless, it got the name "Septuagint," a term adopted from the legend in the *Letter of Aristeas*. The translation, which was as good as the original version, is said to have been completed in the third century BCE. However, it must be said that this was revised several times and had been the Bible of the early Greek-speaking converts to Christianity for a long time, until the New Testament was added to it. Since then the two together constituted the Christian scripture while the Old Testament remained the scripture of the Yahwists. Although the two stories differ on who mooted the idea of translation or how the translation work was done, the biblical scholars agree on the point that it was translated in the third century BCE.

Why is it that the two main books constituting the Bible are called the Old Testament and the New Testament? The word "testament" is derived from the Latin word *testamentum,* meaning "covenant." So the most important factor in the Bible is the covenant, that is, testament. For those who consider the Bible the word of god, this denotes the special relationship that god had with man, or in other words, a compact or a contract between god and man. In secular terms, however, it is a contract between man and man, which means a "social contract." It must be clarified that *man* in this context refers to the "person of one of the Hebrew tribes" and so this contract regulated the economic, social, political, religious and personal life of the Hebrew tribesmen. The first Testament was the four promises that god is believed to have made to Abram, which name was since changed to Abraham.[19] This may be regarded as a covenant because the fulfilment of these promises was subject to certain conditions that man had to observe and any breach of the covenant slowed down their fulfilment. Subsequently, it is believed, a new covenant came into effect by and through the birth, death and resurrection of Jesus.

These two covenants are, in the eyes of the Christians, intrinsically connected, the second one being the natural culmination of the first. The Judaists, on the other hand, consider the term "Old Testament" pejorative and it implies its supersession by the New Testament, which the Judaists do not accept and is not part of the Hebrew scripture. The Hebrew religious leaders have classified the Old Testament, which is the Hebrew Scripture, into three groups: the first is what the Judaists call *Tanakh*, an acronym coined with the initial five Hebrew letters of the three texts that constitute it. The three texts are *Torah*, the "Law" (also called the Pentateuch derived from the Greek word *pentateuchos*), which comprises the first five books of the Old Testament, *Nevi'im* (the "Prophets") and *Ketuvim* (the "Writings" or Hagiographa). Tanakh, thus, consists of the twenty-four books of the Old Testament.[20] To this was added the teachings of Jesus, called the New Testament, and the two together constituted the Christian (Protestant) Bible. The Catholics added one more book, the Apocrypha. The Christians divided the twenty-four books of the Judaist Bible into thirty-nine books.

The Christian Bible comprising both the Old Testament and the New Testament may be defined as a syncretic scripture. It is, in fact, a supreme example of syncretism. The Bible cleverly syncretises a series of Mosaic principles with Jesus' tenets, as for example it attempts to reconcile Moses' *lex talionis*[21] that is, the Law of Retaliation, with Jesus' the Law of Non-Resistance.[22] The reason for this is not difficult to understand. Looking at it from a materialist perspective, a scripture of whatever religion it is, contrary to the belief that it is a revelation of god, is a human document like any literary work. As such it is a product of the society in which the composer lived and worked and is bound to reflect the thoughts and culture of that society.

Man, after all, is a social being and there is a dialectical relationship between the collective ideas, feelings, aspirations, fears and recollections that constitute social consciousness of the people of a given society and the economic structure of the society. Marx writes, "in the social production that men carry on, they enter into definite relations that are indispensable and independent of their will; these relations of production correspond to a definite stage of development of their material forces of production. The sum total of these relations of production constitutes the economic structure of society; the real foundation on which rises the legal and political superstructure and to which correspond definite forms of social consciousness....It is not the consciousness of men that determines their being, but, on the contrary, the social being that determines their consciousness. At a certain stage of their development, the material forces of production in society come in conflict with the existing relations of production....Then begins an epoch of social revolution. With the change of the economic foundation, the entire immense superstructure [and the corresponding social consciousness] is more or less rapidly transformed".[23] This is true not only of ordinary men and women but also of intellectuals like artists and litterateurs, scientists and philosophers. Hyman Levi observes, "Writers, musicians, painters and scientists, however individual and personal their creations may be, are nevertheless expressing through their work, features of the world about them, of a social nature. They may be unaware of it – indeed, they usually are – but they can't escape it."[24]

And that explains the syncretism in the Bible, the subjective reason for which shall be dealt with presently later. Inevitably, the cumulative thoughts of the society in which the bards whose compositions constituted the Old Testament lived are bound to be reflected in their works. The rhapsodists who composed the episodes of the Old Testament lived in a society which differed fundamentally from that of the period of Jesus. To put it differently, the society that Jesus and the Evangelists saw and in which they lived and worked was very different from that of the rhapsodists who composed the Old Testament. In other words, the Old Testament and the New Testament were produced in two different historical eras and under totally different socio-economic conditions – the former during the period of barbarism and the latter after mankind, including the Hebrews, had progressed into the stage of ancient civilisation.

So syncretism was inevitable in the Christian Bible. It happened because a new religion, born in a new socio-economic background, did not reject but clung to and built upon the scripture of a religion born in an earlier and totally different socio-economic environment. The ethical, theological and political ideas of bards who lived in the civilised society of Jesus' period, therefore, could not but have been different from those of the barbaric society of the bards who composed the Old Testament. The contradictory tenets in the Bible are, thus, the reflection of the thoughts and culture of the two respective periods. When the preceptors of Christianity that rose in the period of civilisation broke away from Yahwism, a religion that was the product of the period of barbarism, they did not want to repudiate the traditions and tenets of the religion of the barbarians. The editors and the ecclesiastical councils that subsequently finalised the Christian Bible did not try to or want to reconcile those contradictions.

Until about the latter half of the twelfth century, the Bible was held so sacred that any translation of it was considered sacrilegious. Nevertheless, supported by people who were unhappy with the policy of the official Church that prevented the common man from comprehending the Bible, several new versions of the scripture in the local languages appeared. In about 1170 CE, Peter Waldo of Lyons along with his followers formed a Waldersian Church, which was subjected to acrimonious persecution for many years by the official Church. Waldo got the Bible translated into Provencal, a Romance language spoken in Provence, a region in southeastern France, for which he was excommunicated in 1184. Nearly two centuries later, John Wycliff (1329-1384), a theologian of England, thought it imperative to translate the Bible into English for the benefit of those who did not know Latin, and he did it in collaboration with Nicholas of Hereford and John Purvey. This translation of the Latin Vulgate Bible was completed in 1384. It was later revised by Purvey, which, however, was banned by the synod of the Church. In southern Bohemia, a region now in the Czech Republic, Jan Hus (1359-1415), the then Rector of the Prague University, was influenced by Wycliff and started a movement to translate the Bible into the language of the common man but the Church nipped it in the bud by burning him at the stake. However, his followers continued with the work of translation that he had begun and the Czech New Testament was brought out in 1475.

The first English version made by direct translation from the original Hebrew and Greek was made by William Tyndale (1490-1536), a contemporary of the leader of the Reformation Movement and the father of Christian Protestantism Martin Luther, a German. Educated at the University of Oxford, Tyndale worked as instructor at the University of Cambridge. He and some biblical scholars thought that the Englishmen who espoused Christianity should be able to read the Bible in their mother tongue. But the Church did not approve of the idea and dissuaded him from the venture. However, in 1524 he managed to get financial aid from some wealthy Englishmen and went to Germany to translate the New Testament, which he completed in

1525 and published at Cologne. But the Catholic Church accused him of wrongfully translating it by misinterpreting the Scripture, and all copies were ordered to be destroyed. He, however, again got it printed at Worms and the copies were distributed in England the next year. He then began working on the translation of the Old Testament but, betrayed by some Christian bigots, he was captured in Antwerp and burned at the stake in 1536. However, by that time a large number of copies of the New Testament had already been printed. This was the first English translation of the original Bible and almost all subsequent English versions have been based on this.

The Greek version of the New Testament was first brought out in 1516 by Desidorius Erasmus (1456-1536), a contemporary of Martin Luther. He vehemently criticised the Catholic Church, thus paving the way for the Reformation, but Luther accused him of cowardice as Erasmus refused to cut himself off from the Catholic Church. So he was spurned by the Catholic Church as well as the Lutherans. Nevertheless, all these men including Erasmus, many of whom were martyrs to the cause, may be regarded as avant-couriers of the Reformation. Martin Luther's translation of the New Testament in German appeared in 1522.

The devout Judaists and Christians implicitly believe that the Bible is the "word of god," like those who profess other religions consider their scriptures. And Abraham, the biblical character, in whose covenant with god lies the seeds of Judaism, is considered a prophet and patriarch not only by the Judaists and the Christians, but also by the Muslims. But Islamic tradition regards Abraham, who is called Ibrahim in the Qur'an, as a proto-Muslim and a prophet or Hanif, that is, the propounder of monotheism rejecting the polytheism and idolatry of his father without being prompted by god, unlike as it was in the case of Moses.[25]

According to the Islamic tradition, Allah, the Lord of the Mankind and jinn,[26] commanded Ibrahim (Abraham) to take his son Ismail (Ishmail in the Bible) and his mother Hajar (Hagar in the Bible) to the wilderness. Hajar in the Qur'an was his wife and not his slave like Hagar who was a slave, euphemistically called handmaid in the Bible. During their journey in the desert, they could not find a drop of water anywhere, but on reaching Mecca, miraculously there appeared the well of Zamzam and they quenched their thirst. The Qur'anic version of the story of Abraham differs from that of the Bible in that it was Ismail that Ibrahim offered (not Isaac as the Bible states) when god wanted Ibrahim to sacrifice his son. And lying on the sacrificial stone, Ismail consoled his father and he is portrayed as a paragon of piety.[27] Since Judaism, Christianity and Islam accept Abraham (Abram/Ibrahim) as the prophet, these religions are sometimes referred to as Abrahamic religions.

In course of time, both Christianity and Islam split to form two sects. The breakaway sect of Christianity came to be known as the Protestants, as it was a protest movement against the priesthood, while those who remained loyal to the Establishment constituted the Roman Catholics. The Protestants again split into several sects and so the Catholics. The two sects of Islam are called the Sunnis and the Shias; there are other minor sects too like the Ahmediyas or Qadianis, but they are quite insignificant and are considered heretics by the Muslims. The Bahai sect, which originated in Iran, is an offshoot of the Shias, but the Muslims regard those who profess Bahaism as apostates. The (Christian) Protestants accepted all biblical prophets while the Sunnis and Shias, the two groups of Islam, whose scripture is the Qur'an, accepted some of the biblical prophets only. The Judaists do not accept Jesus as a Messiah.

The Protestants, however, held the Bible as their scripture, unlike, for example, the Buddhists and the Jains, both of which also were, so to say, groups of protestants. Although these two religions, Buddhism and Jainism,[28] had been the offshoots of Hinduism, none of those religions regarded the Vedas, the sacred books or scripture of the Hindus, as sacrosanct. In fact, the two religions Buddhism and Jainism, the protestant movements against Vedic rituals and the corrupt priesthood of the Hindu Brahminical religion, rejected the Vedas, the scripture of Hinduism. Surprisingly, unlike the Buddha and Mahavira, who led the protestant movements against corruption of Hinduism, Martin Luther, the leader of the Reformation Movement of the sixteenth century CE, which was the protestant movement against corruption of Christianity by the decadent Church, did not attempt to found another religion. And he, who accused Erasmus of cowardice for not breaking off from the Church, was himself a coward as he did not have the courage to renounce Christianity; nor to repudiate the Bible (Old Testament).

The five principles on which Luther based his movement were *Sola Scriptura* (according to scripture alone), *Solus Christus* (in Christ alone), *Sola Gratia* (by grace alone), *Sola Fide* (through faith alone) and *Sola Deo Gloria* (for god's glory alone). The first and second of these pointedly show his determination to stay within the fold of Christianity and emphasise his adherence to the Bible while distancing himself from the Church. He vehemently condemned the venality, simony, lechery, sale of Indulgences and such other corrupt practices of the Roman Catholic clergy. However, he did not reject the Bible but repudiated the Church. He disagreed with the Church's assertion that the Church alone had the authority to interpret the Bible, saying that the Scripture alone was its authority, or *sola scriptura*. And he refused to accept the role of the Pope as the mediator between god and man, asserting that Christ is the sole mediator between god and man, or *solus christus*.

Opposing the autocratic hold of the Roman Catholic Church, he along with his followers formed a parallel Church independent of the parent body and liberal in its approach to religious matters. The Protestants, who continued to accept the Bible as the word of god, rejected the Deuterocanonical books that include most of the Old Testament Apocrypha, for they did not consider them canonical and omitted them from their Bible altogether. It must be pointed out in this context that this was the period of Renaissance when absolutism and serfdom was being supplanted by liberalism and equality, and the Reformation Movement of Luther was a reflection of that trend in the European religious thought.

As stated above, the Protestants accept the Bible as scripture, deleting from it the seven Deuterocanonical Books. The Old Testament is an anthology of the bardic compositions, which were passed on from generation to generation by word of mouth. These were originally the compositions of many bards who flourished long before the Hebrew tribes had an alphabet. All the bards being of one or the other of the Hebrew tribes, the verses had naturally been composed in the Hebrew language but obviously it had not been written down then. Schniedewind writes, "The classical Hebrew language does not even have a word that means 'author.' The nearest term would be *sofer*, who was a transmitter of tradition and text (that is *mesorah*) rather than author. Authorship is a concept that derives from a predominantly *written* culture, whereas ancient Israelite society was largely an *oral* culture"[29] And even after the Hebrew language had a script of its own, these bardic compositions were not written down for a long time, the reason for which is discussed in Chapter 3, "A Virtual Tower of Babel." Those bardic compositions that later constituted the Bible (Old Testament) that we have today, were collected, compiled, edited, altered and reduced to writing by various individuals at a later period and at different times, a few centuries after they were composed. The scribes, however, produced a medley of various subjects.

It is said that the compilation of The Book of Daniel, which was written in Hebrew and Aramaic, marked the completion of the Old Testament. Traditionalists date it back to the sixth century BCE. Schniedewind goes a step further and says the writing of biblical literature was "closely related to the urbanisation of Jerusalem, to a growing government bureaucracy (and) to the development of a more complex global economy" and argues that biblical literature was largely written down between the eighth and the sixth centuries BCE. This is indubitably an exaggeration, for traditionalists of all religions tend to do so to show that theirs is the most ancient of all religions. He also disputes "a fashionable trend among a minority of scholars" that hold the view that biblical texts "were not composed until late into the Persian and Hellenistic periods, that is between the fourth and the second centuries BCE.[30] Several modern scholars, however, ascribe it to *circa* the second century BCE, which, however, does not tally with the theory that it was translated into Greek in the third century BCE. So it must have been reduced to writing some time between the sixth and the fourth centuries BCE – between the accepted date of the compilation of The Book of Daniel and the date of translating the Scripture into Greek. The controversy over the chronology apart, no one questions the fact that the primary source was the oral traditions and that contradicts the claim that the Scripture is the word of god.

Several centuries after the Old Testament was composed, the New Testament was added to the Bible by the Christian clerics, flavouring it with their theology and ethical principles. The Bible that has come down to us across a period of several hundreds of years, no doubt, has gone through a long process of editing and revision and contains a fund of information about certain peoples of the ancient world. Incidentally, in the course of it, much of the pristine beauty of the rhapsodies must have got drained off through the fingers of the scribes and editors. The description of Joshua's war in defense of the Gibeonites[31] is a good example of this. The poetic beauty of the description of the war in the original rhapsody would, perhaps, have been lost to some extent when it was written down in the book of Jasher, which unfortunately is not extant today. And the author of the book of Joshua who drew on it in describing the war must have further edited out much of it, losing a great deal of the literary beauty of the original. There is no doubt that the author of the book of Joshua must have mercilessly decapitated the lyric as he was more interested in emphasising the power of god and mythicising the character of Joshua than in the aesthetic elements that must have embellished the original.

For a long time, however, the authorship of each book was ascribed to the person with whose name it was associated, as for example, the "Five Books of Moses" and the "Book of Joshua" were thought to be authored by Moses and Joshua respectively. Those who attributed the authorship to Moses had based their arguments primarily on three verses in Deuteronomy.[32] This, however, was not taken as the last word and investigations into the sources continued. First of all, the historicity of the prophets and many other biblical characters had not been proved and the internal evidence too did not corroborate the assumption that attributed the authorship to those biblical characters. Defying the vehement opposition of the Church and threats of excommunication and even risking their lives, biblical scholars had been splitting hairs and arguing about the original sources and the hands that put the stories and other matter contained in the Bible in black and white.

If Moses (in case such a person had ever lived at all) had written the Pentateuch, he would have narrated it in first person singular, but the four books in which Moses appears are written in third person. It may be argued that those who edited those books later changed the person, but there is ample evidence, as many scholars had pointed out, to believe that the authorship cannot be attributed to the biblical character Moses. Above all, the assertion that Moses is the author does not hold water because in that case it had to be conceded that Moses himself had described his death and burial at the end of the chapter, "Deuteronomy" unless it was conceded that it had been interpolated later. The historicity of the biblical character known as Moses who is believed to have drafted the laws, which were imposed upon the Hebrew society that was in a flux and at a critical stage then, as pointed out above, was itself called in question. Similarly, there was no extra-biblical documentary or archaeological evidence of the Hebrew liberation movement in Egypt and the Exodus. This is discussed in Chapter 4, "Consolidation of Slavery." It was the absurdity of attributing the authorship of the Pentateuch to a fictitious character that prompted the scholars to investigate it.

That the myths and legends as well as the historical events that comprise the book have been drawn from more than one source is evident from the several doublets or two sets of narratives presenting the same story. The creation myth, the difference in the number of animals on Noah's Ark and the story of Moses drawing water from the rock are but a few of such instances. Moreover, it has been observed that one set of stories always referred to the Hebrew god by the word Jehovah (Yahweh) while the other used the word Elohim for god. The two strands that the doublets indicate were later put together to form a single document. But both these traditions have borrowed the stories about creation[33] from various sources, mostly from those of the Sumerian and Mesopotamian civilisations. The word *Yahweh,* meaning "Creator," for example, is possibly an adaptation of the name of the Babylonian rain god Jahu.[34] Graves states *Yahweh* meaning "creator" is an adaptation of the name of the Sumerian goddess Iahu.[35]

Moreover, it has been accepted by biblical scholars that the myth of creation – why, the entire Genesis – was borrowed from the Sumerian story of Genesis, which Jacobsen calls *The Eridu Genesis* to differentiate it from the "First Book of Moses called the Genesis" in the Bible. It was so called because the Eridu City, the earliest known city of Sumer figures importantly in the story[36]. The Sumerian myth was put together by scholars when a fragment of the story of Genesis inscribed in cuneiform script was found on the clay tablets of the libraries of Nippur in Babylon. Another tablet with the fragment of the story inscribed on it in Sumerian was exhumed from Ur. Besides, there were the bilingual ones, Sumerian with Akkadian translation, found in the Assur-bani-pal's library in Ninevah. These tablets, which date back to circa 1600 BCE[37] were unearthed in the late nineteenth century and the inscriptions were deciphered in 1912. All these, Jacobsen states, "tell the same story; creation, earliest cities, the flood (although) they vary a good deal among themselves in explicitness and must be taken to represent not one but several versions" of the same theme as that of the biblical Genesis.[38]

In addition to these, on Tablet XI of the *Epic of Gilgamesh*, the earliest known literary work, which, needless to say, predates the Bible, a story remarkably similar to the biblical story of the flood, has been found. This epic is based on the life of Gilgamesh, a ruler of Sumeria, during the third millennium BCE. The gods of the polytheistic Sumerians are angry with mankind and decide to eradicate the human race by inundating the world and drowning them. Enlil, the ruler of the "World of Gods,"[39] calls an assembly of gods and announces his decision to ask Adad, the rain god,[40] to cause continuous rain and flood the earth. There is no dissenting voice. However, Ea who loves human beings does not see eye to eye with the others but keeps his own counsel. Enlil asks Adad to carry out what has been decided upon. Meanwhile Ea warns his human friend, Utnapishtim, the king of Shurippak, and suggests to him to build an ark to escape the flood, which he does. So when it begins to rain, Utnapishtim along with his family, a few artisans and various animals, gets into the boat. When the rains abate and the floodwaters recede Utnapishtim sends out three birds to find out the flood situation. The story ends when the boat runs aground on a mountain; and Utnapishtim finds that those on board are the only survivors. So the source of the myths of creation and the flood was indubitably the Sumerian mythology and it cannot be denied that the *Eridu Genesis* from which the biblical book of Genesis has adapted the creation and others myths, predates the biblical *Genesis*. The authors of the book of Genesis could have been rhapsodists who flourished, probably, long before the biblical character called Moses is believed to have lived. Presumably, therefore, Moses himself was a fictitious character created by these rhapsodists.

The traditionalists aver that it was in *circa* the ninth century BCE that the scholars of the Hebrew priestly class began to compile the myths, legends, folklore as well as a few romanticised or mythicised stories of historical personalities and incidents brought down to them through generations by word of mouth.[41] These are believed to have formed the nucleus of the Bible or to be precise, the Old Testament. So the material that formed the nucleus must have originated long before Israel had discovered the art of writing. It implies that those stories must have been known to the people in verbal form when the tribes were in the stage of barbarism. In the early nineteenth century, biblical scholars by analysing the language, the themes dealt with, story sequences and historical time frames came to the conclusion that the documents that had come down to us were drawn from not less than four different sources. They came to this conclusion because they could identify four different versions of recorded oral traditions.

These four documentary sources are classified as J, E, P and D. Of these four different versions, the one associated with those living in the kingdom of Judah, who had used the generic term *Jehovah* (*Yahweh*) or *the Lord* for the Creator, is referred to as the J source document and is considered the earliest of all. According to the traditionalists' theory, it is believed to have been written down between the tenth and the eighth centuries BCE. The next one, connected with those living in the kingdom of Israel who used the word *Elohim* or *God* for the Creator, is called the E source document. Though this too is said to have been reduced to writing during the same period, J source document is said to be the earlier one and so the earliest of the four source documents. The third one is the P source document, which is dated back to between the eighth and the seventh centuries BCE. This is what a later group of priests (P) who, using both the J and E sources, edited and compiled, adding their interpretations too from the point of view of the clergy.

Finally we have the Deuteronomistic or the D source document, the fourth one, written by someone whose identity, as in the case of the scribes of the other source documents, is not known but to which also several hands seem to have contributed. This, the D source document, is ascribed to the beginning of the seventh century BCE and is a comprehensive exposition of the covenant. This is believed to have been proclaimed by Moses, as it begins with the sentence, "These are the words which Moses spoke to all Israel on this side of the Jordan in the wilderness..." But as stated above, there is no evidence whatsoever to say that a person like the biblical Moses ever walked on this planet.

Several biblical scholars dispute the dates ascribed to these sources by the traditionalists and they argue that the oral traditions were reduced to writing at a much later date. It is but natural that when dealing with documents of such early periods, scholars seldom agree and each one would bring up seemingly convincing arguments to corroborate his theory and there is no possibility of scholars coming to a consensus on such points. Suffice it for us to know that the oral traditions were written down a few centuries before the Common Era of which there is no dispute. The controversy over the chronology apart, no one questions the fact that the primary source of the Bible (Old Testament) was the oral traditions, which as all scholars agree, were bardic compositions. And that, as stated already, contradicts the claim that the Scripture is the "word of God." If we accept that it was the "word of god," we also have to accept that god dictated these verses not to the prophets but to several barbaric bards.

It had also been pointed out that each of these source documents, which had been reduced to writing whenever it was, had not only been interpolated by scribes who wrote them down but blended with their own thoughts and interpretations as well. There are wide differences in the narratives of these various sources, which is inevitable because, first of all, there could have been many differences in the oral traditions that each of them relied upon. When a poetic composition is passed on orally from generation to generation, the narrators are likely to add, delete, alter, improve or even corrupt certain verses, resulting in a multiplicity of versions, which again get altered and revised by the scribes who write them down using their editorial prerogative. The editor who collected and brought together all these four documents, that is the Redactor or what is generally referred to by the letter R, is believed to be Ezra, a lineal descendant from Eleazar, the son of Aaron. This, presumably, is a conclusion drawn from the book of Ezra that refers to Ezra as "a skilled scribe in the Law of Moses, which the Lord God of Israel had given."[42] But the historicity of Ezra like that of Eleazar and Aaron themselves, not to speak of many other biblical characters is a moot point. Besides, different versions of written documents have been found. This could have happened because the scribes would have added, deleted or altered many passages when they made copies, or it could have been due to the mistakes that the transcribers made. These, naturally, are reflected in the recension of the Bible that has come down to us. Anyway, this study is not intended to delve into that problem.

The exercise to determine the authorship of the Torah, though traditionally attributed to Moses, as stated above, has been going on since the beginning of the Common Era and expression of any view that did not concur with that held by the Church was not tolerated by the priesthood; nor was it accepted by the faithful. Culled from more than one source and written down by diverse hands, the authorship of the Old Testament cannot be attributed to any individual or to the scribe(s) who wrote it down because it was not the work of any one of the composers or the scribes. And of course no biblical scholar claims it to be so. Friedman, in his book, enumerates some of them,[43] which were considered heresy. The history of the investigations into the sources and authorship of the Bible is, thus, a long story of persecutions, excommunications, social ostracism and condemnations of the scholars who held views on the authorship of the Bible different from that of the Church.

In the eleventh century, Isaac Ibn Yashush, a Jewish physician at the court of a Muslim king in Spain, stated that the list of Edomite kings[44] was added by someone who flourished after the period in which Moses is believed to have lived. He was condemned by the Church. When Andreas van Maes, a Catholic scholar of Flanders, pointed out in his book written in the sixteenth century that a later writer had interpolated and even made some alterations in the Pentateuch, the book was promptly placed on the *Index Librorum Prohibitorum.*

In the next century, Thomas Hobbs, an English philosopher, referring to certain phrases used in the Pentateuch, argued that it could not have been written by Moses. A book written in the same period by Isaac de la Peyrere, a French Calvinist, in which he argued that Moses was not the author of the Pentateuch, was banned and burned. This vandalism was decried by Baruch (Benedictus) Spinoza, another philosopher, a contemporary of Hobbs and Peyrere, who wrote that the internal evidence indisputably showed that Moses was not the author of the first five books of the Bible. This was frowned upon by both the Christians and the Judaists. His book was promptly placed on the *Index* by the Catholic Church and a writ of *cherem* or excommunication was issued against him by the Jewish (Sephardic) community of Amsterdam. Besides, thirty-seven edicts were issued against his book and the intolerance of the religious institutions was so much that they went to the extent of making an attempt on his life, which fortunately failed. However, even after his death he was not spared; three of his works were proscribed in Holland where he had been living till his death since his family had immigrated there when he was a child.

Julius Welhausen, in the nineteenth century, pointed out that these four sources indicated the different stages of development of the so-called books of Moses. He asserted that the matter contained in J and E marked the "nature-fertility" stage of religion, the matter contained in P marked the "priestly-legal" stage and the matter contained in Deuteronomy or D marked the "spiritual-ethical" stage. This method of theorising about the authorship of the Pentateuch, by viewing it as having been composed by combining and editing the source documents by scribes at different times, is what the scholars call the Documentary Hypothesis. This *ipso facto* dismisses the view that Moses authored the book and accepts the theory that the Pentateuch was produced by drawing upon and putting together several strands of tradition. In fact, the differences in geographical and historical interests, in theology and language and above all the doublets and contradictions indisputably prove the correctness of Documentary Hypothesis.

In the nineteenth century itself, John Colenso, an Anglican bishop in South Africa, was regarded as wicked for holding views similar to those of Julius Welhausen, which regarded Judaism as having developed in three stages because, he argued, the related documents had been written in three different periods. Subsequently, Richard Simon, a Protestant who embraced Catholicism and became a priest, repudiated Spinoza but conceded that scribes who were prophets "guided by the divine spirit" had made some additions to the Mosaic text. He was considered a heretic and expelled from the order and his book placed on the *Index*. He was refuted by the Protestants as well and almost all the copies of his book were consigned to the fire. There had been many other cases like Karl Heinrich Graf, Wilhelm Vatke, K.H. Oral, *et al.*, all of whom looked at the problem defying the official view, but the Church maliciously discarded them, as the orthodox priesthood refused to accept any of those theories. But their opposition did not deter the search for the brains and hands behind the Bible (Old Testament). In course of time the Church became a little tolerant – perhaps finding the validity of those scholars' arguments or the futility of trying to curb free thought – and began to take a relatively more lenient view of scholarly investigations of the problem of the authorship of the Bible (Old Testament).

Apart from the above mentioned four sources, the compilers of the Bible had leaned on various other source books, which in turn could be compilations of several other compositions of minstrels who flourished earlier. No copies of those source books have been found so far but we know that the biblical scribes, who reduced the bardic compositions to writing, did draw upon those books because they ask the readers to refer to those books for more details. Obviously, therefore, those books contained many historical facts that are not given in the Bible. All copies of those manuscripts were perhaps deliberately destroyed by those who finalised the text of the Bible because they probably contained many unsavoury remarks about the Hebrew tribes and their prophets. A list,[45] which, of course, is not comprehensive, of those source books cited in the Bible, is given below:

Book of the Generations of Adam
Book of the Covenant
Book of the Wars of the Lord
Book of Jasher
Book of the Acts of Solomon
Book of the Chronicles of the Kings of Israel
Book of the Chronicles of the Kings of Israel and Judah
Book of Samuel the Seer
Book of Nathan the Prophet
Book of Gad the Seer
Book of Shemiah the Prophet

Annals of the Prophet Iddo
Book of the Law of the Lord
Book of the Prophet of Esaias[46]

The Bible panegyrises the legendary and mythical heroes of the Hebrew tribes, and celebrates the events of its ancient past. As we shall see in the course of this study, the stories in the Bible were intended primarily to glorify the Hebrew tribe and projecting it as the chosen people, to whom the land of Canaan was gifted by god. That was said to be the justification for their invasion and occupation of Canaan, driving away the tribes that had been dwelling there for many generations. Obviously, therefore, those bardic composers were Hebrews who were proud of their Hebrew ancestry and composed the songs to infuse a sense of pride in their tribesmen. Most of the main protagonists in the Bible – both the Old and the New Testaments – belong to this tribe and the Bible presents their exploits in glowing terms, often sacrificing historical veracity and mythicising by attributing supernatural powers to them. Needless to say the authors of the documentary sources of the books in the Bible and perhaps most of the composers of the oral tradition were not contemporaneous with the events described in the biblical episodes.

The historicity of many important characters, including Abraham and Moses and even John the Baptist and Jesus that appear in the Bible has not been *irrefutably* established so far, although there is no lack of archaeological and literary evidence of many kingdoms and settlements mentioned therein. If these biblical characters that seem fictitious were historical figures, the stories that were recorded about them in the Bible must have passed through the mouths of several generations before they were written down. And as those stories passed from mouth to mouth, facts must have got drowned in myths. Of course, those characters, had they ever existed, must have been like any of us – men and women sans supernatural attributes and with all the faults and foibles of normal human beings. And those characters must have been men and women who, in some way or the other, had caught the imagination of the masses of the period in which they lived. By the time the stories about them reached the scribes who put those stories in black and white, all those personalities had been attributed supernatural powers and mythicised beyond recognition.

Let us ignore the problem of the historicity of the biblical characters and proceed with the interpretation because as explained in the Preface, the historicity or otherwise of the characters has no bearing on the interpretation.

As stated above, the Bible is primarily the history of the Hebrew tribes, whose emergence as a distinct tribe is associated with the name of Abraham. It can be said with certainty that the tribes that existed before Abraham were all polytheists and idolaters. Suffice it to point out here, that the Hebrews had only one god, Yahweh, but the tribes that existed in the periods in which the stories of Adam and Eve have been set, had many gods. Or, it would be correct to say that they had neither god nor religion, for god and religion presuppose worship, about which we shall discus in Chapter 2, "The Universe and God." Assuming that Adam and Eve – two fictitious characters that symbolise mankind in the stage of savagery as we shall see in Chapter 3, "A Virtual Tower of Babel" – were real man and woman in flesh and blood, we do not find them worshipping anybody, either an embodied being or a disembodied spirit; nor did they worship the god that is said to have frequently visited them. On the other hand, they treated god who interacted with them as a person of a higher status, like a feudal landlord, whom they were constrained to obey because they were beholden to him for having given them on lease a piece of land to stay and provided them with facilities for gathering their food. In other words, their relationship was like that of a landlord and his tenants.

The second section of the Bible, the New Testament, saw the light of day about twenty years after the death of Jesus, who led a religio-political movement, which as we shall see in Chapter 8, "Anti-Imperialist Movements" subsequently turned itself into an exclusively religious movement which in due course came to be called Christianity, the reasons for which is explained in Chapter 9, "The Son of Man." As more and more Judaists and Gentiles (non-Israelites or pagans) accepted the new religion swelling its ranks, it was found necessary to prepare a code of doctrines based on the teachings of Jesus and it is said, this arduous task of documenting them took nearly seven decades. That brought forth a body of literature, which formed the basis of what is known today as the New Testament comprising as stated already twenty-seven books, of which only six are said to have been composed in as early as the second century CE.

Today more than three thousand manuscripts of the New Testament in the Greek language are extant of which some are uncials – that is, written in a kind of script resembling modern capital letters but heavier and more rounded, a style adopted by Latin and Greek scribes between the fourth and the eighth centuries CE. There are one hundred and seventeen New Testament papyri dated between the second century and fourth century CE, which are preserved in libraries, museums and universities of different countries of the West. One papyrus that was in Berlin, Germany, was lost, probably during the Second World War. There are also many extant codices dated later than the fourth century CE, of which four are rated high. These are Codex *Sinaiticus*, Codex *Vaticanus* both of the fourth century CE, Codex *Alexandrinus* of the fifth century CE, and Codex *Bezae* of the sixth century CE. Of these, the first and the third are in the British Museum and the other two at Cambridge. Besides, there are several cursives, which are manuscripts written with the letters joined together and with flowing strokes.

The language of the original New Testament was not the classical Greek; nor was it the Greek of the beginning of the Christian era. It is said to be similar to *koin*, the form of Greek spoken by the common man, the masses, of the eastern parts of the Roman Empire. However, a recent study of the language used in the extant papyri reveals that there were subtle differences between *koin* and the language of the Bible. Many biblical scholars now assert that traces of Aramaic, the language spoken by the Jews of Palestine and, it is believed, of Jesus himself, are seen in the language.

The exact date of the composition of the New Testament has not been determined, and even internal evidence as the language for example, has not been very helpful in arriving at the date. But scholars agree on one point: The New Testament was not written by one man or a group of men on a time-bound basis; nor was it the product of any organised effort. The writings of the followers of Jesus, among whom there was no unanimity of ideas and views, accumulated over a period of about half a century. The style of their writing as well as the reasons for writing also differed widely. Although it is conjectured that the earliest are the Epistles attributed to Paul, it has not been confirmed and scholars are of the view that the books were not written in the order in which they are given in the Bible.

Initially the New Testament had consisted of many books, several of which were discarded as they were of doubtful authenticity and some, for want of theological soundness. And finally, the New Testament took its present form some time in the second half of the fourth century CE, bringing the number of books to twenty-seven. This essentially was the same that had been in use till then. All these were, however, perused, examined, edited and brought out in a consolidated form and that is what we know today as "The New Testament." It was called *new* because the writers of the code of Christian doctrine considered it an addition to the testament that god had made with man through Abraham, as recorded in the Hebrew scripture, which they now called the *Old* Testament to distinguish it from the *New*. It could also have been to make the Jewish converts believe that it was another testament that god had lately made with man and was different from the earlier testament that their erstwhile god, Yahweh, had with man. And possibly the editors themselves being Yahwists earlier, continued to revere the old scripture and did not want to discard it altogether. Besides, they must have thought that abandoning the earlier one would repel those Judaists who wished to join them, and the new converts might find it difficult – as they themselves perhaps did – to give up their faith in Yahweh, the god that they believed in and worshipped till then. This, needless to say, is a problem most converts would naturally have. This could have been one of the reasons why although the teachings of Yahweh as recorded in the Old Testament contradicted the teachings of Jesus to a great extent, the followers of Jesus did not reject the old, resulting in syncretism.

It is futile but interesting to conjecture, presuming that Jesus was a historical personage, how Jesus, had he been involved in writing or editing the New Testament, would have dealt with this problem. Born of Jewish parents[47] and being a Jew himself, Jesus would not have repudiated the earlier covenant just as the Evangelists and later, the editor(s) of the New Testament had done. He would have said what Matthew put into his mouth: "Think not that I have come to destroy the law, or the prophets: I have come not to destroy but to fulfill."[48] However, in Chapter 8, "Anti-imperialist Movements" we shall see what his political compulsions were for not rejecting Moses as he, being a revolutionary leader was fighting on two fronts – for the liberation of the Jews and for eradicating corruption among the rabbis.

The dates of all the episodes of the ancient period narrated in the New Testament, as in the case of the Old Testament, cannot be ascertained. However, many of the incidents described in the New Testament are found recorded in non-biblical documents too. But there is a consensus of opinion among biblical scholars regarding the date of transformation of the uncompromising Jewish persecutor of Christians, Saul of Tarsus, known to us as Paul, into an ardent follower of Jesus, who even became a Christian missionary. It is presumed that his conversion to Christianity, as can be understood from the myth about the change that took place in him on the road to Damascus, which he himself describes,[49] was around 33 CE. And in *circa* 46 or 47 CE he along with Barabbas embarked on his missionary journey. The answer to the question why he wrote those epistles is, no doubt, obvious – to persuade the Christians to practise what he had been preaching and to preclude neo-converts being misled by pseudo-prophets. It is generally accepted that the earliest of the letters addressed to the Christians in the Greek city of Thessalonica (Modern Greece's Macedonian port Salonika) was written in 52 CE. However, the date of the second letter to the Thessalonians remains a question mark. Anyway, his letter to the Galatian Christians, which he is supposed to have written from Ephesus, was in *circa* 53-54 CE and about the same time, his first letter to the Christians in Corinth was dispatched, followed by another in *circa* 55 CE. A third letter written after he was insulted and defied seems to have been lost. His letter to the Romans was composed at Corinth in *circa* 57 CE and the rest of his letters are believed to have been written probably in the early 60s when he was a prisoner in Rome.

According to most authorities, the Epistle to the Hebrews, although included in the New Testament and attributed to Paul, is the work of a Jewish Christian, probably an associate of Paul. That this letter composed in the first century CE is not the work of Paul is clear from its reference to Jesus' perfect priesthood and its stress on faith and Mosaic Law, for these are not typical of Paul. And the letter to the Philippians, addressed to the congregation that he himself had founded in Philippi, is not included in the New Testament, maybe because it is a later collection of fragments of his correspondence. Apart from Paul's there are other Epistles, attributed to James, his brother Jude, Peter and John in the New Testament. Some scholars are of the view that the book of James could be one of the earliest, antedating those of Paul. This, however, has been disputed by other authorities who assert that it is a later work. All these Epistles, long instructive letters, were written in a language which, as stated above, is a form of Greek, on sheets of papyrus, nine inches long and five inches wide. These were carried by a reliable messenger to the Christian assembly, which on receipt were perused, discussed and expounded. After that these were copied out and widely circulated.

It was around the same time the four Gospels were committed to writing. These four Gospels are the heart and brain of the New Testament. The root of the word "gospel" is the Anglo-Saxon term *godspell*, which means "good story," the equivalent of the Latin *evangelium* and the Greek *evangelion*, both meaning "good telling." The authorship of these Gospels could not be ascertained although these were for a long time supposed to have been written by the four Evangelists, Matthew, Mark, Luke and John. The scholars now agree that all the four Gospels are anonymous and orally communicated through generations. It was, perhaps, the four Evangelists, Matthew, Mark, Luke and John, who wrote down the Gospels, adding some of their own ideas and material collected from the oral Gospels, of the existence of which we come to know from the writings of Papias, Bishop of the Hieropolis in Phyrgia, who flourished in the first century CE. The scholars, who surmise that the language of the originals was Aramaic, argue that in such a case all the four were possibly written prior to the Romans under Titus invaded and pillaged Jerusalem. This was in 70 CE, and according to them it was about that time the Gospels were written down.

All these Gospels, which are vaguely biographical in content, present a series of vignettes of Jesus. They vividly describe the dramatic events leading to Jesus' capture as well as his execution. We find little information on Jesus' parents and siblings, education and his rise as a popular revolutionary leader. Luke, to whom the third Gospel is attributed, states that he collected his material from eye-witnesses. He writes, "Even as the eye-witnesses and ministers of the word delivered them to us..." Does he mean himself and Paul, of whom he was believed to be the physician, when he says "us"? Could it be Theophilus, whom he mentions but of whom he does not give any other information? Or, were these Evangelists contemporaries and does "us" refer to the four of them? He does not clarify.

Interestingly, Tatian, a Syrian who flourished in the second century CE, has two extant works to his credit, one of which is *Oratio ad Graecos* and the other, *Diatesearon* (a Greek term meaning "out of four"), a compilation of the four Gospels as a single narrative written in *c.*150 CE. The Syrian churches had been using that as the standard text till about 400 CE, when it was replaced by the four separated ones. The language in which this work was originally composed is in dispute. Some scholars opine that it was composed in Greek and later translated into Syriac, probably during the lifetime of Tatian itself while the others are of the view that it was originally written in Syriac and translated into Greek later. Except a few fragments, the Syriac version is practically lost. However, a manuscript, *Codex Fuldensis*, based on the Latin vulgate version, closely related to *Diatesseron* is extant and is in the monastic library at Fulda in the province of Hesse-Nassau in Germany. Two manuscripts of an Arabic version of this work are also extant today. *Diatesseron* is the only known text of the Gospels used in Syria during the third and the fourth centuries CE.[50]

Since the late eighteenth century, the first three of these have been classified as "Synoptic Gospels." The word "synoptic" is derived from the Greek *synoran*, meaning "to see together, all at once," for they are strikingly similar in their accounts of the life and work of Jesus. The fourth one, "The Gospel According to John," is distinctly different from the earlier three with the result, scholars consider it unreliable as history – not that the others are pure history – but they concede its theological value. Of course, it does not in any way contradict the three synoptic Gospels but gives a bird's-eye view of Jesus' life from a totally different angle. That his emphasis is more on theology than on the biography of Jesus is evident from the opening verse itself, which says, "In the beginning was the Word. And the

Word was with God, and the Word was God."[51] His objective is basically evangelistic, which he reveals when he says, "...these are written that you may believe that Jesus is the Christ, the Son of God, and that believing you may have life in his name."[52]

Some scholars believe that Luke and Matthew had freely and profusely drawn from Mark while some others hold that all the three Evangelists had relied on the same source which has been subsequently lost. The controversy about the mutual relationship between the first three Gospels is generally known as the Synoptic Problem, which remains unsolved although there is no dearth of theories put forward to solve it. The problem arises because of the lack of evidence for the source or sources of the biographical facts presented in these Gospels. Neither Jesus nor any of his twelve Apostles who were contemporaneous with him is known to have left any written account of his life or teachings. In fact, we do not know if Jesus was literate as nothing of his writings has been found so far. In case he was and had written down his experiences and thoughts, possibly whatever was found after his death had been destroyed by the rabbis and the Hebrew Chauvinists who were responsible for his crucifixion, for he was a heretic and a danger to the society in their eyes. So they wanted to erase all memory of him from the minds of the people and did not want the future generations to know of him or his "pernicious" ideas.

After Jesus' death, his Apostles, who did not want to be identified with him, had gone underground for some time and did not care to preserve his writings, if there were any. They did not also leave any written document about him or about his teachings, presumably fearing that the Herodians and the Chauvinists would use those as evidence of their association with Jesus[53] to get them arrested and put them behind bars; and of course, to execute them. Or perhaps, the Apostles and his followers might have strongly believed that his Parousia would be during their generation and did not think it necessary to write an account of his life and teachings. But with the gradual spread of Christianity and with the hope of his Second Coming receding, the need for a biography of the man whose ideas had gripped the people was being badly felt, and as some scholars surmised it was in *circa* 50 CE that the first attempt was made to write one. This was believed to have been done in Palestine and is referred to as "Q," the first letter of the word *Quelle*, the German word for "source" as it is supposed to have been the source of the bulk of the material found in Mathew and Luke. But no copy of this document is extant today. It is believed that this was a compilation of the sayings of Jesus as remembered by the contemporaries who had heard him. But most scholars seem to think that it is only a hypothetical document.[54]

Although arranged in the order Matthew, Mark, Luke and John in the Bible, there is no certainty about the chronology of those compositions. It is generally believed that though placed second, the oldest and incidentally the shortest is *The Gospel According to Mark*, which is ascribed to *circa* 70 CE. The scholars are also of the view that the last few verses had not been written by Mark but were interpolated by someone to account for the Resurrection. And if at all Mark himself had composed them, they assert he did not do it at the same time as he had written the earlier verses. There is also a controversy about the language of the oral tradition as well as of the original version of the composition, which need not be gone into as it is beyond the scope of this study.

Be that as it may, today, most biblical scholars tend to accept what is known as the Two-Document Hypothesis, or 2DH as it has come to be known. This theory, first put forward by a German scholar, H.J.Holtzmann in 1861 and "popularised for the English-speaking world by B.H.Streeter in his work, *The Four Gospels* (1924)," caught the attention of the scholars sometime in the second decade of the twentieth century and ever since it has been widely discussed but is yet to find acceptance by the biblical historians. According to this theory Mark's Gospel was the first to be written and it was used by Matthew and Luke, both of whom had access to the Q source, mentioned above. This theory, the scholars assert, has solved the problem of the synoptic Gospels. There is, however, no irrefutable proof to say that the Q source, the premise on which this theory stands, existed at all and as such it is preposterous to pretend that the synoptic problem has been solved.

Apart from the Gospels, the Acts is the only other source of the history of the Church – perhaps, the first authoritative one written – though its historical accuracy has been questioned in recent times. Ascribed to the first century CE, it deals with the history of early

Christianity – the history had been brought up to the beginning of the sixth decade only – and its authorship is attributed to Luke. Of all the books constituting the Bible, the most commented upon is the Revelation of St. John the Divine. An example of apocalyptic literature, it betrays the author's animosity towards the Romans. His prophecy about the decline and fall of the Roman Empire and the possibility of establishing a "new heaven and a new earth"[55] on the ashes of the old, of course, were what the writer wished to see happen. This desire to see the fall of the Roman Empire makes it possible to date the book approximately to the period of Nero (*circa* 54-68 CE) who is said to have executed Peter and Paul or a few years later to the reign of Domitian (*circa* 81-96 CE) because both of them were persecutors of Christians.

Until the cuneiform inscriptions of Babylon and Assyria were deciphered, scholars regarded the Old Testament as a collection of fables and legends and had not given credence to it as historical documents. But the cuneiform inscriptions proved the historicity of most of the places mentioned in the episodes in the Old Testament and it was subsequently corroborated by archaeological findings. Since the turn of the nineteenth century, archaeologists have uncovered the remains of many of the biblical cities, providing corroborative archaeological evidence of the historicity of several of the events like the Assyria-Judah battle of Lachish,[56] described in the Bible. So today, the historical veracity of some of the episodes of the Old and the New Testaments have been generally accepted. However, the details as presented in the Bible and the historicity of many protagonists in the biblical stories, especially in the Old Testament, remain to be proved beyond doubt.

Yet, there are many scholars who regard biblical episodes as pure history, and some early historians have traced the ancient history of the Hebrews depending solely on the material given in the Bible. They have treated all biblical characters appearing in the Bible beginning with Terah and his descendants as historical personalities. Those scholars who hold the view that the biblical episodes are to a great extent true to history are known as the "maximalists." As opposed to this, there is another school of thought, which questions the maximalists' contention that the biblical episodes could be accepted as true history and rejects the Bible as a reliable source of history. These scholars, who are generally identified as the "minimalists," assert that the biblical episodes are purely fictitious and the Bible cannot be accepted as a source of history. But they concede there could be traces of history in the Bible.

Both of them are correct to some extent – while the former group exaggerates the historical value of the Bible the latter totally denies its value as a source of history. There is no gainsaying the fact that the Bible does throw light into the remote past of mankind and gives us glimpses of the ancient history of the peoples of the West Asia, the mythification notwithstanding. In fact, even some of the myths allegorically present the history of those times as we shall see in the chapters that follow. But the bards, whose compositions had been the original sources, were more interested in mythicising individuals and glorifying the Hebrew tribe than in historical veracity. They fictionalised historical events, romanticised and mythicised historical personalities. Their intention was to present Israel as the pre-eminent tribe and naturally, their narratives were blatantly biased. They did not care much for factual accuracy, nor were they expected to, as they were not historians or chroniclers. They were, basically rhapsodists and their compositions were masterpieces of creative literature that presented before the readers a phantasmagoric picture of the men and events of the period.

The scribes who wanted to document those stories, which were being circulated by word of mouth till then, either did not take the trouble of separating or were not able to separate the two disparate strands of fact and fiction tightly entwined with each other in the bardic compositions. Presumably, the motive of those Hebrew scholars of circa the ninth and eighth centuries BCE, who first documented these versified stories, was not to cull historical facts from those oral traditions. They were also not interested in presenting historical facts or in verifying the historical truth of the bardic compositions. They only wanted to record what was being narrated orally, lest all those stories got lost. So they collected and compiled all that came down to them without delving into the historical veracity of those stories. In fact, their interests also lay in glorifying the Hebrew tribe and projecting their theological ideas against the backdrop of fragments of history. If they had written historical facts as such and portrayed the characters as ordinary human beings, their purpose would have been defeated. In due course, "a moral and religious tone crept into the stories" and "historians became preachers and their histories became sermons. The idea of retribution was introduced and good and bad fortune was attributed to piety and sinfulness."[57]

The Bible is thus a beautiful work of informational cum imaginative literature – history, a little though, and myths and legends presented allegorically in a versified form with all the beauty that poetry entails. As a work of informational literature, the Bible gives us a glimpse of the evolution of mankind and the history of the tribes and the monarchies that flourished in West Asia and Egypt, constantly focusing light on the Hebrews, showing their contemporaneous tribes in the background. Here we meet man living like a beast in the forest, man in the state of savagery, man in a barbaric state and man in a civilised society. Here we find the food-gathering economy based on flint and stone tools developing into the food producing economy with the development of sophisticated tools like ploughs and knives of bronze and iron. Here we see an egalitarian society based on collectivism and equality, being supplanted by a stratified society based on private property and slavery. And here we see the rudiments of absolute monarchy factitiously grafted upon the Hebrew society. In short, we get a kaleidoscopic view of the Hebrew society from the earliest times to the first century CE.

Despite being informational, the value of the work as *belles-lettres* is not diminished; perhaps, it is enhanced. The Bible brings to the reader, information about the past symbolically and allegorically. Paradoxically, history is fictionalised in the Bible but it is not historical fiction. The Hebrew rhapsodists' portrayal of the fluctuating fortunes and the final disintegration of the Hebrew tribes that the Bible reflects is comparable to and contrasts with, to take an example from English literature, John Galsworthy's[58] depiction of the tide of fortune of the English middle-class society in his two trilogies. The first one, *The Forsyte Saga*, with two connecting lyric interludes was followed by a second trilogy, *A Modern Comedy*, with two further interludes. These two trilogies vividly present the rise and finally the disintegration of a British middle-class family of the Victorian era.[59] The only difference between the Hebrew bards and Galsworthy is that while the former eulogises and glorifies the Hebrews, covering up the faults and failures of the tribe under the cloak of myths and allegories, Galsworthy satirises and condemns the English middle class. In other words, the difference lies in the fact that the biblical bards looked at the tribes of which they were a part subjectively while Galsworthy, though belonging to the affluent middle class himself, portrayed his class objectively.

The belletristic aspect of the Bible rests on the stories and poems, myths and legends, the myriad figures of speech, the allegories, the symbolism, the imagery and the play of words with which the work abounds. There is no gainsaying the fact that splashes of incomparable poetic beauty lie hidden in the work. The two examples, randomly chosen and given below are studded with figures of speech. Apart from similes, with which these verses abound, the former is embellished with figures of speech like apostrophe, metaphor, anastrophe, tautology and rhetorical questions and the latter, with exclamation, and alliteration in addition.

> *"Give ear, O heavens,*[60] *and I will speak; and hear, O earth,*[61] *the words of my mouth.*
> *Let my doctrine drop as the rain,*[62] *my speech distil as the dew,*[63] *as raindrops upon the tender herb,*[64] *and as showers upon the grass,*[65]
> *As I proclaim the name of the Lord: ascribe greatness to our God.*
> *He is the Rock,*[66] *his work is perfect; for all his ways are justice: a god of truth and without iniquity, just and right is he.*[67]
> *They have corrupted themselves, they are not his children; they are a perverse and crooked generation.*
> *Do you thus requite the Lord, O foolish people and the unwise?*[68] *Is not he your father who has bought you?*[69] *Has he not made you, and established you?"*[70]

These were the words with which Moses began his long disquisition[71] that he gave to the tribe before he is believed to have gone up Mount Nebo to get a view of the "Promised Land." In this he admonishes the people for their perversity and calls upon the tribe to implicitly obey the leader (which is what he means when he says "the Lord") who, he says, is perfect and just.

The following is taken from "The Song of Solomon."

"How beautiful are your feet in shoes, O prince's daughter![72]
the curves of your thighs are like jewels,[73] *the work of the hands of an ingenious workman,*
Your navel is like a round goblet,[74] *which lacks no intoxicating drink; your waist is like a heap of wheat set about with lilies.*[75]
Your two breasts are like two young roes that are twins,[76]
Your neck is as a tower of ivory, your eyes like the pools in Heshbon, by the gate of Bathrabbhim: your nose is like tower of Lebanon,[77] *which looks towards Damascus.*
Your head upon you is like Carmel[78]*, and the hair of your head, like purple;*[79] *the king is held in its tresses.*
How fair and how pleasant are you, O love, with your delights!
This, your stature is like a palm tree,[80] *and your breasts like bunches of grapes.*[81]
I said, I will go up to the palm tree, I will take hold of the boughs:
let now your breasts be like clusters of the vine,[82] *and the fragrance of your breath like apples;*[83]
And the roof of your mouth like the best wine for me beloved,[84] *that goes down sweetly, causing the lips of those that are asleep to speak.*
I am my beloved's, and his desire is toward me.
Come, my beloved, let us go forth to the field;[85] *let us lodge in the* villages.
Let us get up early to the vineyards, let us see if the vine has blossomed. Whether the tender grape has appeared, and the pomegranates are in bloom: there will I give you my love.
The mandrakes exude a fragrance, and at our gates are all manner of pleasant fruits, new and old, which I have laid up for you, O my beloved."

This song[86] reveals the degeneration of monarchs who, as these words connote, indulge themselves in wine and women. Inebriated with affluence and a harem of many women, Solomon, for instance, had begun to neglect the clergy, a powerful social force backed by the affluent class then. This provoked the clergy to foment rebellion and to a great extent that contributed to the strengthening of the clergy's hands leading to the split of the Hebrew kingdom. We shall come back to this in Chapter 7, "The Rise of Imperialism."

The biblical stories have inspired writers, artists and artistes and have been the fountainhead from which flowed thousands of works of adult and juvenile literature in all languages of the world, and many episodes from it have been the themes of visual and performing arts. Apart from these, many a biblical episode has also appeared on the silver screen and the small screen. The works of almost all Western writers are replete with allusions to biblical episodes, and not a few of their works are based on biblical episodes. Familiarity with the biblical episodes and characters is as much essential as knowledge of Greek mythology, to fully appreciate the literary works, be it poetry, drama, fiction or essays of many a Western writer. Dawkins calls attention to the three books written by Naseeb Shaheen, anthologising biblical references in the comedies, tragedies and histories of Shakespeare. Interestingly, Shaheen states, there are more than thirteen hundred biblical references in Shakespeare's works.[87] And episodes like those of Cain and Abel, and David and Goliath have also enriched juvenile literature of many languages. Besides, many biblical expressions can be found in the works of most writers of the world, particularly of the Western world. Interestingly, numerous biblical expressions and proverbs have crept into the vocabulary of all living languages into which the Bible has been translated. And not only the educated but even the uneducated and the illiterate as well use them without being conscious of the source. In other words, they have become household expressions.

As a work of literature, the Bible cannot be classified as an epic or a novel, a drama or a biography, a lyric or any of the familiar genres; but it has the characteristics of all these genres. Of course, Shakespeare ridicules the genre-mania of the literary critics of his times when he makes Lord Polonius, a character in Hamlet, say, "The best actors in the world, either for tragedy, comedy, history, pastoral, pastoral-comical, historical-pastoral, tragical-historical, tragical-comical-historical-pastoral, scene undivided or poem unlimited...."[88] Shakespeare's sarcastic barb is obviously aimed at splitting hairs in determining the genre and not at the idea of classifying literary works by genres. Be that as it may, the Bible may be classed into the genre of sacred writing or *scripture*.

So far so good. But what school of literature does this belong to? It cannot, for example, be fitted into the Romantic, Naturalist, Surrealist, or Absurdist school. Looking at it critically we find, in composing these stories the bards switched back and forth, in an attempt to fuse the rational and the grotesque, the real and the fantastic. So viewing the Bible strictly as a piece of literature, it is tempting, though it may seem asinine, to categorise this ancient work as a work of magic realism, which is a product of the twentieth century.

En résumé, the interests of the ancient rhapsodists as well as the scribes who wrote down the compositions of those bards lay in glorifying the Hebrew tribe and projecting their religious and ethical ideas against the backdrop of fragments of history. And that indubitably brought out a beautiful work of literature. In due course, however, more and more religious ideas were injected into these episodes with the result what was originally a series of romanticised historical episodes, mythological stories and poems, was surcharged with theological thoughts. Eventually, squeezing in more and more theological thoughts by the priestly class helped overshadow everything else and a scripture was born. The scripture, as stated in the beginning, is believed to be infallible and unalterable, but like the scriptures of all religions the Bible was altered, edited, translated and even interpolated by many.

NOTES

1. This was composed c. 1000 BCE, nearly 200 years before the Homeric epics appeared and is eight times longer than both the Iliad and the Odyssey put together.
2. Vide Appendix for the genealogical tree.
3. Qur'an, Surah 4, an-Nisa, 1-36, tr., by M.T. Hilali and M.M. Khan, Madinah Al-Munawwarah, Madinah. (Italics added)
4. Mathew Arnold, Literature and Dogma, An Essay Towards a Better Understanding of the Bible, Preface, New York, 1924, p. xiii.
5. Dan.1:5-16; Lev.11:1-47/17:10-16.
6. The word 'drama' in this context does not mean the literary form designed for the theatre. It suggests the dramatic situations in several

of the episodes presented in the Bible, e.g., I Sam. 24:1-22; Mt. 26:20-52, etc.

7. These are Num. 6:24, 25, 26.
8. The author had the opportunity to visit the exhibition of the Dead Sea Scrolls on September 30, 2006 at the Pacific Science Centre in Seattle, Washington state, USA. The information given here is mostly based on what was gathered at the exhibition. Starting with a replica of the cave from which the scrolls were recovered, there were ten original scrolls. Apart from these scrolls, among the exhibits there were also various artefacts like cooking vessels, pottery, leather sandals and Roman shekel found at the site.
9. Qur'an, Surah 14. Ibrahim, tr. By M. T. Hilali and M. M. Khan. Madinah Al-Munawwarah, Madinah.
10. The Latin translation of the Bible, primarily from the Hebrew, Greek and Aramaic text made by St, Jerome in circa 405 CE, revised subsequently.
11. I. Asimov, *Guide to the Bible*, New York, 1981, p. 283.
12. This is the English form of darwish, a Persian word meaning 'poor.' A dervish is a member of the Sufi order. It also denotes a faqir, which is an Arabic word meaning 'poor.' Members of the tribe of Upper Egypt and Sudan who followed the Mahdi and rebelled against the British during 1880-1885 were also known as the Dervishes.
13. A. Robertson, *The Origin of Christianity*, London, 1953, p. 23.
14. I Sam. 10:11-12.
15. I Sam. 2:12.
16. I Sam. 8:3 5.
17. Latin. Septuaginta interpretes– seventy interpreters.
18. E. Bevan, Hellenistic Judaism. *In The Legacy of Israel*, ed. by E.R.Bevan and C. Singer, Oxford, 1928, p. 40.
19. The significance of changing the name shall be discussed from a materialist perspective, in Chapter 3, "The Virtual Tower of Babel". In the Quran this character is known as Ibrahim, which is the Arabic version of the name.
20. Torah: Genesis, Exodus, Leviticus, Numbers, Deuteronomy; Nevi'im: Joshua, Judges, Samuel (I & II), Kings (I & II), Isaiah, Jeremiah, Ezekiel, The Twelve Minor Prophets (Hosea, Joel, Amos, Obadiah, Jonah, Micah, Nahum, Habakkuk, Zephaniah, Haggai, Zechariah, Malachi); Kethuvim: Psalms, Proverbs, Job, Song of Songs, Ruth, Lamentations, Ecclesiastes, Esther, Daniel, (Ezra, Nehemiah), Chronicles I & II.
21. Ex.21:23-25; Lev. 24:19, 20; Deut.19:21.

22. Mt.5:38-44.
23. K. Marx, A Contribution to the Critique of Political Economy, In "Selected Works," V.1, Moscow, pp. 356-357.
24. H. Levy, *Social Thinking*, London, 1945, p. 37.
25. Qur'an, Surah 3, Al Imran, 67, tr., by M. T. Hilali and M. M. Khan, Mdinah Al-Munawwarah, "Madinah. Ibrahim (Abraham) was neither a Jew nor a Christian, but he was a true Muslim Hanifa and he was not of Al-Mushrikun (the idolaters, polytheists, disbelievers, in the Oneness of Allah, pagans, etc.)." Surah 3 Al Imran, 68.
    "Verily among mankind who have best claim to Ibrahim (Abraham) are those who followed him, believed (Muslims). And Allah is the Wall (Protector and Helper) of the believers." Surah 3 Al Imran, 95. Say (O Muhammad): Allah has spoken the truth; follow the religion of Ibrahim (Abraham) Hanifa and he was not of Al-Mushrikun." Besides these, there are several references to Ibrahim, that is Abraham, in the Qur'an – vide Surah 14, Ibrahim.
26. Jinn is the Qur'anic term for the biblical Satan.
27. Newby, G.D., *A Concise Encyclopaedia of Islam*, Oxford, 2002, p. 95.
28. The Buddha (c. 6th century BCE) opposed classifying human beings into four hierarchical classes or varnas as it is called, and preached equality, which the Sangha exemplified; he also opposed Vedic rituals. Traditionally Jainism traces its origin to the Hindu mythological character Rishabha (Adinath) mentioned in the Puranas and regards him as the first tirthankara who is believed to have flourished contemporaneously with Moses. But historically Mahavira, a contemporary of the Buddha, is known as the founder of this religion. This too, like Buddhism, was a protestant movement against many Vedic practices or rituals, for example human and animal sacrifices, and practised ahimsa or non-violence to a fault.
29. W. M. Schniedewind, *How the Bible Became a Book*, Cambridge, 2004, p. 7.
30. W. M. Schniedewind, *When Was the Bible Written*? Cambridge, 2004, p. 17-18.
31. Josh. 10:11-14.
32. Deut. 31:9, 24, 26.
33. Gen. 1-3.
34. A. Robertson, op. cit., p. 31. Jahu is one of the gods/goddesses in the Babylonian pantheon.
35. R.Graves, *The Greek Myths*, Baltimore, 1955, p. 28.
36. T. Jacobson, Eridu Genesis. In *Journal of Biblical Literature*, V. 100, No. 4, 1981, pp. 513-529.

37. Old Babylonian Chronology.
38. Ibid., pp. 514, 515, 526. William Whitson, a scientist, in his book, 'A New Theory of the Earth,' 1708, puts forward the preposterous theory that the flood the Bible describes was caused by a comet.
39. Enil is analogous to Indra of the Indo-Aryans, Zeus of the ancient Greeks and Jupiter of the ancient Romans.
40. Adad is analogous to Varuna of the Indo-Aryans; Zeus and Jupiter themselves are the rain gods of the ancient Greeks and Romans respectively.
41. It was in circa 850 BCE that Homeric poems appeared, followed by Hesiodic poems a century later. The Mahabharata, the Sanṣkrit epic, appeared nearly two centuries earlier, in circa 1000 BCE. Production of literary records is an indication that the tribes concerned had acquired phonetic or hieroglyphic alphabet and progressed into the stage of ancient civilisation.
42. Ezra 7:6.
43. R.E. Friedman, *Who Wrote the Bible*? New York, 1987, pp.18-27. The information given in this and the subsequent three paragraphs on the church's refutation of the views of and its punitive action against the scholars who carried out researches on the authorship of the Pentateuch is based on this work.
44. Gen. 36:1-43.
45. The order in which the source books are listed has no significance. The list given here is in the order in which each of the source books is referred to in the Bible for the first time.
46. The books listed in the text are referred to in (i) Gen.5:1; (ii) Ex.24:7; (iii) Num.21:14; (iv) Josh.10:13; (v) I Kgs.11:41; (vi) I Kgs.14:19; (vii) I Chr.9:1; (viii) I Chr.29:29; (ix) I Chr.29:29; (x) I Chr.29:29; (xi) II Chr.12:15; (xii) II Chr.13:22; (xiii) II Chr.34:14; (xiv) Lk.4:17 respectively.
47. Although the Bible does not say who his biological father is, we shall probe into his paternity in chapter 9 "The Son of Man."
48. Mt.5:17.
49. I Cor.15:10; Gal.1:15-16; Eph.3:7-9; I Tim.1:12-16.
50. *The Catholic Encyclopaedia*, V.XIV, New York, 1912.
51. Jn.1:1.
52. Jn.20:31.
53. It may be recalled how Peter disowned Jesus, repeatedly saying "...I know not the man..." Vide Mt.26:70, 72, 74.
54. C. Tuckett, *Reading the New Testament*, Philadelphia, 1987, p. 79.
55. Rev. 21:1.

56. II Chr. 32:1-23. The intervention of god and angels spoken of in the Bible may be ignored.
57. A.L. Sachar, *A History of the Jews*, New York, 1965, p. 11.
58. English novelist, dramatist and critic; born 1867, died 1933; pseuds. John Sinjohn, A.R.P.-M; Nobel laureate (1932), declined a knighthood, accepted the Order of Merit.
59. Ralph Fox, *The Novel and the People*, Moscow, 1956.
60. apostrophe.
61. apostrophe.
62. simile.
63. simile.
64. simile.
65. simile.
66. metaphor.
67. inversion.
68. tautology; rhetorical question.
69. rhetorical question.
70. rhetorical questions.
71. Deut.32:1-6.
72. exclamation.
73. simile.
74. simile.
75. simile.
76. simile.
77. simile.
78. simile.
79. simile.
80. simile.
81. simile.
82. simile.
83. simile.
84. simile.
85. alliteration (A figure of sound).
86. Song. 7:1-13.
87. R. Dawkins, *The God Delusion*, Boston, 2006, p. 344.
88. W. M. Shakespeare, *Hamlet*, Act II, Sc.II.

2

The Universe and God

The Bible commences with a theory of creation, which states that "in the beginning God created the heaven and the earth," which was an empty space, devoid of form.[1] The empty space that god created was enveloped in darkness. The spirit of god pervaded the waters, and from the depth of darkness came the voice of god, "Let there be light..." And there it was! The emptiness was suddenly illuminated. Next, god separated light from darkness and he called the light, Day and the darkness, Night. That ended his work on the first day and on the second day he created a firmament in the midst of the waters and divided waters from the waters and he called the firmament Heaven, that is, the sky. Thus the second day passed. The next day, the third day of creation, he commanded the waters to confine itself to one side and the dry land to appear and it happened as god decreed. He called the waters 'seas' and the dry land, 'earth.'

After that he brought forth all kinds of plants as well as their seeds to ensure their continued existence. The fourth day saw the creation of the sun, the moon and the stars in the sky – the sun and the moon to light the earth during the day and the night respectively. The fifth day, he created all those organisms, big and small, that live in water as well as the various birds and blessed them saying "be fruitful and multiply." On the sixth day, he commanded: "Let the earth bring forth the living creatures" and there appeared all kinds of animals that lived on land. After that he said, "let us make man in our image" and he did it.[2] That man was called Adam.

After creating Adam, god made a garden on the east of Eden and diverting a river from Eden he split it into four branches to water the garden. He put Adam in charge of the garden and told him to tend the plants and trees that were there. He also wanted Adam to replenish the earth and rule over the other creatures on the earth and told him that all the herbs, trees and fruits "shall be your food" as well as the food of the birds and animals. But he strictly forbade Adam from eating the fruit of 'the tree of knowledge' and warned him that if he ate that fruit he would die. Six days of hard labour! On the seventh day, satisfied with all that he had created, god took rest.[3] Later, realising that Adam was lonely and needed "a helper suitable for him," god created a woman[4] and she was named Eve. Thus god created the whole universe in six days. This is the biblical theory of creation, which is generally known as the Theory of Special Creation or Creationism. We shall analyse this theory and discuss the fallacies, the contradictions and irrationalities in it when we deal with scientific theories of creation.

Theories about the origin of the universe and living beings can be seen in the scriptures of all religions[5] with a few differences in their details but essentially similar. Of course, the people of different cultures had different myths to explain the way god created the earth and the living beings, which we need not go into as it is not relevant to this study. These theories were not put forward to deliberately misinform the people of those times or with the intention of preaching theism. Those were the considered and honest views of the "philosopher-scientists" of those days about the origin of all that they saw around them in nature. Their logic was simple. They had seen, for example, that a potter or a blacksmith was required to make a pot or a sword respectively and so they reasoned that nothing came into being by itself; there should be someone to make it. The mud and iron were there but they did not on their own form into a pot and a sword; it needed the potter and the smith to turn them into a pot and a sword respectively. Again, where did the mud and iron come from? Those too, they conjectured, must have been made by someone.

The early thinkers had also seen that the "creation" of a baby called for coitus between male and female entities and so they imagined that the creation of the mud and iron too needed these two factors, male and female, which predetermined polytheism. So they deduced that the mud and iron or the universe could not have come into being without male and female 'artificers' and not knowing who or what they were, they arbitrarily called those artificers *god and goddess*, supernatural beings, that they thought were existing in a world of their own, which was somewhere out of this world. The scriptures of all religions give the impression that the world of these supernatural beings is in the sky, which, they thought was a solid structure. A reader of the Bible is convinced of it when he reads, "the Lord came down to see the city and the tower...."[6] If god were to come *down*, he cannot but be living *up* above the world. Where else could it be but the sky?

Those philosopher-scientists who conceived of god and goddess are not to be laughed at or ignored because it has been through such assumptions that many discoveries are made. In fact, when man is not able to understand or explain certain phenomenon he tries to explain it by assuming the existence of 'something' and that *assumed reality* is given a name. Phlogiston was the name given to such a 'reality' that man assumed in recent times. It was supposed that this hypothetical colourless, odourless, weightless substance was the combustible part of all flammable substances and was given off as flame during burning until Antoine Lavoisier, in the eighteenth century, discovered the role oxygen played in combustion. *Assumed realities* may be said to have been born out of ignorance and fear; in the case of Phlogiston it was ignorance of the cause and fear of fire.

Though these theories of creation seem palpably irrational and mythical to the thinking man of today, when these theories were put forward, presumably they were considered by the intellectuals of those days, the most acceptable explanation of the fundamental problem of the origin of the universe. No one could conceive of a more plausible theory to account for the existence of all that he or she saw around him or her. Notwithstanding all the illogicalities and flaws immanent in these theories, they are not to be ridiculed or condemned outright. On the other hand all these theories of creation that the scriptures of various religions put forward have to be seen and appreciated as honest attempts of the thinkers of the period of ancient riparian civilisations to explain the origin of the universe. They recorded those theories and bequeathed this "discovery" to posterity.

These theories which look ludicrous today motivated the subsequent generations of thinkers, philosophers and scientists who, finding these theories inadequate, built upon it various theories of creation. There is no doubt that it was these theories of creation propounded by the thinkers of the ancient riverine civilisations of Sumeria (Mesopotamia) and Egypt for instance, that had inspired the philosopher-scientists of the later civilisations like those of India and Greece. As a result, they mulled over further the mysteries of nature and propounded more sophisticated theories of creation. However, these too could only be speculative because science itself lay buried in speculative thought in those days. In fact, philosophers were the scientists of the period of those civilisations. Hence the earliest theories about the origin of the universe put forward by the philosopher-scientists of those civilisations – be it Indian or Greek – were basically speculative thoughts. Although anchored in materiality, they were more speculative than empirical and an invisible hand, a supernatural power known to different people by different names, played a role in all these speculative theories of creation.

The religions of almost all peoples of the ancient world were polytheistic and the gods conceived by them were of both sexes, male and female. The polytheistic religion of the Canaanites, a civilised tribe, had, in their pantheon, male and female gods, which includes goddesses like Anath and Asherah and gods like Shemesh, Haron, El and Baal. Of these El was the creator of all other gods and goddesses and mankind. He had two wives and so the involvement of the male and female factors is implicit in the Canaanite theory of creation.

The Sumerian religion, like that of the Canaanites, was polytheistic and of the many gods in its pantheon, the four more important were An, Enlil, Enki and Ninhursaga also called Nintur. Of these, the last one was a goddess and had the same status as the three male deities. However, the Sumerians believed the goddess Ninhursaga alias Nintur "did the actual work of creation," because she says "*my* creatures" when she speaks of mankind; and they had seen it was the female factor that helped bring forth the universe. But the male too had a role, and as other Sumerian myths suggest, Enki, a god, also had played a role in the work of creation.[7] Interestingly, this indicates that the Sumerians believed in the involvement of the female (Nintur) and male (Enki) factors in the process of creation.

The biblical theory of creation is the first step that the barbaric tribe of West Asia that later came to be called the Hebrews or Israel, which was at the threshold of the Status of Civilisation, took in their attempt to explain the fundamental question about nature. As stated in Chapter 1, "The Book of Books," it was borrowed from polytheistic Sumerians who had long back progressed into the Status of Civilisation. That they had adopted the Sumerian theory of creation indicates they had imbibed and accepted polytheistic idea of the religions of all other tribes. Robertson writes, "...From their first settlement in Palestine the Hebrews, as was natural, adopted the cults of the country in which they had settled. Jahveh was only one *baal* (lord) among many... (Significantly) Jahveh had female consorts... Papyri, discovered at Elephantine in Upper Egypt show that as late as 408 BCE, after the time of Nehemiah, a colony of Jews, settled there for more than a century, worshipped along with Jahu two variants of the mother-goddess, Anath and Ashima."[8] Besides, the word Elohim (Eli), the other word by which the Hebrews identified their god, was originally plural in form[9] which confirms the fact that the Hebrews too were polytheistic like any other tribe of those times. It was much later, before the tribe led by Abram was forced out of Haran – the legend of which we shall deal with in Chapter 3, "A Virtual Tower of Babel," – that it repudiated polytheism and embraced monotheism. Yet they grafted the same theory of creation on their monotheistic religion. Obviously they were oblivious of the logic – the imperative of the involvement of male and female in the process of creation – behind the Sumerian theory of creation and so they did not realise the incompatibility of the Sumerian theory with monotheism.

In the polytheistic religion of the Indo-Aryans (Hindus) that has a plethora of gods and goddesses in their pantheon, none of them was directly involved in creation. Brahma was in charge of the 'portfolio' of creation and hence considered the Creator. He created twenty-one prajapatis to assist him in the task of creation. All these prajapatis had wives, and human beings are said to be the progenies of one of the prajapatis called Manu,[10] while the other prajapatis created everything else in the universe, including all other living beings. So according to the Hindu mythology the two sexes are involved in the creation of the universe.

Ahura Mazda, the Zarathustrian god, is an amalgam of both male and female sexes. *Ahura* is masculine gender while *Mazda* is a feminine noun. That these two are spoken of as one is suggestive of copulation. And so in the process of creation by this god, male and female participation is implied.

The Qur'an, the scripture of the Muslims, which has blindly adopted the biblical myth of creation, calls the Creator "Allah, the One, eternal and unequalled" that substituted Yahweh in the biblical theory of creation. Allah is addressed as "Lord" or referred to as "He" thereby implying masculinity. So according to the Islamic theory also like that of the Yahwists there is no involvement of the female element in the process of creation.

Hence, whether the male and female elements are involved in the act of creation or not, the common factor in the creation myths of different peoples of the ancient world is god. In other words, god is the cornerstone of all theories of the origin of the universe that are found in the scriptures of various religions, polytheistic or monotheistic. Hence, the theories of creation conceived by the peoples of all ancient civilisations are based on blind belief in god. And the biblical theory of creation, like its source the Eridu Genesis, is also based on blind faith in god.

When did man conceive of a being called god? Archaeologists have unearthed burnt bones of animals, which date back to the period when the Neanderthal man wandered the earth between *circa* 200,000 BCE and 40,000 BCE. These burnt bones, some archaeologists assume, were sacrificial offerings. They, therefore, assert that it suggests the Neanderthals' belief in god and that thousands of years before modern man appeared, the Neanderthal man had thought of a deity or deities. However, all those archaeologists who hold that view seem to have arrived at the conclusion that those were sacrificial offerings, on the basis of a preconceived notion that the Neanderthal man had the necessary intellect to conceive of things beyond what they saw and experienced.

Darwin writes, "There is no evidence that man was aboriginally endowed with the...belief in the existence of an omnipotent god. On the contrary there is ample evidence, derived not from hasty travelers, but from men who have long resided with savages, that numerous races have existed, and still exist, who have no idea of one or more gods, and who have no words in their languages to express such an idea."[11] Anthropologists are unanimous in their opinion that the savage had no god. In fact, today most anthropologists affirm that even the modern man during the period of barbarism had not thought of god. The Neanderthals, anthropologists unequivocally say, were constrained to spend all their time gathering and hunting for food or searching for a mate and had no time to speculate on matters beyond what fell within the sphere of their experience. Moreover, the Neanderthals' brains had not sufficiently developed to conceive of supernatural being or think of anything other than their basic necessities.

Significantly, however, several graves of Neanderthals that had been unearthed were seen to contain tools and weapons, along with burnt bones. The burnt bones should not, therefore, be looked at in isolation. When seen along with the tools and weapons, there is no doubt that the Neanderthals did imagine a world beyond, but not of a supernatural being. Possibly, what would happen after death and where would those who die go, must have been a problem that haunted them. Obviously they must have thought that there existed a world, mysterious but material, other than the one they lived in and knew – not a world of spirits and divine beings but a physical world similar to their own, inhabited by men and animals akin to those seen in their world. They were, perhaps, sure that those who died would be going to that world. Although those are burnt bones of an animal it can be said with certitude that they were not sacrificial offerings, for as anthropologists say, the Neanderthals could have had no god or a supernatural being to give burnt offerings to. So the Neanderthal man did not even think of a being other than what he saw around him. And the burnt bones found in Neanderthal graves do not prove that he had conceived of a supernatural being.

The possibility is that the burnt bones could be what remained of a boar or any other animal roasted and kept in the grave for the departed relative or companion to eat on his way to the other world. Some of the finds like weapons and tools, in the graves of Neanderthals along with the burnt bones, seem to suggest this possibility. The roasted meat kept in the grave was only for the journey and would not last long after that. The weapons kept in the grave could be for him to hunt for his food and to defend himself if necessary, from any hostile people or beasts that might possibly attack him on the way. After his arrival in the other world also, the departed person would need the weapons, for he would have to hunt for his food and to defend himself from enemies and predatory animals there. Those weapons may be what he had been using during his lifetime in this world. If Neanderthals had not conceived of god, the idea of a supernatural being must have occurred to the *Homo sapiens* at a later period. However, there is no possibility of determining the exact point in time when this idea had occurred to man but it can be said with certainty that god was the brainchild of the modern man. We shall discuss this problem a little later.

Before that let us see what was it that impelled man to think that a supernatural being that he called god was governing us and to start worshipping that being. How did such an idea take shape in the mind of man? Did he suddenly conceive of it one day? Or was it an idea that gradually developed? It is wisely said that necessity is the mother of invention and god, of course, is an invention prompted by certain necessities. Let us see what those necessities were and trace the steps that led to the concept of god. It is a long story that had its beginning in the period of savagery.

During the early period of savagery, anthropologists observe, the many hostile forces like thunderstorms, diseases, wildfires, earthquakes and such other intimidating natural phenomena that man had to face, were incomprehensible to him. All these imperilled his life and frequently wreaked widespread havoc on his surroundings, often causing the death of his fellow beings and wild animals. He was helpless, for he did not know what they were and what caused them. In addition to these, he had to contend with aggressive rivals in foraging for food and in the competition for a mate, as well as defend himself from predatory animals. However, all those hostile forces that made his life difficult and even caused death and distress so plagued him that he was compelled to think of ways and means of controlling them and of protecting himself from them. It was a problem that baffled him immeasurably but with his limited intelligence and knowledge, he could not comprehend those phenomena or find a solution to them. He was living in constant fear – the fear of these natural phenomena against which he was helpless.

This inability of man to find a way to protect himself from those phenomena brought forth the magician claiming magical powers to control all those furies of nature and man found that sometimes the magic worked. Needless to say, it was not his magic that worked; the result was coincidental. But the magician claimed it was the result of his power. A tribal magician who was believed to have such magical powers is also referred to by anthropologists as a sorcerer or a shaman. The magician or shaman was also the physician of the savage, for he claimed that his magical power would cure any kind of ailments and sometimes he did succeed. That too was, of course, coincidental. In his role as the healer of diseases he is called a medicine man or a witch doctor. Incidentally, the sign or miracle that the Bible speaks of is in anthropological parlance magic, sorcery or shamanism. The savage relied on the shaman and shamanism to protect him from all those hostile forces that were beyond his comprehension and from the furies of which he was powerless to defend himself.

Magic was, thus, the product of man's sense of insecurity, which was caused by,

(i) the incomprehensible natural phenomena that perpetually threatened his/her very existence,
(ii) the danger to his/her life from the carnivores prowling all around, in the midst of which he/she had to exist,
(iii) the possibility of being attacked by fellow human beings with whom he/she had to compete for food (occasionally for mate too, and
(iv) the uncertainty of getting food.

Apart from using magic as protective armor to defend oneself from hostile natural forces, it was also used to protect individuals and ensure the tribe's success in inter-tribal wars.

Ergo, the primitive man, scared of all these dangers and finding no alternative, sought refuge in the magic of the shaman who, he thought, had all the power to restrain the antagonistic forces of nature and protect him from elemental furies as well as to cure him of any diseases. He was also certain that the shaman had the power not only to save him from wild beasts and human foes but help him achieve success in hunting and wars as well. The shamans were equally confident that "the performance of the proper ceremony accompanied by the appropriate spell would inevitably be attended by the desired results..."[12] Not much thought was involved in the genesis of the idea of magic and of the belief in the power of the practitioner of magic; it was, so to say, the result of man's knee-jerk reaction to the forces that endangered his life.

But shamans did not, naturally, always succeed. Occasional failures were of course, overlooked. Sometimes failures were attributed to the interference of witches and wizards or even to the magicians of the enemy tribe. But these excuses would not be accepted by the tribesmen for long. They would lose faith in that magician who failed too frequently and they would throw him out of the tribe or kill him.[13] This practice was found even during the time of Jesus as the following episode illustrates.

The news of Jesus' miracles, especially his miraculous healing touch that cured all sorts of diseases and physical disabilities spread all over Judaea. When he went to Nazareth where he preached in the synagogue, he said, "The Spirit of the Lord is upon Me because He has anointed Me to preach the Gospel to the poor...He has sent me to heal the broken-hearted, to proclaim...recovery of sight to the blind...."[14] He, therefore, rightly expected the people to ask him to show some signs. But he wanted to avoid it, obviously because he knew that his sorcery did not always achieve the desired result. So at the end of the sermon he said to the freemen of the city who had assembled there to listen to him: "You will surely say to me, Physician, heal yourself. Whatever we have heard you have done in Capernaum, do also here in your country." And he continued, "No prophet is accepted in his own country," adding that there were many lepers among Israel in the time of Elisha but he did not cure any of them as he did Naaman the Syrian. His excuse was not accepted by the crowd that had assembled in the synagogue and was looking forward to seeing him perform miracles. They were disappointed and furious. They dragged him out of the synagogue and brought him to the brow of the hill on which the city was built, intending to push him down the precipice to his death. But in the confusion that prevailed, he cleverly slipped out of the crowd and fled to the security of Capernaum in Galilee, where he had many followers.[15] If Jesus was a historical personality, which doubtless he was, as we shall see in chapter 9 "The Son of Man," this episode exemplifies the treatment meted out to failed magicians of primitive societies.

Man would not have started the practice of magic before he learned to make fire and began to verbalise his thoughts, both of which were prerequisites of magic – fire for performing the various rites and speech for chanting incantations associated with magic. Although there are many legends in the mythologies of ancient civilisation attributing the discovery of fire to one of the mythological characters,[16] nobody knows for sure who first mastered the technique of making fire. But we know when it was discovered. Morgan states man learned the use of fire in the lower stage of savagery; however, it is difficult to say where and when exactly the technique of making fire was discovered.

It may not be irrelevant here to visualise how this discovery was made. After a wildfire, the savages must have kept the fire going in their caves for a long time and used it for keeping themselves warm to begin with but later for cooking also. It could also have been used as a weapon to ward off predatory animals as well as to attack or defend themselves against other tribes. But they would not have been able to keep that fire all through the year, as quite often it must have got extinguished by strong winds or heavy rains and that must have motivated them to try to make a fire themselves. Some of them who were comparatively more intelligent and observant – the savage 'scientists' so to say – must have noticed how the trunks of two trees rubbing against each other in the wind produced sparks that started wildfires. So they must have tried out using two pieces of wood or stones to kindle a fire. And ah, there it was – fire! Anyway, after trying for many days, they succeeded in making a fire! This would not have been a one-time discovery, as discoveries are today. The tribe(s) that discovered the secret of making fire would not have divulged it to the other tribes because fire must have proved to be as dangerous a weapon then as nuclear weapons are today. And so the tribe or the tribes that had acquired the knowledge of the art of making fire did not want other tribes to acquire that know-how and must have kept it a secret. Apart from keeping themselves warm, fire must have proved not only an effective deterrent against attacks by predatory animals but also a decisive weapon in inter-tribal wars. However, in course of time, various savage tribes inhabiting different regions must have mastered the technique of making fire on their own at different times. But as the art of writing had not been discovered at that time, no record of this discovery was left for the information of posterity and so we cannot pinpoint the person who first discovered the art of making fire.

The other prerequisite for the practice of sorcery was articulate speech, which is communication through conventional vocal or oral symbols, presupposes language without which ideas could not have been formed in the mind. Of course, before the acquisition of language also, man would have been thinking as any other animal did and still does but not as he did after the commencement of articulate speech, which was made possible with the invention of verbal expression, that is spoken language. Language may be defined as any means, vocal or other, of expressing or communicating thought or feeling[17] and it helped him form ideas because language is the vehicle, as it were, of ideas. "Several writers, more specially Prof. Max Mueller, have lately insisted that the use of language implies the power of forming general concepts; and that no animals are supposed to possess this power...."[18] Speech is not possible without language; these two go hand in hand and as articulate speech developed during the lower stage of savagery, language too must have developed at that time.

Both these, mastery of the technique of making fire and articulate speech, were acquired by man late in the lower stage of savagery pushing him up to the middle stage of savagery.[19] It was, presumably, at that time, during the period of transition from the lower to the middle stage of savagery, that the magician and magic appeared and eventually became a part of human culture. No doubt, hundreds of thousands of years must have elapsed since his advent on earth, by the time man reached that stage. This stage of social development also witnessed the herding together of man in its most primitive form, the development of which we shall discuss in Chapter 3, "A Virtual Tower of Babel."

That was a period when revolutionary changes had been taking place, leading to mankind's leap forward from savagery to barbarism. In the course of this long, long journey from savagery to barbarism, man had won many battles in his incessant war with nature. During this period, he enslaved fire, extracted metals and learned to make alloys with which he made the bow and arrow, invented the wheel and began to make pottery and chariots. He learned to cook, domesticated animals and cultivated plants. He irrigated the land, baked clay in the sun and made bricks with which he constructed houses, and he discovered iron. Along with this he developed art also. All these activities did have a tremendous impact on his brain and the dexterity of his hands. As Morgan points out, "with the production of inventions and discoveries, and with the growth of institutions, the human mind necessarily grew and expanded; and we are led to recognise a gradual enlargement of the brain itself, particularly of the cerebral portion."[20] In fact, this went on along with the development of the hand. In other words, his interaction with nature helped improve the adroitness of his hands and sharpen his brain, taking him to the portal of abstract thought.

Until then, frequent failures of the magicians to control the elements of nature, or to ensure the safety of the tribe and the tribesmen, for which whatever excuse that the magician had given were accepted by the tribesmen. But now, thanks to his developed brain and enhanced intelligence, he realised that the magician was incapable of controlling nature and he began to look elsewhere for protection. All attempts of the shamans to explain away those failures to protect the people of the tribe from elemental fury and other dangers did not satisfy them anymore. The magicians had lost their credibility. This set the "philosophers" among the tribesmen thinking and they mulled over the problem. They must have asked themselves what these natural phenomena were and how those were caused; above all, how they could control them and save themselves from those deadly forces of nature. It was a problem common to all tribes. So the more intelligent among them must have discussed this problem with the members of other friendly tribes.

This question was uppermost in the minds of the thinking men of all tribes, for all of them must have been losing faith in the magician and his magic. Having seized of this problem that affected their very existence, they put their heads together to find a solution. They, with their more developed brains and increased intelligence, now concluded that there was something more than meets the eye in all those natural phenomena. They now realised that trying to control the furies of nature by magic was futile and that there was something more powerful than the magician, which resided in each of these natural phenomena and objects.

Man now thought there was a power of some kind in each of the objects that was existing, be it tree, animal or even an inanimate object like a river as well as various natural phenomena. The barbaric tribes had a word to denote this power. Among the Melanesians it was known by the term *mana*; the Algonquins called it *manitou*; to the Iroquois it was *orenda* and in the language of the Sioux, it was *wakanda* – these did not imply personalities but were invisible 'spirits' and were the nearest that the barbarian got to an idea of god.[21] But his worship did not go beyond certain magical incantations and rituals. So the power to control natural phenomena did not lie with the magician any more; that power, the power to control each of the phenomena lay with the spirit concerned. However, they still needed the help of the magician to intervene on their behalf to keep those spirits in good humour. Frazer too had come across certain cases of magic in which the operation of spirits was assumed and attempts were made to win their favour by prayer and sacrifice.[22] Instances like these are interim stages in the process of transformation of sorcerer and sorcery into priest and religion, which presupposes god. The sorcerer, now, tries to placate or to threaten a spirit on the assumption that each spirit had the power over what that particular spirit controlled. This, incidentally, sowed the seed of nature worship.

It took many years for man to realise that those spirits to whom he had attributed the power to control the forces of nature also are not the answer to his problem. The spirits too failed him as did the magician earlier. He surmised there were some other forces or powers beyond all those spirits and they controlled not only all those natural phenomena but mankind as well. He began to imagine some supernatural power or powers residing beyond all that he perceived and controlling those natural objects and forces. As was the case when magic and the magician failed, this time it was the perceived inability of the "spirits" to stand up to the hostile natural forces which those spirits were believed to rule over that called for a rethink. In other words, the provocation for such a rethink must have been man's realisation that propitiating the spirits that were believed to be residing in and controlling the natural objects and phenomena too was quite futile.

This rethink prompted him to isolate the spirits from the objects and phenomena over which they were believed to have control and to conceptualise embodied spirits existing independently of those objects and phenomena. He called those embodied spirits "gods," and he thought each god controlled a particular object or phenomenon; hence there were for example, the god of thunder, the god of the seas, the god of wind and so on. These embodied spirits or gods were the personifications of the earlier spirits, which, he now thought, stood aloof and above the objects or the phenomena that they controlled. All these personified phenomena and objects were then deified.

The birth of god, however, created a problem for man. He was left in the lurch with no one to go to for help against the furies of nature or for protection from his enemies because god, the protector, was somewhere. The spirits that man had conceived earlier were supposed to be residing in the objects concerned. But the new embodied spirit or god was not there, for had he been there, being an embodied one, he would have been visible; but he was invisible, incommunicado and inaccessible. He was not approachable like the sorcerer of the olden days who was believed to have the power to control nature had been; nor like the spirit whose abode was known. Moreover, he imagined these gods to be schizophrenics with pronounced contradictory traits, benign and wicked, like Jekyll and Hyde.[23] When those beings were in good humour they were like Jekyll, pleasant and benevolent, but if they were not, they would be like the misanthropic Hyde, grisly and malevolent. The Jekyll in those gods would turn into the Hyde in them! So these gods had to be kept happy lest they turned sinister and noxious.

So in order to persuade the gods to help man, he thought, they needed to be propitiated by supplication. Out of this necessity to placate god, grew certain forms of worship, rites and rituals. These, of course, are not very different from, but more complicated than those of magic, the performance of which called for a specialist. That was the priest; he knew all the rites and rituals as well as the incantations or the invocations to accompany those rituals that helped please their gods. He, thus, had the power to liaise with god on behalf of man and he acted as the interface between god and man. He was, to use a cliché, old wine in a new bottle; this new player, the priest, was *mutatis mutandis* the shaman or magician of yesteryears.

How do they differ? The shaman was an independent person who claimed to have the power to control and subdue the various phenomena of nature. On the other hand, the priest in general did not have the power to subdue the various phenomena of nature as the shaman claimed to have. Unlike the shaman, the priest represented and was supported by an Institution of which he was a full-time employee. These institutions were known by various names like the church, mosque, synagogue and temple depending on the organisation – which is what we call 'religion' – that maintained these institutions and each of these organisations employed its own priests and had its own god(s). "The priest is the socially initiated, ceremonially inducted member of a recognised organisation, where he holds a certain rank and functions as the tenant of an office..."[24] The priest of a particular religion had the power only to appeal for help to the god or gods of the members of that religion and he dubbed the gods of the other religions as spurious to justify his inability to influence those gods.

The magician and magic of the primitive man did not, one fine morning, suddenly turn into the god and religion that subsequently replaced the discredited magician and magic. The rise of god and religion was not the result of man's spontaneous reaction to elemental fury as had been the case with the origin of magic. This transition from magician and magic to priest, god and religion had taken myriad years. It was a long process that took as many years as man did for its long, long journey from savagery to civilisation. The transition from barbarism to civilisation was a critical period in the history of the evolution of human society, lasting hundreds of years that witnessed a drastic change in the socio-economic structure. The tribal communes of an egalitarian society based on collectivism had been supplanted by a stratified society based on private property and slavery when absolute monarchy and political institutions emerged. It is, however, difficult to say precisely at what point in time man conceived of god. We can conjecture that it could in the beginning of the stage of ancient civilisation that the idea began to take shape and it took a concrete form some time during the period of the ancient civilisation.

All evidence points to the infancy of the ancient civilisation when the transformation of spirits into gods and the magician into the priest took place. The archaeological finds like the cave drawings and inscriptions discovered hitherto, of the period of barbarism do not suggest the concept of god. But apart from the ruins of temples and idols of gods of the period of ancient civilisations, documents like the clay tablets and papyrus scrolls of the period of ancient civilisations that have been retrieved and deciphered prove that they had conceived of gods. Indubitably, therefore, it was during the period of ancient civilisations that man for the first time conceived of god. As stated above, he personified and deified the spirits that they believed controlled every phenomenon of nature. As a result, there arose a pantheon of gods like that of the ancient peoples of Mesopotamia, Egypt, India, Greece, Rome or Scandinavia. So we find that the earth, the sun, wind, rivers, trees, lightning, thunder, rain, flood and all such natural objects and phenomena had been personified and deified. Those were the early gods that the ancient man worshipped in those bygone days and in due course, social and cultural factors also began to be deified and worshipped bringing forth the god of war, the god of wealth, the god of love and such other gods with social and cultural attributes.

No god had been conceived *ex nihilo*. The omnipotent god that we see in the Bible was a replica of an absolute monarch that the Hebrew bards saw. Although the Hebrew tribes were in the status of barbarism and had no kings, when the bards composed the biblical verses, there were many contemporaneous tribes that had progressed into the stage of civilisation and were being ruled by autocratic kings. Those absolute monarchs provided the models for the omnipotent god of the Old Testament. For the barbaric Hebrew bards and the Evangelists of the period of civilisation, who created the biblical (the Old and the New Testament) gods, the kings or the emperors that they saw, were the role models on which the character of their gods was moulded. And that is why Yahweh, the god of the Old Testament, was cruel, jealous, totally devoid of compassion and used violent means to subdue those who did not accept his supremacy and bow to him.[25]

The god of the New Testament too was not different, for like the despotic kings and emperors in the days of absolute monarchies and imperialism, he regarded those who opposed him or even dissented as iniquitous and punished them in a way that today is considered inhuman and fiendish. To punish those who question his authority, he "will send out his angels who will gather out of his kingdom all things that offend and those who are involved in unlawful acts; And will throw them into a furnace of fire: there will be wailing and gnashing of teeth."[26]

These are not the traits of the biblical gods alone; gods of all religions are in no way different because all gods, of whatever religion they are, were the products of the period of monarchy and were modelled on the despotic kings and these gods in turn provided the religio-philosophical justification for the monarchies. Incidentally, we do not find a democratic god because no god was created after absolute monarchy passed into history and democratic institutions took its place. In fact, no god can afford to be democratic because omnipotence is the very essence of god. Be that as it may, the origin of god and religion also, like that of the magician and magic, can be traced to fear – the same four fears that gave rise to magic and magician. After man deified these phenomena, the priestly class began to weave yarns around these deities to show that these unseen beings with immense powers controlled everything that is seen including man and interestingly, these myths in course of time began to be cited to prove the existence of these invisible beings known as god. Eventually, these myths formed what is today known as the scripture and became the grammar as it were, of religion. The Bible, like the scriptures of all religions, as we saw in the previous chapter, "The Book of Books," was originally an anthology of such myths and legends. It can, therefore, be said that god fathered religion and is the pedestal on which religion, whatever religion it is, stands; and religion became the source of income that sustained and nourished the priesthood.

In fact, every religion grew out of a god or gods; and there is no religion without god. However there were two exceptions, Buddhism and Jainism, both of which were born without being fathered by god. Neither the Buddha, who founded Buddhism, nor Mahavira the founder of Jainism spoke about god. These religions which were protestant movements against Hinduism were, paradoxically, atheistic in its original form but they found it impossible to sustain themselves without gods, which, incidentally, shows religion is inseparable from the concept of god.

Obviously, *ashtangamarga* or the Eightfold Path, which is nothing but a code of ethical principles that the Buddha preached rejecting god, was a poor substitute for god as far as the ordinary man was concerned. They were not satisfied with it; and all of them being converts from polytheistic Hinduism, wanted a deity to whom they could look up to for help in times of difficulty. So after the Buddha's *nirvana* or death, gradually god was brought in by the back door and ironically the Buddha who was radically averse to the idea of god, was himself deified by his followers and worshipped as god! Chattopadhyaya points out that even the Mahayana Buddhists who posit no god have in their monastery pictures and images of "a whole host of ghosts, goblins, and demigods crowding the Mahayana pantheon – the Herukas, Hevajras, Taradevis and what not!"[27]

Similarly, Jainism, a religion of which Mahavira, "a senior contemporary of the Buddha" was the last of a series of tirthankaras (prophets), "as a philosophy is a form of stark atheism, notwithstanding all that is quaint about it."[28] But in the absence of a god, there was no binding force among the devotees and the ordinary man was left helpless with no one to whom he could go for help in times of difficulties. Besides, all those who embraced Jainism, like the Buddhists, were also previously polytheistic Hindus. The priesthood was, therefore, constrained to create a god that would hold together the devotees and preclude their return to the Hindu fold. So the Jain priesthood created what is known as Adhishtayaka Deva as for example, Nakota Bherav Deva in Rajasthan (India), a supernatural being analogous to the gods of other religions who is the protector of the temple and the devotees. In each Jain temple there is one Adhishtayaka Deva, with the result they have not one but many gods.

If Confucianism can be called a religion, that too can be said to be an atheistic religion. However, although Confucius (Kung-futze, as his name is in Chinese) did not speak of god, he preached ancestor worship, which is tantamount to worshipping a supernatural power or being. In Confucianism, therefore, the spirits of the dead ancestors are substituted for god(s). Shintoism, which has deified the sun and the principal deity of which is the Sun goddess, is based on animism and can be considered a polytheistic religion. No religion can sustain itself without a divine being or god, or at least some symbol of a supernatural power, which is the foundation on which all religions are built. In other words, god is an integral factor, an inevitable concomitant of religion, or to put it differently, religion presupposes belief in god and in fact religion is a byproduct of god.

One of the most distinguished philosophers of the twentieth century Bertrand Russell agrees that god is the product of fear. He writes, "... It is partly the terror of the unknown and partly, as I have said, the wish to feel that you have a kind of elder brother who will stand by you in all your troubles and disputes. Fear is the basis of the whole thing – fear of the mysterious, fear of defeat, fear of death."[29] The 'elder brother' that Russell speaks of is obviously god and 'the mysterious' is undoubtedly not the natural phenomena or the wild beasts that the savages and the barbarians feared. Thanks to the spread of education and the developments in science, today man is certainly not intimidated by many of the natural phenomena that once terrified the primitive man because the forces behind most of these are no more a mystery to him. He knows what causes them, he can foresee to a great extent when they would appear and he knows how to escape from their fury while those that are yet to be understood are being probed into. In order to escape from the furies of nature, now he looks up to science and the scientist, not to the magician or spirit as the savage and the barbarian did; nor does he seek the help of the priest or god either. For example, after the recent catastrophic tsunami, the monstrous tidal wave of 2004 that killed not less than 225,000 people in South Asia, it was not to god or religion that man looked to for help. It was to the scientist and science that he turned to, to warn him of and protect him from such calamities in future.

Yet god did not die. As ancient civilisation progressed into modern civilisation, consequent upon the Industrial Revolution (1760-1850), the root of which may be traced back to the period of Renaissance, fundamental changes occurred in industries, transportation, agriculture and economic policies that brought about drastic changes in the socio-economic structure of society. With the advent of the

Industrial Revolution and the changes it brought about in the socio-economic structure, a new force had come up that was unseen, unpredictable, and incomprehensible, in one word, a delitescent force that man began to fear. The mysterious force that he now feared was evidently not any of those natural phenomena or the wild beasts that the savages and the barbarians feared. The wild beasts had been kept away, confined to their habitat, the forest, long back. He had discovered the secret of the natural phenomena; and he knew that whatever remained a mystery still, would eventually be found out and that there is no supernatural power behind them.

The new force, the delitescent or the mysterious *bete noire* that he now feared was the hidden social phenomenon – the blind market force that behaved erratically and was unpredictable. The man, rich or poor, feared the market force, which controlled him and over which he had no control. He cannot see it, nor can he feel it; but he knows it is there as he experiences its vagaries. The market threatened his life every moment. He could not foresee when it would crash and if it crashed the entire society would be thrown into disarray, bringing in its trail unemployment, beggary, prostitution, misery, starvation deaths, suicides and what not. Ignorant of the fact that this market force was a societal phenomenon, he turned back to god and prayed to save him from the sufferings caused by the erratic behaviour of the new dreaded force. The economists who were supposed to have some knowledge of this phenomenon seemed to be as helpless as the hapless layman. They failed to diagnose the cause of this social malady and tried to treat the symptoms rather than the cause. And even if it was subdued for the time being, a recurrence could be expected any time, and without fail the expected happened periodically. The only remedy that would eliminate the possibility of its relapse was a fundamental change of the socio-economic structure, which, naturally, the vested interests resisted and still resists. Hence the fear persists and god continues to exist along with its concomitants like religion and the priest.

Desmond Morris, a renowned zoologist, looks at the development of the concept of god from an ethological perspective. Although he does not state it overtly, it is evident that he too attributes the birth of god to fear – fear of the dangers lurking in forests. After describing religious activities as "coming together of large groups of people to perform repeated and prolonged submissive displays to appease a dominant individual" Morris turns to our biological ancestors to explain the birth of god. He asks: "since none of these gods exists in a tangible form, why have they been invented?"[30] Long before primitive tribal groupings called gentes or communes, based on hunting-gathering economy took shape, savages must have formed loose groups in response to the dangers posed by other beasts in the forest. This herd instinct exhibited by man was inherited from his animal ancestors as we find, for example in several other species of animals like the elephants.

And each of these groups, whether it was of men or of any beasts, was dominated by a strong male. The male that dominated the herd or group acted as the leader and all members of the group had to propitiate him. In return, he took upon himself the responsibility of protecting the group or perhaps those who clung to him expected him to protect them. The whole group looked upon him as their guardian and saviour. However, they were not different from the other animals, as each individual in the group was an independent unit gathering food for himself, finding a mate for himself but living in the group for security. Slowly, as they found the advantage of co-operating with one another for successful hunting, they developed a cooperative spirit and this brought about a change in the relationship between the erstwhile leader and the members of the group; the strongman became irrelevant and a more tolerant leader emerged. Desmond Morris thought it was this leader that eventually became god.[31] Incidentally, that is the ethological explanation for regarding the king as god when absolute monarchy emerged.

The classical scholar, George Thompson, however, explains it differently. Describing this development, he writes, "...more advanced forms of worship develop in response to the rise of a ruling class – hereditary magicians, priests, chiefs and kings. The totem is now tended with prayer and propitiation. It assumes human shape, and becomes god. The god is to the community at large what the chief or king is to his subjects. The idea of godhead springs from the reality of kingship, split as it now is by the cleavage in society, the relation is inverted. The king's power appears to be derived from god and his authority is accepted as being the will of god."[32] The people of ancient

Egypt, for example, identified the Pharaoh – which was the generic name that came to be used for all Egyptian kings – with god, to be precise, with Horus[33] as well as with their gods like Re, the sun god. The Pharaoh was believed to have magical powers with which he could control nature. When a Pharaoh died or was killed (that there had been conspiracies and rebellions, sometimes resulting in their assassination, although the Pharaoh was looked upon as god, is a different matter) he became god. Osiris, the son of Re and father of Horus, who was the god of the dead was believed to be the divine incarnation of a dead Pharaoh. There are several myths about the Pharaohs becoming (Egyptian) gods after their death.

And, as stated above different religions grew out of the gods of these various cultures. Some mythologists and anthropologists tend to equate the *rites de passage* of the primitive tribes, which could best be described as magic or sorcery, with the religious rites of the period of civilisation. Most anthropologists, as pointed out above, are of the view that primitive man had no god. Religion, in its ancient form, was "an incongruous mixture of magic, totemism, ancestor-worship, nature-worship, and rationalising but contradictory myths."[34] This must have been a passing phase in the transformation of magic into religion. Over the years, religion shed or modified many of the assumptions, beliefs and rituals – in one word, the various elements – that constituted magic. As Caudwell says, in its early stage religion was mythology and showed all the spontaneous inventiveness and recklessness of self-contradiction which is characteristic of mythology. He continues, "Early Christianity shows the same insurgent proliferation of mythology...A new form of religion begins when the mythologising era ends. The mythology is taken over, but it ossifies. Religion has become 'true' religion."[35] Robertson points out that by the time "civilisation emerged from barbarism, religion is already an amalgam of contradictory elements. Firstly, it is a body of ritual traceable to primitive magic and carried out by priests or priest-kings, the civilised counterpart of tribal magicians, in order to ensure food-supply as well as subsidiary advantages to the community which they rule. Secondly it is a body of myths relating to the ritual."[36]

A few vestiges of magic are still seen in religious beliefs, practices and rites, in modern religions. For example, today the Christians believe in the power of miracles like those claimed to have been performed by some nuns or priests. It was on the basis of the belief in the miracles they are supposed to have performed, that the Church canonises them and confers them with sainthood! Capland, who speaks of the ancient Hindus as a "highly civilised people, famed for their philosophical systems, their dramatic poetry, (and) their epic lays," points out "the agreement between the magic ritual of the old Vedas and the shamanism of the so-called savage. If we drop the peculiar Hindoo (sic) expressions and technical terms, and imagine a shaman instead of a Brahmin, we could almost fancy that we have before us a magical book belonging to one of the tribes of North American red-skins."[37] Such beliefs and rites are seen among all religious groups even today. This is an irrefutable proof of the fact that the magician with his offspring magic which is a product of the confused savage mind and god with its concomitant religion of the civilised man, are intrinsically connected. It may not, therefore, be wrong to say that magic carried religion in its womb and when religion is born, the mark of the umbilical cord is seen in the incantations, rites and rituals that are not very different from what a magician performed during the periods of savagery and barbarism. As Caudwell says, "religion was always latent in magic. We call it religion only when it shows an organisation, a coherence, a tough visible structure."[38]

What, then, is religion? Religion, which may generally be defined as a belief in or reverence for a supernatural power or being(s), constitutes, in its visible form, a set of songs and incantations, supplications and rites, rituals and forms of public worship. Frazer, in discussing the relation between magic and religion, however, does not attempt a definition of religion. He writes, "...there is probably no subject in the world about which opinions differ so much as the nature of religion, and to frame a definition of it which would satisfy everyone must obviously be impossible. All that a writer can do is, first, to say clearly what he means by religion, and afterwards to employ the word consistently throughout his work. By religion, then, I understand a propitiation or conciliation of powers superior to man which are believed to direct and control the course of nature and human life." He adds, religion has two aspects – one, a belief in a godhead and the act of propitiating it and two, practice. In other words, religion constitutes both a belief and the rites connected with it. But the rituals need not consist in the offering of sacrifice and such other ceremonies; it may consist in ethical conduct if that would help appease the deity.[39]

Haskins also says, "it is hard to define religion. Ten different people will give ten different meanings. For one person, religion is a complete way of life, determining what he eats, who his friends are, whom he marries, even his daily schedule. For another, religion means going to church, the synagogue, the mosque or the temple and observing religious holidays. For another, religion is simply a way of living in the world; for another it is a belief in god. For still another, it is not a belief in god but a feeling of oneness with the universe. And for some, religion is just something that other people need to provide meaning for their lives."[40] Karl Marx looks at religion through the eyes of a political philosopher that he was, and relates it to the society as he saw it. He writes, "Religion is the sigh of the oppressed creature, the heart of a heartless world as it is the spirit of spiritless conditions. It is the opium of the people."[41] According to him, therefore, religion creates illusory fantasies for the deprived and the poor masses seek refuge in religion, which is a palliative that helps mitigate their misery. To the oppressed people, it is an opiate that helps them forget their wretchedness.

The most holistic definition of religion is given by Frederick Engels. He relates religion to both nature and society and tersely defines it as a distorted reflection of the natural phenomena as well as social forces in the human mind. His definition also explains the phenomenon of presiding deities of cultural factors like love, wealth, music and education. He writes: "All religion, however, is nothing but the fantastic reflection in men's minds of those external forces which control their daily life, a reflection in which the terrestrial forces assume the form of supernatural forces. In the beginnings of history it was the forces of nature, which were at first so reflected, and in the course of further evolution they underwent the most manifold and varied personifications among the various peoples. Comparative mythology has traced back this first process, at least in the case of the Indo-European nations, to its origin in the Indian Vedas, and has shown its detailed evolution among the Indians, Persians, Greeks,

Romans, Germans and, so far as material is available also among the Celts, Lithuanians and Slavs. But it is not long before, side by side with the forces of nature, social forces begin to be active; forces which present themselves to man as equally extraneous and at first equally inexplicable, dominating them with the same apparent necessity, as the forces of nature themselves. The fantastic personifications, which at first reflected the mysterious forces of nature, at this point acquire social attributes, become representatives of the forces of history. At a still further stage of evolution, all the natural and social attributes of the innumerable gods are transferred to one almighty God, who himself once more is only the reflex of the abstract man. Such was the origin of monotheism which was historically the last product of the vulgarised philosophy of the later Greeks and found its incarnation in the exclusively national God of the Jews, Jehovah."[42]

Nonetheless, there is a fundamental difference between magic and religion. Curiously, in spite of germinating from the same seed, that is *fear*, the shoots that grew up were remarkably different. Frazer states "that in the mental evolution of humanity an age of magic preceded an age of religion and that the characteristic difference between magic and religion is that, whereas magic aims at controlling nature directly, religion aims at controlling it indirectly through the mediation of a powerful supernatural being or beings to whom man appeals for help and protection."[43] Malinowski endorsing the above view writes, "Early man seeks above all to control the course of nature for practical ends, and he does it directly, by rite and spell, compelling wind and weather, animals and crops to obey his will. Only much later, finding the limitations of his magical might, does he in fear or hope, in supplication or defiance, appeal to higher beings; that is to demons, ancestor-spirits or gods. It is in this distinction between direct control on the one hand and propitiation of superior powers on the other that Sir James Frazer sees the difference between religion and magic."[44] In simple terms, as Robertson puts it, in the case of magic, which does not conceive a deity there is only ritual whereas deity or god being an integral part of religion, ritual is inevitably accompanied by worship.[45] Worship includes chanting or singing paeans to the deity accompanied with appropriate gestures. These gestures vary depending on the religion. It may be kneeling as the Christians do, kneeling and touching the floor with the forehead as the Muslims do or prostrating as the Hindus do. In essence, all these have the same objective; these are meant to show submissiveness to god whose help is being sought.

As already stated, each religion has its own god or gods and goddesses. Gods are of many forms and several gods of the people of ancient civilisations were grotesque figures; some were theriomorphic, meaning "in the form of beasts," and some, therianthropic, that is half-human and half-animal, and a few, anthropomorphic, that is resembling human beings in form and behaviour. There are also gods that are amorphous. Significantly, even those gods that the believers claim to be formless are addressed as or referred to by the term "Lord" and by the pronoun "he" whatever be the equivalent words in the languages concerned, as if the formless god is an anthropomorphic male deity. This contradicts the amorphism of god; and hence in effect, there is no amorphous god. In polytheistic religions like that of the Indo-Aryans (later, of Hinduism), ancient Greeks, Romans, Scandinavians and Egyptians, each of whom had a galaxy of gods and goddesses and all types of deities – theriomorphic, therianthropic, anthropomorphic – can be seen in their pantheons.

Interestingly, several of the gods that once reigned supreme have been subsequently discarded by the devotees in favour of some other god or gods. Those gods have disappeared for good, while a few that did not exist earlier, have been created. The discarded gods are not worshipped any more. Those gods as for instance, the Greek gods, the Egyptian gods or the Norse gods are practically 'dead.' Their 'bodies' have been removed from their heavenly abode and are not entombed or placed in tombs but embalmed and preserved as mythological characters in tomes. Parodying H. W. Longfellow, it can be said, 'myths thou art, to myths thou returnest.' With the death of those gods, the religions that grew out of those gods passed into oblivion because all religions sprouted from the concept of god. Religion as we saw cannot sustain itself without god and if any god dies the religion based on that god loses its relevance and is forgotten.

That brings us to the question – what is god, the premise on which the biblical theory of creation stands? Augustine defines god as follows: "What then, brethren, shall we say of God? If thou hast been able to comprehend it, thou hast comprehended something else instead of God. If thou hast been able to comprehend Him as thou thinkest, by so thinking thou hast deceived thyself. This then is not God, if thou hast comprehended it; but if this be God, thou hast not comprehended it."[46] In one word, he could not define god or say what it is and to cover up his inability he is beating about the bush as it were. In short, what his verbal jugglery makes absolutely clear is his vain attempt to admit the non-existence of god. Theologically speaking, god is considered eternal and as such is unborn and deathless; in addition, god is omnipotent and omnipresent, immutable and indestructible, imperceptible and incomprehensible. As far as an ordinary man is concerned, a definition of god is not difficult. He considers god – as theists irrespective of the religion they espouse would agree – the creator, the sustainer and the governor of the universe.

However, there is no unanimity among the theists and theologians about the appearance and attributes of god because god is conceived differently by different peoples or different religions and different cultures. Hence, we find for example Christian god and Muslim god, or Hindu god and Buddhist god. As such, the bedrock on which the creation myths of all religions stand is not an objective reality like calcium or ozone, about the appearance and properties of which there is no difference of opinion. There is, for example, no Christian calcium or Muslim calcium, Hindu calcium or Buddhist calcium. This element is represented by the symbol *Ca* and it has certain physical and chemical properties which remain the same irrespective of the person who deals with it. In other words, it is an objective reality, unlike god, which is a subjective category, the symbol of which changes depending on the religion of the person who pictures god in his mind. This imperceptible, subjective category called god is the foundation on which the biblical theory of creation, like the theory of creation found in the scripture of every other religion, stands. It cannot, therefore, be called a theory and is appropriately called a *myth* or creation myth.

This creation myth that we find in the Bible states, "In the beginning God created the heaven and the earth." That implies that god preexisted the heaven and the earth. But from where did the creator that is called god come or who created god and who was the creator of god's creator? It is a question that recurs endlessly which falls into a bottomless pit called *ad infinitum retrogression*. A hypothesis that does not require or admit an antecedent hypothesis alone could escape this fallacy and would be credible; the concept of a creator is not such a hypothesis. The theologians explain away that fallacy, by asserting that god is eternal; it has neither beginning nor end. But as our experience shows, there is nothing eternal and everything changes constantly, which fact the famous Greek philosopher Heraclitus had graphically expressed saying "one cannot step twice into the same river."

Be that as it may, another preposterous statement in this theory is that "the earth was without form, and void" when god created it. The word *void* means "emptiness" or "vacuum." A void or emptiness is not expected to have a form and to say that it was a void without form is redundant. It is also beyond one's comprehension how the heaven and the earth that he created were not solid, liquid or gas but just void! To add to this confusion, it is said, "the spirit of god moved upon the face of the waters." We are not told where the waters came from because as we understand from the Bible, there was only void or emptiness till then. Let us also ignore this illogicality, which cannot be explained in any way. It is said god caused a firmament on the surface of the waters and that was lifted up to form the sky, which was just an empty space over the earth till he created all the other heavenly bodies. So according to this theory, earth is the oldest of all the cosmic bodies that constitute the universe, which contradicts the generally accepted scientific theory of the origin of this planet.

Subsequently, he created the sun and the moon to illumine the earth – the sun to give light during the day and the moon to light up the earth in the night. But he seems to have forgotten that he had already created light or that part of the electromagnetic spectrum ranging from radio waves to gamma rays and so these two sources of light – the sun and the moon – are superfluous. However, let us assume that now he divided the light that he had already created, giving a greater share to the sun and the remaining portion to the moon. Incidentally as can be understood from what is said, the moon is not a satellite of the earth that reflected the light coming from the sun but like the sun it is a star that emitted light. Next, he created the stars and so according to him the sun is not a star.

After creating all that, the Bible states, god created man whom he called Adam. It must be understood that Adam is not a historical personality as the Bible would like us to believe; he is a mythological character and a symbol. We shall return to this point when we deal with the scientific theory of the emergence of man on this planet and more of it when we discuss the connotation of this myth in chapter 3, "A Virtual Tower of Babel." After creating Adam, god told him that he was free to make use of all plants and the fruits that they bear as food except the fruit of the tree of knowledge, for if he ate that he would die. There is no doubt that Adam had not understood what god meant by saying that he would die. It does not seem to have occurred to god, that the phenomenon of death was totally unknown to Adam, for he had not seen death, either of a man or of any other creature so far and god did not explain to him what he meant by saying that he would die. Strangely, Adam also did not ask god what he meant when he said, "the day that you eat that you will surely *die.*" A doubt arises in this context. Adam and Eve ate that fruit in consequence of which human beings are condemned to die and they have been dying. But how is it that the poor animals which have not eaten that fruit have also been dying? Maybe, it applies only to human beings.

Anyway, on the basis of this myth biblical scholars as well as priests and theologians had been researching to ascertain the exact time when this work of creation was carried out by god or when exactly the universe came into existence. Various scholars came out with different dates, all of which were rejected by the church. "The Samaritan Pentateuch plans this primordial epoch BC (BCE) 4700; the Septuagint, 5872; the Talmudist, 5344, Scatiger, 3950; Petavius, 3984; Dr. Hales, 5411 who enumerates about 120 various opinions on this subject, the difference between the latest and the remotest date of which, is no less than 3268. The generally received epoch of 4004 BC (BCE), however, seems to be as well established as any other; it is worthy of remark that the celebrated astronomer Laplace has observed that that year was distinguished as a remarkable astronomical epoch; the earth's orbit then coinciding with the line of equinoxes and consequently the true and mean equinoxes being united."[47] This date was arrived at by Archbishop Ussher of Ireland (1581-1656) in the seventeenth century. It must be borne in mind that Laplace had not made any suggestion connecting the astronomical phenomenon and the origin of the universe but Archbishop Ussher referred to Laplace's observation to give the illusion of a scientific basis for his computation of the date.

Probably that trick clinched the issue and 4004 BCE was accepted as the most likely one of all the dates computed by biblical scholars. The Archbishop, however, did not stop with the year. After a deep study of the scripture, he concluded that god had begun the task of creation precisely at nine o'clock on Wednesday the 26th of October in the year 4004 BCE![48] He, however, had not explained *how* he arrived at the date, the month, the day of the week and the exact time of creation. He came to this conclusion long before scientists came up with the Big Bang theory and theory of evolution that are supported by irrefutable evidence. Since then, the people knew that the universe had come into being millions or billions of years before 4004 BCE when, according to Archbishop Ussher, Yahweh or Elohim created the universe.

By the middle of the nineteenth century, as a result of scientific developments, especially in the spheres of palaeontology, archaeology, geology, physics – in short, all branches of physical and biological sciences – it had been accepted that the biblical theory of creation like those seen in the scriptures of all religions, was pure myth. And today no one gives credence to the biblical story about creation except those who have a vested interest like the priesthood concerned, the *raison d'être* for whose existence is belief in god. Even though they know that the biblical theory is a myth, they do not question its veracity; they pretend to believe it. In fact, today no other educated person believes or pretends to believe that god created the universe, except those who are blinded by faith or who have some selfish motive. And no one would deny that this planet, which had come into existence trillions of years before man appeared on it, has been and will continue to be a silent witness to the emergence and extinction of several forms of life.

While magic to religion, as we have seen, was a smooth path, the one leading from religion to science was tortuous and full of hurdles. Science in its infancy was as stated already, diluted with speculative philosophy influenced by religion as the early theories of philosopher-scientists, be they of India, Greece or any other culture, exemplify. Religion was not just a drag on science but was the biggest impediment to the growth of science as a peep into the history of science would show. Gradually science freed itself from the shackles of speculative thought, matured and diversified itself into different branches of knowledge mentioned above. That made it easy for scientists to concentrate on and probe into various aspects of nature. On the basis of empirical knowledge, physical scientists had put forward the Big Bang theory of the origin of the universe and biologists Charles Darwin and Alfred Russell Wallace propounded the theory of the evolution of the flora and fauna. Finally, Wöhler paved the way for the Oparin-Haldane theory of the origin of life that bridged the wide, gaping chasm that few believed was possible. These theories scientifically explain the origin of the universe and the emergence of life and the evolution of different forms of life on the earth. It is, therefore, imperative in this context to explain as briefly as possible these scientific theories to enable the readers to understand the inadequacy and the mythical character of the biblical concept of creation.

The Big Bang theory states that there existed a region of space of infinitesimal volume that was inconceivably dense and intensely hot. The scientists called this "singularity."[49] Looking at it from a different angle, a singularity is a point in space-time surrounded by a region of space distorted by gravity to such an extent that nothing can escape from it. This region is what constitutes the black hole.[50] This black hole suddenly began to expand about forty billion years ago[51] and it still continues to expand at an ever-quickening pace. We are not concerned with the structure or properties of singularity; suffice it for us to know that it is a physical category or a natural phenomenon and not anything spiritual or supernatural. This continually expanding singularity is the universe that we see today, which comprises myriad galaxies, solar systems, planets, comets, meteorites, cosmic dust, gases and what not. This phenomenon of the continual expansion of the universe, which was observed by the American astronomer Edwin Hubble (1889-1953) in 1929, proved the prediction made seven years earlier by a Russian cosmologist and mathematician, Alexander

Friedman (1888-1925.) The force behind this or what caused this continual expansion is dealt with elsewhere.

But the singularity from which our universe came into being may not be the only one of its kind; nor could it have been the first or the last. There could be other such singularities that have been expanding and as you are reading this there could, perhaps, be a singularity undergoing big bang. There could, thus, be other universes apart from ours. But we do not know yet how much this universe of ours will expand and what would happen to it in the future. Anyway, all that is beside the point.

Theists may argue that a Prime Mover or god is what started the expansion of the singularity and created the universe. This as we discussed already, gives rise to a recurring question and is an absurd fallacy. In all natural phenomena, it is not god but chance that plays a decisive part within the parameters and limits set by the laws of nature. Chance is inextricably linked to Necessity. To give an example, birth is a chance while death is a necessity. For instance, which sperm or pollen fertilises which ovum as well as how, when and where it takes place or whether fertilisation would take place at all is a chance. And even after fertilisation takes place, birth is not a necessity because the law of cause and effect comes into play then and so there is an element of chance in that too. There could be abortion or miscarriage and whether this would happen at all and if it happens when, where and how it happens is, of course, a chance. So birth is dependent on all those factors and to that extent it is chance. Death, as stated above, is a necessity but here also chance plays a role because how, when and where death occurs is a chance. Necessity asserts itself through the interaction of myriad chances, each of which is the consequence of an inevitable sequence of causes. It was not as a result of an experiment in nuclear fission or fusion that god conducted in his heavenly laboratory that the Big Bang happened; it was the result of what may be called *chance* that brought about the conditions necessary for triggering the big bang. Big bang, however, is not a necessity, for not every black hole in the universe would undergo big bang.

Millions of years after the big bang, particles in the solar nebula condensed to form solid grains, which clumped to form lumps of rock mainly as a result of gravitational pull. These chunks of rock developed into planets and one such planet is the earth on which we live. This is estimated to have formed more or less five billion years back. The surface of the earth was originally molten and as it cooled, volcanoes spewed large quantities of ammonia, carbon dioxide, methane and steam, which in course of time condensed into water and this eventually formed the seas. All that existed then is what we call inorganic elements. Hence, to begin with there were only inorganic substances on the earth and in course of time, certain inorganic elements (necessarily including carbon and hydrogen) present in the sea water slowly got synthesised when physical conditions conducive to the process happened by chance to be present bringing forth various new compounds. And as this process continued, little by little, changes took place in the proportion of these elements. When such gradual changes in the proportion of the elements constituting the various compounds reached certain critical points, changes in their properties occurred changing the inorganic compound into an organic compound. The changes in the properties of a substance are determined by the changes in the proportion of the elements contained in them. This is a law of nature.

The most important point is that the external agents that cause the change, or catalysts as they are called, are physical substances and nature works without any supernatural, immaterial or spiritual force behind it but based on certain physical laws, which are the laws of nature. Incidentally, when it is said *laws of nature*, it must not be misconstrued that these laws are statutes imposed upon or fiats decreed by a ruler or rulers of the universe. Nor are they like the civil and criminal laws of the various countries, which are regulations made by the governments or rulers of the countries concerned to protect societal structures. The laws of nature are not enacted by anyone to protect the structure of the universe. They are simply the principles by which nature functions and these principles are not extraneous to but inherent in nature. Therefore unlike the civil, criminal or constitutional laws, the laws of nature cannot be repealed, even amended or in any way altered. In other words, these laws of nature are nothing but mental reflections of the laws governing the development of nature, which are discovered by men in the course of their investigative interaction with nature.

These laws of nature also operate in the process of the formation of organic compounds from inorganic elements. It has been proved that organic or animal substance can be produced from inorganic elements *in vitro*. The possibility of such a change – the change from inorganic to organic substance – that had been thought of as impossible till then was demonstrated in 1828 by the German chemist Friedrich Wöhler. Incidentally, his serendipitous discovery exploded the hitherto held doctrine of vitalism, which asserted that living matter contained a non-material vital principle – what the French philosopher Henri Bergson (1859-1941) called *elan vital* – that was neither a physical nor a chemical category. Wöhler prepared urea, an organic substance found in the urine of many animals, from inorganic compounds. When he treated silver cyanate, an inorganic compound, with a solution of ammonium chloride [NH4CNO], another inorganic compound, another inorganic compound, ammonium cyanate [NH4Cl], was obtained:

AgOCN(aq) + NH4Cl(aq) → AgCl (s) + NH4CNO (aq).

And when this crystalline inorganic substance ammonium cyanate, was heated, at a critical temperature it completely changed, transforming itself into urea [CO(NH2)2], an organic compound. In other words, the ionic bonds in it changed to covalent bonds in urea. The disposition and connection between the elements in these compounds are different, although the compositions of both are fully identical as the equation given below shows.

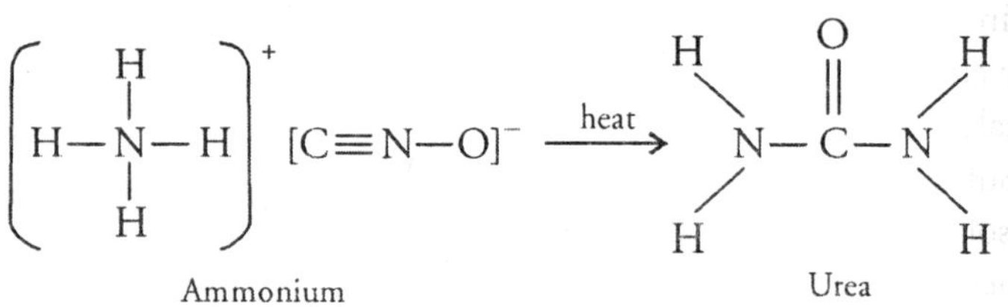

$$\left(\begin{array}{ccccc} & & H & & \\ & & | & & \\ H & - & N & - & H \\ & & | & & \\ & & H & & \end{array}\right)^{+} [C\equiv N-O]^{-} \xrightarrow{\text{heat}} \begin{array}{ccccccc} H & & & O & & & H \\ & \diagdown & & \| & & \diagup & \\ & & N & - \; C \; - & N & & \\ & \diagup & & & & \diagdown & \\ H & & & & & & H \end{array}$$

Ammonium cyanate   Urea

Both the inorganic and organic compounds ammonium cyanate [NH4CNO] and urea [CO(NH2)2] being identical, are called isomers. That is, they are composed of the same chemical elements in the same proportions by weight and having the same molecular weight but differ only in the configuration of their atoms. Yet their properties are fundamentally different; in other words, they are qualitatively different. Here again the law of nature comes into play, for the amount of each element constituting the inorganic compound and those that constitute the organic compound are combined in different proportions, as analyses of these two compounds, ammonium cyanate and urea, showed. In ammonium cyanate, nitrogen (four atoms) was 46.781%; carbon (two atoms), 20.198%; hydrogen (eight atoms) 6.595%; and oxygen (two atoms) 26.425%. In urea, on the other hand, nitrogen (four atoms) was 46.5%; carbon (two atoms), 20.00%; hydrogen (eight atoms) 6.71%; and oxygen (two atoms) 26.64%. In other words, the quantities of each of the elements that make up these compounds are different and those differences cause the difference in the properties of the two compounds although the ingredients that constitute them are the same. So ammonium cyanate, an inorganic substance, has changed into an organic substance as a result of the changes in the proportion of their components. This has been brought about by the same law of nature that transformed inorganic compounds into organic substances in nature that we discussed above.

Following Wöhler's path-breaking discovery, a series of experiments were conducted by chemists synthesising a variety of organic compounds from inorganic substances, proving that organic matter is basically a combination of inorganic elements. These experiments, thus, broke down the barrier between inorganic and organic substances. We know, today, that organic substances are nothing but chemical compounds containing carbon and one or more other elements, most often hydrogen, oxygen, nitrogen, sulphur or the halogens and sometimes others as well.

Subsequently, Marceli Nencki (1847–1901), a Polish chemist, had isolated albumin, nitrogenous material, salts of sodium, potassium, magnesium and phosphorous from the protoplasm of putrefactive bacteria, the composition of which, he says, may depend on the species of the bacterium. This observation undeniably showed that protoplasm, which is the basis of life, is also made up of inorganic elements, which as stated above, combined to form organic compounds. Life is a peculiar form of motion. It is a mode of existence of albuminous substances and it exists as long as metabolism, which is the totality of the opposite phases, anabolism or the constructive phase and catabolism or the destructive process, continues to be active. In common language these two opposite processes may be described as assimilation and disintegration of body substances; assimilation begins with the intake of food and disintegration necessitates excretion of the products of disintegration. So two mutually exclusive and antagonistic processes stay united in the phenomenon called life. This, the co-existence of two mutually exclusive and antagonistic processes or forces, is another law of nature.

However, there is a very wide gap that needs to be bridged. How did non-living matter get transformed into a living organism? Again the law of nature that we saw in action in changing the inorganic substances into organic substances came into play here also. No doubt, after the earth was born, aeons passed before life first appeared on the earth. The problem of the origin of life baffled biologists for a very long time. Darwin-Wallace's theory of evolution that explains how the different forms of life came into being does not say how living organisms first came into existence. Several scientists in an attempt to solve this problem proposed various theories but none of them was acceptable to the scientific community.

In 1924, Alexander Ivanovich Oparin, a distinguished Russian biologist, asserted that there was no fundamental difference between a living organism and non-living matter and propounded his theory of the origin of life. He writes, "to be sure, in the primitive ocean, which was a solution of elementary organic substances (that some scientists called the 'primeval soup'[52]) reactions took place not according to any definite sequence or order but to a large extent, in a chaotic manner. Organic substances were simultaneously undergoing several chemical transformations, following various chemical courses, which yielded a great number of different products. But from the very outset there was a definite general tendency towards the synthesis of more complex and highly molecular compounds. This tendency led to the appearance in the warm waters of the earth's primitive ocean, of highly molecular organic compounds similar to those which we now find in the bodies of plants and animals."[53]

About the same time that Oparin published his theory of the origin of life, J.B.S. Haldane, a British scientist, working independently put forward a similar theory. So the theory of the origin of life, which has now been accepted by the scientific world, may be referred to as the Oparin-Haldane theory. Today, scientists are at the threshold of producing life in the laboratory.

Chance, as explained above, does play an important role in all these processes and occurrences in nature. It was chance that caused the big bang and turned inorganic elements into organic compounds, finally giving rise to protoplasm. By the time various inorganic elements combined and turned into what scientists consider organic compounds that eventually brought forth protoplasm that is *life* on earth millions of years, not less than four thousand million years, must have elapsed after the earth came into existence. It was not necessity but a series of chances that caused this.

As far as we know today, the first protoplasmic life in the form of unicellular prokaryotes emerged in the oceans approximately two billion years ago as a result of a series of chance occurrences. The Prokaryote is an organism of the kingdom *Monera* (also called *Moneran*) or *Prokaryote*, comprising the bacteria and cyanobacteria characterised by the absence of a distinct, membrane-bound nucleus or membrane-bound organelles and by DNA that is not organised into chromosomes. The mode of existence of this matter, protoplasm is what we call "life." Hence it may not be wrong to say, protoplasm is the physical basis of life and life does not exist in the absence of this physical basis. One of the unique characteristics that protoplasm is endowed with is reproduction. All these living beings, plants and animals, including man, that we see today did not suddenly appear on the earth in one day or a week but evolved from the primordial form of protoplasm as the Theory of Evolution states.

Some organisms in their struggle for existence perished and vanished from the earth while some withstood the rigorous 'selection' by the environment. As Darwin puts it, "It may be said that natural selection is daily and hourly scrutinising, throughout the world, every variation, even the slightest; rejecting that which is bad, preserving and adding up all that is good; silently and insensibly working, whenever and wherever opportunity offers, at the improvement of each organic being in relation to its organic and inorganic conditions of life. We see nothing of these slow changes in progress, till the hand of time has marked the long lapse of ages, and then so imperfect is our view into long past geological ages, that we only see that the forms of life are now different from what they formerly were."[54] This process, known as Natural Selection, that has brought forth a diversity of living beings, has been incontrovertibly corroborated by subsequent palaeontological and geological findings. The process that causes the diversity is mutation which, "formally defined as a heritable change in the genetic material (DNA or RNA) of an organism, is the ultimate source of all variation."[55]

The Bible, however, states that god moulded Adam in his own image and this was dated back to 4004 BCE by Archbishop Ussher. Alfred Russell Wallace writes: "Anthropologists are now, indeed, pretty well agreed that (modern) man is not a recent introduction into the earth. All who have studied the question now admit that his antiquity is very great; and that, though we have to some extent ascertained the minimum of time during which he must have existed, we have made no approximation towards determining that far greater period during which he may have, and probably has existed."[56] Palaeo-anthropologists, based on the study of recent archaeological finds, confirm that hominoids or the first human-like species appeared on this planet more than three and a quarter million years ago. And the first modern man as pointed out above, about two hundred thousand years back or a little earlier. So the modern man, known to the zoologists as the species *Homo sapiens sapiens*, must have appeared on the earth two hundred thousand years or more before the fictitious biblical character Adam is believed to have been created by Yahweh.

The Bible categorically states, "So God created man in his own image...."[57] This is said only about man and no other living being, which implies that the fish, beasts, birds, insects, protozoans – in short, all living beings other than man – were not made in his image and evidently god does not look like any of those creatures. Since god had moulded man in his own image, as the Bible has not given a description of what god looks like, it may be presumed that god generally resembles us – or any human being that we find on the earth today. The differences in the physiognomy, cranial measurements, colour of the skin, eye and hair and even the stature of human beings of different races show that there was not one but more than one creator at work and each one of them had made man in his own image. The existence of different races like the Dravidian, the Aryan, the Mongoloid and the Negroid may, therefore, be attributed to the multiplicity of races among gods too. In that case, the human beings are products of different races of gods, like the Dravidian god, the Aryan god, the Mongoloid god and the Negroid god! We are not told which god created Adam. As the Bible does not specify to which race Adam belonged we can only guess. Accepting Darwin's theory that the first man appeared in Africa as we shall see in Chapter 3, "A Virtual Tower of Babel," Adam being the first man, must have been of the Negroid race and so the god that created Adam too belonged to the Negroid race.

Now let us look at the problem from a different angle. Palaeo-anthropologists, based on the study of recent archaeological finds, have come to the conclusion that the extinct species of man's direct ancestors, the earliest of the Hominind began to roam the forests of Africa nearly three and a quarter million years ago. They are *Australopithecus afarensis*, *A. africanus* and *Paranthropus bosei* but like the other animals, as these were of the Homini and not the *Homo* genus, probably the god that created the Homo genus did not create them in his own image. Nevertheless, the general appearance of those Hominis whose figures palaeontologists have attempted to recapture and sketched on the basis of the skeletons unearthed by them shows a marked resemblance to human beings. However, the decisive point of departure was the advent of *Homo habilis*, the first in the genus *Homo* known to have produced some crude tools, for which they had to use their hands and to a great extent they resembled modern man. Incidentally, this, perhaps, marks the beginning of the Palaeolithic Age and the lower stage of savagery. Close on their heels appeared *Homo ergaster*, followed by *Homo erectus*, which are known to have lived in caves and tamed fire. Then came our closest ancestors, *Homo sapiens neanderthalensis* or the Neanderthals. The Neanderthals are said to have invented language, which must have enabled them to speak and so the lower stage of savagery must have ended with the Neanderthals.

However, it must be understood that each of these species did not appear one after the other. So the previous one would not have vanished from the earth before the next species appeared; there was overlapping of species. Some biologists suggest that *H. erectus*, Neanderthals and the modern man must have been coexisting for thousands of years. So *H. erectus* lived through the period of the Neanderthals and continued to exist during the infancy of the modern man. And both these species very closely resembled man. It may, therefore, be presumed that they have been created in the image of the god that created the modern man.

If god had created Man in his own image, he must have started his work on man with the creation of *Homo habilis*. And he proceeded step by step until he created *Homo sapiens sapiens*, after which, as the Bible says, he took rest and did not resume duty. Are we to understand, therefore, that the creator too had evolved as the *Deus habilis*, *Deus ergaster*, *Deus erectus* and *Deus sapiens neanderthalensis* and finally *Deus sapiens sapiens*,[58] creating at each stage of his evolution the corresponding species in his own image? If that were so, *Deus erectus*, *Deus sapiens neanderthalensis* and *Deus sapiens sapiens* too had co-existed and created *Homo erectus* as well as both sub-species of *Homo sapiens*. And could it be that the two species *H. erectus and H. sapiens neanderthalensis* are not being created now because the corresponding species of gods too are extinct?

Significantly as stated above, archaeologists have not hitherto exhumed any cave paintings of gods by the several species of the genus *Homo* that existed before the period of riparian civilisations; it may be, therefore, presumed that in pre-historic times, man had not conceived of what we call god. The earliest pictures of gods that have been found so far belong to the period of riverine civilisations and most of those pictures are of theriomorphic and therianthropic gods with a few anthropomorphic gods. Pictures of anthropomorphic gods were those of the later civilisations, for example the Indo-Aryan and Greek. The point being made here is this. If god had created man in his own image, the men of ancient Egypt for example, would have looked like those theriomorphic and threianthropic gods – some of them looking like weird beasts and some having partly animal and partly human forms. Earlier, we saw that it was man who created god or man conceived of god out of fear of nature or invisible social forces. So it can be said that it was not god that made man in his own image but *vice versa*, that is, it was man who pictured god in the image of what he imagined god to be like. And the god that resembles modern man is what the modern man created in his own image.

All these developments, the origin of the universe, its continuing expansion and the transformation from inorganic compounds to organic compounds, the synthesis of various elements to form life and the evolution of living beings have not been simple processes as they seem when they are described here. These are extremely complex processes in which chance played an important part; and hundreds of thousands of years must have elapsed for these processes to have brought the universe to the present state. However, the last word on the origin and continual expansion of the universe and of the origin and evolution of life on earth is yet to be said. In the future, scientists may chance upon certain facts that may call for revision or modification of the present theories. Nevertheless, from what we know already, it can be said with certainty that these processes – the origin of the universe and life on the earth and the evolution of living beings – do not need the intervention of god, an imaginary supernatural power, at all.

In this study, we are looking at god not as a theological subject or an amorphous category but as a concept and the Bible not as a scripture. The Bible, as we had discussed in the previous chapter, "The Book of Books" is as much a work of informative and imaginative literature as it is a scripture. And when you look at the Bible as a literary work, god appears as one of the most important *dramatis personae* in the long drama that unfolds through the chain of episodes presented in it.

NOTES

1. Gen. 1:1-2.
2. Gen. 1:26-27/2:21-22..
3. Gen. 2:3.
4. Gen. 2:21-22.
5. Such creation myths are part of the traditions of all tribes and are usually found in all scriptures. In the Vedas and in the Qur'an however, unlike as it is in the Bible, the myth of creation is not described in continuous verses. In the Rigveda, for example, see mantras 10:72, 81, 82, 90, 121, 129, 130, 190, etc., and in the Qur'an, Surah 7:10,11; 32:5-9; 41:9-12, etc.

6. Gen.11:5.
7. Ibid., pp. 514-516.
8. A. Robertson, *The Origins of Christianity*, London, 1953, pp. 21-22.
9. *The New Compact Bible Dictionary*, Grand Rapids, 1967.
10. Mahabharata, Shanti Parva, Ch.335. Prajapatis are supernatural beings and involvement of sex is not a necessity for their creation or coming into being, they may even be swayambhoo, that is "self-born." Hence Manu is also called swayambhuvan or "self-begotten."
11. C. Darwin, *The Descent of Man*, Akron, 1874, p. 95.
12. J.G.Frazer, *The Golden Bough*, Pt.1 The Magic Art and the Evolution of Kings, V.1, New York, 1963, p. 230.
13. A. Robertson, op. cit., p. 14.
14. Lk. 4:18.
15. Lk. 4:23-31.
16. In Hindu mythology Angiras is said to be the discoverer of fire. Vide V.M. Mohanraj, The Warrior and the Charioteer, New Delhi, 2005, p.81. Greek mythology credits Prometheus with the discovery of fire. (He stole fire from the god Zeus and gave it to humans). Similarly, mythologies of different peoples attribute the discovery of fire to one of their culture heroes.
17. In this context, we are concerned with the vocal means of expression only. The other means of expression is the sign language that must have preceded speech. Even arachnids and insects are said to be using their own communication system that may be considered a king of 'sign language.' For example, the 'courtship dance' of the male spider can be regarded as a kind of sign language inviting the female to mate. This should not be confused with the sign languages that man has developed. The spiders are not known to have the faculty for thinking as humans do and theirs is an instinctive act.
18. C. Darwin, op. cit., p. 90.
19. L.H. Morgan, *Ancient Society*, Palo Alto, 1978, p. 10.
20. L.H. Morgan, ibid., p. 37.
21. A. Robertson, op. cit., p. 12.
22. J.G. Frazer, *The Golden Bough*, Pt.1 The Magic Art and the Evolution of Kings, V. 1, New York, 1963, p. 220.
23. A novel by Robert Louis Stevenson, which portrays a psychopath with such contradictory traits. In this novel, both the benign and wicked traits are found in the personality of Dr. Jekyll.
24. J. Campbell, *The Masks of God, Primitive Mythology*, Hammondsworth, 1969, p. 231
25. Ex.7:13 ff. Vide also Complete Lectures of R.G.Ingersoll, Rhodes and

McClure, 1895. (Recent paperback reprints are available.)

26. Mt.13:41-42.
27. D. Chattopadhyaya, *Indian Atheism*, Calcutta, 1960, p. 8.
28. Ibid, p. 162.
29. B. Russell, *Why I Am Not a Christian*, ed. by P. Edwards, London, 1964, p. 16. (Brackets added.)
30. D. Morris, *The Naked Ape*, Dell, New York, 1972, pp. 146-147.
31. D. Morris, *The Naked Ape*, New York, 1972, p. 147.
32. G.D. Thompson, *Aeschylus and Aathens*, Berlin, 1977, pp. 42-44.
33. The Egyptian sky god, the god of light, also regarded as the grandson of Re or the youthful sun born afresh every morning.
34. A. Robertson, op. cit., p. 18.
35. C. Caudwell. *Illusion and Reality*, Berlin, pp. 43-44.
36. A. Robertson, op. cit., pp. 16-17.
37. W. Capland, Altindisches Zauber-ritual, p.ix. Quoted in J.G.Frazer, op. cit., p. 229.
38. C. Caudwell, *Further Studies in a Dying Culture*, Calcutta, 1990, p. 31.
39. J.G.Frazer, *The Golden Bough*, Pt.1 The Magic Art and the Evolution of Kings, V.1, New York, 1963, pp. 222-223.
40. J. Haskins, *Religions*, Philadelphia, 1973, pp. 13-16.
41. K. Marx, A Contribution to the Critique of Hegel's Philosophy of Law. Introduction, Moscow, 1976. p. 39.
42. F. Engels, *Herr Eugen Duhring's Revolution in Science*, London, 1934, pp. 346-347.
43. J.G. Frazer, op. cit., p. 423.
44. B. Malinowski, *Magic, Science, and Religion*, New York, 1954, p.19.
45. A. Robertson, op. cit., p. 18.
46. Augustine, Sermo LII, vi, 16. Quoted in "Catholicism," ed. by George Brantl, New York, 1962, p. 36.
47. The Comprehensive Holy Bible, Old and New Testaments, revised corrected an improved by Dr. Blayney, Samuel Bagster, London. Year of publication and pagination are not given. [Presumably, it was printed in the late eighteenth or early nineteenth century as Samuel Bagster, the printer, lived 1772-1835 (See on-line). A copy of this voluminous tome is in the Nilgiri Library, Ootacamund, India.
48. Ibid.
49. S. Hawking, *A Brief History of Science*, London, 1989, p. 50.
50. The scientists define this as a Planck sphere, which had a radius equal to what they call the Planck length denoted by the symbol lp measuring 1.66×10^{-35} m.
51. This is said to have happened at 6.4×10^{-44} second, which the scientists

call the Planck time denoted by the symbol tp

52. E. Nisbet and C.M.R. Fowler, *The Early History of Life*, University of London, 2003, p. 15 (On-line)
53. A.I. Oparin, *The Origin of Life*, Moscow, 1955, pp. 44-45.
54. C. Darwin, On the Origin of Species, Ch. 4, (On-line)
55. N.H. Barton, *Evolution*, New York, 2007, p. 325.
56. A.R.Wallace, *Contributions to the Theory of Natural Selection*, London, 1870, p. 303.
57. Gen. 1:27.
58. Deus is the Latin word for 'god.' Deus sapiens sapiens denoted god of the species sapiens sapiens.

Part Two

WIZENED COLLECTIVISM

3

A Virtual Tower of Babel

The Bible, which is basically considered a scripture, as stated in Chapter 1, "The Book of Books," is virtually a blend of theology and various mundane matters of which the most conspicuous is history – glimpses of prehistory of mankind and a smattering of the early history of West Asia. The book commences with allegorical presentation of the prehistory of mankind and gradually narrows down to focus light on the proto-history of the tribes, especially of the Hebrews, that existed in the Fertile Crescent as well as the history of the contemporary kingdoms and empires that overpowered the tribes, decimating and even exterminating some of them. The belief that the mythical and historical drama that we see in the Bible had been played out in this region has been confirmed by archaeological evidence. Biblical archaeologists have exhumed the hitherto hidden worlds of the Old and the New Testaments bringing to light the undocumented history of man that lay buried for thousands of years in Western Asia. The pioneer of biblical archaeology, Paul-Emile Beta of France, exhumed in 1843 reliefs of Sargon II the king of Assyria who pillaged the kingdom of Israel.[1] This was followed by several others. A team of British archaeologists, led by Sir Charles Leonard Woolley, after unearthing Ur of the Chaldees continued the excavation revealing the ruins of the Sumerian temples,[2] beneath which, he assumed, lay telltale signs of the Flood,[3] believed to have occurred around 4000 BCE.

Further below was found evidence of human habitation, of a period far back into time, long before the biblical god is said to have carried out the task of creation. Artefacts like handmade jars and primitive implements of hewn flint and absence of any metal remains proved that the habitation belonged to the Stone Age.[4] Flint tools are characteristically of the Middle Palaeolithic or Mesolithic period, which came to a close, "on one chronology" about 140,000 years ago,[5] when Neanderthal man coexisted with modern man in the continents of Africa and Asia. And today no one doubts that since the Palaeolithic period, human beings had been living in that part of the world, where the historical episodes described in the Bible are said to have taken place. Here, in days of yore, life throbbed – men and women in flesh and blood lived, loved, fought and died very much like what is happening in the world of today! The stories about those men and women and the life they led then, had been originally composed by Hebrew bards with the intention of eulogising and romanticising those whom the people of the region considered the heroes of their times as well as to project Israel as a pre-eminent tribe. Naturally, therefore, their narratives were totally biased and highly exaggerated while the historicity of most of those characters remains unconfirmed. In fact, those are fictitious characters.

Over the years, archaeologists have exposed a panoramic view of the settlements and habitations lying scattered underground in deep slumber for centuries all over the region, popularly known as the Fertile Crescent, that provided the stage for the human drama, which unfolded then. It is this drama that is reflected in the Old and the New Testaments. All these archaeological remains of the biblical times exhumed from there, however, do not prove the historicity of the biblical characters, many of which as stated above are but fictitious. Nonetheless, when we delve deep into the Bible we find the type of society in which the people of those times lived. But it has to be borne in mind that there were myriad tribes at different stages of development existing in the region in which, as archaeological remains prove, many, though not all, of the biblical episodes are known to have taken place.

The evolution of each tribe depended on the progress it had been making in developing the tools for the collection and production of food and in melting ores of metals for making weapons. The tribes being nomadic, the geographical locations and the duration of camps at each of these places had an impact on the development of those tools, which in turn inevitably and profoundly affected the progress of the tribe concerned. Besides, the status of the other tribes in the midst of which a tribe had been and with which it happened to be interacting for a long period, were also factors that influenced its evolution. However, the tribe would move up to a higher socio-economic stage only if the material conditions of the tribe itself were ripe for the upward leap.

The Bible presents those events through symbols, myths and allegories while some of the events of the biblical period are distorted or falsified versions of historical facts. In other words, what we find in the Bible are symbols, myths and allegories with a sprinkling of raw and cooked-up history of the Hebrew tribe and the tribes contemporaneous with it, wrapped in theology. Nevertheless, from these myths and allegories mixed with bits and pieces of historical events and developments that we find in the book, we can get a very clear picture of mankind exemplified by fictitious characters symbolising the pre-Hebrew tribes, in the period of savagery. The focus then narrows down to the barbaric Hebrews, giving us a vivid close-up of the tribe. We get a glimpse of the emergence of the Hebrew tribe and its evolution – its progress from barbarism to civilisation; we also see the tribe in its heyday, its decline and its partial recovery against the backdrop of the rise and disappearance of several other tribes, kingdoms and empires. And finally we find the tribe poised for a headlong collision with Rome, the most powerful imperialist power of the period.

Those historical events described in the Bible had taken place mostly in the Fertile Crescent, which was the crescent-shaped stretch of land lying between the rugged mountains in the north and the arid sandy waste of peninsular Arabia in the south. For centuries, there had been civilised tribes like the Sumerians, the Akkadians and the Elamites, living in this region, occasionally leading to clashes with one another thanks to their hunger for land. And to add to the prevailing confusion, the comparative fertility of this region known as the Fertile Crescent had been understandably attracting the tribes inhabiting the unfriendly mountainous North and those living in the wilderness of Arabia in the south. It was in the early second millennium

BCE that the influx of various barbaric tribes into the Fertile Crescent and the tribal movements in the entire western Asia as well as the region south of it occurred.

This is what the biblical story of the Tower of Babel metaphorically reflects. When the human beings built the skyscraper called the Tower of Babel, and were living in it happily, god thought that it would help unite the human beings and that "now nothing will be restrained from them, which they have imagined to do." So he said to his fellow beings, the other gods, that he would go down to the Tower to "confound their language...and the Lord scattered them abroad from there all over the face of the earth."[6] The Fertile Crescent was virtually the Tower of Babel flattened and spread out on *terra firma*, truly reflecting the condition of the Tower of Babel after, as the myth says god sowed the seeds of disunity among the human beings residing in the biblical Tower. Here, in this region called the Fertile Crescent, various tribes speaking different languages inhabited, like the people who were in the mythological Tower of Babel after god successfully confounded their language fearing that a united mankind would pose a danger to him and his fellow gods.

The plurality of tribes in this "Tower of Babel" called the Fertile Crescent was, however, not the result of an imaginary paranoiac and vicious god's machinations but the handiwork of innocent and blind socio-economic forces. These nomadic and semi-nomadic barbaric tribes that descended upon the Fertile Crescent from in and around this region had been getting embroiled in conflicts with one another and contending with the indigenous peoples, for pieces of pastoral or/and arable land to settle down. So the history of the tribal peoples in the Fertile Crescent is a long story of the incessant wars between the immigrant barbaric tribes and the indigenous barbaric and civilised peoples in those bygone days, vying with one another for possession of land. Until the Fertile Crescent became part of the Roman Empire the entire western Asia was in convulsions as it were – tribes replacing tribes, kingdoms sprouting and crumbling, empires supplanting empires – as a result of tribal migrations and the inevitable armed conflicts between various peoples for land and natural resources.

It is enigmatic how the Semitic barbarians who began pouring into the Fertile Crescent in the second millennium BCE, succeeded in absorbing or overpowering the more advanced and civilised pre-Semitic peoples like the Sumerians and the Babylonians who had been dominating the region for centuries. A discussion of the cause of the decline and ultimate extinction of those pre-Semitic riparian civilisations is not relevant here. However, it may, incidentally, be pointed out that this is similar to what happened to the highly civilised people of the Indus Valley who were drowned by the waves and waves of barbaric Aryan migrants that flowed into the valley and inundated the region.

The society of that period – to be precise, the economic, social and political structure of the biblical society – was fundamentally different from what human society is today. This is but natural. As pointed out in Chapter 2, "The Universe, Man and God," nothing is absolute and all phenomena in the universe are subject to change. So is human society. It had been progressing from savagery to barbarism and to civilisation due to the impact of social, geographical, demographic and above all economic factors. As Morgan puts it, "by re-ascending along the several lines of human progress toward the primitive ages of man's existence, and removing one by one his principal institutions inventions and discoveries, in the order in which they have appeared, the advance made in each period will be realised."[7] Instead of going into a detailed theoretical exposition of this process, which is beyond the scope of this book, let us go back in time and try to glean from biblical stories, the pre-history of mankind and the early history of West Asia.

In the Bible, the character that is introduced to the readers first is Adam who, the Bible says, was the only human being living in a garden called the Garden of Eden along with various kinds of animals and birds. But Adam was not a human being that existed in flesh and blood. A man, an individual, called Adam never existed. He is a symbol – he symbolises the earliest human beings. When we look into his life and the generations that followed him, we see mankind in its infancy. In the person of Adam we meet face to face the most primitive man, the savage of the Palaeolithic period. In other words, Adam is the personification of the mankind that existed in the beginning of what according to Morgan's periodisation, is called the Lower Status of Savagery. Interestingly, the word *Adam* means 'mankind' and hence it may be said he personifies all species from *Homo habilis to Homo sapiens Neanderthalensis.*

There is also no evidence to say that the Garden of Eden which the Bible speaks of was situated somewhere in the Fertile Crescent or that there was such a geographical region that the Bible calls the Garden of Eden existed at all anywhere on the earth. The Bible simply says a river that flowed out of Eden and branched into four distributaries watered the garden.[8] One of these was the river Euphrates, which is a river approximately 2,750 kilometres long that today flows from Turkey and passing through Iraq, Syria and Iran discharges itself into the Persian Gulf. The other three rivers, the Pison, Gihon and Hiddekel, remain a mystery and are probably mythical rivers, for no such rivers are known to have existed in the historical or even in the pre-historical period. Some scholars assume that one of those three, the Hiddekel, is what is known today as the Tigris. The Pison, it is said, may be a river in Arabia while the fourth, the Gihon, was the river Nile. Different biblical scholars identify the Pison with different rivers, which are in the region that forms the background of the biblical episodes. But associating Pison with the river Sindhu (now known as the Indus) as some biblical scholars are inclined to do is preposterous, as the region through which the river Indus flows is far from the Fertile Crescent. Presuming Eden to be in the Euphrates-Tigris Valley, it is conjectured that the Gihon was a small stream in that region, perhaps a tributary of the Euphrates-Tigris that subsequently dried up. Some scholars surmise that it was the name of the spring near Jerusalem where Solomon was anointed the third king of the undivided Hebrew kingdom.[9] As it is said in the Bible that one of the rivers was Euphrates, it may be assumed that the biblical Garden of Eden was on the bank of the river Euphrates. The Garden was, presumably, a small part of the Fertile Crescent, covered with thick forest and inhabited by savages that Adam symbolises and wild animals.

We cannot emphatically say that the other three rivers, the Pison, Gihon and Hiddekel, had not existed in pre-historical times because the possibilities of changes in the geographical features of any region cannot be ruled out. Hence, it is possible that those rivers did exist once but geological factors like tectonic disturbances coupled with siltation, soil erosion, creeping desertification, climatic changes and such other natural phenomena had caused the disappearance of those rivers. And had they been small rivulets, to some extent, human interference with nature, howsoever insignificant it was, could also have contributed to their disappearance. Even if archaeological probes and hydrological researches were to prove that once upon a time those rivers did exist, we can say for certain that a place called the Garden of Eden that the Bible describes had not existed at all. The Garden of Eden is as much a mythical concept as the biblical story of creation or the fictitious character Adam in the Book of Genesis and is nothing more than a figment of the author's imagination.

However, if the phrase *Garden of Eden* simply means the region where man first appeared on the earth, it is not a mythical concept because man must have appeared somewhere on the earth. And the place where he had appeared may be called the Garden of Eden. Incidentally, the word "appeared" does not mean that one fine morning man just popped up from the bosom of the earth or came out of the blue from no-one-knows-where or descended from outer space or as the Bible says, was created by god. Interestingly, Charles Darwin, in his monumental book, when dealing with the advent of man on the earth, suggests that the "Garden of Eden," which may be understood as the birthplace of man, was most probably in Africa!

He states, "We are naturally led to enquire, where was the birthplace of man at that stage of descent when our progenitors diverged from the Catarhine stock? The fact that they belonged to this stock clearly shows (sic) that they inhabited the Old World; but not Australia nor any oceanic island, as we may infer from the laws of geographical distribution. In each great region of the world the living mammals are closely related to the extinct species of the same region. It is therefore probable that Africa was formerly inhabited by extinct apes closely allied to the gorilla and chimpanzee; and as these two species are now man's nearest allies, it is somewhat more probable that our early progenitors lived on the African continent than elsewhere. But it is useless to speculate on this subject; for two or three anthropomorphous apes, one the Dryopithecus of Lartet, nearly as large as a man, and closely allied to Hylobates, existed in Europe during the Miocene age; and since so remote a period the earth had certainly undergone many great revolutions, and there has been ample time for migration on the largest scale."[10]

As Darwin had suggested, the human fossils unearthed lately point to the Sub-Saharan region as the cradle of man, and the genetic studies of patterns in the DNA of people living in various parts of the world also corroborate the theory that modern man arose in Africa. Hence, today, scientists have unequivocally accepted the fact that human beings originated in Africa and fanned out from there to different parts of the world.[11] The factors that caused the variations in the physical features that we find in the human beings today call for further research. It could be due to mutations. And to some extent this may perhaps be attributed to the food, the climate and other environmental and geographical factors. Let us leave that problem to the palaeo-geneticists to probe into.

However, accepting the biblical story for the purpose of interpreting the Bible as a literary work, let us visualise the imaginary Garden of Eden as a limited area which was a small part of the vast forest that covered the Fertile Crescent, consisting of a large variety of flora and fauna. This garden was skirted on one side by the river Euphrates and watered by a few perennial streams, Hiddekel, Pison and Gihon, that emptied into the Euphrates. As the curtain on this mythical Garden of Eden rises, we find a man called Adam. But the Adam that we see before the appearance of Eve, as stated above, is the personification of the primitive man or what is generally known as the savage. So in the character of Adam we see a few – maybe, a hundred or a few hundreds of – men and women. They were roaming a portion of the vast forest that the Bible calls the Garden of Eden, in the midst of a variety of animals and birds, digging and gathering nuts and fruits for their sustenance.[12] That was the beginning of the period of the lower stage of savagery.

This should not be construed to mean that the composer, whoever it was, of the biblical book of Genesis intended to portray Adam as a symbol of the savages. He had composed the verses hundreds of thousands of years after the earliest human beings or those whom anthropologists call savages had vanished from the face of the earth without any visible trace whatsoever. He could not have seen any individual or tribe that was at the early stages of social evolution; nor would he have known that man had passed through such a stage. The composer was not an evolutionary anthropologist with poetic imagination to present Adam as a symbol of the savages. He would have thought as everyone else, including scientists, did till Darwin published his theory of evolution in the second half of the nineteenth century CE that man and all other living beings were created by god. In fact, no one would have even imagined that genetically monkeys were man's ancestors, or to put it differently, man was the product of evolution, until Darwin shocked the Church and the world by unravelling the mystery of the descent of man. And the bardic composer of the Book of Genesis would not have also thought that mankind had passed through various stages of development before it reached the stage at which he and his compatriots were, when he composed the episode.

Regardless of what the composer intended, the biblical story of Adam and Eve allegorically portrays the period of savagery and if the composer had really intended it to be so, which doubtless is not likely, it speaks volumes for his imagination and creativity. Although this mythical character, Adam, is portrayed as male, he represents both the male and the female of the species and as stated above, personified mankind as a whole in the period of savagery, "the formative period of the human race,"[13] which according to archaeological periodisation is the Palaeolithic Age. Geologically, this period falls within the Pleistocene epoch and the biota of this epoch closely resembled that of the modern ones. A few of them are extinct now. Interestingly, this epoch witnessed the evolution of a new species of animal that the scientists call *Homo sapiens*, which in common parlance is "Man" or "human being." This newly evolved species, Man, had not begun to live in groups, then. Adam as we see in the Bible was the lone human being that existed. This implies the sparsity of human population in those times and the fact that human beings, be it man or woman, lived individually and had not begun to herd together.

So each one, man or woman, had to collect food for himself or herself. He subsisted on nuts and fruits that he gathered as much as he required or as much as he could from all over the territory over which he had established his or her right to forage for food. Occasionally, he might have had to fight with a poacher. Adam and all his fellow beings went around, alone and naked, facing the dangers possibly lurking behind every bush in the forest. He had no permanent roof over his head and so had to find his own abode, living sometimes in trees, sometimes under some natural rock overhangs, staying wherever he found himself while wandering in search of food. He had no permanent mate. He mated like any other species of animals did and lived with his mate during the period of her gestation and as long as the instinct of parental care impelled him to, after the baby was born. Possibly, the man and his mate had continued to live together until the baby had learnt to walk or till it was able to fend for itself. The period of parental care among the savages must have been much longer than that of other animals.

The appearance of Eve,[14] the female character, symbolises a new stage in the evolution of mankind. There is a conspicuous difference between the manner in which the two human beings, Adam and Eve, were created. Significantly, it is only in the case of human beings that god is said to have created, or the author describes the creation of, the two sexes separately. The male and female of the species were created on different days and in different ways. It may be recalled that Adam was moulded out of dust and in its nostrils god breathed the breath of life.[15] He created Eve not out of dust but out of Adam's rib, which, the Bible says, god took from his body putting him to sleep.[16] This too should not be taken literally. It does not mean that god administered anaesthesia to Adam and performed a surgery! The sleep indicates the passage of time. That "god caused a deep sleep to fall on Adam and he slept" before god created Eve, therefore, indicates that after the appearance of Adam, hundreds or even thousands of years must have gone by when Eve appeared. After creating Eve, as he did for Adam, he did not find the necessity for "breathing the breath of life" in her nostrils; she was alive when she was created. No one can say with certitude if the bardic composer who authored this myth intended it or not, but the differences in the manner of creation of these two is remarkable.

It is significant that Eve had been moulded out of Adam's rib instead of being created out of dust as Adam was and that she was addressed as "the mother of all living things." Had Eve also been created out of dust, it would indicate an increase by just one individual.

On the other hand, one human being produced from the body of another metaphorically connotes procreation and multiplication of the species. As "the mother of all living beings," she symbolises fertility and motherhood. And as a symbol of fertility and motherhood, her creation points to an explosion of human population. No, not that alone; it has other significance too. It unmistakably reveals the progress of human society and social structure of the period.

Adam and Eve being structurally different–the former, a male and the latter, a female–and viewing both of them as personifications of mankind in the early stage of savagery, the biological difference connotes differentiation of mankind and the rudimentary stage of human society. Adam and Eve, thus, indicate the beginnings of the process of herding among the human beings that were till then living individually. Man had learnt by experience that there was strength in numbers and the survival of the species demanded living in groups. Now they would not fall an easy prey to the ferocious animals, their offspring could be protected and taken care of better than they could individually as they had to earlier, and they could pool the food they collected. Above all, it assured everyone of his or her food even if one day he or she had failed to get any or was too ill to go in search of food. Both Adam and Eve may, therefore, be considered personifications of groups that may be called the Adamites and the Eveites,[17] each representing a few groups. Anthropologically, Adam and Eve were still savages, in the Lower Status of Savagery, which symbolically presents a picture of a more advanced stage of social evolution than that of the period of Adam.

It was actually kinship groups that the Adam-and-Eve duo symbolises, for as Eve was created out of Adam's rib, they could be considered related by blood and their consanguinity is confirmed when Adam says, "this is now bone of my bones and flesh of my flesh."[18] The kinship units may be regarded as nuclear family units, which presumably, gradually developed due to the imperative of prolonged parental care. Each of these kinship groups, to begin with, comprised in all probability, only the man, woman and their offspring, which today is called a monogamian family. But in those days it was just a grouping of convenience and should not be deemed a monogamous relationship. It may be described only as a nuclear kinship unit, the formation of which is allegorised in the story of the forbidden fruit, which we shall discuss presently. In course of time, a few such kinship units that had been living in adjacent caves or rock overhangs must have joined together, forming a fairly large unit or extended family because obviously it gave them a higher sense of security. Many such kinship units constituted the Adamites and the Eveites. This was the band society – a simple society that arose during the period of savagery, "lacking the integrative devices of higher levels of socio-political evolution" – which is "a familistic order in terms of both social and cultural organisation."[19] Consanguineous families were the pattern of family life in those days and in these nuclear kinship units, incestuous relationship could not have been forbidden, for the sexual behaviour of man in those days was not different from that of the other animals. It was this familistic orders that presumably formed the nuclei for the development of a little more expanded social organisation of tribal societies called the communes or gentes.

The herding together of man in kinship units necessarily presupposes communication among the members of the group. We hear articulate speech only after Eve was created, when Adam says, "She was the bone of my bones and flesh of my flesh...." This is the first time that we hear the inhabitants of the Garden speaking and after that we hear the serpent and Eve discussing the fruit that god had forbidden them from eating. Later Adam was saying to god, "I heard your voice in the garden, and I was afraid, because I was naked, and I hid myself."[20] Again, before going out of the Garden of Eden, "Adam called his wife's name Eve; because she was the mother of all living."[21] Until Adam spoke about Eve, it was only god that had been talking and the others were just listening without uttering a word. For example, earlier, when god asked Adam to name the birds and beasts, the author says, "Whatever Adam called every living creature that was the name thereof."[22] But we did not hear Adam vocalise, for he did not speak out the name of even one of those creatures. This denotes that at that stage, the savages had mentally classified all the living beings that they found in the forest as all other animals, perhaps, do.

These episodes, the terse "monologue" of Adam and the dialogues between the serpent and Eve and again between Adam and god, show unmistakably that language was discovered and that man had commenced to speak. This, the beginning of articulate speech, reveals an important fact. It indicates that the savage had taken an upward step leading to the middle stage of savagery. Mankind was, thus, at a transitional stage now and was in the process of slowly moving up from the lower stage to the middle stage of savagery.[23] Apart from that, the development of speech, which presupposes language, was undoubtedly an important factor that helped keep together and eventually consolidate the kinship units and tribes. And now they could interact with one another and exchange ideas. This would give an impetus to make improved tools and weapons, which would help steer them to higher levels of social organisation.

The Adamite tribes and the Eveite tribes, thus, could be considered the earliest predecessors of the Hebrew and the other non-Hebrew tribes of West Asia that we meet in the Bible. In fact, tribes similar to the Adamites and the Eveites, that is, human beings living in groups, had existed all over the world, beyond the West Asian region, maybe at different times. We saw in Chapter 1, "The Book of Books," that Adam or the Adamite tribe was not of the Hebrew stock, although according to the Bible, Adam was the earliest known ancestor of Abraham,[24] the son of Terah and the first Patriarch. Terah too was not a Hebrew; nor was Abraham at birth. Yet, Abraham is considered the progenitor of the Hebrews, for legend has it that it was he who founded the tribe of Israel, which we shall discuss in detail when we deal with the story of Abraham.

Coming back to the myth of Adam and Eve, the duo had been living in the Garden of Eden without any problem whatsoever when one day god suddenly walked in and ordered them out of their limited habitat. What was the provocation? God said that he was expelling them from the Garden of Eden as punishment for disobeying him by eating the fruit that he had specifically told them not to eat. The habitation of Adam and Eve – that is, of the Adamite tribes and the Eveite tribes – known as the Garden of Eden was restricted to a small area of the vast forest in the Euphrates-Tigris valley, which the tribes of Adamites and Eveites must have cleared for themselves long back. It is but natural that through the years the tribal population had increased unprecedentedly as the creation of Eve symbolises, resulting in a steep increase in the density of population. At the same time, their lifestyle, economy and social structure had also been changing.

The story of the forbidden fruit allegorically explains these and other changes taking place in the human society over the years since we first met a small population of savages that Adam personified. After eating the fruit Adam and Eve became conscious of their nakedness. It connotes that they realised the disadvantages of exposing their bare bodies to the changes in weather and to insects like the bees, wasps and mosquitoes which must have infested the forest and had been stinging them. And so to protect themselves against the capricious weather and the vexatious insects they "sewed fig leaves together"[25] but soon finding it quite inadequate to protect their bodies and not durable they began to clothe themselves in "coats of skin."[26]

The story, however, implies much more than that. It may be noted that after eating the forbidden fruit Adam and Eve not only covered themselves with fig leaves but also "hid themselves from the presence of the Lord God." The traditional scholars who consider sexual activity as "original sin" interpret this story in a very narrow and limited sense as denoting, to put it in simple terms shorn of all theological frills, sexual impulse in the two protagonists called Adam and Eve. Such a shallow interpretation is the result of isolating Adam and Eve from their social background and looking at them as individuals. In order to see the real import of the story, Adam and Eve must be placed in the historical context and viewed against the backdrop of the evolving tribal society. No doubt, there is an element of sex in the episode but not raw sex that the traditional scholars tend to impute to it. The sex that is implicit in this story is symbolic of a change that had come about in the then prevailing society of the Adamites and the Eveites.

The story, therefore, has a much deeper significance than what the traditional biblical scholars perceive, for it connotes increased procreative activity (which, of course, implies sex) among the human beings, resulting in the demographic growth. Evidently, the herding of man forming kinship units and extended families must have contributed to the birth rate far exceeding the death rate among mankind thanks to the easy availability of partners for mating and promiscuity. To cap it all, the fact that human beings have no mating season as all other animals have, had also helped immeasurably the increase in population.

After the creation of Eve, it is said, "Therefore a man shall leave his father and mother and shall cleave to his wife and they shall become one flesh" and immediately after that, the Bible says, "...they were both naked...and were not ashamed."[27] It is significant that they were not ashamed, though naked. The word *cleave* in this context means "hold fast" or "cling" and the word *wife* here is used in the archaic sense meaning "woman." There was nothing to be ashamed of because they were man and woman living together to form a kinship unit, which marked the beginning of the herding together of the animal species called the *Homo sapiens.* The appearance of Eve that marks the escalation of population and proliferation of tribes also witnessed the sprouting of many nuclear kinship units when men and their mates left their parents and formed separate nuclear kinship units. But these pairs cannot be regarded as husbands and wives because the institution of marriage was alien to the savages. But the bards who composed this episode flourished in the upper stage of barbarism when family system that possessed some of the characteristics of the monogamian family[28] was practised. The syndiasmian family "was founded upon marriage between single pairs, but without an exclusive cohabitation. The marriage continued during the pleasure of the parties."[29] The syndiasmian family system, no doubt, appeared in the lower stage of savagery but the Adamite and Eveite tribes were in an earlier stage when the nuclear kinship units had been springing up. Those kinship units were the natural offspring of the instinct of parental care, which in human beings lasts for a much longer period than in other animals. In course of time these nuclear kinship units developed into what resembles syndiasmian families, which eventually coalesced to form gens, which set the stage for the growth of consanguine family. As we shall see in Chapter 9, "The Son of Man," Jesus (or to be precise, the author, whoever it is, of The Gospel According to Matthew) who flourished after mankind entered the stage of civilisation when monogamy was the norm, also mistakenly regards the male-female partners of these nuclear kinship units as married couples of monogamian families.

It may be noted that after eating the forbidden fruit Adam hid from god when god visited them because he said he was afraid to meet god.[30] Significantly, after they ate the fruit (of the knowledge of reproductive function), when god cursed the woman, he referred to Adam as her "husband."[31] This implies only procreative activity and not the institution of marriage. Adam, perhaps, had suspected that god wanted to prevent procreative activity of the human beings and escalation of human population that may result in human beings outnumbering the gods. That would endanger their (gods') existence, for the human beings might, then, get together and conquer the world of gods. So god was trying to restrict the human population and that was why he forbade them from procreative activity. This suspicion of Adam was proved correct as the story of the Tower of Babel reveals. But Adam or man had done what god did not want him to do with the result the human population had increased. So he was feeling guilty and he hid. Interpreting this materialistically, "god" in this context represents the original tendency of man to live independently of his fellow beings or to put it differently, man's lack of herding instinct. This episode, as stated above, allegorises man's recognition of the advantages of herding together and the revolutionary changes taking place in society in those times.

On the eve of leaving the Garden, it is said, "Adam called his wife's name Eve, because she was the mother of all living."[32] This and the statements quoted in the last paragraph are perhaps what misled the traditional scholars to interpret these two persons' sudden consciousness of their nudity as just sexual impulse. This misinterpretation by traditional scholars is understandable. Those scholars, as already pointed out, look at Adam and Eve as two individuals divorced from society. They also fail to see the social norms of the period when the Adamites and the Eveites flourished. The traditionalists think in terms of the modern, civilised society in which monogamian family is the norm while those were the times when man was just slowly moving up to the middle stage of savagery. Man was then beginning to form small consanguine units or kinship units, which has been discussed already. As such, the concept of monogamy was unknown to them and the family system must have been of the consanguine type. This "was founded upon the intermarriage of brothers and sisters, own and collateral in a group."[33]

These episodes have a sociological import. Eve being referred to as Adam's wife confirms the interpretation of "mother of all living" as symbolising fertility and motherhood. This connotes a burgeoning of population due to the increased birth rate among both the Adamite and the Eveite tribes. Hence the expulsion of Adam and Eve from the Garden of Eden connotes the incremental demographic growth of these two sets of tribes that necessitated occupation of a wide area of forest land beyond the confines of the Garden of Eden. Naturally, therefore, they were constrained to leave their hitherto limited habitat, the Garden of Eden, and spread out into the forest far beyond the Garden of Eden. That was the period when mankind in groups began to leave the original habitat and move to different parts of the world.[34] This happened, according to Morgan, at the commencement of the middle stage of savagery after man acquired knowledge of making fire and began to eat fish.

Meanwhile, further changes in their economy had also been taking place. When Adam and Eve were expelled from the Garden of Eden, god said, "...you shall eat the herb of the field; in the sweat of your face you shall eat bread..."[35] As the artefacts unearthed by archaeologists reveal, the savages in general had been inventing newer and newer tools; the tools of wood, bone and perhaps some soft, pliable materials were gradually replaced by tools of hard stones. Tools of tougher material were required when mankind began to produce food by cultivation. So far Adamites and Eveites did not have to sweat for their food but now they had to till the soil, for which they needed tools of tough material. All these years human beings had been sustaining themsleves by gathering nuts and fruits, the ready-made food provided by nature, and that did not involve hard labour that cultivation demanded.

But now the increased population made it incumbent upon them to work hard and literally sweat for getting their food. The hitherto foraging herbivorous human beings had necessarily become cultivators producing their food by the sweat of their brows. They now had to prepare the ground, sow the seeds, water the plants, guard them from being eaten or damaged by birds and animals, and finally harvest them. Apart from this with the new weapon like the javelin and the bow and arrow, man had also become hunters. They cultivated to supplement the food they gathered and so they not only went gathering food but also began to produce food, auguring a new form of economy

– food-producing economy. The direction of god that they had to find food "in the sweat of your face" indicates the evolution of society to a higher stage symbolised by the two brothers Cain and Abel, the personifications of the more advanced phase of human society.

The two mythical progenitors of mankind, the Adam-and-Eve duo represents the entire tribal population of the world in the remote past. As the story goes, after their eviction from the Garden of Eden, the couple, Adam and Eve, begot two sons, Cain and Abel. These two characters are as much fictitious as Adam and Eve and like their mythical parents, they too are but symbols. With the appearance of Cain and Abel, the number of biblical characters has become four, symbolising the increase, again by not less than one hundred percent, in the tribal population of the region and the consequent proliferation of tribes that the Cainites and the Abelites symbolise. We shall now see how much the tribes that the brothers, Cain and Abel personified had evolved after the Adamites and the Eveites or the human beings inhabiting the Garden of Eden spread over different parts of the forest in the Euphrates-Tigris valley and beyond.

But now further changes had taken place in the sphere of both economy and family. The mode of subsistence of Cain and Abel shows the socio-economic development of the tribes. The Bible says, Cain was a "tiller of the ground" and Abel, a "keeper of sheep," indicating that the tribes that these two characters symbolised were in the middle stage of barbarism, characterised by domestication of animals and cultivation by irrigation. We saw that the food-gathering economy of the period of the Garden of Eden began to change when the Adamites and Eveites spread from their limited habitat over a larger part of the Fertile Crescent. It had now been necessarily and completely supplanted by the food-producing economy of the Cainites and the Abelites to meet the increased demand due to the explosion of population.

The Bible, however, does not mention the use of any metallic implements by the Cainites and the Abelites at that time but it may be inferred from their mode of subsistence. The Abelites were not keeping sheep for dairy products alone; meat must have become an important part of their daily meal and so they would be using a knife to butcher the sheep and cut its meat for food. This is confirmed when Abel offered meat to god who visited him.[36] The domestication of animals and the development of weapons like bow and arrow had made them hunter-gatherers and meat and dairy products had become a regular item on their *carte du jour.* So man had now learned to cook, for unlike the digestive systems of other carnivorous animals the digestive system of human beings cannot digest raw meat. As we saw in Chapter 2, "The Universe and God," maybe hundreds of years before the barbaric tribes of Cainites and Abelites appeared, in the last lap of the lower stage of savagery, man had mastered the technique of making fire when, Morgan says, fish had become a part of his diet. But, in the Bible, we were not given even a hint that they had been cooking and eating fish. This is the first time there is a suggestion of cooking, for without cooking Abel would not have served meat.

Nonetheless, they were still in what the archaeologists call the Neolithic Age and were beginning to use metal implements but anthropologically in the barbaric stage. This is not an unusual phenomenon, though rather rare. Childe states that in the economic sense at least, Neolithic does not correspond to a period of time and he points out the example of the Maoris of New Zealand who were Neolithic in equipment and economy in 1800 CE. He adds, "many societies that economically are still barbarian have learned to use iron or bronze tools and weapons...."[37] This is found to be true even in the case of a tribe that is in the stage of savagery. For example, the Sentinelese,[38] a fiercely hostile tribe on the North Sentinel Island of the Andaman and Nicobar archipelago, a centrally administered region of India, is an exemplification of such a tribe today. They go about naked, hunt, fish and gather food using weapons like the spear and bow and arrow made from scraps of iron collected from two cargo ships that ran aground near the island sometime in the 1980s. But they are found to be in the stage of savagery even today. So the Cainite-Abelite tribes had used metal to make ploughshares, knives and weapons like bow and arrow. They were, however, in the Neolithic Age and in the middle stage of barbarism. Although they were ignorant of the technique of smelting, they were perhaps skilful at smithery.

Abel being the "keeper of sheep" the Abelites were evidently pastoral tribes and must, necessarily, have been nomadic or semi-nomadic. They moved from place to place camping wherever lush green grass for their flocks was abundant. But the Cainite tribes of Cain the "tiller of the ground," that had learned to cultivate must have begun to lead a sedentary life that agriculture demanded. Agriculture required these tribes to stay in one place seldom migrating, unless of course drought, war or epidemic forced them to move out and go in search of flat arable land near a perennial water source. The Cainites and the Abelites representing farming and pastoral tribes respectively now needed more land not because of the escalation of population; they needed land for production of food or for grazing their flock, as the case may be. The pastoral tribes wanted wet and grassy land preferably in the plains to graze their herds. The agricultural tribes also needed wet land free from weeds like grass. However, they needed pastureland also for grazing their cattle that they used for ploughing.

The Adamites and the Eveites were groups of extended kinship units. The pressure of unprecedented demographic growth that necessitated breaking out of the boundaries of the Garden of Eden and the continued escalation of population began to impact the societal structure by the time Cain and Abel appeared on the scene. So several extended kinship units of the period of lower stage of savagery merged giving rise to large socio-economic units. These are gentes or communes which came into being as mankind progressed into the middle stage of savagery. The Cainites and the Abelites were groups of such gentes held together by bonds of kinship.

The gens or the commune was the most ancient *socio-economic* organisation that came into existence after man began to live in groups. The gens was a "body of consanguinei descended from the same common ancestor distinguished by a gentile name and bound together by affinities of blood,"[39] as Morgan succinctly defines it. It was the smallest or the primary unit of a tribe, the essential feature of which was collectivism, that is, collective production and collective consumption. In this society there was no private property, no private family, no political organisation and no class division; but division of labour caused by sex and age differentiation sprang up gradually. Interestingly, "liberty, equality and fraternity, though never formulated, were cardinal principles of the gens."[40] This social organisation must have come into existence during the middle stage of savagery. Considering the population then, the tribes would not have been very large.

According to Morgan's periodisation, the middle stage of barbarism was characterised by animal husbandry and agriculture as well as metallurgy. Although Cain and Abel are said to be the offspring of Adam and Eve, when looked at as symbols of tribes, hundreds of thousands of years must have elapsed by the time we meet the more advanced Cainite and Abelite tribes. In sociological terms, mankind had traversed a long distance in time since the period of Adam as it had passed through the middle and upper stages of savagery and the lower stage of barbarism to enter the middle stage of barbarism. This progress had been achieved as a result of the discovery of new tools like the ploughshare, the knife and the bow and arrow. While the bow and arrow and knife helped food gathering by hunting, the plough and knife made the production of food by cultivation possible, thus turning food diggers and gatherers into food producers.

Morgan, however, states that domestication of animals was the peculiarity of the Eastern Hemisphere while cultivation of plants by irrigation was confined to the Western Hemisphere. He, thereby, implies that *vice versa* was not a feature of the barbaric tribes of these two hemispheres in the stage of barbarism. Morgan came to that conclusion because during his lifetime, it was not known that the barbaric tribes in the Eastern Hemisphere too were cultivating. It was five decades after his death that archaeologists chanced upon evidence of cultivation long before riverine civilisation sprung up in Mesopotamia or Sumeria. Archaeological findings of the early twentieth century point to the fact that out of the nearly seven hundred important cultivated plants, not less than four hundred of them originated in southern Asia and five principle regions of cultivated plants have been identified in the continent of Asia. Moreover, from the cuneiform writings on the clay tablets unearthed by archaeologists in the early twentieth century, in the Euphrates-Tigris valley, we understand, there was a widespread irrigation system with canals and dams, in the kingdom of Mari when the semi-nomadic barbaric tribes that Abraham symbolises had been moving about there.

Archaeologists have also found that the pre-Semitic Babylonian Civilisation that dominated the Fertile Crescent from the eighteenth to the sixth century BCE had maintained a well-developed irrigation system with canals, dams and reservoirs. They are said to have inherited this from the Sumerian civilisation that thrived earlier. Possibly, therefore, on seeing this and realising the advantages of irrigation in agriculture, some of those pastoral tribes of the Eastern Hemisphere must have taken to agriculture and settled down in the plains of the Euphrates-Tigris. The barbaric tribes, living side by side with these civilised societies, had naturally emulated the irrigation system. Indubitably, therefore, cultivation by irrigation was practised in the Mesolithic and Neolithic ages (*circa* 8000-4000 BCE) in the Eastern Hemisphere too by the barbaric tribes in the region. So contrary to what Morgan said, cultivation by irrigation was not unknown to the barbaric tribes of the Eastern Hemisphere also. Understandably, Morgan (1818-1881), who flourished in the nineteenth century, was not aware of these because, as pointed out above, the archaeological discoveries were made several years after he died.

The tribes that we have now come across in the Bible were in the Eastern Hemisphere and some of them, the Cainite tribes, were engaged in cultivation, as Cain being "tiller of the ground" denotes farming. So the Cainites being agricultural tribes cannot be regarded as an anachronism although there are quite a few anachronistic episodes in the Bible.[41] The increased population and the need to find pastoral and cultivable lands for the pastoral and the farming tribes respectively, created unforeseen tension between them. This was inevitable. Both the pastoral and the agricultural tribes needed wet lands and so the two groups were bound to clash in their bid to occupy good fertile land.

Thus the antagonism between the two fictitious characters Cain and Abel and the murder of Abel was not just a fratricide impelled by personal animosity due to jealousy as suggested in the Bible.[42] It is symbolic of the tribal struggle for land, and hence this fratricide allegorically depicts the inter-tribal war and annihilation of the Abelites by the victorious Cainites.[43] This predated the system of slavery and so the defeated tribe was exterminated, and the murder of Abel exemplifies this. As each of these brothers represented pastoral and farming tribes, the fight between them leading to Abel's death further signifies the end of pastoralism of the pre-Israel tribes of that region, bringing about a change in the economy and habit of those tribes. They had given up nomadism necessitated by pastoralism and began to settle down in areas congenial for tillage.

Thousands of years must have gone by after Cain murdered his brother and moved away, when we come across some pre-Israel tribes in the descendants of Cain, each representing a few tribes. By this time, these barbaric tribes, according to the Bible, had become experts in metallurgy as symbolised by Tubelcain, who was "an instructor of every artificer in brass and iron."[44] This too may not be an anachronism because there is anthropological evidence for it as many anthropologists have found barbarian tribes using bronze and iron weapons and tools. Childe points out, "...it is not surprising that in the earliest historical societies, as among contemporary barbarians, metallurgists are always *specialists*."[45] In the case of Tubelcain it is explicitly said that he was the artificer of *brass and iron*, which is a clear indication that the tribe had knowledge of metallurgy and so we can say with certainty that they had passed the Bronze Age and entered the Iron Age. Yet it cannot be said the Tubelcainites had already progressed into the stage of civilisation because there is no mention of the tribe having acquired the art of writing because "civilisation commences with the use of phonetic (or hieroglyphic) alphabets."[46]

The many generations that followed one after the other beginning with Seth indicate that the human population had been increasing and many new tribes had come into existence while several must have got extirpated when defeated in tribal conflicts. The span of life of each of those characters denotes the wide hiatus of time between the periods of the Adamites and the Noahites, another non-Hebrew tribe. During the generation of Noah, who is said to be the ninth descendant of Adam,[47] a flash flood inundated the region inhabited by these tribes. This may be a fictitious story adopted from the *Eridu Genesis*, which was dealt with in Chapter 1, "The Book of Books." Incidentally, the Indo-Aryan (Hindu) tradition also speaks of a flood, the Sanskrit term for which is *pralaya*.[48] In the flood that the Bible describes, a large number of inhabitants of that region were drowned.

After the flood, according to the Bible, the only human beings that existed on the face of the earth were Noah, his wife, his three sons, Shem, Ham, and Japheth, and their spouses, with the result their progenies constituted the entire population of the world.[49] It may be borne in mind that for the author(s) of "The First Book of

Moses called Genesis," the world did not extend beyond the stretch of land extending from the Euphrates-Tigris to the Nile Valley. The Noahites were agricultural tribes, for we find that Noah was a farmer and had a vineyard.[50] The offspring of Noah too like Noah himself, and their descendants were not individuals who really existed. They symbolise the Semitic and non-Semitic tribes.[51]

As descendants of one person, Adam, all these should have been only one tribe but the pre-history and history give us a different picture of mankind. We know that the world extended beyond West Asia and mankind comprised not one but many tribes spread over the world. It is said, "...these are families of the sons of Noah, after their generations, in their nations: and by these were the nations divided in the earth after the flood."[52] The composer of the story thus acknowledges the multiplicity of tribes. The word "nation" used in this context may be taken to mean "tribe," for at that time, nations, in the sense that we understand it today, had not come into existence. Each tribe constituted a "biblical nation" as it were, and the story of the Tower of Babel allegorically describes the multiplication and differentiation of tribes.

The multiplicity of languages that resulted after god is believed to have gone to the Tower to "confound the language" of those living there, is indicative of the blossoming of various cultures among mankind. This must have happened over a period of thousands of years. The mastery of the technique of making fire, knowledge of cultivation, farinaceous food, domestication of animals and the consequent consolidation of the food-producing economy immensely helped the process of human migration.[53] Now man was able to settle down wherever he wished to, for his food supply was assured. The population explosion that must have taken place at that time compelled the human species to spread over a large part of the earth. This migration, it may be recalled, began with the expulsion of Adam and Eve from the Garden of Eden. The dispersal of tribes naturally resulted in the development of different languages and cultures.

Many years after the flood, we meet the nomadic tribes symbolised by Terah, that is, the Terahites, which were barbaric, in Ur of the Chaldees. Those were the times when waves and waves of nomadic and semi-nomadic tribes, as mentioned above, were moving from place to place. So the tribes that Terah represents, along with many other tribes, must have flowed down to the Fertile Crescent carried on the crest of one of those waves of Semitic migrants from the Arabian wilderness. Although the Bible does not specify the nativity of all those tribes, Terah, we know, was a descendant of Shem. The tribes that Shem and his progenies represent were not natives of Ur but were Semites originating from Noah's son Shem[54] and were a diverse group of peoples of desert origin as has been borne out by a couple of lines in the Old Testament.[55]

It is futile to place these characters chronologically because there is no archaeological or documentary evidence of their existence. Prior to this period, we came across several other tribes, of which we know through myths and legends only, beginning with the story of Adam and Eve, which we have already discussed. However, looking at Shem and his descendants as personifications of tribes, anthropologically speaking the Terahite tribes were still nomadic barbarians. The Terahites entered the turbulent Fertile Crescent hundreds of thousands of years after the Adamites and the Eveites exited the placid atmosphere of the Garden of Eden.

However, the commune of Terah broke up and Terah's family left Ur. The Bible states that Terah with his son Abram,[56] his daughter-in-law Sarai and his grandson Lot moved to Canaan.[57] Why did he leave Ur with only a few members of his family leaving the rest in Ur? The composer does not say what caused them to leave Ur for an unknown town in a strange land. It does not speak of a famine or any other natural calamity like earthquake, epidemic, drought or flood that could have compelled them to move out of Ur. In short, there was no apparent reason for the tribe to migrate from there and the Old Testament too is silent about it. But in the New Testament, we hear of Stephen, one of the seven deacons, saying that "the God of Glory" asked Abraham to move out of Ur.[58] The composer of Acts has made a mistake, as it was not at the instance of Abraham that Terah migrated from Ur.

Let alone the myth of god telling Abram. First of all the author of the Pentateuch does not say so and it is crystal clear from what he says that it was Terah and *not* Abram who took the decision to move out of Ur. It is said in unequivocal terms that Terah took Abram, Sarai and Lot when he left Ur, which makes it abundantly clear that Abram had no voice whatsoever, in it. Luke or whoever had authored the Acts of the Apostles, it was written many years after the Pentateuch was composed. As internal evidence suggests, the author[59] wrote it after 62 CE, for at the end of the book he mentions Paul's stay under house arrest in Rome. Paul was sent to Rome in 60 CE and he "dwelt two whole years in his own hired house..."[60] Besides, the biblical character of god that he calls "the God of glory," did not 'interact' with "our father Abraham when he was in Mesopotamia." It must be understood that Stephen, whether a historical or a mythico-historical character, who was repudiated by the Sanhedrin, was a staunch Christian for he cried out, "Lord Jesus receive my spirit,"[61] when stoned by the members of Sanhedrin. Hence, if anything, this could be construed as pure imagination of the author and was intended to mythicise Abraham and relate him to Christianity. In order to give it a semblance of credibility, the author put it in Stephen's mouth so that credulous believers accept it as a historical fact.

So we can only guess why they left Ur. Human population had been increasing over the generations from Shem to Terah's father Nahor, who alone had many sons and daughters. It must be borne in mind that one offspring does not mean an increase by one individual; it denotes an escalation of population. That Terah begot three sons indicates the further burgeoning as well as the increased rate of growth of the population and the proliferation of tribes. This undoubtedly resulted in the unwieldy growth of certain tribes, including the Terahites but does not seem to have caused a struggle for land.

Nevertheless, the tribe of Terah that had settled in Ur, as stated above, left the place heading for Canaan. The most plausible reason for this migration could be the social forces and the demographic factor that caused the division of the 'communistic household' of Terah. Engels points out "Every primeval family had to split up after a couple of generations, at the latest. The communistic common household...determined a certain maximum size of the family community, varying according to the circumstances but fairly definite in each locality. As soon as the conception of the impropriety of sexual intercourse between the children of a common mother arose, it was bound to have an effect upon this division of the old and the foundation of a new household communities (which, however, did not necessarily coincide with the family groups)...In this or some similar way the form of the family which Morgan calls the punaluan family developed out of the consanguine family."[62] So it was these socio-economic factors that compelled Terah to split the commune and leave with Abram and others. In order to distinguish from the larger section of the Terahite tribe that remained in Ur, let us call the breakaway section that moved out of Ur, the Abramites because next to Terah, Abram was the oldest member in the group.

But on reaching Haran, which was an important town at that time, Terah decided to stay there, for he must have found fertile land suitable for pasture and cultivation. The tribe was in Haran till Terah died, when Abram with the rest of the family left Haran and proceeded to Canaan, which, as mentioned above, was their original destination. The Abramites had comfortably settled in Haran and there should have been a compelling reason for him to leave that place and go to Canaan. As the legend goes, after the death of Terah, god is said to have stepped in and spoken to Abram who, it is believed, was god's chosen one. "Now the Lord said to Abram, Go away from your country, and from your kindred, and from your father's house, to a land that I will show you: And I will make you a great nation...."[63] Here too the word "nation" as elsewhere earlier, denotes "tribe," and the land that was spoken of was the land of Canaan.[64]

The myth of god appearing and telling Abram must be interpreted as what goes on in Abram's mind. So when it is said that god wanted Abram to cut himself off from his kith and kin so as to make him a great nation, it means that Abram was thinking of discarding his tribal traditions and reforming the tribe. Many of the tribesmen, perhaps, thought of going back to Ur but Abram was strongly opposed to the idea; he wanted to go far away from his kindred and from his father's place. Abram's insistence on getting out of his country and away from his "kindred" and his father's house is significant. Abram was in the process of what may be described as an ideological metamorphosis. He was having a rethink on the ideas of his tribe – its traditions, conventions, customs, and above all religious beliefs and practices and seemed to have decided to breakaway from his ideological past. He was planning an ideological revolution as it were, which, he knew, would make him unacceptable in his country, in his father's house and to his kindred.

The story of Abram shifting his camp to Canaan at the behest of god was as much mythical as the character itself. It was intended only to mythicise Abram. At Ur itself Terah had planned to go to Canaan; maybe, he had heard of the fertility of the land of Canaan from various nomadic tribes. Obviously, there must have been some compelling reason for the Abramites to leave Haran all of a sudden and go to Canaan, their originally planned destination. What could be the reason for the tribe to move out of Haran? It could not have been the death of Terah, for a nomadic or semi-nomadic tribe did not move out from one place just because one of the members, even if it happened to be the tribal chief, expired. It must be noted that the god that entered into a covenant with Abram was different from the god that interacted with Adam and Eve, for he was, as pointed out in Chapter 1, "The Book of Books," one among many other gods. This god that is said to have spoken to Abram had no fellow beings of his status. There were only angels that lived with him as we later learn from the Bible[65] but they were his subordinates whose duty was to carry out his orders. He was the one and only god, who presided over all other supernatural beings like angels and even his equally powerful rival, Satan.

So the idea of "one god" or monotheism of the Hebrews and the rejection of idolatry by that tribe is believed to be the product of Abram's brain. In fact, it was these revolutionary ideas that brought forth the tribe of Israel and differentiated it from other contemporary tribes. There is, however, no evidence that an individual known as Abram ever existed. This character as well as the other Patriarchs, Isaac, Jacob and Joseph, are as mythological as for example those of the Greek heroes. There is absolutely no authenticated archaeological or extra-biblical documentary evidence to confirm that such a person called Abram or Abraham had ever existed; hence Abram (Abraham) is a fictitious character as many other biblical characters are. But ideas are formed only in the minds of human beings and cannot arise or exist independent of or without human mind. And this idea of monotheism must have sprouted in the brain of an individual but no one knew and still knows who it was. The Hebrew bard who composed this episode, therefore, created a fictitious character called Abram and attributed the idea of monotheism and iconoclasm to him.

So the new religio-philosophical ideas were supposed to be the outcome of the rethink of this fictitious biblical character called Abram (later renamed Abraham, the reason for which we shall discuss presently), on the religious ideas and practices of the tribe into which he was born. These new ideas occurred to him after the death of Terah when he was the chief of the tribe of Abramites and he persuaded the tribe to accept these ideas. In order to attract them he said, his god, whom he called Yahweh, would make them great and give them a fertile land to settle down. It must have, no doubt, taken quite some time for him to convert his own tribe to this new religion.

After that he and his tribe must have preached monotheism, proclaiming that there was only one god, Yahweh, which was superior to all other gods and condemned idolatry as a loathsome practice. Presumably, several members of other tribes too were influenced by what the Abramites preached and accepted his religious ideology, rejecting their gods and idolatry. So a few of the communes of other tribes broke away from their parent tribes accepting Yahweh as their god, and some individuals of other tribes who accepted the new religion were perhaps absorbed by the Abramites. However, as new converts always are found to be, the Abramites and other newly converted monotheists-cum-iconoclasts must have been fanatics and quite explicit and vociferous in the condemnation of polytheism and the practice of idol worship prevalent among the other tribes around there.

The majority of the other tribes, however, must have stayed away from these revolutionary ideas and clung to their traditional beliefs. So those that had become converts to this religion were regarded as apostates and despised by the polytheistic and idolatrous tribes. Obviously, therefore, they must have invited the wrath of those tribes that believed in many gods and were idol worshippers. All those polytheistic tribes that far outnumbered the monotheists must have boycotted and totally isolated the latter whom they regarded as apostates and a threat to their long-held beliefs and traditions. Consequently, the apostates would have been prevented from entering wet, pastoral lands for grazing their cattle and sheep. The traditionalists must have assailed them making it difficult for the Abramite tribes to continue to live in the midst of such hostile surroundings and forcing them to move out of Haran. Incidentally, those were the days when tribes from the eastern steppes were descending on the land of the Canaanites and the regions around it. It is this historical fact that is allegorised by the story of Abramite tribe's migration into Canaan.

When the Abramites moved into Canaan,[66] the Canaanites referred to this group of nomadic Yahudim tribes of the ancient northern Semitic stock that migrated from the east to the land of Canaan led by Abram, as the "Hebrews." It is generally believed that the Canaanites, the tribal people that "dwell by the sea and by the coast of Jordan"[67] had actually used the term "Hebrew" when referring to Abram[68] because he had come from beyond the river Euphrates. The word *Hebrew* may be traced to the Aramaic root, *Eber*, which means "one from beyond" [the river] indicating they came from the other side of the river Euphrates.[69] And they called Abram and his descendants who were trans-Euphratian immigrants by this term to distinguish between the peoples that inhabited the two sides, east and west, of the river Euphrates. A few inscriptions of the Pharaonic period and some Egyptian and Canaanite documents extant today refer to them as *apiru* or *hapiru*.

Some scholars assert that the Habiru, a nomadic Semitic tribe mentioned in Mesopotamian tablets, were ancient Hebrews or their close ancestors. But it is a moot point if all the Hebrews who were in Egypt or who are believed to have emigrated from Egypt can be identified with the Habirus. Another view is that the Hebrew tribes were all Habirus but not all Habirus were Hebrews. According to them, the Habirus did not constitute any particular ethnic group or tribe; nor did they speak a common language. But the term "Habiru" referred to marginalised individuals or groups of outlaws, plunderers, mercenaries and slaves. Most probably the Canaanites, who were polytheists, must have called them Hebrews meaning outcasts because this nomadic tribe being monotheists, were outcasts in their eyes. They could have used the term "Hebrews" in the sense of plunderers or bandits also, as the Abramites might have attacked their camps and even carried away their cattle and the grains stocked by them. Anyway, whatever be the origin of the term, in course of time, the Abramite tribes came to be referred to as "Hebrews" by all other tribes.

Presumably, faced with the hostile polytheistic tribes of Canaan, they could not stay there for long but moved from there further south to Egypt,[70] symbolising the beginning of the migration of the Hebrew tribes to Egypt. The Abramites' stay in Egypt impacted on their socio-economic structure and was a turning point in the history of the Hebrew tribes. During their sojourn in Egypt, the Hebrews witnessed the rise of private property and slavery and the beginning of the disintegration of the tribal communes and collectivism in their society. Many years later, after the two communes, the Abramites and the Lotites had come out of Egypt, the Lotites had shifted their camp to the plains of Jordan and the Abramites were dwelling in the plain of Mamre in Hebron.

In keeping with the decision to cut off from his tradition altogether and as a sign of it, Abram decided to change his name to Abraham.[71] Having changed his name, Abraham thought it was but proper that he changed his wife's name too and he told her that thenceforward her name would be Sarah.[72] Abraham's decision to change the names of his wife and himself was very significant because it is an indication that they had completely abjured all the beliefs, doctrines, customs—why, all that they held sacrosanct till then—and their entire past. So Abramites shall hereafter be referred to as Abrahamites. They had entered into a new life. The covenant god had with Abraham is the myth of the origin of the Hebrew tribes but it may not be wrong to say, with the birth of the tribe the seed of a new religion, Judaism, was sowed. This mythical character, thus, came to be regarded as the founder of the religion of Yahwism or Judaism.

The covenant with god was actually what Abraham had decided to do to differentiate his newly formed tribe from his ancestral tribe as well as other polytheistic and idolatrous tribes. He wanted his tribe to be away from the polytheistic tribes, lest his new religion got corrupted by the old. He perhaps feared that some of the members of his own tribe and new converts from other tribes might relapse into polytheism and idolatry. To preclude that, he wanted them to circumcise so that even if they wished to go back to their parent tribes, those tribes would not accept them. When his tribe was forced to leave Haran, he decided to go far away to the land of Canaan, of which he had heard his father speak and had intended to go and settle. Incidentally, some of the ethnologists are of the view that the Covenant of Abraham dates back to a period long before that of Abraham. This theory, however, is not accepted by scholars, as there is no documentary evidence to show that Judaism originated before the period when Abraham is believed to have flourished. Hence we shall presume that the origin of Judaism is connected with the mythical character of Abraham who is considered a Patriarch. The rhapsodist who composed the story of god entering into a covenant with Abram gives the readers the point in time of the origin of the tribe of Israel and a hint about the prospective conquest of the land of Canaan by the Hebrew tribes.

Naturally, therefore, Abraham was not a Yahudim or a Hebrew at birth, and so we understand from the Bible too. The Abrahmites were, therefore, the first set of Hebrew tribes. Although we meet the tribe of Terah in Ur, the Terahite tribes were immigrants from the wilderness of Arabia and there is no indication to say that Abraham, regarded as the progenitor of the Hebrews or Israel, was born in Ur. All his ancestors were pagans and so was he at birth. A peep into his ancestry as revealed by what he himself says and what we understand from Joshua's words confirm it. The Bible tells us that when Abraham was dwelling in Canaan he thought of finding a suitable bride for his son Isaac. He did not want his son to marry a girl of Canaanite ethnicity. So he called the oldest servant of his house and told him to go to "my country," the "land of my kindred," where "my father's house" was and look for a suitable girl for Isaac. This land, to which his servant went, was not Ur but Nahor,[73] a city in Mesopotamia. The words that the bard put into the biblical character Joshua's mouth, that Terah lived on the other side of the flood,[74] too, seems to corroborate the view that Abraham's ancestral house was in Nahor. Much later we hear Joshua telling all the tribes of Israel, "Thus says the Lord God of Israel. Your fathers dwelt on the other side of the flood in old times, even Terah, the father of Abraham and the father of Nachor and they served other gods."[75] Again, we hear Joshua say, "...Thus says the Lord God of Israel,...And I took your father Abraham from the other side of the flood in old times...." Obviously, therefore, Abraham's place of birth was on the other side of the flood, and that could only be Nahor because his ancestral house was there.

This does not mean that Abraham was a historical personality. Notwithstanding all such details given in the Bible about Abraham and although his name is associated with three religions in the absence of any evidence of his historicity, biblical scholars and historians had cast him into the realm of pure mythology. However, the excavations carried out in the 1930s at Tel Hariri brought to light Haran, a place mentioned in the Bible (Old Testament) where Terah, with Abram, Sarai and Lot are believed to have lived, tempted some scholars to revise their views on the question of Abraham's historicity and led to a rekindling of the belief that Abraham and all the other patriarchs were in fact historical personalities. It is tantamount to asserting that Shylock and Portia, characters in Shakespeare's play *The Merchant of Venice*, were historical personages just because the cities of Venice and Belmont, against the background of which the story is set, existed in the sixteenth century CE. Simply because a certain site of the period when a fictional character is believed to have existed has been exhumed, it cannot be presumed that he or she really existed then.

On two of the clay tablets discovered from the same site, names of about two thousand people were found. But there was no mention of Terah or Abram (Abraham) or any person with at least a similar name in any of the nearly twenty-five thousand documents recorded on the clay tablets. All the tribes, including the one into which he was born, that existed then were polytheists and idol worshippers. Being a staunch monotheist and an iconoclast at that time, he must have been a notorious person as all revolutionary thinkers always had been in the eyes of traditionalists and conservatives. If such a person, who is believed to have founded a new religion, repudiating that of his tribe and the tribes around him, had flourished in that region around that time, his name would have been mentioned once, at least in a bad light.

Assuming that such a person existed, a glimpse of his economic status shows the stage of development of the tribes of Israel. The history of Israel, therefore, commences at this stage of social evolution. He had many servants or slaves and he was very "rich in cattle, in silver and in gold."[76] He could afford to pay a large sum of money "four hundred shekels of silver, current money" for the cave of Machpelah, which he purchased as a place of burial for Sarah.[77] In addition, his wealth is reflected in the raiment and the gold and silver jewelry he had[78] as well as in the food he ate, which consisted of corn cake and meat, butter and milk.[79] He also possessed sheep and oxen, asses and camels, and slaves,[80] both men and women, to work for him and implements like knife indicating the use of metal. All these show that the degree of development of the tribe "corresponds substantially with that of the Homeric Greeks,"[81] which was the upper stage of barbarism. The possession of private property and prevalence of slavery do not mean that the tribal communes based on an economy characterised by collective production and consumption had disintegrated altogether. So the period of Abraham or the Abrahamites, marks a critical stage in the history of the Hebrews – the transition from a tribal society based on collectivism and equality to a stratified society based on private property and slavery. Nevertheless, it was still a gentile society, "in which the government dealt with persons through their relations to a gens and tribe. These relations were purely personal."[82]

The Hebrew marriage custom as is seen in the case of Abraham purchasing Rebekah as a wife for Isaac, according to Morgan, indicates that the tribe still had the gens in its archaic form as the gifts were given not to the bride's father but to her mother. Again, when Abraham said, "And yet indeed she is my sister; she is the daughter of my father, but not the daughter of my mother; and she became my wife,"[83] he was not lying but was speaking a truth. Pointing out this, Morgan concludes, "with an existing gens and descent in the female line, Abraham and Sarah would have belonged to different gentes, and although of *blood kin* they were not of *gentile kin* and could have married by gentile usage." In the cases of Nahor who married his niece, his brother's daughter, and Amram, Moses' father, who married his aunt, his father's sister, the descent being in the female line, the "persons marrying would have belonged to different gentes; but otherwise with descent in the male line." These cases do not, however, prove the existence of gentes but the latter does lead us to presume that the gentile organisation must have existed in its archaic form.[84]

Be that as it may, whatever can be gleaned from the Bible indicates that the Hebrews or Israel lingered for a long time as nomadic or semi-nomadic barbarians. However, as Morgan points out, "when the Mosaic legislation was completed, the Hebrews were a civilised people but not far enough advanced to institute political society" like several other contemporaneous tribes.[85] The Hebrew society was organised as consanguine groups, which had been preceded by a gentile system. That system continued to exist and a system of governance similar to that of a gentile society formed of consanguine groups bound by personal relations had been established, for they were ignorant of any other governmental structure.[86] Significantly, while the Hebrews colonised Palestine, the locality occupied by each of the tribes was named after one of the twelve sons of Jacob, from whom the tribe concerned is said to have originated. This proves that they were organised by lineages and not into a community of citizens, which explains why the protohistory of the Hebrews is associated with the names of Abraham, Isaac and Jacob, and the twelve sons of Jacob but not with any geographical units.[87]

A large number of barbaric Hebrews, the Bible says, had been living in Egypt for about four hundred years ever since the Hebrew migration to the Nile valley that the immigration of Abraham symbolises. They existed side by side with the Egyptians, who were, according to the Bible, the descendants of Ham's son, Mizraim. Incidentally, *Mizraim* is the usual Hebrew word for Egypt. The Egyptian society had progressed into the stage of civilisation as is evident from the fact that it was a monarchic slave society and had a script. Although the Hebrews were in the lower stages of barbarism when they first migrated into Egypt, they progressed into the upper stage of barbarism as could be understood from the allegorical story of Abraham. Being in the upper stage of barbarism, the Hebrew society too was riven into two classes, freemen and slaves that Abraham and Hagar symbolise. In the post-Abrahamic period, the entire tribe was oppressed by the Egyptians. Nonetheless, several of the Hebrew freemen had amassed wealth. It is said that among the Hebrews there were usurers, a class that would not have come up unless there were wealthy individuals who had enough money to lend[88] and these wealthy individuals were hiring servants as well as keeping slaves.[89] So the collectivist tribal communes among the Hebrews in Egypt were on their deathbeds.

This was the society in which Moses, the liberator and lawgiver of the Hebrews, *if he were a historical figure*, was born. Or, it may be said, he was the hero of the biblical story, fictitious though it may be, of the mass movement for the liberation of the enslaved Hebrews in Egypt and the leader who planned and executed their mass emigration from that country. We shall deal with the story of the struggle of the Hebrews for liberation and their migration under Moses' leadership in detail, in the next chapter, "Consolidation of Slavery."

As Morgan said, they could be categorised as civilised tribes inasmuch as their social structure and civil laws were in harmony with the culture of the status of civilisation although their political structure was yet to be. But the other determining criterion of civilisation, according to Morgan, is the invention of a phonetic or hieroglyphic alphabet and the production of literary records. Whether in those times the tribes of Israel that Moses is believed to have led out of Egypt had an alphabet of their own has been a controversial point. In Chapter 1, "The Book of Books," we saw that the ancient society of Israel was not a written culture, implying that the Hebrews in those times had no alphabet. However, it is said, "Moses wrote all the words of the Lord" "and he took the Book of the Covenant and read in the audience of the people."[90] Besides, he spoke quite a few times about writing down the laws. Again, after enjoining his tribe to "set a king over you," he said, "...he shall write him a copy of this book...."[91] And almost at the end of his life, it is said "...Moses wrote this law and delivered it to the priests the sons of Levi..."[92] Are all these anachronisms? The answer depends on when the Hebrews learned the art of writing.

The Bible gives a conflicting message. Many biblical historians argue that the Mosaic Law was reduced to writing for the first time after the exiles returned from Babylon and the Temple was rebuilt, during the period of the Roman Emperor Artaxerxes in the third century CE. They, thereby, imply that the Hebrew language had no script before that time, and their contention was based on a couple of verses from Ezra.[93] This law had, since then, become a social contract for the Hebrews, regulating the lives of individuals in relation to the society and the relationship between man and man. However, in the third decade of the twentieth century, thanks to the excavations carried out at Ras es-Shamreah (which was Ugarit, a cosmopolitan city in biblical times) the archaeologists had unearthed clay tablets with documents recorded in a cuneiform script, which had been deciphered. They aver that one of these bilingual documents was written in what is said to be pre-Mosaic Hebrew script[94] and hence, it may be inferred, the Hebrew tribe must have had its own script prior to the Mosaic period. Had there been no Hebrew script, the composer would not have made Moses repeatedly exhort the tribe to put down the Mosaic Law in black and white. And it is also said that Moses wrote down the laws in the Book of the Covenant.

Describing the condition of the Hebrew society of the Abrahamic period, Morgan compares it with that of the Homeric Greeks but states that "writing in this branch of the Semitic family was probably, then unknown."[95] Yet, he points out that when the Mosaic legislation was completed, the Hebrews were a civilised people, "but not far enough advanced to institute political society."[96] These archaeological discoveries of pre-Mosaic Hebrew script vindicate Morgan's claim that the Hebrews were a civilised people, although theirs was still a gentile society. These discoveries had not been made when Morgan was alive but yet he considered the Hebrew society civilised taking into cognizance various other characteristics which were similar to the Greeks of the Homeric period. Incidentally, that speaks for Morgan's incredible insight into the prehistory of mankind. Now that we know they had an alphabet it can be said with certainty that although they did not institute political society, the Hebrews were a civilised people, because the use of alphabet is one of the main criteria of a civilised society. Nevertheless, doubt arises regarding the claim that the tribe had an alphabet during Abrahamic times because there are no extant Hebrew literary records of the period; nor are there any Hebrew documents of the Mosaic period extant today. Biblical scholars are of the view that whatever had come down to the historical period was the oral tradition that was reduced to writing in the ninth century BCE.

What could be the reason for the absence of non-biblical documents on the history of the tribe in Egypt or any sort of document whatsoever written in the Hebrew language, if as is claimed by several scholars, they had a script? The tribe lay scattered and had not been able to get together to carve out a territory for itself and settle, as all the contemporaneous civilised tribes had done but was compelled to continue to be nomadic or semi-nomadic. Documentation would cause an inevitable though gradual accumulation of literary records but a nomadic way of life is not congenial to the proper storage and preservation of those documents. Being nomadic, the Hebrews moved from place to place and it would be too cumbersome to cart around all the accumulated documents. That must have deterred them from keeping any written records of the history of the tribe or chronicling the events related to the tribe. Succeeding generations were, therefore, left with the tribal history passed on from generation to generation orally. It had to wait, as said above, till about the ninth century BCE for the scribes to reduce it to writing and this has come down to us in the Bible, which is the only information that we have about the early history of the tribe, although the historical information that it provides is very meagre.

The Hebrew tribes of Egypt were organised in a series of consanguine groups in an ascending scale, analogous to the gens, phratry and tribe of the Greeks. The tribe of Levi consisting of eight gentes, for example, was organised in three phratries: Gershonite phratry comprising two gentes, Libni and Shimei; Kohathite phratry consisting of four gentes, Amram, Izhar, Hebron and Uzziel; and Merarite phratry with two gentes, Mahli and Mushi. The groups are sometimes described in a descending order. For example, "the children of Simeon with their generations constitute the tribe, the families are the phratries and the house of the father is the gens."[97] A conglomeration of consanguine groups, the motley crowd that Moses led, taken as a whole, was, therefore, neither a gens nor a phratry. During the four centuries that they had been in Egypt their population had burgeoned so much that it was an assemblage of gentes, each of which organised in phratries. Presumably, these Hebrew tribes that had been living in Egypt spoke the same dialect and not dialects of the same stock of language or of a different family of languages. In short, it was "a gentile society (*societas*) as distinguished from a political society or state (*civitas*)."[98] It was this conglomeration united by a common language and culture that Moses is supposed to have liberated from slavery and led out of Egypt.

In the Fertile Crescent, as it was in the Tower of Babel confounded by god, there were people speaking different languages or to put it differently, there were many tribes and peoples contemporaneous with the Hebrews. The territory that Moses and his tribe had to pass through was that of the Moabites who were biblically the descendants of Lot. This territory consisted of three geographical regions. A part of it was skirted by ranges of hills on the east and the south, the Dead Sea cliffs on the west and the gorge of the river Arnon on the north. A stretch of land lying between the river Arnon and the hills of Gilead constituted another part of their settlement and the third was the valley of the river Jordan. When the Hebrews approached the territory of Moab, Moses told them, "distress not the Moabites, neither contend with them in battle." He seemed to have known of their strength. They were too powerful for Israel to confront in a battle, for they had occupied that land after overthrowing many powerful tribes like the Hormims as well as the Zamzummims, Emims and Anakims, the tribes of men of gigantic stature.[99] So as advised by Moses, Israel took a detour along its borders. We shall see more of this tribe and its interaction with Israel when we deal with the topic elsewhere.

Canaan "was accounted a land of giants" as "giants dwelt therein in old times."[100] It was a tribe known, as mentioned above, by the names, Emim, Anakim and Zamzummim, who were tall and for a long time they had been occupying the region into which the Philistines had now thrust themselves. These tribes were collectively known as the Canaanites. This suggests that they had been living there from very early times and in fact they were the earliest known inhabitants of this part of the Fertile Crescent. Presumably that was why the region got its name, Canaan. The Canaanites who were related to the NW Semitic peoples of northern Mesopotamia and Syria had settled in this coastal region some time in the Early Bronze Age, in *circa* 3300 BCE. As many archaeological findings indicate, the Canaanites were a highly civilised tribe, which according to the Bible were the descendants of Ham's son, Canaan. And from Canaan arose the various Canaanite clans: Sidon, Hittites (Heth), Jebusites, Amorites, Girgashites, Hivites, Arkites, Sinites, Arvadites, Zemarites, and Hemathites.[101] At Ugarit or Ras Shamra, for example, archaeologists have found the ruins of a sprawling mansion consisting of many rooms believed to be of the Canaanites, which shows how developed the tribe was at that time.

At this site, a large number of (baked) clay tablets with cuneiform inscriptions on them, which are said to belong to the fourteenth and fifteenth centuries BCE, have also been unearthed. We understand from these clay tablets that the literature of the Canaanites consisted mainly of myth, epic, saga and ritual, providing us a vivid picture of their religion. Their political structure was a sort of a monarchy, each of their city-states, the most important of which was Jerusalem, being ruled by a king. These settlements were to some extent comparable to the city-states (*polis*) of ancient Greece, which had first claim on citizens' labour and loyalty. Incidentally, it was this reality that prompted Aristotle to define man as a political animal. The city-states owed their origin to agriculture, unlike the modern cities, which grew around industrial complexes. A city-state was a territory surrounded by a strong wall with a gate, which was closed by sunset. The city in which the people lived was ruled by a king, who had a standing army. In times of external aggressions, usually a few of these city-states joined together under the strongest that had suzerainty over the others, to defend themselves. For instance, Jabin, the king of Hazor, as we shall see in Chapter 5, "A Period of Crisis" had forged a coalition like this when he thought that the Hebrews were planning to attack Hazor.

Basically an agriculture-based society, there were among them craftsmen skilled in weaving, carpentry, smithy and pottery. The cities, Bethshan, Gezer, Megiddo, Shechem and Hazor, each of which had its king, were strongly fortified by massive rampart. Megiddo, for example, enclosing an extensive area was protected by incredibly thick walls that could help the city withstand the assault of any invader, howsoever powerful his army was. Of these city-states, however, the last mentioned, Hazor, was the largest and the most powerful, with the hegemony of all the other cities in the hands of its king.[102] The Canaanites were starved of the strategic material, iron, which, despite their close relationship with the neighboring Philistines, the latter did not supply to them. As a result, the Canaanites had to depend upon bronze weapons, importing copper mainly from Egypt and Cyprus. Their military power, of course, was based on chariots. However, in course of time, gradual incursions by the Philistines,

Israel and the Aramaeans had reduced the extent of the territory of the Canaanites to nearly a quarter of its original size.

The Philistines (Palestina[103] or Palestine[104]), the tribe that Moses feared would prevent Israel from taking the shortest route to Canaan, was one of the most powerful "Sea Peoples," so called because they came from beyond the sea. Historically, the Philistines originated from Cyprus or Crete, spoke a non-Semitic dialect, and were of mixed ethnicity, though predominantly Aegian and South-Eastern European. Biblically, they, the Philistines, or Philistims as they are called in the Bible, were the descendants of Casluhim.[105] They arrived in the Mediterranean region by about the Middle Bronze Age, in the seventeenth or eighteenth century BCE, when the Iron Age had supplanted the Bronze Age. In anthropological terms, they arrived when societies in the region were slowly moving from the middle stage of barbarism to the upper stage, which coincided with what the archaeologists call the Iron Age.[106]

They settled – almost at the same time as the Israelites did in the highlands of Judah – in strongholds, which were fortified towns, five in number mostly in the coastal plain of the southern part of Canaan. Some scholars observe that it was these fortified towns that in course of time became city-states, the three important ones of which were Ashkelon, which had a harbour that helped the residents trade with other nations, Ashdod and Gazawas. The other two, Gath and Ekron, lay a little off the coast, in the interior. All these five city-states together are known as the Pentapolis. Apart from these five city-states (there were some others too) the most conspicuous of which were Yavneh and Tell el-Quasile because of their economic importance – the former, a fertile area and the latter, a harbour town on the bank of the river Yarmuk. The social environment and the location of their settlements helped the rapid growth of the tribe as a strong mercantile community.

The city-states of the Philistines functioned, to a great extent, as single, autonomous units each of which was ruled by a "seranim" or lord, an institution that was somewhat analogous to a king. Nevertheless, politically all the five main city-states were loosely allied with one another, with a well-equipped and powerful army and a unified command. The early stages of the Iron Age saw the Philistines who had mastered the art of smelting of iron preventing other tribes from getting it. Israel too had knowledge of smelting iron but because of the Philistine embargo as it were, on supplying this metal to the Hebrews, they were not able to equip their army with strong weapons of iron. Their strategy of monopolising iron, which they imported from Egypt, by denying it to the other tribes and refusing them the help of blacksmiths[107] for making weapons and tools, paid dividends. It helped them maintain their superiority in weaponry and military might over the other tribes. Taking advantage of this, the Philistines had been making constant forays into the territory of Israel, and the growing tension between these two tribes often flared up into open armed conflicts. Incidentally, some historians believe that these conflicts helped unite Israel tribes and the establishment, in due course, of a united Hebrew kingdom.

The Philistine language, which is extinct, was perhaps related to Mycenaean Greek or is said to be non-Semitic and part of the Canaanite dialect continuum. The Philistines, in course of time, mixed with the Canaanites and even intermarried with them; they adopted Canaanite dialect as well as the cuneiform writing and even gave Canaanite names to their Aegean gods! Archaeolcgical findings at Ashod bear witness to the extent of the impact of the Canaanite culture on this non-Semitic tribe. Judging by their socio-political structure and cultural development, they can be said to be a civilised tribe.

Coming from the fringes of the Arabian Desert, the Armaeans, mentioned earlier, were a nomadic tribe with a mixed ethnicity, speaking a Semitic language and their culture was a mixture of that of the Babylonians, Assyrians and Canaanites. After the collapse of the Hittite, Egyptian and Assyrian powers, they moved northwards into Mesopotamia and from there proceeded to the west to occupy the Syrian plains, where they established several powerful kingdoms. This they could do without much difficulty because of the absence of any other strong power in the region, except Israel tribes that were their northern neighbours. The two tribes often clashed, border skirmishes developing into wider armed conflicts for expanding their territories until Israel decisively defeated the Armaean king, Ben-Hadad I (Hadadezer) and annexed that territory.[108] This victory gave Israel control over the copper mines of the Armaeans and helped establish suzerainty, as it were, over other Armaean kingdoms too, thus bringing a large part of Syria under the control of Israel. But embers of opposition to foreign domination were not extinguished altogether. It burst into flames under the leadership of Rezon who held his own, establishing himself in Damascus as the king of Syria[109] and proved to be a thorn in the side of Israel which he detested.

A tribe that the Hebrews would come into contact with off and on was the Amalek, a nomadic tribe that dwelt in the wilderness of Sinai, and according to some scholars, Amalek was the eponymous chief after whom the tribe was named.[110] Amalek, according to the Bible, was the grandson of Easau and son of Eliphaz and Timna, the concubine of Eliphaz.[111] However, if the involvement of this tribe in the inter-tribal war that occurred in the days of Abram (Abraham) were historically true, it must be accepted that the tribe existed long before Amalek is said to have been born, in which case, Amalek got his name because he happened to be the Duke (Chief) of the Amalek tribe. This is the background of the tribe that we shall have the opportunity to meet more than once, later.

Another tribe, the Amorites, whom the Mesopotamians called "Amurru" were the descendants of the settlers of Canaan. Their incursions into Mesopotamia were in the third and second millennia BCE. They harassed but failed to overthrow the Third Dynasty. But after its downfall that created a political vacuum, the Amorites nudging away the many tribes that converged on the region, each one trying to find some elbow space so to speak, for itself, succeeded in getting a firm foothold in Lasar,[112] a city-state in southern Mesopotamia. And in course of time, under the leadership of Gungunun they overran Ur. However, the sixth king of the Semitic dynasty, Hammurabi of the Babylonian Empire, who is remembered for his "Code," subdued Larsa, integrating all the Akkadian-speaking[113] peoples of Mesopotamia.

By the time man stepped from prehistory into history the whole of Western Asia, except the peninsular Asia Minor, was inhabited by the Semitic peoples. There are no extant records that give the information as to when these tribes first came there; it must have been some time in the early historical period, for we are pretty sure that by 3000 BCE, the Semites had struck deep roots in Babylon. However, we know that they were the Mediterranean people as they were generally called. They are said to have come from the African continent to the Arabian Peninsula crossing the Straits of Bab-el-Mandeb long back, sometime between *circa* 30,000 and 20,000 BCE, bringing in the Sebilian culture.[114] The Semites and the Arabs, it is surmised, were the descendants of these Mediterranean people. The Semites are said to be the group of peoples, who according to the Bible, had descended from Noah's son Shem[115] and spoke languages that are closely related to one another. Linguistically, the Semites may be broadly divided into four groups: East (Babylonian-Assyrian) Semites, North (Aramaic) Semites, West (Canaanite) Semites, and South (Arabian) Semites. It is generally accepted that the original home of all these groups was Arabia and so all the Semitic tribes were the offshoots of the desert tribes.

Over the centuries, one by one, waves of these tribes descended on the region called Mesopotamia, often fighting among themselves, primarily for land and other natural resources, pressured by the escalating population. The first of these was the settlement in Babylon by a motley group of various tribes, like the Semites and Kassites. The Sumers had already been here for hundreds of years, perhaps since the barbaric period, dominating the region politically and culturally while the Akkads, who were of Semitic ethnicity, were latecomers. They came probably at the dawn of civilisation but they carved out a niche for themselves in the northern part, pushing the Sumers to the south to the Babylonian plains. They adopted the cuneiform script of the ancient Sumerian tribe and established a monarchic slave state, typical of ancient civilisations. The unification of the Sumerian and Semitic tribes was brought about by Sargon and his grandson, Naram-Sin. However, as stated above, it was left to Hammurabi of the Third Dynasty to expand the territory by establishing its hegemony over Syria and consolidate the Babylonian Empire.

In short, it is the fascinating story of the peoples that inhabited the western part of the Asian continent in the early days of historical times that the Bible unfolds before us. We meet several tribes in this virtual Tower of Babel called the Fertile Crescent but as stated above, the biblical account is centred on the Hebrews. In other words, the rhapsodists who composed these myths, legends and chronicles that constitute the Bible, being Hebrews, looked at the history of the period from the point of view of their tribe. So they naturally romanticised and glorified the Hebrew tribe and its achievements; they portrayed Israel as the "chosen people" and the fictitious character Moses as a great leader who guided by their god Yahweh, liberated the tribe from Egypt. He is supposed to have given them a code of law and brought them to the border of the land that the tribe claimed was gifted to it by god.

NOTES

1. W. Keller, *The Bible as History*, tr. by William Neil, New York, 1964, Introduction, p.8. The word Israel denotes the Hebrew tribes.
2. Ibid., p. 41-44.
3. Gen. 7:11-24. Interestingly stories of a flood that inundated the world are found in Sumerian and Indian mythologies too. It is generally believed that the source of the Indian version of the flood is also like that of the biblical story, the Sumerian tradition.
4. W. Keller, op. cit., p. 50.
5. Gordon Childe, *What Happened in History*, Hammondsworth, 1975, p. 40.
6. Gen. 11:6-9.
7. L.H. Morgan, *Ancient Society, Palo Alto*, 1978, pp. 29-30.
8. Gen. 2:10.
9. I Kgs. 1:38-39. "...and caused Solomon to ride upon King David's mule, and brought him to Gihon," where he was anointed.
10. C. Darwin, *The Descent of Man*, Ohio, 1874, pp. 158-159.
11. Gary Stix, Traces of the Distant Past. In *Scientific American*, July 2008, V. 299, N0. 1, pp. 56-63.
12. Gen. 2:16, "And the Lord God commanded the man, saying, Of every tree of the garden you may freely eat."
13. L.H. Morgan, op. cit., p. 41.
14. Gen. 2:18. "It is not good that the man should be alone; I will make a suitable help for him."
15. Gen. 2:7.
16. Gen. 2:21-22. "And the Lord caused a deep sleep to fall upon Adam, and he slept; and He took one of his ribs, and closed up the flesh in that place. And with the rib, which the Lord God had taken from man, He made a woman."
17. It may be borne in mind that no tribe as "Adamites" or "Eveites" had ever existed and the terms like Adamites and Eveites are used for the

purpose of distinguishing the various types of tribes that must have existed before the formation of the tribe of Israel. And each of these names represents not just one but more than one tribe. These words are coined on the lines of the biblical practice of calling tribes after their progenitors as for example, the Ephramites after Ephraim or the Moabites after Moab.

18. Gen. 2:23.
19. Elman R. Service, *The Hunters*, Englewood Cliffs, 1966, pp. 7-8.
20. Gen. 3:1-4, 10.
21. Gen. 3:20.
22. Gen. 2:19.
23. L.H. Morgan, op. cit., p. 10.
24. Vide Appendix I, Genealogy. Abraham was the twentieth descendant of the fictitious character Adam.
25. Gen. 3:7. It is not that they used only fig leaves; this may be taken to mean any kind of leaves thick enough to be attached together.
26. Gen. 3:21. The word 'skin' here means 'bark' of trees, for man had not begun to hunt to get the skin of animals for their clothing.
27. Gen. 2:24, 25.
28. L.H. Morgan, op. cit., p. 453.
29. L.H. Morgan, ibid., p. 384.
30. Gen. 3:10.
31. Gen. 3:16. The bard used the word "husband" because he lived when the institution of family had come into existence and he would not have known that the relationship of cohabiting man and woman in biblical times was different from that of his days.
32. Gen. 3:20.
33. L.H. Morgan, op. cit., p. 384 ff. A description of these types of families is given. Vide See also "Systems of Consanguinity and Affinity of the Human Family" by Morgan.
34. L.H. Morgan, ibid., p. 10.
35. Gen. 3:18-19.
36. Gen. 4:4.
37. G. Childe, What happened in History, Hammondsworth, 1973, p. 30.
38. This tribe inhabits the North Sentinel Island of the Andaman and Nicobar archipelago and their population is estimated to be approximately 300. They go about naked and are hunter-gatherers. Racially they are considered to be Negritos.
39. L.H. Morgan, op. cit., p. 63.
40. Ibid., p. 85.
41. For example, Gen. 20:2. "And Abraham said of Sarah his wife, she is

my sister: and Abimalech king of Gerar sent and took Sarah." Assuming the protagonists are historical personalities, this is an anachronism because the Philistines, of which Abimalech was the Chief, had not come to the Mediterranean yet. The Philistines had not come to the Mediterranean at the time when the Hebrews were believed to have come there. This episode, like many in the Old Testament is, obviously fictitious. However, it shows the social norms among the Hebrew tribes of those ancient times.

42. Gen. 4:5. "...And Cain was very angry, and his countenance fell..."
43. Gen. 4:4-6, 8.
44. Gen. 4:22. "And Zillah also bore Tubalcain. An instructor of every artificer in brass and iron...."
45. G. Chide, *What Happened in History*, Hammondsworth, 1975, p. 85.
46. L.H. Morgan, op. cit., p. 12.
47. Vide Appendix I.
48. Agni Purana, Ch. 368.
49. Gen. 8:16/10:1.
50. Gen. 9:20. "And Noah began to be a husbandman and he planted a vineyard."
51. Gen. 10:1-32.
52. Gen. 10:32.
53. L.H. Morgan, op. cit., pp. 21-27.
54. Gen. 9:18, 19/10:21-31/11:10-27.
55. Deut. 32:10. "He found him in a desert land and in the wasteland, a howling wilderness..."/Jer.2:2. "I remember you, ... when you went after Me in the wilderness, in a land that was not sown."
56. This was the original name of the character and his wife's original name was "Sarai" until both names were changed to "Abraham" and "Sarah" respectively. The reason for changing the names is dealt with elsewhere in the text.
57. Gen. 11:31.
58. Acts. 7:1-4. In reply to the High Priest, Stephen says, "The God of glory appeared to our Father Abraham, when he was in Mesopotamia, before he dwelt in harem."
59. All biblical scholars agree that The Gospel according to Luke and the Book of Acts are authored by the same person, namely, Luke the beloved physician," for in the latter, the story narrated in The Gospel of Luke is continued.
60. Acts. 28:30.
61. Acts. 7:59.

62. F. Engels, The Origin of the Family, Private Property and the State, Moscow, 1948, pp. 56-57.
63. Gen. 12:1-2.
64. The original name of this region was Canaan (Gen12:5), It was also Called Palestine, a name derived from Philistinia (Ps.60:8) as it was occupied by the Philistines. After it was conquered by Israel tribes it came to identified by that name (I Sam.13:19). In the Greco-Roman period it was known as Judea, maybe because, after the Hebrew kingdom split, the northern kingdom of Israel was conquered and occupied by the Assyrians who took the people into captivity. The southern kingdom of Judah lasted for a little more than another two centuries and perhaps that was why the name Judea lingered in the memory of subsequent generations.
65. Ex. 3:2. "And the angel of the Lord appeared to him in a flame of fire..." There were several other angels too, as for example Gabriel.
66. Gen. 12:5-8.
67. Num. 13:29.
68. Gen. 14:13.
69. *World Book Dictionary.*
70. Gen. 12:10, 14.
71. Gen. 17:4-5. "As for Me, behold, My covenant is with you...you shall be a father of many nations. Your name shall not any more be called Abram, but your name shall be Abraham..."
72. Gen. 17:15. "...As for Sarai your wife, you shall not call her name Sarai, but Sarah shall be her name."
73. Gen. 24:4, 7, 10.
74. The word "flood," in this context, means "river."
75. Josh. 24:2. The biblical scholars opine that the flood in this context refer not to the flood of Noah's time but to the river Euphrates. In several other places in the Bible where the word "flood" is used, it denotes the river Euphrates.
76. Gen. 13:2.
77. Gen. 23:16.
78. Gen. 24:53.
79. Gen. 18:6, 8.
80. Gen. 12:16/22:6. As pointed out in the Preface, the Bible in its English KJV version uses the word "servant" for the word "slave." So it must be understood that 'servant" in the former verse means "slave."
81. L.H. Morgan, op. cit., p. 367.
82. Ibid., p. 62.
83. Gen. 20:12.

84. L.H. Morgan, op. cit., pp. 367-368.
85. Ibid, p. 368.
86. L.H. Morgan, ibid., p. 366.
87. Ibid., p. 366.
88. Ex. 22:25-26.
89. Ex. 12:44-45.
90. Ex. 24:4, 7.
91. Deut. 17:18.
92. Deut. 31:9.
93. Ezra 7:11-12. "Now this is the copy of the letter that the king Artaxerxes sent to Ezra, the priest, the scribe, even a scribe of the worlds of the commandments of the Lord, and of his statutes to Israel."
94. W. Keller, op. cit., pp. 262-263.
95. L.H. Morgan, op. cit., p. 366.
96. Ibid., p. 368.
97. Ibid., pp. 368-369.
98. Ibid., p. 66.
99. Deut. 2:9-23.
100. Deut. 2:10-11, 20.
101. Gen. 10:15-18.
102. Josh. 11:1, 10.
103. Ex. 15:14; Isa.14:29, 31.
104. Joel 3:4.
105. Gen. 10:14; 1 Chr.1:12. "Philistim" is another form of the term "philistines."
106. L.H. Morgan, op. cit., p. 11.
107. I Sam. 13:19-20.
108. II Kgs.13:25.
109. I Kgs. 11:23-25.
110. Gen. 36:16. "... and duke Amalek; these are the dukes that came to Eliphaz, in the land of Edom..."
111. Gen. 36:12.
112. Some scholars associate Lasar with Ellasar (vide Gen.14:1) but this has not been confirmed.
113. Akkadian language, of which the Babylonian and Assyrian were dialects, is one of the group of Semitic languages.
114. J.W. Swain, *The Ancient World,* V.1., New York, 1950, p. 29.
115. Gen. 10:21-31.

4

Consolidation of Slavery

The fictitious story of the journey of the Hebrew tribes led by Abram to Egypt symbolically marks the beginning of intermittent influx of the Hebrew tribes from Asia to Egypt in subsequent years, driven by drought and famine. The history of the migration and struggles, successes and failures of the Hebrew pioneers in Egypt is allegorised in the story of the immigration of the Abramites to Egypt. On entering Egypt, the Hebrews encountered no opposition from the king or the princes and palace officials. On the other hand, enamoured of the beauty of the tribeswomen that Abram's wife Sarai symbolised, the Pharaoh and the officials of the palace welcomed the Hebrew tribe with open arms.

Seeing the welcome accorded to them by the king, the people too did not resist, though they were naturally not very happy to have an alien tribe in their midst – more so because of the special treatment given to them by the Pharaoh. In return for the "services" rendered by the Hebrew women who stayed in the palace and "pleased" the Pharaoh and the palace officials, the immigrant tribes got many privileges. The king provided them all facilities to settle in the territory and even gave them many gifts including "sheep, and oxen, and he-asses, and men servants, and maidservants, she-asses, and camels."[1] The extraordinary freedom that the Hebrews enjoyed helped them exploit the people of Egypt and accumulate wealth. Egyptian society was in the stage of civilisation, then. As a result of the help given by the Egyptians, the development of the Hebrew tribes had been accelerated and the Hebrew society, which was perhaps in the lower or middle stage of barbarism slowly progressed. As we understand from the Bible, in due course, thanks to the Pharaoh's generosity, as pointed out in the previous chapter the tribe moved up to the upper stage of barbarism and was at the threshold of civilisation.

That the Hebrew women were accommodated in the palace for "pleasing" the king and his officials, however, should not be misconstrued as prostitution, for the Hebrews were at a stage of development when there were no sex taboos. In other words, they should not be judged on the basis of the ethics of the present society, or even that of the Hebrew society of the period after the Mosaic Code was ratified by the tribe; they have to be viewed in the context of the Hebrew society of the pre-Exodus period.[2] The Hebrew tribes of the Abrahamic period when they entered Egypt were most probably in the lower or middle stage of barbarism. Anthropologists and social philosophers assert that each form of society has its own ideas of ethics. Generally speaking, changes in the social structure necessarily bring about changes in the sphere of ideas. For example, it is obvious that the ideas – especially political and legal, not to speak of ethical and philosophical ideas – which were compatible with the tribal communes based on collectivism and equality would not be in consonance with that of a monarchic society based on private property and slavery. New ideas sprout, out of the compulsions of the changed configuration of social forces and their inter-relationship. Hence, inevitably, changes in the social structure bring about corresponding changes in the realm of ideas but these changes, in a field like ethics that is not directly related to the social structure, do not happen *pari passu* with structural changes.[3]

Be that as it may, from the legend of the Abramites, we come to know that in course of time they became very wealthy, possessing cultivable land, livestock and many male and female slaves. Incidentally, all these domesticated animals — like donkeys, sheep, goats, camels, oxen and pigs — once constituted the wealth of each commune. But in course of time, livestock became part of the property of the head of the commune. It is debatable if Abram held the herds as his property owing to his being the head of the family community or because he was the hereditary head of a commune. To quote Engels, "But private property in herds must have developed at a very early stage. It is hard to say whether Father Abraham appeared to the author of the so-called First Book of Moses as the owner of his herds and flocks in his own right as head of a family community, or by virtue of his status as actual hereditary chief of a gens."[4] However, when mankind was on the verge of stepping into the historical period, livestock had been the property of the heads of families like certain personal effects and even slaves. Whatever it was, he cannot be equated with the property owners of the period of civilisation. Nonetheless, this was the infancy of the institution of private property which entailed slavery among the Hebrews.

The native tribes were naturally unhappy with the favouritism that was being shown by the Pharaoh and the palace officials to the immigrant Hebrew tribe which, consequently, was thriving at their expense. They were particularly critical about the heinous role being played by the Hebrew women. Although pre-marital or extra-marital sex was not taboo in the then Egyptian society, they knew how the Pharaoh could be influenced by women. It was evident that the undue favour being shown to the Hebrews was due to the influence of the Hebrew women over the Pharaoh and the palace officials. These Hebrew women had been in the Pharaoh's harem since the tribe arrived in Egypt and the members of the royal family including the Pharaoh as well as the palace officials were charmed by them. Above all, these foreign women were depriving the Egyptian women of the opportunity of being taken into the harem, which was deemed a privilege and a matter of pride for the families concerned in those times, apart from the benefits they derived both in kind and in cash.

Consequently, the people of Egypt seethed with anger. The spies had been giving the Pharaoh secret intelligence that there was a whispering campaign against his association with the Hebrew women. And the rising anti-Hebrew sentiment among the Egyptian freemen was causing sporadic riots in different cities. Eventually, it erupted into an open revolt.[5] The people revolted, protesting the privileged position of the Hebrew women whom Sarai symbolises and the preferential treatment given to an immigrant tribe. And they must have openly showed their animosity towards the exploitative alien tribe, forcing the Pharaoh to take immediate action. The Pharaoh decided to send off the Hebrew women from the harem and expel from Egypt the Hebrew clans to which these women belonged. He called Abram and said that the people of Egypt were not happy that he took the Hebrew women into the harem and ordered Abram to take the Hebrew women away and quit the country at once.[6]

The Pharaoh had no choice but to command his soldiers to drive out of the country those Hebrews who exploited the local people.[7] Consequently, led by Abram and Lot, the communes that had sent their women to the Pharaoh's harem and had enriched themselves at the expense of the local population by enjoying the protection given by the Pharaoh and his officials had to move out of Egypt. The majority of the Hebrew clans that had not sent their women to "please" the Pharaoh and had not been favoured by him was not as rich as the Abramites. They had not exploited or infringed upon the rights and interests of the local population and neither the Pharaoh nor the people objected to their continuance in the country. They were mostly Hebrew freemen like petty traders and craftsmen as well as the poor who had been working as hired servants or slaves of the Hebrew and Egyptian freemen. In fact, the Egyptians did not want them to leave, for they were a good source of slaves or cheap labour for the rich Egyptian freemen. So the communes to which these men and women belonged stayed back in Egypt.

Leaving the Egyptian territory, the two Hebrew communes, the Abramites and the Lotites, travelled north and encamped between Bethel and Hai, where they had been earlier and had even built an altar for Yahweh then. But now that the livestock of the tribe had increased considerably and the population of the two gens put together had also grown, the land available at their campsite was not enough to accommodate the increased population of men and animals of the two communes comfortably and for grazing those animals. The pastureland was not extensive enough to feed the herds of both the Abramites and the Lotites, and water too was insufficient to meet the requirements of the two communes. The competition for pasturage and water resulted in frequent clashes, especially between the herdsmen of the two communes. That could have led to a fratricidal war.

Anticipating such an eventuality and eager to prevent it, Abram talked it out with Lot, and they decided to settle the problem amicably. Abram said he would shift to the plains of Jordan but he gave the choice to Lot, who was asked to choose between the plains of Jordan and the land of Canaan. The plains of Jordan was fertile, the fields covered with lush, verdant grass and there were many water sources. Naturally that was Lot's choice and he decided to leave with his commune, slaves and livestock.[8] So the Lotites moved to the plains of Jordan with all the wealth that they had acquired and pitched their tents at a place near the city of Sodom. The Abramites "dwelled in the land of Canaan" and they shifted their camp to Mamre, near Hebron.[9]

The Lotites could not, however, stay there for long. At that time, an inter-tribal war broke out involving all the tribes in the region including Sodom, who were not far from the site at which the Lotites had pitched their tents. The victorious tribes pillaged the land of Sodom, carried off all the wealth of the land including that of the Lotites who were camping nearby and the tribesmen of all the vanquished tribes as well as the Lotites had been taken prisoner. As soon as the news reached Abram, he mobilised his men, pursued the enemy and slaughtered them. The prisoners of war were all rescued and the plunder recovered. When the king of Sodom heard of it, he went to welcome the victorious Abramites and the king of Sa'lem feasted Abram and his men. They told Abram and his men to take for themselves all the wealth that they had brought back. But Abram declined, saying "that I will not take from a thread even to a shoelatchet and that I will not take anything that is yours,"[10] because he did not want the king of Sodom to say later that he made the Abramites rich. The composer intended to portray Abram as generous and noble by making him refuse the plunder that was offered to him, but he failed when he made Abram say "lest you say, I have made Abram rich." This statement actually betrayed his egoism and the readers see conceit and not generosity or nobility in his refusal to accept the offer of those kings.

Soon, however, the Lotites had been constrained to move their camp from the plains of Jordan near Sodom. One day, some people of Sodom warned the Lotites of an impending disaster and advised them to escape from there.[11] They said they were all leaving as they had seen signs of an earthquake – probably there was a mild quake of very low intensity that the Hebrews, not having experienced a quake so far, did not even notice. So Lot went to his sons-in-law who were in the city and said to them that he was told an earthquake was imminent and that he and his tribe had decided to move out of this place at once. He asked them to accompany his tribe but they refused to go with the Lotites. They had heard their grandfather speak of quakes that had occurred when he was young but neither he nor anyone of the family had run away from the place then. So Lot's sons-in-law did not think it necessary to leave the place on account of an impending earthquake.[12] Lot was in two minds, but soon, urged by his tribesmen,[13] he too with his wife and daughters along with the entire tribe fled from there. Lot's wife was trailing behind. Somewhat later, maybe because she was finding it difficult to keep pace with the others or perhaps to try again to persuade her sons-in-law to join them, she returned to Sodom. The earthquake struck the area just at that moment and she was buried under the debris of one of the houses that were destroyed in the quake.[14]

From the description in the Bible, it may be surmised that either a volcano had erupted or an earthquake had occurred there. There is no history of any volcanic activity in that region, but geologists have observed that the region, the Dead Sea basin, had been prone to earthquakes since ancient times.[15] We shall have occasion to discuss this in detail in the next chapter, "A Period of Crisis." Suffice it to say now that it could have been an earthquake that forced the Lotites to leave the place. However, Lot along with his two daughters, the bulk of the tribesmen, the slaves and the livestock arrived safely at a village called Zoar by dawn the next day. It was not very far from Sodom. In the meantime, the two cities of Sodom and Gomorrah were completely destroyed by the catastrophic earthquake of very high intensity.

During this period, Abram had decided to change his name as well as his wife's to Abraham and Sarah respectively, indicating his complete rejection of his pagan heritage. So the Abramites will, hereafter, be known as the Abrahamites. The day the earthquake struck the Jordan valley, unaware of what had happened there, the Abrahamites were going about with their daily chores. The morning after the earthquake as the sun rose, when Abraham woke up he could see "smoke" rising up to the sky from the plains of Jordan. The dust thrown up in the air by the quake was obviously what he thought was smoke. The Abrahamites knew of the quake only when those who had taken refuge in the nearby villages gave them the news. Abraham was happy when they told him that the Lotites along with Lot and his two daughters had escaped the calamity.[16] During his stay in Zoar, Lot begot two sons in his two daughters. (Incest became taboo among the barbaric Hebrews much later, to be precise, only after the Mosaic Law came into force.) The babies were named Moab and Benammi who, incidentally, were the progenitors of the Moabites and the Ammons respectively.

Meanwhile Abraham, who was in Mamre, had also begotten in his slave Hagar, a son whom he named Ishmael. (Ishmael,[17] who married an Egyptian girl, had twelve sons who became princes and progenitors of as many tribes that inhabited Northern Arabia and the Arabs claim to be the descendants of those tribes.) The birth of these children indicates not just the birth of three individuals; it implies that the Hebrew population had increased threefold because during this period, naturally, many children would have been born to the other members of the tribe also. The bard mentions the birth of only these children not only because Abraham and Lot are the two main protagonists in the episode but also because these children would be the progenitors of several tribes.

After the earthquake in Sodom, the Abrahamites did not want to stay in the region any more. They moved into Gerar, between Kadesh and Shur. Here again, the Hebrew women were allowed, as was done in Egypt, to "please" the Chief of the local tribe who took Sarah.[18] Sarah, in this context too, symbolises the Hebrew women. So when it is said the Chief took Sarah, it implies that he took as many Hebrew women as he wanted. In return, the Chief gave the Hebrews "sheep and oxen and menservants and women servants" and allowed the women who "pleased" them to go back to their tribe, giving Abraham "a thousand pieces of silver."[19] There was no reason for giving Abraham the livestock and such a large sum of money except as remuneration for the "services" rendered to the Chief and the elder tribesmen by the women of the Hebrews. Moreover, as the Pharaoh did, he gave the Abrahamites the liberty to pitch their tents in any part of the land that they wished. The Abrahamites stayed there for a long time, during which period, Abraham begot a son in Sarah and they named him Isaac,[20] indicating further demographic growth of the Hebrew tribe.

The local tribesmen, naturally, resented the undue favour being shown to an alien tribe, but now when the Hebrews began to aggrandise themselves by exploiting the locals the resentment grew into open protest. Nevertheless, the Chief continued to support the Hebrews and so the people took law into their own hands. They cut off water supply to the Hebrews by violently expropriating the wells that the Abrahamites had dug for their use.[21] The Chief seemed helpless and so the Hebrews could not stay there any more; they left the place and went to Beersheba where they encamped. It was during their stay there that Sarah died.

Abraham was now quite old and he got his son, Isaac, married to Rebekah, a girl from his father's native place, because he did not want Isaac to marry a Canaanite girl. Meanwhile Abraham took a concubine and in her he begot many children; these children too married and had children. He sent away the children he begot in his concubine giving them some gifts and deeded all his wealth to Isaac. It was not that Abraham alone had been getting children and grandchildren; all members of the tribe too must have got, perhaps many more children and grandchildren. So the Hebrew population had been increasing by leaps and bounds. After Abraham's death, the Abrahamite tribe, which may now be called the Isaacites, moved south to camp by the well Lahairoi,[22] where Rebekah gave birth to twins, who were named Easau and Jacob.

A few years after the death of Abraham, another famine broke out in Canaan. But the Isaacites did not dare take the tribe back to Egypt, for he had heard his father and other elders telling about the treatment meted out to the Abrahamites there.[23] So the Isaacite tribe went back to Gerar between Kadesh and Shur, where the Abrahamites had been earlier, and stayed there.[24] When the Chief of the local tribe asked Isaac who Rebekah was, he said she was his sister.[25] There is a hint in this statement, that as it was in Egypt and earlier in Gerar itself, this time also the Hebrew women that Rebekah symbolises, had been allowed to "please" the Chief and the elders of the tribe. As the Abrahamite and Lotite tribes did in Egypt, here too the Hebrews exploited the local people and amassed wealth. The local people tolerated the exploitative alien tribe for a long time but finally they protested. They attacked the Hebrews; they filled with earth the wells that the Hebrews had dug, thus cutting off the sources of water that irrigated their land. And Isaac was prevented from digging another well.

The increasing opposition of his tribe to the Hebrews alerted the Chief, and he told Isaac to call back the women who had been engaged in "pleasing" the Chief and the elders of the tribe. He also asked the Hebrews to leave the place forthwith.[26] Finding themselves in the midst of a hostile population and an unsympathetic Chief, the Hebrews were constrained to leave the place. So leaving Gerar, they went to Beershebah and encamped there.[27] The elders of the Gerar tribes were, however, nervous. The Isaacites had become wealthy and powerful and the tribe in Gerar feared that the Hebrews would come back, and forcibly driving them out, would occupy their land. So the Chief and the elders of the Gerar tribe went over to Beershebah to meet Isaac and pacify the Hebrews. The meeting was cordial; there were no hard feelings. The elders of both the tribes swore to maintain peace between them and sealed a bilateral non-aggression pact as it were, with a grand feast.[28]

It was in Beershebah that Isaac spent the rest of his life with his wife and two sons, the twins, Easau and Jacob. The Bible says, when their mother, Rebekah, was pregnant, "the children struggled together within her" and god told her "two nations are in thy womb and two manner of people shall be separated from thy bowels,"[29] of whom the younger will dominate the elder of the twins. The twins symbolise two tribes and the "two manner of people" indicates the differences between the two tribes. As pointed out in the previous chapter, "A Virtual Tower of Babel," at a certain stage a primeval household was bound to split, each section forming a household or commune. This episode of Easau and Jacob is the mythico-poetic way of indicating the possibility of the formation of a punaluan family out of a consanguine family.[30]

Coming back to the biblical story, the reason for these twin boys' mutual antagonism, we come to know later, was the greed for property, the inheritance of which, among the Hebrews, "was strictly among the phratry, and probably within the gens, namely the 'house' of the father."[31] Besides, by nature they were different as could be judged by their deeds. Easau was simple to the point of naïveté, while Jacob, considered one of the Patriarchs, was inhuman and crafty. For example, when Easau, the elder of the twins, felt faint and was on the verge of death, Jacob refused to give him the pottage that would revive him, until he promised to give up all the legitimate privileges as the first born in favour of Jacob. Again when Isaac, their father, old and practically blind, was on his deathbed, Jacob, persuaded by and with the connivance of his mother, got his father's blessing.[32] The blessing in this context means the wealth and property.

In ordinary language, Jacob got the entire wealth and property of his father by deceit, leaving nothing for his brother Easau. Later, only when Easau came with the cooked meat that his father had asked for and requested his father to bless him, Isaac realised that Jacob had duped him. When Easau implored his father for a small share of the property, Isaac said to him that a little earlier Jacob had come slyly and cheated him of all the wealth that he wanted to give Easau.[33] And Isaac said that there was nothing left with him and advised Easau to serve Jacob! This episode highlights the problem that the rise of private property had created in the barbaric society that had so far been based on collectivism.

Consequently, Easau hated Jacob and decided to murder him after their father's death. Sensing Easau's grudge against Jacob and fearing that his life was in danger, Rebekah found a pretext to send him to a distant place. She told Isaac that she did not want Jacob to marry a Canaanite girl and so requested him to allow Jacob to go to Padanaram, her father's place to find a suitable bride for him. Isaac thought it was a reasonable request and told Jacob to go to Padanaram and ask for the hand of Rebekah's cousin Laban's daughter. He went there and married Rachel, the daughter of Laban. He stayed with the Labans for seven years, during which period, he also married Rachel's sister Leah and got involved with their maids, Bilah and Zilpa. Rachel was barren but Jacob begot twelve sons and a daughter in the other three women. Their twelve sons were Reuben, Simeon, Levi, Judah, Dan, Naphtali, Gad, Asher, Issachar, Zebulun, Joseph and Benjamin. Jacob now decided to go back to his parents' home in Beersheba with his two wives, two concubines and twelve children.

On the way, at Jabbok as the story goes, he wrestled with god, who appeared in the form of a man, and prevailed. At that time god renamed him saying, "Your name shall no more be Jacob, but Israel,"[34] meaning "the man who fights with god." This myth helped the tribe rid itself of the ignominy of being identified by the term "Hebrew," which had an odious connotation, as the term referred to outlaws and plunderers in those days. This is also intended to mythicise Jacob. Anyway, since then the Abrahamite tribes, known to the Canaanites as the Hebrews, called themselves *B'nei Yisrael*, meaning "the people or the tribe of Israel," because they were the descendants of Jacob[35] who was Abraham's grandson and who god renamed Israel. They did not want to be known as "Hebrews" any more. And these twelve sons of Jacob are regarded as the progenitors of the twelve tribes of Israel, which patronym came to be used thereafter to denote the followers of Judaism, one of the Abrahamic religions.

Of all his sons, Joseph was his father's favourite and Jacob was blatantly partial towards Joseph. Jacob was now quite old and bedridden and all his other sons thought their father would bequeath his entire property to Joseph who, they knew, was their father's pet. So they planned to kill him. On second thoughts, however, they decided not to kill him but get him out of the way. One day when they were grazing their sheep, all eleven of them as planned, pushed him into a dry well; and they sold him to Ishmaelite traders[36] who happened to pass by, at that time. The Ishmaelites took the lad, who was then seventeen years of age, to Egypt from where Pot'i-phar, a captain of the palace guard bought him as a slave in his household. This episode again brings into focus the problem caused by the rise of private property – a problem that as stated above, the barbarians did not encounter in their communes, which were based on collectivism that was now a fading socio-economic system.

When Joseph was brought into Egypt, there was a fairly large population of the Hebrews in the country. The Hebrews had been trickling into Egypt in groups, large and small, after the first influx that the immigration of Abraham symbolised and settling in that country along with those Hebrew communes that had stayed back when the Abrahamites were forced out of Egypt. Apart from this, many Hebrew men and women were brought into Egypt – some were bought as slaves by Egyptian traders from other countries as exemplified by the episode of Joseph and the rest were those taken as captives during wars and enslaved. There were, therefore, several Hebrew gentes existing side by side with the monarchical civilised society of the Egyptians. Presumably, whenever palace officials and some rich Egyptian families needed more labour force, men and women from among Israel must have been either forcibly captured and enslaved or bought and made to work for them as slaves.

However, all the Hebrews in Egypt were not slaves; there were several rich, middleclass and lower-middleclass Hebrews too. The Hebrew clans existing on the fringes of the Egyptian society had inevitably been undergoing gradual changes not only by internal contradictions but influenced by the more advanced Egyptian society as well. The institution of private property and slavery that had begun to sprout during Abraham's time among the Hebrews had now grown fully. As a result a new wealthy class had come up and the system of slavery had struck deep roots among the Hebrews, the slaves being the poorer section of the tribe. Many of the slaves, particularly Hebrew slaves, were badly ill-treated and some, imprisoned for various crimes, sometimes alleged crimes as in the case of Joseph.[37] Needless to say, the affluent Hebrew freemen did not have the freedom and the privileges that the ruling class, the Egyptians, enjoyed. The Egyptians treated even the affluent Hebrews with contempt and this often led to clashes. Moses' fight with an Egyptian,[38] which we shall deal with presently, exemplifies this, and obviously it could not have been the first or the last. The Hebrew freemen generally, resented the treatment being meted out to them by the Egyptians and were becoming restive.

The Pharaoh must have been getting reports of the simmering discontent among the Hebrew freemen through his intelligence officers. Stray incidents of skirmishes between the Egyptians and the Hebrews, the oppressors and the oppressed, were also being reported, and the Pharaoh feared that these might one day flare up into a widespread rebellion. This, the Pharaoh thought, would imperil his position and the stability as well as the security of the kingdom, and so he hit upon a plan. He decided to utilise the services of any intelligent men that he could find among the Hebrews, including those slaves currently held as prisoners.

The story of the imprisonment of Joseph and his release has to be viewed against this backdrop. The fictitious story of his ability to interpret dreams is, evidently, aimed at mythicising the character of Joseph as well as showing that he was incredibly brilliant. The Pharaoh, who must have heard of the extraordinary intelligence of Joseph from his prison staff, decided to release him and appoint him to a high post. This was done as a matter of policy dictated by political imperative and not because as the Bible says, Joseph was "a man in whom the spirit of God is."[39] He was, it may be surmised, not the one and only Hebrew to be released from the prison; there could, certainly, have been several Israelites serving prison terms who were found to be intelligent and were released and given responsible positions in the government by the Pharaoh.

Joseph was appointed the vizier or governor, who was second only to the Pharaoh in power and position. Saying, "...only as regards the throne will I be greater than you," the Pharaoh took the signet ring from his finger and put it on Joseph's finger.[40] Apart from delegating to Joseph immense powers as the vizier, the Pharaoh gave him a ring, a gold chain and expensive clothes of exquisite silk, lest he shifted his allegiance to his tribe and turned against the Egyptian government. This was a very clever move on the part of the Pharaoh, for he knew that better than the Egyptians, the Hebrews in positions of authority would be able to hold down the restive Hebrews without creating more bitterness against the Egyptians in general and the government in particular. On the other hand, the ire of the Hebrew freemen who were reprimanded or punished for any misdemeanor or disloyalty to the king would now be directed against the Hebrew officials. That, he calculated, would help divide the Hebrew community and thus obviate the danger of the Hebrews uniting against the government.

Whether Joseph was a historical personality or not is immaterial. The story of his life in Egypt is an allegory, reflecting the life of the Hebrew immigrants in Egypt. His life, therefore, symbolises the trials and tribulations as well as the failures and successes of the subjugated Hebrew freemen who were struggling to find an honourable place for themselves in the land of the Pharaohs. It is specifically symbolic of the lives of the Hebrews of the lowest rung of society, from which some self-seekers like Joseph subsequently rose to become wealthy and powerful or got into high official positions in Egypt with the support of the Egyptian nobility. Naturally, they were beholden to their Egyptian patrons and acted as their agents. In other words, Joseph exemplifies the servile class of Hebrews that the Pharaoh built up as a bulwark against the disaffected and freedom-loving Hebrews. But the Pharaoh did not realise that this was a double-edged sword.

By the time Joseph died, with his help many Hebrews had become quite wealthy and this affluent class of Hebrew freemen became a powerful force too dangerous to be ignored. Meanwhile the population of the Hebrews too had burgeoned so much that, if left unchecked, there was a distinct possibility of the tribe soon outnumbering the Egyptians. At that time, "there arose a new king over Egypt, who did not know Joseph." He was not tactful but blunt in his dealings and he did not trust the Hebrews, many of whom had become rich and powerful, some occupying key positions in the officialdom. He eased the Hebrews out of all the official positions they had been holding. He warned his people, saying that the Hebrews had become a powerful community that was becoming more and more powerful. The situation was, in fact, getting worse by the day and if no remedial measures were taken, they would soon dominate the kingdom. In the event of an invasion by a hostile country, he feared, they might even collaborate with the enemy and fight against Egypt.[41]

So the Pharaoh decided to check the growth of the Hebrew population. He summoned Hebrew midwives and ordered that all male children being born to Hebrew women should be done away with at birth itself. Yet the Hebrews "multiplied and waxed very mighty" because the midwives did not obey the Pharaoh's orders. The king, who was furious at the midwives' impunity, summoned them for interrogation. When questioned as to why they refused to obey him, they said that the Hebrew women would have given birth before they arrived on the scene.[42] So he commanded the people to drown all newborn Hebrew boys in the river Nile and the subsequent Pharaohs also continued all repressive measures against the Hebrews. This, however, proved to be counterproductive and helped only make enemies of loyal Hebrews too. They became more and more estranged and began to think of fighting for their freedom.

And to lead them in their struggle for freedom there appeared on the scene a man by the name of Moses. No one can say with certainty that Moses was a historical personality, for there is no documentary evidence whatsoever, except what is found in the Bible, about his existence; nor is there any archaeological evidence. The Bible speaks of his birth and death, but these events are so mythicised that it is difficult to accept them as anything other than poetic imagination. In fact, his entire life is a series of myths and legends with no concrete evidence of any sort to corroborate those stories, including the story of the Exodus that he is supposed to have led.

As the legend goes, Moses was born to an Israelite woman of Levi, wife of a man of the Levite tribe. That was the time when the Pharaoh had ordered all the newborn Hebrew children to be drowned in the Nile. So the parents managed to keep the baby hidden at home for three months. But finding that this could no more be kept a secret, the mother made a small boat of bulrushes and placing the little one in it, kept the boat on the bank of the Nile. Her daughter, Moses' elder sister, was told to stand at a distance and watch to see what happened to the baby. Soon one of the Pharaoh's daughters, who came to bathe in the river, happened to see the baby. She took him and assuming that the baby was disowned and discarded by his mother or perhaps the mother, leaving the baby on the bank, had got into the river for a bath and was drowned, decided to adopt the child.[43] At this time, the baby's sister approached the princess as if by chance and asked if she would like to have a woman to nurse the baby. And she brought her mother. The princess did not know it was the baby's mother. So the baby's life was saved and his mother herself became his wet nurse! This story, which is stranger than fiction, is intended to touch a tender chord in the hearts of the readers and also to show that at his birth itself he had the grace of god.

At the time of Moses' death, the Bible tells us, there was god's presence. As the story in the Bible goes, just before his death Moses climbed up the mountain of Nebo and god showed "him all the land of Gilead up to Dan, and all Naphtali and the land of Ephraim and Manasseh and all the land of Judah up to the utmost sea. And the south and the plain of the valley of Jericho, the city of palm trees, up to Zoar."[44] It is said Moses died when god was showing him the Promised Land and was buried by god himself "in a valley in the land of Moab."[45] There is no archaeological evidence to confirm that Moses was buried there, for no remains of a sepulchre or anything that could be construed as a sepulchre, vault or an ossuary has been found in this region so far. The belief that he was buried there is based purely on what is said in the Bible, which itself says, "but no man knows of his sepulchre to this day."[46] In fact, neither the Bible nor extra-biblical literature provides any documentary evidence about the place and time of his death. So we can be certain that this biblical character named Moses was only a mythological figure.

However, Moses was regarded primarily as a prophet and a religious preceptor. Grant writes, Moses "came to be regarded as primarily a priest, the true founder of the Yahwist faith" and equates him with the founders of other religions, the Buddha and Zoroaster, that is Zarathustra.[47] It is precisely because of such a belief that the Hebrews called him *Moshe Rabbeinu*, meaning "Moses, our Preceptor/ Rabbi." That he is considered a preceptor, however, has tempted many scholars to regard him as the founder of Yahwism or Judaism and they began to equate him with founders of religions, which cannot be justified in any way. We can positively say, for example, Muhammad (570-632 CE), the Buddha (563-483 BCE) or Lao Tze (604-531 BCE) was the founder of Islam, Buddhism or Taoism respectively because there is ample irrefutable evidence of their historicity. The founder of Yahwism lies hidden in the sepulchre of Time. Moses cannot, under any circumstance, be considered the founder of Yahwism or Judaist faith because first of all, there is no evidence whatsoever to say that such a person ever trod the earth. Apart from that, the origin of Yahwism or Judaism is associated with the name of another mythological character, Abraham. Moses, as we see him in the Bible, was, at best, a fictitious tribal chieftain and lawgiver of Israel, for there is no proof of the historicity of the biblical character called Moses. However, there should have been a person who was responsible for codifying the laws known to us as the Mosaic Laws just as Hammurabi had done years back for his people. Since the lawgiver of the Hebrews would have had a name and that the Bible tells us was Moses, let us call him so although we consider the Moses of the Bible as much a mythological character as Abraham or Adam.

Reverting to the story of the life of infant Moses who was being nursed by his mother, when the baby grew up the mother took him to the princess who named him Moses "because," she said, "I drew him out of the water"[48] and looked after him as her own son. Although he was brought up by the Pharaoh's daughter, he had a strong predilection for the Hebrew tribe and had imbibed the Hebrew culture and spirit, maybe because he spent the impressionable period of his life with his Israelite parents. And of course, when he grew up, he would have come to know that he was born to Hebrew parents. He, therefore, identified himself with the Hebrews. As a result, he could not tolerate the arrogance of the Egyptian masters and the merciless and degrading oppression that the tribe with which he identified himself had been subjected to. Moses, in fact, personifies the feelings, the growing anti-Egyptian sentiments and the aspirations of the Hebrews living in Egypt at that time. One day "when he was grown and went out to his brethren, he looked on their burdens, and he saw an Egyptian smiting a Hebrew." He was furious and could not contain himself. His anger got the better of him. He looked around to see if anyone was watching them and finding that none else was nearby, he killed the Egyptian and buried him there.[49] He went back to his foster mother thinking that no one had seen what he did, but the next day when he went out, he was stunned to hear that some persons, probably an Egyptian or a Hebrew working for the Egyptian government, did see what he had done. He was told that the Pharaoh too had come to know of it. Obviously the information was conveyed to the Pharaoh by the person who had seen the incident and the king was after Moses' blood to avenge the killing of the Egyptian. It is strange that the Pharaoh did not know that his own daughter was Moses' foster mother and that the young man was living in the palace. Surprisingly the persons who carried the news to the Pharaoh also did not seem to know this!

Moses knew that his tribe was too powerless and timid to defend him. Under the circumstances, thinking that discretion was the better part of valour he fled the country and took refuge in Median[50] where the writ of the Pharaoh did not run. He soon endeared himself to the people of Median, because of his service-mindedness as the story of the help he rendered to the daughters of Reuel (Jethro), the priest of Median, reveals. Pleased with Moses, the priest gave one of his daughters, Zipporah, in marriage to Moses.[51] So Moses settled with the family of the priest in Median but he never ceased thinking of his tribe back in Egypt. He had always empathised with the sufferings of Israel and was distressed at the pitiable plight of his brethren.

When he got the news of the Pharaoh's death, he thought he could now go back to Egypt and bring his tribe out of that country. He was now safe because to the new Pharaoh he would be a stranger. He hated the Egyptians for mercilessly oppressing the Hebrews. He had seen the miserable plight of his tribesmen and the inhuman treatment meted out to them by the Egyptians.[52] By a quirk of circumstances he had married a non-Yahwist girl and had settled in Median, but he remained a good Yahwist and a religio-purist at that and his heart and mind had always been in Egypt with his tribe, the Hebrews. Moses considered it his duty to liberate the enslaved Hebrews and take them out of Egypt.[53] He had, therefore, been planning to go to Egypt and fight for the emancipation of his tribe. He wanted to settle them in the land of Canaan, a land flowing with milk and honey, where several tribes – the Canaanites, the Hittites, the Amorites, the Perizzites, the Hivites, and the Jebusites – inhabited in those days. Moses had not so far visited Canaan. Assuming that Moses was a historical personality, the question arises as to how he would have come to know that Canaan was a land flowing with milk and honey. There is only one possibility. He must have heard of the fertility of the land from various nomadic tribes that, coming via Canaan, camped at Median.

However, he was in two minds and did not know what to do. Ever since he heard of the death of the Pharaoh who wanted to kill him, Moses had been toying with the idea of going back to Egypt and confronting the new Pharaoh.[54] He wanted to ask the Pharaoh to let him take the enslaved Israel out of Egypt. But he asked himself what right or authority he, an insignificant person had, to do that.[55] If, however, he failed to get the permission of the Pharaoh to allow the Hebrews to leave Egypt, he thought he would ask the elders of Israel to accompany him to the Pharaoh. But he was doubtful if the tribesmen would trust him; they might look upon him as a coward who fled when his life was threatened. So he thought of appealing to the tribe in the name of their god, Yahweh, and telling them that their god would certainly stand by them. But he was sure they would turn back and ask him who this god was and where he had been all these years, leaving them to the mercy of Egyptian oppressors.[56] If he succeeded in convincing the elders of the tribe, he thought he would lead a delegation of the elders of his tribe so that all of them together could meet the Pharaoh and request him to allow the tribe to leave Egypt.[57]

He was in a dilemma. He kept debating in his mind for many days. He wondered what he would say if the Pharaoh were to ask him why he wanted to take them out of the country. He should have a credible reason for requesting the Pharaoh to permit the Hebrews to leave Egypt, for he was sure the Pharaoh would not easily allow the Hebrews, be they freemen or slaves, to leave Egypt. He thought of a good excuse. But how to carry it out was his problem now. The delegation of the elders, he thought, could tell the king that they only wanted to be allowed to go to the wilderness for three days to offer a sacrifice to Yahweh.[58] He doubted if the Pharaoh would believe them and allow the Hebrews to leave Egypt. If that too failed, he thought, he would ask the Hebrew freemen to demonstrate in front of the Pharaoh's palace against his adamant refusal to allow them to offer sacrifice to their god.[59] But then how could he persuade them to do that? He thought he would tell them, the men and women of his tribe that if the king allowed them to go, they could plunder the Egyptian homes and carry away all gold and silver ornaments and other valuables when they leave Egypt.[60] And once they went out of the country they would not go back and all that they plundered would be theirs. That would be a good ruse to tempt them to join the protest. But he was not sure if his tribesmen, even the elders, would accept his leadership to demonstrate against the Pharaoh.[61]

It was easy to plan to meet the Pharaoh and to ask him to permit the Hebrews to leave Egypt. But on meeting the Pharaoh how he could convincingiy put forward to the Pharaoh what he wanted to say, was a problem. Moses knew he was "not eloquent" and was "slow of speech and slow of tongue."[62] So he thought of asking someone who would be able to speak fluently and convincingly, to accompany him. He wondered if there was anyone among the elders who was capable of speaking to the Pharaoh boldly and convincingly.[63] He could not think of anyone. Suddenly it struck him that his brother Aaron could speak well and he decided to take Aaron along when he goes to meet the Pharaoh.[64] If the Pharaoh did not comply with their request to release the Hebrews, he decided that he would launch a mass movement to liberate his tribe and planned out in detail how he would proceed.[65] Anyway, he finally decided to go to Egypt and taking leave of his father-in-law, he left with his wife and two sons.

Back in Egypt as planned, Moses, along with Aaron, met the Pharaoh and asked him to let the Hebrews leave Egypt. They warned the king that if he did not agree to allow the Hebrews to leave, they would be compelled to take to the streets.[66] But the Pharaoh did not take the warning seriously and ignored their threats. So Moses with the help of Aaron whipped up anti-Egyptian sentiments among the Hebrews. He carried on a vigorous campaign telling the Hebrews that he would lead them to a land flowing with milk and honey, a fertile land where everyone would have a piece of land to cultivate. There would be no oppressors and they themselves would be their masters. The Hebrew freemen were enthused and they rallied behind Moses and Aaron. Moses now called upon the Hebrews to come out on the streets and protest. The response was far beyond their expectation; all tribes and sections of the Hebrews joined them in large numbers. There were angry demonstrations and protests against the Pharaoh all over the country.[67]

The Pharaoh responded by sending the army to disperse the protesters.[68] But the Hebrews could not be cowed down by force; they turned violent.[69] The liberation movement drew into its vortex freemen of all strata of the Hebrews and they attacked the Egyptians.[70] The rebels destroyed the farms and cattle, aimed at creating panic among the people.[71] They attacked, with sticks and stones and whatever they could get hold of, not only the soldiers but also the Egyptian freemen who had been oppressing them.[72] Many soldiers were wounded and an equal number of Egyptian civilians too.[73] Thanks to the tenacity and strong leadership of Moses and Aaron, the freedom fighters were making steady progress. At last, Moses and Aaron brought out swords and spears that they had secretly collected and kept hidden in a cache and distributed to the partisans of freedom struggle. Armed with those weapons, they fought desperately, inflicting heavy casualties on the Pharaoh's army and also attacked the Egyptian people at large.[74]

The soldiers found it difficult to curb the widespread violence. The people of Egypt became restless and grumbled; they asked the Pharaoh how long he would be leaving them at the mercy of the Hebrews[75] and they urged him to let the Hebrews go. Nevertheless, the Pharaoh did not move and he refused to allow the Hebrews to go. Moses was infuriated at the intransigence of the Pharaoh and warned him of serious consequences. The insurrectionists made the final thrust; they destroyed the standing crops and indiscriminately killed the Egyptians, young and old. They did not spare even babes in arms and the newborns. This continued for three dark, dreadful days. The soldiers were helpless. The death toll of the Egyptians was frighteningly high and governance became impossible.[76] The soldiers found it difficult to curb the violence and their morale plummeted. The Pharaoh ordered them back to the barracks and conferred with his ministers till late into the night.[77] He called Moses and Aaron in the night itself and said that he wanted to see the back of the Hebrews at the earliest.

The Hebrews had been liberated! Having successfully led the Hebrews in their struggle for freedom with the promise of leading them to the land where, he said, they would be masters and would have abundant food, he was naturally looked upon by the freemen of the tribe as their leader. In other words, men and women, young and old, of the Hebrew tribes unquestioningly accepted him as the chieftain of the tribe. He thus became the chieftain of the Hebrews, a position that made him both the temporal and the spiritual head of the tribe. He, however, paid more attention to the secular aspects like the governance, delegating the task of carrying out the routine administrative duties connected with spirituals to Aaron. But as a prophet, he retained for himself the right of taking final decisions on all matters concerned with spirituals also.

However, it must be noted, Moses was interested only in liberating the Hebrews, freemen and slaves, from Egypt but he did not intend to emancipate the slaves. He did not try to liberate the Hebrew slaves of Egyptian masters. The leader of the Hebrews, whom the Bible calls Moses, thought and worked within the *de facto* legal bounds of the society of his times. He seems to have realised the consequences of destabilising the social structure and was intent on maintaining the *status quo.* He did not, therefore, make any attempt at abolishing slavery; on the other hand whatever he did was only aimed at buttressing the then prevailing social system. To put it differently, he seemed to have appreciated the necessity of the times and was careful not to mangle the social fabric by dismantling the slave system. That was the period when tribal communes among the Hebrews were slowly but inevitably breaking up and slavery was being accepted by the society. The bard who created this character called Moses could not conceive of a society sans slavery. Hence we see Moses as a progressive leader who took care to consolidate the emerging social order based on private property and slavery. Naturally, therefore, the Hebrew slaves owned by Egyptians continued as slaves in Egypt and those Hebrews who worked for their Hebrew masters continued as slaves even after the Hebrews were liberated from Egypt. And that pleased the Hebrew freemen who now looked upon him as their natural leader.

The liberated Hebrew tribes now felt as if they had won a war and with the consent of Moses, who too must have felt like a commander of a victorious army, the Hebrews ransacked the houses of affluent Egyptian freemen. They appropriated their jewels of gold and silver, and even expensive garments as spoils of war.[78] Collecting all the valuables that they could lay their hands on, the Hebrews from all over the country congregated at Ramses as directed by Moses.

The fictitiousness of the whole episode stands exposed when it is said that about six hundred thousand men alone on foot, besides women, children, the old and the decrepit along with their slaves and livestock congregated in Ramses the same night the Pharaoh informed Moses that he had the permission to take the Hebrews out of Egypt. It is humanly impossible for Moses to have contacted, in such a short time, all the Hebrew freemen living in different parts of the country and to have told them to congregate at Ramses. It is equally impossible for all of them to reach Ramses from all over Egypt with their possessions and to have left Egypt that night itself. And before leaving the country they had also found time to plunder the Egyptian houses! This could have been regarded as a hyperbole employed by the rhapsodist to show the magnitude of the problem that Moses dealt with and to project Moses as a great leader, had there been some archaeological or non-biblical literary evidence of Exodus. In the absence of any such evidence, this only confirms that the story of the Exodus is pure fiction.

According to the Bible, carrying all their booty and belongings the Hebrews headed to Succoth, where they halted,[79] when Moses exhorted the Congregation to observe the Passover feast every year that day to commemorate their liberation. He thought such a feast would bring together the freemen of all the Hebrew tribes on that day and that would help develop in them a sense of belonging and oneness. He demanded that all tribesmen, the freemen and the slaves, should take a solemn vow that they would not worship any god other than Yahweh and would destroy the places of worship of other gods when they conquer Canaan.[80] In other words, he expected the Yahwists not just to be religio-purists but religious fanatics, thus paving the way for the rise of Hebrew chauvinism. However, it has to be conceded that religio-purism (not fanaticism) was certainly a progressive ideology under the circumstances because Yahwism was the only factor common to all the Hebrew tribes and the only force that precluded fissiparous tendencies and ensured their unity.

Although the shortest route to Canaan from Egypt was through the land of the Philistines, Moses decided to avoid that route. There was a reason for it. He knew that the Philistines would not allow his people to pass through their land. That was bound to lead to a clash between the two tribes, in which the Hebrews who had been enslaved and had no training in the use of arms for almost four centuries would not be able to fight the Philistines and were sure to be routed. It would be suicidal. Moses knew that war was not like insurgency. During the insurgency the Hebrews had fought with arms but they succeeded because they did not fight with the soldiers face to face and they also targeted unarmed civilians to bring pressure on the Pharaoh. But with the Philistines, they would be fighting a pitched battle with seasoned soldiers with the possibility of being massacred. And the survivors would have been forced to go back to Egypt to a life of slavery and wretchedness. Moses did not want that to happen and so he led his tribesmen through the desert, fully conscious of the difficulties and the problems involved. The tribe implicitly placed their faith in Moses, their chieftain, who, they thought, knew the route to Canaan, but he was as ignorant of the route as any other person in the Congregation.

So like a cloud in the sky, Moses leading the Congregation, wandered here and there in the desert.[81] Incidentally, if as the Bible says it was god that assumed the form of a pillar of cloud and was acting as a guide, he did not know the shortest and the least hazardous route to Canaan through the desert and was cheating the people who trusted him! Evidently Moses did not know where he was heading to, but he led the Congregation hoping that finally he would reach the land flowing with milk and honey. No wonder they took several years to reach their destination. It is difficult to find one's way in a desert, which a traveller is not familiar with, for there are no landmarks to guide the traveler. The fluctuations in temperature added to their travail. During the day the temperature in the desert usually rises to between 45° to 55° Celsius and in the nights it always drops to 20° C and even to below 0° C depending on the season. The drop occurs so suddenly that without lighting a fire it would have been difficult for the wandering Hebrews to keep themselves warm. The pillar of fire that the Bible speaks of was this campfire that they lit daily beside every tent in the night to protect them from cold and to ward off animals, if any.[82]

As soon as the Hebrews left, the rich freemen of Egypt complained to the Pharaoh that the Hebrews had plundered their houses and carried away all their valuables before leaving the country. The Pharaoh was livid with rage.[83] Regretting his decision to free the Hebrews, he sent a large contingent of chariots in hot pursuit but they failed to intercept the fleeing Hebrews because Moses and his tribe had by then gone too far for them to catch up. There was no Suez Canal then. The area between the Mediterranean Sea and the Gulf of the Red Sea was a stretch of marshy land broken by a few lakes. By the time the Pharaoh's soldiers arrived, the Hebrews had crossed the marshy land[84] but the heavy chariots of the pursuing Egyptian army could not. Anyway, it is futile thinking over this problem because the episode, the sea receding to allow the Hebrews to pass and drowning the Egyptians at Moses' bidding, is pure myth intended to make Moses the mythical hero of the story.[85]

Needless to say, it was an arduous journey, for often they were short of food or water and as expected, the tribesmen almost repudiated Moses' leadership. Walking through the wilderness of Shur without water to drink, they reached Marah where they pitched their tents. They could not stay there for long for want of good drinking water, as the water found there was saline and unfit for drinking. Naturally, the tribesmen, weary and thirsty after the long trek, grumbled against Moses[86]. But he could find a small pool of water that was not salty,[87] which helped quench the thirst of and calm the agitated tribesmen. Soon after, they left the place to camp at Elim,[88] where water was available in abundance. Leaving Elam, *en route* to Mount Sinai, when the tribe was trekking through the desert of Sin, there was shortage of food and the tribesmen openly showed their displeasure. They criticised Moses and Aaron and faulted them for mismanagement.[89] They said they could have happily stayed back in Egypt where they did not have to go without food for days together like this.

Moses told them to gather manna, that could be seen fallen on the ground in the mornings; and in the evenings they could catch quails,[90] flocks of which would come for roosting there at that time. Every morning "when the dew that lay melted, behold, on the surface of the wilderness, there lay a small round thing, as fine as the frost on the ground; and the evenings saw flock of quail."[91] Manna is a natural product of the desert and botanists have suggested the names of a few plants that produce something that resembles the manna that the Bible speaks of.[92] Anyway, it is only to portray Moses as a prophet who is believed to be having a special relation with god that this is said to have been supplied by god at his request for the trekking Hebrews only. He expressly told the tribesmen not to collect more than the quantity of food (manna) that each family would need for its meals in a day – "every man to take according to his need"[93] only. And he told them that if kept overnight, it would be unfit for consumption the next day.

Despite his warning and specifically telling them not to collect more than what was required, some of them took much more than what they could eat apparently with the intention of keeping it for the rainy day. And the next day they found that it was spoiled and unfit for eating as Moses said.[94] Moses severely rebuked them for disobeying his orders. He was a strong leader who would not tolerate contumacy and he intended to keep them under his thumb. No doubt, in the beginning the tribe accepted the leadership of Moses unanimously but during the trek in the wilderness, more than once, rumblings of opposition to his leadership could be heard. For the first time, as we have seen, his leadership was questioned when the tribe had encamped at Marah. Again when they were in the wilderness of Sin, they blamed him for the shortage of food.

This episode is significant in that it betrays a contradiction in the Hebrew society of those times. The tribe was at a critical stage of social evolution when it moved *en masse* out of Egypt, headed by Moses; the old tribal communes were in the process of disintegration but a new social order had not blossomed fully. So the contradiction inherent in a society in transition inevitably manifested itself in the conflict between the tribesmen and Moses. Moses, as any chieftain of a barbaric tribe would have done, should have consulted at least the elders of the various communes before he ordered the tribesmen not to collect manna in excess of their requirements. It was their resentment of Moses' authoritarianism that was behind their flouting his order more than their eagerness to save for a rainy day as future events reveal.

In the tribal communes of yesteryears, no one, including the eldest member of the tribe, took any decision without consulting all members. The tribal society was based on the principle of equality and collectivism. The gens or commune was free from division into classes like freemen and slaves as it was in the Congregation now, there was no government or state and there was a kind of primeval democracy at work. Morgan writes, "Wherever gentile institutions prevailed, and prior to the establishment of political society, we find peoples or nations in gentile societies, and nothing beyond. The *state* did not exist. Their governments were essentially democratical, because the principles on which the gens, phratry and tribe were organised were democratical."[95] So autocracy that Moses practised now was unknown to them. But by the time the Hebrews left Egypt, the physiognomy of the Hebrew society had changed considerably. In fact, these changes had been taking place since the time of Abraham who, we saw, had become quite rich and had been employing slave labour, as symbolised by the Egyptian girl Hagar. So the old egalitarian society of the Hebrew tribes had almost yielded place to a society divided into two antagonistic groups, freemen and slaves, but an appropriate political state was yet to take shape.

The stratification of society inevitably results in social strain, which, if not controlled, may any time flare up into open clashes between the two social forces – the affluent and the indigent – the interests and aspirations of which are not naturally congruent, resulting in anarchy. The Egyptian Hebrew tribes were in such a volatile situation when Moses assumed leadership. It called for a strong leader capable of maintaining peace as well as preventing fratricidal tribal wars and uprisings by the oppressed slaves, both of which could result in social instability and chaos, possibly ending in total disintegration of the tribes themselves. Moses was, by force of circumstances, unconsciously moulding a form of governance suited to the condition in which he found the tribe when the leadership of the tribe fortuitously fell on his shoulders. Thanks to the conditions prevailing then, a new kind of regime that was alien to the tribal genius slowly evolved, making the chieftain an autocrat. In spite of the lack of political structure, Moses controlled and ruled the Congregation of the Hebrew tribes like an absolute monarch.

But he was acting against the spirit of collectivism and democracy of the tribal communes. Many tribesmen still clung to the barbaric principles of collectivism and democracy, which was not practicable in the evolving scenario. In other words, the tribes were in a transitional stage; tribal communes of the barbaric period had practically broken down and a new social configuration was in the making. So the tribesmen had lost their moorings and were yet to adjust themselves to the new situation. And that caused the conflict between the Chieftain and the freemen.

Trouble arose again when they reached Rephidim. There was scarcity of drinking water that gave an excuse for the collectivists to defy Moses' leadership. They questioned him why they had been brought all the way from Egypt to suffer without even drinking water, when they had been living comfortably there. On the advice of Jethro, who came to the camp all the way from Midian on hearing of Moses' problems,[96] Moses decentralised the function of judgment, which he had been doing all by himself so far. He organised the entire Congregation into groups of thousands, hundreds and fifties and appointed a chief judge with assistants proportionate in number to the strength of each group. Moses judged only hard cases and remained as the appellate authority.[97] This decentralisation of judgment duty considerably reduced his workload and was a great relief to him. Soon after that was done, Jethro bade them farewell and returned to Midian.

Resuming their journey, after a long and wearisome trek through the sweaty wilderness in sweltering heat, the Congregation reached the Sinai Peninsula and they set up camp in its wilderness at the base of Mount Sinai.[98] In the course of their journey from Egypt, Moses seemed to have realised that the Hebrews did not have a set of laws consistent with the prevailing social realities and agreed to by all the tribes. That, he thought, was the problem. He had made all proclamations in the name of Yahweh to instill in the people faith in Yahweh whose absolutism gave him the religio-philosophical justification for his authoritarianism. He announced to the Congregation all that Yahweh is supposed to have told him and he said, "God spoke all these words, saying, I am the Lord, your God, which have brought you out of the land of Egypt, out of the house of bondage. You shall have no other god before me." The tribesmen knew Moses was the one who fought to liberate them from Egyptian hegemony and brought them out of that country. So they understood that in the name of god, he was telling them that "he was the Chieftain, their Chieftain who had brought them out of the land of Egypt, out of the house of bondage" and "they shall have no other Chieftain before him."[99] That was exactly what Moses meant. But in the absence of any statutory backing, he found it difficult, well-nigh impossible, to assert his authority.

Anyway, Moses now decided to have the laws drafted in consultation with Aaron.[100] But Aaron advised him to constitute a committee presided over by Moses and consisting of himself and his two sons Nadab and Abihu who would represent the clergy and seventy elders from among the freemen of the various tribes of Hebrews as representatives of the tribesmen. Accordingly, a committee, which may be called the Law Committee, was formed. The members of the Committee retired to the nearby mountain, the Mount Sinai,[101] for drafting a code of laws. Moses in consultation with the Levites, the priestly class, represented by Aaron and his sons, Nadab and Abihu, drafted and presented before the Committee a set of laws. The members formally approved it and empowered him to proclaim it to all the Hebrew tribes in the Congregation and enforce it strictly.

At the end of the conference, Moses, who headed the Committee, wrote down the laws[102] and the Committee requested him to read out what they called the Book of the Covenant to the Congregation. It was, in effect, a covenant between man and man, drawn up by the Law Committee headed by Moses, who presented it to the Congregation for ratification. Thanks to this fictitious story, the Yahwists associate these laws with the mythological character Moses and hence it has been called the Mosaic Code. Incidentally, the story that Musa (Moses), who is considered a precursor to Muhammad the Prophet, was given Tawrat (Torah) by god in Sinai is the Qur'anic version of the biblical myth of Moses going up Mount Sinai where god dictated to him the laws called the Mosaic laws.[103]

As the biblical story goes, in compliance with the desire of the Committee, after invoking god's blessings, Moses read out the Book of the Covenant "in the audience of the people," where "people" denotes the freemen of the Hebrew tribes, for the slaves had no voice in any such matters. When he completed reading it, it was ratified by the assembly of freemen by vowing that "all that the Lord has said we will do, and be obedient."[104] The "Lord" in practice was Moses himself. Israel would thenceforth be guided by these laws and be obedient to Moses. So Moses was happy thinking that now he had a powerful weapon in his hand to deal with revolts or any kind of lawlessness. The tribesmen were made to believe that it was a covenant between Yahweh and the Hebrews. It was, in fact, a social contract – an agreement to regulate the relations of the Hebrew tribes with one another and with their "government" in the context of the disappearing tribal communes.

The Mosaic Code was an important landmark in the history of the Hebrews. By adopting this Code, the Hebrew tribes formally approved the dissolution of communes based on collectivism and legalised the system of slavery, which had been a *fait accompli* since the days of Abraham. In other words, the *de facto* social system based on private property and slavery that had been lacking social approbation had now been granted *de jure* sanction. In the parlance of political science, it can be said that the tribes had given to themselves a *Constitution*, by which the communes had been dissolved and slavery legitimatised. Those upholding or intending to revert to the system of collective leadership as it had been with the tribal communes, who may be called the Conservatives, would now have no constitutional or legal right to stage a counter-revolution as it were.

With the passing of this Code by the entire tribe, it was constitutionally and legally permissible to buy and sell slaves and to keep as slaves those men and women captured after a war or one who was found thieving, if he or she failed to "make full restitution." The laws also specified how to acquire and sell the poor as slaves and made it imperative to give the slaves a holiday on the holy day of Sabbath.[105] The last clause making it obligatory to give the slaves a holiday on this holy day was intended to make the slaves too get a feeling of belonging and to give them an illusion that they were one with the freemen. Significantly, there was a provision in the law that permitted a slave to decide if he or she should continue to work as a slave or "go out free for nothing" after serving the master for six years. If he decided to continue, his master would take him to the judges, "and bore his ear through with an aul; and he shall serve him for ever."[106] This right given to a slave to choose after six years of service his or her future shows it was the early stages of slave system, for in later years a slave had no such right and remained as a salve till his death. Obviously, slavery was only beginning to strike roots in the Hebrew society and the Hebrews were struggling with the 'birth pangs' of a new socio-economic system.

Immediately after that, a complete census of the Congregation was taken,[107] the purpose of which was twofold. It was meant to find out not only the number of combatants but also the population of slaves *vis-à-vis* that of freemen, which information, Moses must have thought, was necessary to hold down the slaves and maintain law and order. The census revealed that the Hebrews could muster a large army of able bodied men who would, if given military training, be a powerful force. Their main problem was lack of good weapons, which was compensated, to some extent, by their numerical strength.

After ascertaining the strength of his forces, with their help a tabernacle facing east was improvised, as per the measurements specified by the religious leaders or clergy. Moses then anointed and sanctified it and performed the necessary ceremonies to propitiate the god for the success of the tribe in the wars that they would have to wage against the tribes that were in the land of Canaan. And after invocation to god, Moses divided the tribes into four groups.[108] Each of these groups comprised three tribes and he arranged them in two circles around the tabernacle, as follows. In the inner circle, he and Aaron as commanders – himself as the prophet-priest and the chieftain of the tribe, and Aaron, being the religious head of the tribe – set up their camps facing the entrance of the tabernacle, on the east. The Merarites, Gershomites and Kohathites constituting the Levites encamped on the north, west and south respectively, of the tabernacle. The outer circle was formed by the Judah, which was expected to lead the expedition, encamped in the east, flanked by the Issachar and the Zebulun; in the west, was the Ephraim with the Benjamin on its left and the Manasseh on the right. In the north the Dan, with the Asher and the Naphtali on either side of it, and the Reuben with the Gad and the Simeon on each of its sides, set up camps.

After that, Moses formed a reconnaissance party consisting of twelve men, one from each tribe, representing the twelve tribes of Israel. They were Shammu of the Reuben, Shaphat of the Simeon, Caleb of the Judah, Igal of the Issachar, Oshea of the Ephraim, Palti of the Benjamin, Gaddiel of the Zebulun, Gaddi of the Manasseh, Ammiei of the Dan, Sethur of the Asher, Nahbi of the Naphthali, and Guel of the Gad.[109] These twelve men were expected to scout and report back to Moses about the condition of the land of Canaan, its terrain and the people inhabiting the land. That would enable him to plan and decide on the logistics for mounting an attack taking into cognizance the layout of the land, the military strength, the preparedness of the enemy and other relevant factors.

It may not be wrong to conjecture from the manner in which Moses arranged the men that before they launched the attack on Canaan, he was giving them necessary military training. Moses was also carefully planning the logistics for the invasion of Canaan, which he knew would not be a cakewalk, because the Canaanites, who were reputed to be good at chariot warfare on which lay chiefly their military might, had a well-organised and formidable army equipped with strong weapons.[110] Although Israel did not have such weapons, their combatants probably outnumbered those of most other tribes; their morale was very high and they had the will and determination to "do or die."

Now on its way from Sinai to the border of Canaan, the tribe halted at a place, when the freemen began to grumble about the non-availability of good food, like what they had in Egypt. They said they were getting fish and a variety of vegetables and fruit in Egypt with onions and garlic to flavour the food. This rebellion ostensibly for the sake of food kindled the fire of fury in Moses, who considered it defiance of his authority. He executed all the ringleaders who, he thought, were behind the revolt.[111] The others who were involved in the revolt pleaded for mercy and Moses excused them.[112] But the people continued to grumble because they were getting nothing but manna, which had become nauseous.[113]

The reason for the tribesmen's ire had apparently been shortage of water or food, but the real reason behind the opposition was not shortage of food or water. They disapproved of his style of leadership. The lack of good food was a problem that the rebel leaders and the Conservatives in general who wanted to revert to collectivism of the barbaric communes, raised to get the support of all sections of the freemen of all tribes. They were actually protesting against Moses' authoritarianism, which contradicted the tribal democratic principles. The Congregation wanted him to follow the old tribal style of governance.

Moses seems to have understood that at last. The mounting pressure to democratise the system of governance was now too much for him to ignore or to take lightly. It might, Moses feared, cost him his position as the Chieftain of the Congregation. This revolt, however, set Moses thinking and he consulted Aaron. He advised Moses to constitute a Council of freemen similar to the Law Committee that framed the Code of Laws, to help in the governance of the tribe.[114] Moses agreed with Aaron. In order, therefore, to preclude such rebellions in the future, Moses, by virtue of the power vested in him as the prophet and Chieftain of the tribe, decided to constitute what may be called a Council of Freemen. And he nominated seventy freemen to the Council. They were now expected to help Moses maintain discipline and manage the affairs of the tribe.

The formation of this council gave a democratic façade to Moses' autocratic leadership, which both of them, Moses and Aaron, hoped would help pacify the tribe, and there would be no reason any more to complain that Moses acted autocratically. Now the Conservatives found another excuse to defy Moses. They said their food had been manna only and they were not getting meat, which they had to their hearts' content in Egypt.[115] They wondered who would give them meat now. Moses told them that when the quails came there to roost at night they could collect any number of those birds and eat as much as they wanted.[116] Moses was aware that there were still some more dissenters, and this he knew was the right time to punish the ringleaders. Now that the tribesmen had got the meat that they had been craving for, Moses rightly guessed the opposition in general had been practically blunted. When the freemen had their food and their seething anger had cooled down, Moses executed the ringleaders.[117] He took this action without referring to the judges that he himself had appointed earlier on Jethro's advice or consulting the newly constituted Council of Freemen. This flagrant violation of democratic principles as understood by the barbaric tribe further enraged the Conservatives, especially the priests.

Soon after this, Aaron conspired with Miriam to oust Moses and assume the chieftainship of the Congregation. Aaron and Miriam, siblings of Moses, two very powerful individuals of the priestly class, took up the cudgel against Moses on the ground that Moses had taken an Ethiopian woman as his wife.[118] By pointing out this, they wanted to show that Moses was not a true religio-purist. Aaron thought he could thus undermine Moses' claim of religious purity and his authority and project himself as a true Yahwist. So he asked: "Has the Lord indeed spoken only through Moses? Has he not spoken through us also?"[119] Moses had no answer; he felt humiliated. Moses' authority was very seriously threatened. At the same time, he was livid with anger; he turned round and walked beckoning to both of them to follow him to the door of the tabernacle to prove to them that it was from Yahweh that he derived his authority to lead the Congregation.

He reprimanded both of them and gave Miriam exemplary punishment;[120] she was socially ostracised and was to be treated as a leper would have been treated in those days.[121] She was expelled from the camp and would go along with the tribe but stay outside the camp forever. This, he thought, would be a warning to Aaron and would deter him from pursuing his ambition. Aaron pleaded for Miriam, saying, "Please do not lay this sin on us, in which we have done foolishly...,please do not let her be, as one dead...." He beseeched Moses to rescind his order or at least commute the punishment, but Moses refused. However, he agreed to reduce the period of boycott to seven days[122] but reserved the right to extend it consecutively for another five terms.[123] This he felt, would meet the ends of justice and act as a deterrent to such rebellions by the clergy in the future. Moses was wary of punishing Aaron, for he knew Aaron commanded great respect among the tribesmen. Yet this revolt failed because the freemen did not find any reason to support Aaron and Miriam. Several influential freemen and Levites were all collectivists and were opposed to religio-purism, which they associated with autocracy. At the same time, they were not opposed to slavery, not realising that collectivism and slavery represented mutually exclusive social practices. Hence although they were unhappy with Moses' religio-purism that spawned the authoritarian style of governance, they could not find common cause with Aaron and Miriam whose ideology was not different from that of Moses.

Aaron and Miriam were obviously religio-purists and were not opposed to authoritarianism. They pretended to be stronger religio-purists than Moses himself, by harping on Moses' marriage with an alien girl. That was, no doubt, a clever move to embarrass Moses, for soon after he took over the Chieftainship of the Congregation, he had told the freemen not to have any dealings with other tribes and even to destroy their places of worship. But he himself had married a woman of a non-Hebrew tribe. They were, thus, questioning his commitment to religio-purism and portraying him as a hypocrite. But it was their claim to their commitment to religio-purism that alienated them from the many lay freemen who demanded reverting to the principles of collectivism of the tribal communes, which were practically disbanded with the adoption of the Mosaic Code of Laws.

Surprisingly, Aaron failed to understand that the powerful among the tribesmen – why, the tribesmen in general – were collectivists who thought that religio-purism was the underprop of authoritarianism. The biggest blunder that Aaron and Miriam committed was not taking up the issue of shortage of food and good potable water – an issue that affected the tribesmen in general, freemen and slaves alike (not that the slaves mattered much), with the result they failed to get the support of all sections of freemen. So Moses had no difficulty in suppressing them. He was, naturally, displeased with Aaron who, he thought, was being treacherous, for it was obvious that Aaron was aspiring to the chieftainship of the tribe. But he continued to consult him as he had been doing so far, lest Aaron might next try to rally the tribesmen against him. Anyway, he waited for an opportunity to avenge the humiliation and remove once and for all the threat to his position.

After Aaron's aborted attempt at capturing power, the tribe left Hazeroth and shifted the camp to the desert of Paran,[124] a place strategically situated on the south of Canaan, from where it was easy for the spies to infiltrate into Canaan. As advised by Aaron who represented the clergy, Moses now called the twelve men he had chosen as spies and instructed them to go into the Land of Canaan.[125] They were asked to find out if the land was fertile or barren, what was cultivated there, what kind of people inhabited the country and whether they lived in tents or strong brick houses. The spies returned after reconnoitering for forty days. Giving all the intelligence that they had collected, they said that the land truly flowed with milk and honey, to prove which they showed the grapes, figs and pomegranates that they had brought from there. But, ten of them said, the people were strong and hefty and the cities were all fortified with thick walls. They concluded saying that it would be disastrous to attempt an attack against them. However, Caleb dissented; he said that they should immediately attack and conquer the land. But the others continued to be sceptical and said that those people were gigantic in stature and Israelites who looked like grasshoppers in front of those people would not be able to subdue them. But Caleb, now supported by Joshua, who till then was silent, reiterated that the land was incredibly good and fertile and it should not be difficult for them to overthrow the tribes that were there.

Moses, however, hesitated. Going by the majority view, he decided against entering the land of Canaan at this juncture, which gave a wrong message to the tribesmen. The tribesmen naturally thought that they had been misled by Moses and the entire tribe was up against Moses and Aaron. They cursed the two leaders for bringing them all the way from Egypt only to be killed by the people of the land that Moses had promised to conquer for the tribe. They were made to understand that the land would be handed over to them on a silver platter as it were. So they decided to elect a leader to take them back to Egypt. Caleb and Joshua now intervened and wanted the tribe not to be disillusioned and exhorted them not to rebel but to repose their faith in Moses. They tried to pacify the rebels saying that they could be sure Moses would help them conquer the land that flowed with milk and honey as promised.[126] Moses found that the tribesmen were getting agitated and again beginning to question his leadership.[127] Cunning as he was, he knew how naïve the tribesmen were and how to deal with them in such situations. So both he and Aaron "fell upon their faces." This apparent show of humility touched the simple tribesmen and they were pacified.

Moses thought that he had liberated these people from bondage in Egypt and leading them through the desert, brought them to the border of Canaan. He wondered why they did not have faith in his leadership still. He was so frustrated and angry that he even toyed with the idea of massacring the entire Congregation.[128] But he refrained from it, thinking that it would reflect badly on his leadership and the Egyptians would forever speak of him disdainfully, saying that he killed them because he could not carry out what he promised them.[129] He, therefore, decided to excuse all the tribesmen who questioned his sincerity and integrity saying that he misled them. He looked for a scapegoat and found ten – the spies who had advised against launching the attack. He held them responsible for creating disaffection among the tribesmen and making them feel so miserably hopeless that they even thought of going back to Egypt. So he executed all those ten spies whose unfavourable report almost led to a revolt.[130]

However, encouraged by what Caleb and Joshua said, a few men decided to enter the land of the Canaanites, defying Moses, who dissuaded them from the venture. He warned them that entering

Canaan without proper planning and preparation would be suicidal. He pointed out that they were disobeying him, the Chieftain of Israel, and said if they wanted to invade Palestine, they could do at their own risk and not expect any help from him. He, thus, refused to render any advice or help to those who wanted to invade Canaan. Nevertheless, those few men got up early in the morning and marched on Canaan. On getting intelligence from the spies that the Hebrews were coming up the mountain to conquer and occupy their land, the Amalekites and the Canaanites joined forces and descending on the invading army of Israel attacked them, killing most of them. The few survivors, who managed to escape with their lives, returned to the camp, weary and wounded. The first attempt of the Hebrews to enter Canaan thus ended in a fiasco.[131] It was a humiliating defeat. Moses was happy they got the punishment that they deserved for defying his authority and so he did not take any further action against them.

This, however, had its repercussion. The tribesmen felt the feedback given by the executed spies was accurate and it was proved correct by what happened to those who ventured into the land. The execution of the spies, therefore, could in no way be justified. They had not done anything wrong; nor had they committed any crime. However, they were executed just because their report was not consentaneous with what Moses made them believe. There were judges and there was a Council of Freemen, but without consulting any of them, the spies were given capital punishment, which most freemen thought was blatantly unfair. Such highhanded actions of Moses who had been ruling like an autocrat and executing with no rhyme or reason, naturally, was not taken kindly to by a vast majority of the freemen.

A powerful group of freemen raised the banner of revolt and questioned his authority to ride roughshod over the Congregation. Led by Korah, a Levite of the Kohathite clan, two hundred and fifty "men of renown" who disapproved of the style of Moses' functioning assembled together and put him on the mat. They questioned his dictatorial method of governance.

Korah asked: "...you take too much on yourself but all the Congregation is holy, every one of them and the Lord is among them: why then you consider yourself above the Congregation of the

Lord?"[132] The rebels by saying that "all the Congregation is holy" recalled the ethos of the tribal communes of the earlier period, in which all members of the commune were equal; there was no high or low, no leader and the led. The rebel leaders pointedly questioned how Moses could assume the role of an absolute ruler and they clubbed it with the problem of food shortage that directly affected the lay tribesmen as well as the Levites, the class of priests. They asked, "...is it a small thing that you have brought us out of a land that flows with milk and honey, to kill us in the wilderness, and *you pose like a prince* over us?"[133] Although Korah and the other freemen leading the revolt would not have thought of the slaves when they said this, it did touch a sympathetic chord in them also, for whatever food they had got in Egypt was better and more than what they were getting all these days in the desert. The rebels continued their verbal attack saying, "Moreover you have not brought us into a land that flows with milk and honey or given us inheritance of fields and vineyards...."[134] This was tantamount to accusing Moses of duping them, and this accusation helped them get the support of a large number of lay freemen. These words of Korah, who was a Levite himself, unlike those of Aaron and Miriam, echoed the feelings of the people who still have the mindset of the days of the communes, which were based on collectivism – collective leadership, collective production and collective consumption. In the Congregation, the leadership was concentrated in one hand and collection and consumption of food were left to each individual. This individualism, naturally, must have led to competition, conflict and even hostilities.

However, Moses played his cards cleverly that created a split in the priestly class as well as the non-Levites. He first "fell upon his face," to show that he was not, as they had accused him of, trying to make himself a prince over the Congregation. The common man was touched by this humility and several of them thought he was being unjustifiably accused of autocracy. Moses asked Korah why all of them assembled there, were agitating against his leadership; and what had Aaron done to them that made them complain against him?[135] That was a masterstroke. By this question he at once succeeded in getting the sympathy of Aaron and his supporters and alienating them from the rebels led by Korah. Aaron was yet to reconcile himself with his failed attempt to overthrow Moses and he was under the impression that Moses was still angry with him. But now he was carried away by Moses' pretence of support for him.

Addressing the people gathered there, Moses asked all of them to assemble in front of the tabernacle the next day with their censors putting incense and fire in them. He said, "Tomorrow morning the Lord will show who is his, and who is holy and will cause that man to come near him; whomsoever he chooses, the Lord will cause to come near to him; ...and it will be that man whom the Lord chooses, who is holy...."[136] So he made it clear that he was chosen by god to rule the Congregation of Israel or to put it differently, god had bestowed on him the right to rule the congregation.

This, however, was a well-organised revolt by the votaries of collectivism to capture power and subvert the emergent social structure. It was a very serious challenge to the leadership of Moses, and it was an equally serious threat to the progress of the Hebrew society. Although the earlier revolts were provoked by Moses' authoritarianism, they did not dare openly express it; they highlighted only the shortage or bad quality of food and water. This time they made it clear by asking if he had brought them out of Egypt to rule over them like a prince.

The opposition to the authoritarianism of the religio-purists that Moses represented had, thus, reached its peak; more and more people who had supported Moses were getting disillusioned and were leaning towards the Collectivists. So, thought Moses, if he did not get rid of these leaders, the Congregation could be overtaken by counter-revolution making the Code of Laws irrelevant. Moses ordered the tribesmen to keep away from the tents of Korah, Dathan and Abiram, the three rebel leaders, to enable him to punish them as per the law. Moses went to their tents, accompanied by the Council of Elders and said, "I have not done them of my own will" but as decided upon by the Council,[137] thus making it clear that he was being democratic. After he made that announcement the members of the Council executed the three of them along with their families and burned them with "all their belongings." The members of the Council then put to the sword the two hundred and fifty men of the noble families who were actively involved in the rebellion.[138] The rest of the tribesmen watching this mass execution vanished from the scene, maybe because they had given moral support to the rebels and were scared that the Council of Elders might find them also guilty and turn upon them.

A large section of the Congregation resented this mass execution. The very next day almost the entire Congregation was up against Moses and Aaron, saying, "You have killed the people of the Lord."[139] Moses did not spare them; he ordered Aaron to execute all of them. Aaron thought this was a good chance for him to get back into the good books of Moses and without any compunction he went on putting the men to the sword. Finally Moses told him to stop and he stopped. By the time Aaron sheathed the sword fourteen thousand and seven hundred heads had rolled![140] This exaggerated number may be taken as an indication that Korah had the support of a large number of tribesmen and those who were in the forefront of the rebellion paid for it with their lives.

This episode is an allegorical presentation of the clash between the forces of progress and those of reaction. Looking at it today, a religio-purist like Moses may be regarded as a reactionary and this defeat of Collectivists led by Korah may be considered a victory for reactionary forces. But viewing it against the background of the times in which this incident took place, Moses, the mythical character, personifies the progressive forces because his authoritarian style of governance was in keeping with the needs of the newborn stratified society. On the other hand, Korah, also a fictitious character of course, represents the reactionary forces that wanted to put the clock back by restoring the moribund social system of tribal communes based on collectivism that had lost its relevance. Most freemen and particularly the slaves, who were unable to adjust to the ethos of a stratified society, longed for the old tribal society, but collectivism was not practicable in a cloven society.

Anyway, this rebellion by the clergy must have again kindled his suspicion about Aaron. Possibly, after Aaron and Miriam challenged his authority on the flimsy ground of his marriage with a non-Hebrew girl, he must have lost his faith in Aaron's loyalty and had suspected that it was Aaron who instigated Korah and the nobles to revolt. He knew Aaron was very popular among the tribesmen and Miriam, although an exile from the tribe was a prophetess and a force to be reckoned with and could not be written off. So with Miriam alive, he must have thought it not prudent to take any action against Aaron, as it would boomerang on him and the entire tribe could be up in arms against him. He, therefore, decided to wait for a good opportunity to strike at Aaron. Instead of taking action against Aaron in haste and precipitating the matter, Moses placated Aaron by confirming his priesthood and making it hereditary.[141] This must have been a tactical move to please the rest of the freemen with whom Aaron was very popular and to get Aaron's unreserved support, thus precluding the possibility of reactionary Collectivists among the clergy and the lay freemen overthrowing him and disintegrating the Hebrew society.

Israel, as mentioned above, was in the desert of Sin, camping at Kadesh, at the border of Canaan, when Miriam died. There was not enough drinking water at the place where the camp was pitched and the freemen held a protest meeting. They faulted Moses and Aaron for this miserable situation and asked Moses if he had brought them out of Egypt into this wilderness only to kill them and their cattle. They asked sarcastically if this place where there was no water to drink was the one that he said where vine and pomegranate and other fruit trees grew. Moses and Aaron went around and saw a pool of fresh drinking water and the tribesmen were pacified.[142] The Congregation had to cross the territory of the Edomites to go to Canaan but the king of Edom threatened to order his army to stop them if they attempted to enter his kingdom. So Israel had to go back to take the route via Mount Hor.[143]

As we had seen, Aaron had fallen from Moses' favour. Now that Miriam was no more and the powerful clans of Korah, Dathan and Abiram as well as their followers had been extirpated, Moses thought this was an opportune moment to get rid of Aaron. As the whole Congregation watched, Moses asked Aaron and his son Eleazar to accompany him and climbed up the Mount Hor. But no one, neither Aaron's son nor the tribesmen, knew why the three of them were going up the Mount but no one dared ask. Moses, however, had told Aaron alone of his intention to strip him of his priesthood and to anoint his son as the priest. He also gave a hint of his intention to execute Aaron when he told him that Aaron would not enter Canaan but Aaron did not comprehend what Moses implied by that. Had he suspected it he would have rallied the people behind him and revolted. At the summit Moses stripped Aaron of his priesthood and executed him.[144] However, in order to placate his kin and preclude the possibility of a revolt by the tribesmen, with whom Aaron was incredibly popular, he conferred the priesthood on Eleazar, Aaron's son, who was too shocked – and presumably scared too – to react to the execution of his father. Aaron's popularity may be inferred from the fact that the tribe observed thirty days of mourning for him.[145] Never before did Israel mourn even for a day the death of anyone, including Korah who was popular as could be judged by the support he had received from the tribesmen or for Miriam who was the sister of Moses and Aaron and above all a prophetess.

After Aaron's execution Moses proceeded taking a route via Arad. The King of Arad, the Canaanite, who had received intelligence that the Hebrews were approaching, mobilised his army to intercept them. He defeated Israel and took some of the men as captives. Israel, however, after regrouping, again attacked Arad and defeated the Canaanites. They completely destroyed all the cities of Arad, after which they moved southward along the road skirting Edom. Meanwhile, the people began to grumble, for the route that Moses took was barren and there was not enough food or water. Moses was exasperated when they blamed him for bringing them from Egypt to suffer like this. He ruthlessly executed the disaffected men and pardoned the rest who pleaded guilty and appealed for mercy.[146]

The tribe continued its march until they reached the valley of Arnon that bordered the northern side of the kingdom of Moab and went further to Beer. Hemmed in between Moab in the north and the Amorites in the south[147] Israel was in a fix. Moses sent a message to Sihon, the king of the Amorites, asking for permission to pass through his kingdom, only to be rebuffed with the threat of deploying the army to prevent them from entering his territory. Moses decided to draw the sword, for he seemed to know that the Amorite army was not very strong. Avoiding the territory of the Moabites, which, Moses knew, was a powerful tribe, he went along the border to the north, attacked the Amorites and defeated them. After that Israel moved into Bashan when Og, the king of Bashan, came out with his men in defence of his land but had to bite the dust. Israel massacred all men, women and children of those tribes, plundered the cities and razed them to the ground.[148]

In the flush of this victory and with their morale very high, Moses decided to give battle to the Moabites and moved the camp east of the river Jordan, near Jericho.[149] Meanwhile, the Moabites, anticipating an attack by Israel, entered into a loose alliance with the Midianites. However, watching Israel's camp, which could be seen clearly from the heights of Kirjathhuzoth, they realised that Israel was too strong for even their combined forces to withstand an Israel assault. So they consulted their priest who advised them to let the women of Moab and Midian to seduce the men of Israel.[150] They approved the idea and it did succeed and many of the young men of Israel even defected to the enemy camp.[151] This invited the wrath of Moses[152] and with his tacit permission Phinehas, the son of Eleazar the priest, executed all those men, thousands of them, who got involved with the Moabite women and were acting as the enemy's agents.[153] Pleased with Phinehas's loyalty, Moses rewarded him by proclaiming that Phinehas and his descendants would hold the posts of priests.

In preparation for launching the final assault to capture the land of Canaan, Moses again took a census of the combatants – all those who were twenty years and above – of the tribes of Israel, except the Levites. And with this census a new convention was created. During the earlier one the Levites too were counted and would have got "inheritance" in Canaan, like the others but not any more; being ministers, they were expected to devote themselves totally to the service of god.[154] The message was loud and clear – the ministers of god were to keep themselves away from mundane activities. This was the first step that Moses took in separating the clergy from the lay freemen; that is spirituals from temporals. He thought that this would prevent anyone of the priestly class not only from aspiring to be the chieftain but also from challenging the authority of the chieftain as Aaron had done or from instigating the lay tribesmen to rise in revolt as he suspected Aaron did, thus playing into the hands of the counter-revolutionaries. Moses, perhaps, was the first 'ruler' to apply divide and rule policy. At the same time, Moses took care to see that the religio-purists continued to have a voice in the governance.

He had become old. He knew that his days were numbered and most probably he would not live to lead Israel into the land of Canaan. Hence he decided to pass on his mantle of chieftainship to one who in his opinion would make a good leader. Realising the problem and having sensed the pulse of the people, Moses appointed Joshua, who was a non-Levite, a lay tribesman as his successor. Joshua who had been Moses' helper for a long time, not being of the priestly class was apparently not a religio-purist. Besides, he had proved to be a good leader and soldier when he successfully repelled the Amalekites who attacked the congregation at Rephidim.[155] The lay freemen, particularly the collectivists, therefore, had no reason to raise any objection, because he was a non-Levite and they did not associate him with religio-purism. As Moses expected, the lay freemen including the collectivists endorsed the choice of Joshua as Moses' successor and were happy. Joshua who was Moses' helper, had been interacting with the priests and Levites for a long time. So they had known him intimately and found him a committed religio-purist. So they too were happy with the selection.

Moses now mobilised a thousand men from each of the tribes of Israel and sent them to attack the Midianites. They defeated the Midianites in the war and brought the booty and the captured Midianites to Moses, who ordered that all male prisoners of war and all the women who "have known man by lying with him" be killed. And he told them to "keep alive for yourselves" all virgin girls of the tribe of Midian.[156] Had Moses said "ourselves" instead of "yourselves," it could be taken to mean "to keep as slaves for the tribe." The words "keep for yourselves" had a dubious connotation. It could not be taken to mean "to keep as wives or as concubines," for as a religio-purist, Moses would not ask the Hebrews to marry those girls who were polytheists and idolaters. It could only mean "to keep for your sexual gratification." So in effect it was a license to rape! Moses also divided the spoils of war "between all the Congregation" including the Levites and took for himself and Eleazar all the gold and the jewels.[157] With this victory, Israel occupied the land "that was on this side of Jordan, from the river of Arnon up to mount Hermon."[158] Moses distributed this land among the various tribes that comprised the Congregation.

The Book of the Covenant that Moses had read out to the Congregation, now popularly called the Mosaic Code, dealt with laws relating to religion, all aspects of civil life, ethics besides containing criminal law, military law, and laws concerning diet. It also gives us a glimpse of Moses' – that is, the ancient Hebrews' – idea of judiciary and statecraft. His life in Egypt had shown him the advantages of monarchy in a slave society and hence he exhorted the tribesmen to choose a king for them after they conquered those parts of Canaan still being occupied by other tribes. He said, "When you come to the land which the Lord your God is giving you, you shall dwell there and say I will set a king over me, like as all the nations that are about me."[159] But he wanted the clergy that is, the religio-purists and *not* the lay tribesmen to choose the king.[160] That was what he meant when he said "whom Lord your God gives you." In fact, by selecting Joshua to succeed him as the chieftain of the tribe without consulting anyone, he had set the precedent for the king choosing his successor. Just as he chose Joshua, the king would have the right to choose his successor and the king naturally chose his son to succeed him, which in course of time paved the way for hereditary succession to the throne in monarchies.

However, he was visualising a polity wherein the political authority and the religious authority did not interfere with the functions of each other so that both the temporal and the spiritual wings would function independently and smoothly. But the power to select a king being in the hands of the clergy, he expected, the king chosen by the clergy would be a religio-purist from among the non-Levites. In order to ensure that the king continued to stick to religio-purism, he said, "...when he sits on the throne of the kingdom...he shall write him a copy of this law in a book[161]...and he shall read it all the days of his life...to keep all the words of this law and these statutes."[162] In other words, the Book of the Covenant was to be the statute book of the prospective Hebrew kingdom.

Moses' objective in fighting for the freedom of Israel from Egypt, as stated already, was not abolition of slavery and emancipation of the Hebrew slaves. He took slavery for granted and even strengthened the system by giving mandatory approval through his code of laws. Judging by the then historical situation Moses cannot be faulted on legally underpinning slavery. In the context of today when mankind is striving to build an egalitarian and democratic society, slavery in any form or of any group of people is considered a despicable practice; it is totally abhorrent and inconsistent with the concept of democracy and modern notions of human rights and dignity of the individual. But in the historical situation, in which the tribes of Israel found themselves during Moses' time, it could not have been wished away, and Moses cannot be faulted on legally reinforcing slavery. As Engels rightly points out, those who inveigh against it today fail to realise how much the modern world owes to slavery; but for slavery the world would not have seen the "flower of the ancient world, Hellenism." And paradoxically, "this was an advance even for the slaves; the prisoners of war from whom the mass of the slaves was recruited, now at least kept their lives instead of being killed as they had been as before or even roasted, as at a still earlier period."[163]

It should, however, be borne in mind that neither the historicity of Moses nor the historical veracity of the biblical story of the liberation of the Hebrews from Egypt and the Exodus under Moses has been established; there is no mention of such an incident in any of the extant Egyptian records. If it were a fact, an uprising of such dimensions would certainly have found a place in Egyptian records. Robertson points out that "the biblical story of the Exodus from Egypt under Moses...cannot be fitted into the Egyptian records. It may contain a dim and distorted tradition of historical events just as the Homeric poems contain a dim and distorted tradition of a real Trojan War. But the authority of the two stories is about on a level."[164]

In recent years, ample non-Hebrew literary and archaeological evidence of the slavery of the Hebrews in Egypt has been found. There is, for example, non-Hebrew literary evidence like the Leiden Papyrus 348 of the period of the third Pharaoh Rameses II which documents an order that food be given to "the Apiru who are dragging stones to the great pylon." And the ruins at Avaris (Tel el-Daba) in the Nile Delta provide Egyptian archaeological evidence of the slavery of the Hebrews in Egypt[165] but researchers have not been able to find evidence of any sort whatsoever of the mass emigration led by a person called Moses. The Exodus could, perhaps, be only an exaggerated and romanticsied version of a revolt led by a slave leader for the emancipation of a few disaffected Hebrew slaves from their master who succeeded in fleeing the country under cover of the dark of night and all the characters may be fictitious. Or it may be a fictitious story composed by a slave rhapsodist who derived a vicarious pleasure by imagining the release of slaves from bondage to live as free men and women in a land flowing with milk and honey.

Whether Abraham and Moses are historical personages or not and whether the sojourn of Abraham in Egypt and the Exodus led by Moses are historical facts or not, the periods in which these two fictitious characters are placed, are milestones in the history of the Hebrew tribes. The period of Abraham marks the beginning of the end of a society based on equality and collectivism and the rise of social stratification and slavery while the Mosaic period witnesses the consolidation and legitimisation of private property and slavery among the Hebrews.

NOTES

1. Gen. 12:15-16. "And the woman was taken into Pharaoh's house. And he treated Abram well for her sake." Italics added.
2. Gen. 34:31. In this verse it is said, "Should we deal with our sister as with an harlot?" There could have been prostitutes in those times but it was perhaps customary for men of the Hebrew tribe to offer their wives to guests or men in high position as a gesture of friendship. Such a custom is known to have been prevalent among some tribes in India but those women were not looked upon as prostitutes.
3. K. Marx, Contribution to the Critique of Political Economy. In *Selected Works*, V.1, Moscow, pp. 356-357.
4. F. Engels, *The Origin of the Family, Private Property and the State,* Moscow, 1949, pp. 77-78.
5. Gen. 12:17. "And the Lord plagued Pharaoh and his house with great plagues because of Sarai, Abram's wife." "The Lord" in this context stands for "the people" and "plagued Pharaoh" indicates a "revolt against the Pharaoh."
6. Gen. 12:18, 19. "And Pharaoh called and said, 'What is this that you have done to me? Why did you not tell me that she was your wife? ... take her and go your way.' "
7. Gen. 12:20. "And the Pharaoh commanded his men concerning him; and they sent him away, and his wife, and all that he had."

8. Gen. 13:11.
9. Gen. 13:18.
10. Gen. 14:23.
11. Gen. 19:1, 12, 13. "And there came two angels to Sodom...and the men said to Lot...whatever you have in the city, take them out of this place...the Lord has sent us to destroy the city."
12. Gen. 19:14.
13. Gen. 19:16.
14. Gen. 19:26. "But his wife looked back behind him, and she became a pillar of salt."
15. Z.B. Begin, et al. A 40,000 year unchanging seismic regime in the Dead Sea rift. In *Geology* (Journal of the Geological Society of America), V.33, No.4, Apr., 2005, pp. 257-260 and E.J.Kagan, et al. Dating large infrequent earthquakes by damaged cave deposits. In *Geology* (Journal of the Geological Society of America), V. 33, No. 4, Apr., 2005, pp. 261-264.
16. Gen. 19:29. "...that God remembered Abraham and sent Lot out of the midst of the overthrow..."
17. Ismail, as he is known in the Qur'an, in which he is considered a prophet, helped his father build the Ka'bah and preached monotheism in Mecca. The Qur'an does not consider Hajar (Hagar) slave of Ibrahim (Abraham). Taken by Ibrahim into the wilderness as commanded by Allah, Hajar along with ismail was wandering in the desert in search of water, when they reached Mecca. There, by a miracle, they found the well of Zamzam. The water of this well is, therefore, considered holy by the Muslims and those who go on Haj collect this water in a bottle to take back home.
18. Gen. 20:2.
19. Gen. 20:16. "Manservants"/"womenservants"–these words mean "slaves." Please see the Preface for a brief discussion about the use of the word "slave" in the Bible.
20. Gen. 21:3.
21. Gen. 21:25.
22. Gen. 25:11.
23. Gen. 26:2. "And the Lord appeared to him, and said, do not go down to Egypt..."
24. Gen. 26:1. "And Isaac went to Abimalech king of the Philistines to Gerar." Earlier, Abraham is said to have interacted with Abimalech. Vide Ch. 3, Fn. 33 and Gen. 20:2-18. Anyway, the historicity of Abimalech itself is questionable.

25. Gen. 26:7. "And the men of the palace asked him of his wife and he said, she is my sister."
26. Gen. 26:15-17.
27. Gen. 26:23.
28. Gen. 26:29-31. "...So he made them a feast, and they ate and drank. Then they rose early in the morning and swore an oath with one another; and Isaac sent them away, and they departed from him in peace."
29. Gen. 25:22, 23. "Two nations are in thy womb..." The word "nation," as stated on earlier occasions, means "tribe" in biblical parlance.
30. F. Engels, *The Origin of the Family, Private Property and the State*, Moscow, 1948, pp. 56-57.
31. L.H. Morgan, *Ancient Society*, New York, 1877, p. 545.
32. Gen. 27:28. "The dew of heaven and the fatness of the earth and plenty of corn and wine."
33. Gen. 27:35. "Your brother came with deceit and has taken away your blessing."
34. Gen. 32: 25-27, 28. The word "Israel" used in the Bible denotes not only Jacob but also the twelve tribes descended from his twelve sons.
35. Reuben, Simeon, Levi, Judah, Dan, Nephtali, Gad, Asher, Issachar, Zebulun, Joseph, Benjamin.
36. Gen. 37:23-28.
37. Gen. 39:7-20.
38. Ex. 2:11-12.
39. Gen. 41:38.
40. Gen. 41:40, 42.
41. Ex.1: 9-10. "...Behold the people of the children of Israel are more and mightier than we; come on, let us deal with them lest they multiply, and it come to pass, that, when a war broke out, they may join the enemy and fight against us..."
42. Ex.1: 16-19.
43. Ex.2: 3-9.
44. Deut. 34:1-3.
45. Deut. 34:1-6.
46. Deut. 34:6.
47. M. Grant, *The History of Ancient Israel*, New York, 1984, p. 21.
48. The meaning of the word "Moses" is "drawn out" or "born."
49. Ex.2: 11-12/
50. This is the land of the Midianites, the descendants of Midian, a son of Abraham in Keturah, his second wife (Gen. 25:1). The tribe subsequently became extinct.

51. Ex. 2:15-21.
52. Ex. 3:7. "...I have surely seen the affliction of my people which are in Egypt, and have heard their cry by reason of their taskmasters; for I know their sorrow."
53. Ex. 3:8. "...I have come down to deliver them out of the land of the Egyptians and to bring them...to a land flowing with milk and honey..."
54. Ex. 3:10. "Come now, therefore, and I will send you to Pharaoh..."
55. Ex. 3:11. "Who am I, that I should go to Pharaoh and that I should bring forth the children of Israel out of Egypt?"
56. Ex. 3:12, 13. "...Certainly I will be with you..." "...and they shall say to me, What is his name?"
57. Ex. 3:16. "Go and gather the elders of Israel together...and you shall come, you and the elders of Israel to the King of Egypt...and you shall say to him...now let us go."
58. Ex. 3:18. "...and you shall say to him, The Lord God of the Hebrews has met us: and now let us go, we beseech you, three days' journey into the wilderness, that we may sacrifice to the Lord, our God."
59. Ex. 3:20. "...I will stretch out my hand and strike Egypt with all my wonders..."
60. Ex. 3:21-22.
61. Ex. 4:1. "And Moses answered and said, But behold, they will not believe me, nor heed my voice..."
62. Ex. 4:10.
63. Ex. 4:12, 13. "Now therefore go, and I will be with your mouth and teach you what you shall say." "...O my Lord, I pray you, please send by the hand of him whoever it is that you will send."
64. Ex. 4:14. Is not Aaron, the Levite your brother? I know that he can speak well..."
65. Ex. 4:3-9.
66. Ex. 8:2, 4. "I will smite all your land with frogs..." (which) "...shall come up both on you and on your people..."
67. Ex. 8:6. "And Aaron stretched out his hand over the waters of Egypt, and the frogs came up and covered the land of Egypt."
68. Ex. 8:7. "And the magicians did so with their enchantments, and brought up frogs on the land of Egypt."
69. Ex. 8:17. "Aaron smote the dust of the earth and it became lice in the man and in beast..."
70. Ex. 8:24. "...and there came a grievous swarm of flies..."
71. Ex. 9:3. "...the hand of the Lord is on your cattle..."
72. Ex. 9:10. "...and they took ashes of the furnace...and Moses sprinkled

it up...and it became a boil breaking forth with blains on man, and on beast."

73. Ex. 9:11. "...the magicians could not stand before Moses because of the boils and the boils were on the magicians and on all the Egyptians."
74. Ex. 9:23. "Moses stretched forth his rod...and the Lord sent thunder and hail and the fire ran along the ground..."
75. Ex. 10:7. "And Pharaoh's servants said to him, how long shall this man be a snare to us? Let the men go..."
76. Ex. 10:14, 22/Ex.12:29. "And the locusts went up all over the land" "...Moses stretched out his hand...and there was thick darkness in all the land of Egypt for three days." / "And it came to pass at midnight that the Lord struck all the first born in the land of Egypt..."
77. Ex. 12:30. "The Pharaoh rose up in the night, he, his servants, and all the Egyptians; and there was a great cry in Egypt, for there was no house where there was not one dead."
78. Ex. 12:35-37; Num. 33:5.
79. Ex. 12:37; Num. 33:5.
80. Ex. 34:11-14. "...I drive out before you the Amorite, and the Canaanite, and the Hittite, and the Perizzite, and the Hivite, and the Jebusite...you shall destroy their altars, break their images and cut down their groves..."
81. Ex. 13:21. "...the Lord went before them by day in a pillar of cloud, to lead them the way..."
82. Ibid, "...and by night in a pillar of fire, to give them light."
83. Ex. 14:8. "and the Lord hardened the heart of Pharaoh..."
84. Ex. 14:21. "And Moses stretched his hand over the sea; and the Lord caused the sea to go back by a strong east wind all that night and made the sea dry land and the waters were divided."
85. Ex. 14:16-28.
86. Ex. 15:23-24.
87. Ex. 15:25. "...And the Lord showed him a tree, which when he had cast into the waters, the waters were made sweet.
88. Ex. 15:27; Num. 33:9-10.
89. Ex. 16:1-2.
90. Ex. 16:12-13; Num. 11:5-9. "...saying, At even you shall eat flesh, and in the morning you shall be filled with bread...And it came to pass that at eve the quails came up and covered the camp; and in the morning the dew lay round about the host." "Flesh" denotes "quail" (Coturnix vulgaris), which is an endogamous bird in that region.
91. Ex. 16:14.
92. Ex. 16:4, 15. 'Manna' is the general term used for many species of trees, the botanical names of which are, Fraxinus ornus (Linn),

belonging to Oleaceae family, F. excelsior, Quercus vallormas, Q. persica, Alhagi naurarum, Tamarix gallica (var. mannifera) and Larix europaea. All these are conjectures and it is difficult to confirm if any of these is the "manna of the Bible. Num.11:7-8. 'Manna,' the Bible says, looks like coriander seeds and is of the colour of bdellium, which can be beaten in a mortar and baked in pans. The cakes made like this, which taste like wafers made with honey, is eaten. However, no one knows what exactly is the 'manna' that the Bible speaks of. It could be any one of these mentioned above or none of them but some other plant.

93. Ex. 16:16.
94. Ex. 16:20.
95. L.H. Morgan, op. cit., p. 67.
96. Jethro was Moses' father-in-law. He came to Moses' camp in the wilderness with Zipporah and her two sons whom Moses had earlier sent to Midiam. How the news of Moses' troubles reached Jethro and how the four of them found their way to and arrived at the camp so soon should not be questioned, for as you know the story of Exodus is a product of bardic imagination and Moses is nothing but a fictional character.
97. Ex. 18:16-26.
98. Ex. 19:1.
99. Ex. 20:2-3.
100. Ex. 19:24. "And the Lord said to him, Away! Get down and come up, you and Aaron with you..."
101. Ex. 24:1.
102. Ex. 24:1-7. cf Qur'an, Surah, al-Isra 17:2.
103. Ex. 24:7-8.
104. Ex. 20:10/21:2-11; Lev.25:39-54.
105. Ex. 20:10. "But the seventh day is the Sabbath of the Lord thy God; in it thou shalt not do any work, thou, nor thy son, nor thy daughter, thy manservant, nor thy maidservant..." The words "manservant and maidservant," as pointed out elsewhere, are used to mean "slaves
106. Ex. 21:2-6.
107. Num. 1:2-3.
108. Num. 2:2-34.
109. Num. 13:1-15.
110. M. Grant, op. cit., p. 19.
111. Num. 11:1. "And when the people complained, it displeased the Lord...the anger was kindled and the fire of the Lord burnt among

them, and constituted them that were in the uttermost part of the camp." "the uttermost part of the camp" denotes the ringleaders.

112. Num. 11:2. "And the people cried out to Moses; and...the fire was quenched."
113. Num. 11:10, 13.
114. Num. 11:16-17. "...the Lord said to Moses, Gather to me seventy men of the elders of israel...and bring them to the tabernacle...and I will speak to you there. I will take the spirit that is on you and will put it on them; and they shall bear the burden of the people with you..."
115. Num. 11:18.
116. Num. 11:19-20.
117. Num. 11:33. "And while the flesh was yet between their teeth...the Lord smote the people with a very great plague."
118. Num. 12:1.
119. Num. 12:2.
120. Num. 12:10. "...Miriam became leprous."
121. Lev. 13:45-46. "...(the leper's) clothes shall be rent, and his head bare, and he shall put a covering upon his upper lip and shall cry, unclean, unclean. All the days wherein the plague shall be in him, he shall be defiled; he is unclean; he shall dwell alone; without the camp shall his habitation be."
122. Lev. 13:4.
123. Lev. 13:5, 21, 26, 31, 33.
124. Num. 10:12/12:16.
125. Num. 13:1-3. "...the Lord spoke to Moses, saying, Send your men that they may search the land of Canaan..."
126. Num. 14:6-9.
127. Num. 14:10. "...all the congregation said to stone them with stones,"
128. Num. 14:11, 12. "And the Lord said...How long will this people provoke me?...I will smite them..."
129. Num. 14:13, 15, 16. "...Then the Egyptians will hear it...the nations which have heard of your fame will speak, saying...the Lord was not able to bring this people into the land, which he swore to them, therefore he has slain them in the wilderness."
130. Num. 14:37. "...those men that did bring up the evil report upon the land, died by the plague before the Lord."
131. Num. 14:40-45.
132. Num. 16:3.
133. Num. 16:13.
134. Num. 16:14.
135. Num. 16:11. "For what cause both you and all your companions are

gathered together against the Lord; and what is Aaron, that you murmur against him?"

136. Num. 16:5, 7.
137. Num. 16:28, 30. "...Hereby you shall know that the Lord has sent me to do all these works, for I have not done them of my own will." The "Lord" in this context denotes the Council of Elders. "But if the Lord makes a new thing and the earth opens her mouth, and swallow them up with all their belongings..." That the Lord caused the earth to cleave and swallow them indicates that the members of the Council themselves executed them.
138. Num. 16:30-33.
139. Num. 16:41.
140. Num. 16:46-49. "...the plague was begun among the people..." "...he stood between the dead and the living; and the plague was stayed."
141. Num. 18:1-4.
142. Num. 20:11. "And Moses lifted up his hand, and with his rod, he smote the rock twice; and the water came out abundantly..."
143. Num. 20:14-23, 25, 26.
144. Num. 20:24-28. "Aaron shall be gathered to the people; for he shall not enter into the land, which I have given to the children of Israel because you rebelled against my word at the water of Meribah. Take Aaron and Eleazar his son, and bring them up to mount Hor in the sight of all congregation; and strip Aaron of his garments and put them upon Eleazar his son; and Aaron died there in the top of the mount..."
145. Num. 20:29.
146. Num. 21:6-7. "And the Lord sent fiery serpents among the people, and they bit the people and many people of Israel died...the people came to Moses and said, We have sinned..."
147. Num. 21:13.
148. Num. 21:35, Deut.3:1-11.
149. Num. 22:1.
150. Num. 25:1.
151. Num. 25:2. "And they called the people to the sacrifices of their gods; and the people did eat, and bowed down to their gods."
152. Num. 25:3. "The anger of the Lord was hot against his people..."
153. Num. 25:7-9/31:16. "And those that died in the plague were twenty and four thousand."
154. Num. 26:62.
155. Ex. 17:8-13.
156. Num. 31:17-18.

157. Num. 31:27-54.
158. Deut. 3:3-9. It may be remembered that the whole story of Exodus is fictitious.
159. Deut. 17:14.
160. Deut. 17:15. "You shall in any case set him king over you, whom the Lord your God gives you."
161. The Book of the Covenant that is, the Mosaic code.
162. Deut. 17:15-20.
163. F. Engels, *Herr Dühring's Revolution in Science* (Anti-Dühring), London, 1934, pp. 202-204.
164. A. Robertson, *The Origin of Christianity*, London, 1953, p. 21.
165. J.K. Hoffmeier, *Israel in Egypt*, New York, 1997, pp. 112-114. (Apiru refers to Hebrew.)

5

A Period of Crisis

Although Moses as the chieftain of the Hebrew tribes acted like an absolute monarch, there was neither a territory over which he had jurisdiction nor a political organisation to help him rule the tribe. They continued to be a congregation of nomadic tribes. Israel was, thus, just a group of tribes divided into two classes, the freemen and the slaves. The freemen comprised the clergy and the affluent laity. Being nomadic, they had no attachment to any territory but identified themselves with their tribes and as such the allegiance of the freemen was more to their respective tribes than to the chieftain. The slaves could be bought and sold like the cattle and were the property of the freemen who owned them. Presided over by the chieftain Moses, this congregation of twelve tribes was to a great extent still based on kinship and was bond together basically by a religion, that is Yahwism, and a set of laws known to us as the Mosaic Code of Laws anchored in the same religion reflecting the social realities of the period. This was the type of society that Moses handed over to Joshua.

The historicity of the biblical character Joshua is as dubious as that of Moses, for there is no evidence of any sort whatsoever, direct or circumstantial, of his historicity or no reason to say that he was a historical figure. No doubt, several cities, like Jericho, associated with his supposed exploits that are mentioned in the Bible have been exhumed by archaeologists. There is also enough evidence to believe that a barbaric tribe known as "Hebrew" or Habiru did exist. All this only proves that such a city or a tribe existed in those days but does not in any way testify that a barbaric tribal chief by name Joshua flourished in that remote past. To argue on the basis of those archaeological finds that a barbaric tribal chieftain called Joshua did flourish is preposterous as pointed out in Chapter 3, "A Virtual Tower of Babel." Had any ruins, like that of his tomb, been unearthed, or had any non-scriptural literary evidence of his existence been found, archaeological finds of cities and other sites connected with his life as we see in the Bible could have been admitted as corroborative proofs of the existence of such a person. But so far no such evidence has been found.

However, although the scholars reject the historicity of the biblical story of Joshua's conquest of Canaan, they concede that the Hebrews had off and on crossed into the territory and attacked the tribes inhabiting Canaan. That could be for looting. Being a large congregation of pastoral tribes wandering from place to place, they must have been subsisting partly on meat and dairy products, as they could take the livestock along with them wherever they went. But they had to forage neighbouring tribal settlements for agricultural produces like grains and vegetables, as they had no land to cultivate. These forays required a chieftain and there had to be one who led the Hebrew tribesmen in Canaan. We could call him by any name, Amar, Akbar or Antony, but as the fictitious character is called Joshua in the Bible, in order to avoid any confusion, let us also stick to that name.

As we see him in the Bible, he was very diplomatic and took care not to ruffle the clergy's or the lay freemen's feathers by adopting a policy of non-aggressive religio-purism. But the clergy was naturally wary of his tribal background. He was not a Levite, and added to that he was an Ephramite, which was one of the powerful and proud tribes among the Hebrews. Hence, although the clergy knew him to be a religio-purist, they were rather suspicious of his loyalty because he did not have a religious background. So in order to obviate the possibility of his reneging from religio-purism, the clergy mustered all the religio-purist forces behind them. That included the Levites, the fanatic Yahwists and the affluent lay freemen of all tribes – in one word, the Hebrew Chauvinists – who had been known to be backing the other fictitious protagonist Moses all these years in the interest of safeguarding the institution of private property and slavery and the integrity of the Congregation. It was a powerful group that the priesthood gathered behind it and with its help, the clergy could checkmate any move on the part of Joshua to ignore them. The clergy, thus, assuming the leadership of the Chauvinists decided to keep the chieftain strictly under its control. So as soon as Joshua took over the chieftainship of Israel, the clergy as the spokesmen of the Chauvinists, magnanimously offered its ostensibly unconditional support to him.

The chief priest on behalf of the clergy ordered Joshua to cross the river Jordan and conquer the land beyond, pointing out that, as 'my servant' Moses was no more, it was Joshua's responsibility.[1] When the clergy said "my servant" it should not be taken to mean that the relationship of the clergy and the chieftain was like that of a master and his servant. It means the 'servant' of the ideology that is, religio-purism the cause of which he was expected to *serve*. The chief priest deliberately qualified the name Moses with 'my servant' to bring home to Joshua that he too was obliged to adhere strictly to religio-purism as Moses had been. By repeating 'my servant,' the clergy stressed the point that he should not waver in his adherence to the ideology.

So although their offer of support was apparently unconditional, there was a conditionality, which was that he accepted the supremacy of the clergy, the embodiment of religio-purism, whose servant he was. Following the example set by Moses, he should not deviate either to the right or to the left but take the middle path.[2] In other words, they wanted him to be like a horse with blinkers on either side. He should neither be a fundamentalist nor a liberal in religious matters but be a religio-purist. The clergy promised Joshua that it would not dither in its support and would not abandon or fail to help him as long as he followed the path of Moses.[3] And the priests exhorted him to strictly adhere to the Mosaic Law and not to stray from the path shown by the religio-purists.[4] This was intended to make him understand that he was subordinate to the clergy and by extension the Chauvinists, and was bound to carry out the tasks that the clergy or the Chauvinists assigned to him. Joshua took the hint.

The bard who composed this story had portrayed him as a master of diplomatic finesse. As suggested by the clergy, he always sought its advice and acted accordingly. He was, thus, correct in his relationship with the clergy and so the Chauvinists stood solidly behind him in all his expeditions with the result there was no friction between him and the clergy. In effect, therefore, he was not an independent leader like Moses who was the head of the clergy. Joshua being a non-Levite could never be a priest, let alone be the head of the clergy and so he adapted himself to the situation in which he found himself. Hence his style of governance too was different from that of Moses because the conditions and the circumstances under which each of them, Moses and Joshua, functioned were very different.

The tribes that Moses had to lead were a motley group of communes that had lost their moorings, with no set of laws common to them until Mosaic laws were accepted by all the tribes and implemented; yet they were not coherent groups. Moses, guided by his instinct, had eliminated all such individuals and groups that stood in the way of progress. Looking back from this distance in time with the mindset of today's society, it may seem undemocratic but it was inevitable under the circumstances to maintain the integrity of the Hebrew Congregation. Besides, with the disintegration of tribal communes which were based on collectivism and the birth of slave system, primal democracy that the tribals practised lost its relevance. Joshua, on the other hand, could afford to be democratic because he inherited a Congregation that was free of counter-revolutionary elements like the collectivists of Moses' time. What Joshua led was a comparatively more well-knit congregation governed by a Code of Laws, which was suited to the stage of development that the society was in at that time, and was to a great extent strictly observed by all the tribes. He had, therefore, no difficulty in maintaining law and order and consequently during the period of his chieftainship there never had been a revolt or even a mild protest.

The Hebrews had at that time pitched their camp at Shittim. Reassured of the support of the Chauvinists, Joshua called upon the freemen to muster courage and be prepared to cross the river Jordan to conquer the land that flowed with milk and honey. He also told them that the "mighty men of valour" must leave their wives, children and the cattle on this side of the river Jordan when they crossed the river to launch the attack. The lay freemen who were under the illusion that they now had a lay tribesman as chieftain, a non-Levite free from the influence of the clergy, gave him *carte blanche* and the freemen of all the tribes responded to Joshua's call saying that they would obey whatever he commanded and would go wherever he sent them.[5]

Joshua said they must strictly observe the Mosaic Law and anyone who dared break the law would be put to death.[6] This stress on the law and the threat of stringent punishment to lawbreakers were specially meant as a warning to the slaves not to defy the old and decrepit freemen and shirk work when all the able-bodied young men would be off on the battlefront. After being assured of the support of the people, Joshua detailed two spies to go to Jericho to reconnoiter the territory of the enemy and report back. The two men crossed the river Jordan and at Jericho they lodged in the house of a prostitute called Rahab.[7] She said to the spies that the king and the people were aware of the strength of Israel and the people of Jericho in general are scared. From what Rahab said, it was clear to the spies that the morale of the enemy was very low and they had almost reconciled to their possible defeat.[8].

The King of Jericho seems to have had an efficient counter-espionage service, for he got the news of the Hebrews staying in Rahab's house within hours of their arrival there. No sooner was he informed of the two Hebrew men staying with Rahab than he sent his soldiers to Rahab's house with orders to arrest the two men who, he suspected, were spies of Israel. When she saw the king's men coming to her house, she guessed their intention and hid the two spies. Clever as she was, Rahab did not deny that two men had come to her house but said to them that she did not know who the two men who came to her were. And she told them that those men had left "about the time of shutting the gate" in the evening, adding that if they pursue without tarrying at her house further, they should be able to overtake and catch those men. As soon as the soldiers left, she let the spies down by a cord through her window at the back of the house, out of the city wall on which her house was built. However, she advised them to hide in the mountain for three days, by which time, she guessed, the pursuers, not finding them, would return. But before they left, in return for all the information and help that she gave, she got an assurance from them that Israel would not harm her, her parents and her siblings. Not just that; the Israelite army would not also plunder their houses and take away their possessions when the soldiers pillaged the city after defeating the king of Jericho as victorious armies usually did.

This episode is significant, for it shows that the settlement of Jericho, with walls around the territory, was obviously a sovereign city-state ruled by a king. The Amorites were, therefore, a civilised tribe and so the individuals were not known by their gentile names, as they had grown into a state in which the members identified themselves with the territory. Rahab considered herself a citizen of the city-state of Jericho rather than a member of the Amorite tribe and her psychology was attuned to the ethos of this new socio-political structure. So she had no compunction in betraying the tribe of which she was a member because her attachment was to the territory and her loyalty was primarily to her property and the narrow circle of her family and only then to the state; the tribe came last, if at all it did. Seldom would a member of a barbaric tribe have betrayed his or her tribe because all members of the tribe as pointed out in Chapter 3, "A Virtual Tower of Babel," were related by blood and as such, was like a family. But it was not so in the case of citizens of a monarchic state.

The spies came back and gave their assessment of the enemy's strength and morale based on what Rahab had said about the situation in Jericho. The report of the spies emboldened Joshua. The next morning Joshua, along with all men, women and children as well as their slaves and the livestock, shifted the camp to the river Jordan and he told them to keep themselves ready for the expedition and requested the clergy to guide them.[9] Confirming their support, the Chauvinists said, they had accepted him as their undisputed leader and the chieftain of the Congregation.[10] Encouraged by the report of the spies and assured of the support of the Chauvinists, Joshua told the tribesmen in general that they would have to fight one by one all the tribes that inhabited the land of Canaan at that time. He added that they had the unconditional support of the Chauvinists and hence the clergy too. It should not, therefore, be difficult for them to subdue and drive out all those people.[11] The main problem was to cross the river, which Joshua said should not be difficult and as directed by the clergy, the Hebrew forces crossed the river.[12]

The Bible says the Israelites crossed the river as if on land. How could the Hebrews have crossed the river as if on land? Did the flow of the river Jordan stop because the feet of the priests carrying the Ark touched the waters as stated in the Bible? That obviously is a myth[13] but there is a basis for this myth or to put it differently, a geological phenomenon was made use of by the composers of this episode to weave this yarn. Considering the seismicity of this region that caused the earthquake in Sodom, which we discussed in the previous chapter, "Consolidation of Slavery," some biblical scholars have opined that, in those days, there could have been temporary interruptions in the flow of the river Jordan caused by earthquakes. Israel took advantage of that and crossed the river. This vain attempt at rationalisation is preposterous.

Many geologists who have studied the geology of this region agree that the region is prone to earthquakes. There is ample evidence of earthquakes that had occurred in the Jericho region since pre-biblical times but such tectonic disturbances, they opine, were not very frequent. Their investigations have revealed that geologically Jericho lies near a major fault and had experienced several earthquakes since very early times.[14] The last one, a severe earthquake that occurred in 1927 CE, was caused by rupture on a fault segment beneath the north basin of the Dead Sea. The flow of the Jordan River had stopped for twenty-one and a half hours then, thanks to landslides caused by seiches in the northern basin of the Dead Sea. Earlier too, in 1546 CE, as a result of a severe earthquake in the region, the flow of the river Jordan had stopped for two days. Unmistakable evidence of very ancient earthquakes has been found in the region of Jericho. "Older seismically triggered slumps buried beneath the 1927 slump show that a record of ancient Jericho earthquakes can also be found in the sedimentary record." However, such tectonic disturbances were not very frequent, for the geological features "suggest a long average earthquake recurrence time."[15] So those biblical scholars who try to rationalise say it was at such a time that the Hebrews had crossed the river but to suppose that such a phenomenon had occurred so opportunely is rather farfetched. However, it could be argued that it was just coincidental that an earthquake caused the obstruction of the flow of water in the river Jordan, when the Hebrews had come to cross the river. That too is incredible though not improbable. However, it is implied in such explanations that the Hebrews waited for such an occurrence and consciously planned their campaign to coincide with it or that the earthquake occurred just in time to help the Hebrews cross the river Jordan. All such seemingly rational explanations do not carry conviction.

The one reasonable explanation is that the bardic composer of the story might have witnessed this phenomenon himself during his lifetime or heard his parents or grandparents talk about it. Or they must have heard of the phenomenon from some other elderly persons who had seen it. Calamities like earthquakes and strange occurrences linger in social memory and grandmothers or mothers narrate what they had heard in their childhood days about such occurrences to their grandchildren and children. The bard who composed this episode too would have heard such stories in his childhood. Obviously, ignorant of what caused earthquakes they attributed it to god, for in ancient times, as pointed out in Chapter 2, "The Universe and God," all natural phenomena that could not be explained were attributed to some supernatural power. This occurrence when churned in the imaginative brain of the rhapsodist turned out to be an excellent idea that helped mythicise the clergy as well as the character of Joshua and bolster faith in the Hebrew god because as the feet of the priests who bore the ark dipped in the edge of the water, the flow of water stopped and the rhapsodist used it in this context with telling effect.

Presumably, they had crossed the river as the two Hebrew spies did three days back – under cover of the dark of night in boats or on some improvised catamarans or rafts. The scribes, who reduced the oral tradition to writing, unquestioningly wrote down exactly as it had come down to them and the authors of the Bible understandably accepted it, for it suited their purpose well. Anyway, it is immaterial for us to know how they crossed the river, for the historical veracity of this episode is doubtful; so is the historicity of Joshua himself. Suffice it to say, the Hebrews crossed the river Jordan stealthily. They camped at Gilgal on the eastern border of Jericho[16] and for seven days they laid siege to the city. On the seventh day, with a mighty thrust they succeeded in breaching a part of the fortification around the city.

That the wall collapsed "when the people shouted and the priests blew the trumpets,"[17] is nothing but the composer's imagination meant to keep up the myth of Joshua's character. The archaeologists who excavated the site in the early twentieth century had reported that they found a part of the wall collapsed. They also reported having seen some of the houses adjacent to this part of the wall fallen, seemingly by an earthquake[18] and now that historians have rejected the historicity of Joshua, it can be said with certainty that the destruction of the wall was caused by an earthquake. The bard who composed this story would not have even known about it. He, as any poet would do, concocted the story of the wall collapsing when priests blew the trumpet, to add mythical spice to the story and bolster faith in Yahweh. Coming back to the story, the Hebrew soldiers succeeded in breaching the defences of the Jericho army and poured into the city. They freely indulged in indiscriminate carnage of the entire population of the city, save Rahab and her kin. They burnt down the city after plundering all the households, leaving untouched the possessions of Rahab alone.[19]

The biblical statement that the city was completely destroyed by the Israelites has been proved wrong. A team of archaeologists who excavated the region in 1953 had found a large part of the wall and other structures resembling houses that were about seven thousand years old, intact.[20] The invasion of Jericho by Israel, according to the biblical chronology, should have been between *circa* 1300 and 1190 BCE, when Joshua, the mythical character, is said to have flourished.[21] When houses built in the early sixth millennium BCE have been found in good condition, even conceding an error of forty percent in dating the ruins, it can be said with certainty that this story of Israel burning down the entire city is fictitious. Or, the Hebrews had not invaded Jericho at that time.

Leaving aside the question of the historicity of the event, let us go back to the story and continue analysing it to see what it reveals about the character Joshua. When the spoils of war were brought, neither Joshua nor the soldiers were given their due shares. All the booty collected from Jericho were appropriated by the house or tribe of Levites, the clergy, giving nothing whatsoever to anyone, including the soldiers who brought the booty.[22] Joshua was not even consulted. It may be recalled that after defeating the Midianites, when the Hebrew soldiers brought the booty, Moses told them to share the man and the beast equitably. Later, the officers brought "an oblation for the Lord what every man found, of jewels of gold...to make atonement for our souls before the Lord." Moses and Eleazar "took the gold from them and all the wrought jewels" and shared between themselves.[23] And the warriors took whatever spoils that each of them had taken. On the contrary, Joshua had no voice in sharing the spoils of war, which indicates that the Chieftain's abject servility to the clergy.

Joshua's subservience to the clergy was glaring when he was forced to take action against Achan who had taken "a beautiful Babylonian garment and two hundred shekels of silver and a wedge of gold of fifty shekels weight" and hid them buried in his tent.[24] It was paltry compared to the amount of spoils that the clergy had got, but the priests, greedy as they were, did not want to lose even that. Thanks to the pressure brought upon him by the clergy, Joshua reluctantly summoned Achan for interrogation but the manner in which he questioned Achan shows that his sympathies were with the accused. It is significant that Joshua addressed him "My son" and said, "I beg you." Apart from that, he told him to confess to the clergy and not to him.[25]

No tribal chieftain would have addressed an alleged culprit accused of theft as "my son," and spoken so politely; nor would he have told the accused to confess to the clergy. And seldom would a chieftain have spoken to a known pilferer or any offender without showing his ire. Joshua's words sound as if he viewed this misdemeanor rather sympathetically and might have even condoned it, using his discretion. In fact, it was not a misdemeanor in the eyes of a soldier like Joshua, for conventionally the soldiers were entitled to the booty that they collected. But he seemed helpless, with the clergy breathing down his neck[26] and at their instance, in accordance with law, Joshua ordered Achan, his children and his cattle to be stoned and set on fire.[27] Presumably, the priests were watching from the wings to make sure that he punished Achan severely. They did not come out, perhaps because they did not want to be seen by the people of the tribe as greedy for wealth.

Picking up the thread of the story of Israel's expedition in Canaan, the victory of the Hebrews over Jericho made Joshua famous and also made him overconfident as is evident from what followed.[28] After conquering Jericho, he turned his attention to Ai. Of a settlement like Ai, no archaeological evidence has been found so far. Maybe, there was no city-state with thick brick walls and houses but only a vast territory, a settlement of a tribe, with a few houses built of adobe-bricks and stone or even tents. As the biblical story goes, Joshua sent two spies to explore the city of Ai and assess the strength of the tribe. The spies reported that the enemy did not seem very strong and so a small contingent of about three thousand men would be able to subdue them. Trusting the spies, Joshua sent as they advised three thousand men, but the men of Ai fiercely defended themselves, inflicting heavy casualties on Israel. The spies had underestimated the enemy's strength. The invaders had to flee for their lives and they returned considerably depleted in strength. Joshua was disheartened and he was worried that it would demoralise his men.

The Chauvinists, and the clergy in particular, were furious. They told Joshua that the reason for the defeat of his men was the result of his not seeking their advice. Obviously, Joshua had ignored the Chauvinists as well as the clergy and relying on the report of the spies, he took the decision to send a small contingent only. He must have thought of ridding himself of the vise-like hold of the Chauvinists and the clergy who truly treated him like their servant and not like the chieftain of the tribe. What Joshua did was illegal or impertinence in the eyes of the Chauvinists because he had gone beyond the limits of his authority given to him by the clergy. He was not expected to act independently, especially in matters connected with wars. Whatever it was, this failure further weakened Joshua and correspondingly enhanced the power of the Chauvinists. Probably it was a gamble that Joshua tried but it failed.

Anyway, Joshua decided to attack Ai again but was not confident of confronting the enemy in a pitched battle. He sought the advice of the Chauvinists. They said victory was sure and he would be able to defeat them as he did the king of Jericho if he strictly adopted the stratagem that they advised him to.[29] So this time he decided not to take any risk and planned his moves exactly as the Chauvinists had advised him. He chose thirty thousand valorous men and sent them to hide in the bushes near the city.[30] And with the rest of the army he marched towards the city. When the men of Ai came out to defend, Joshua and his men feigned to be fleeing and as could be expected, the men of Ai followed the enemy in pursuit. At that time, as planned earlier, those hiding in the bushes nearby entered Ai and set the city on fire. On seeing the city in flames, the men of Ai turned back to put off the fire and join battle with those inside the city. At once Joshua and those with him turned back and attacked them from behind.[31] The army of Ai was caught between the two divisions of the Israelite army and they panicked and ran helter skelter, with the result they fell an easy prey to the Hebrew sword. The entire population of Ai – men, women and children – was mercilessly done to death. The king of Ai was captured and brought to Joshua, who ordered the vanquished king to be executed in public.[32]

The news of the capture of Jericho followed by that of the rout of Ai and the ruthless massacre of those people reached "all the kings, which were on this side of Jordan." They were alarmed. Knowing that it would be impossible for them to face the belligerent Hebrew tribes separately, they formed an alliance, comprising "the Hittite, the Amorite, the Canaanite, the Perizzite, the Hivite and the Jebusite" to defend themselves in case the Hebrews attacked them.[33] But on hearing of the carnage at Jericho and Ai as well as of the earlier wars of the Hebrews with the kings of Heshbon and Bashan, the Gibeonites[34] were unnerved and were wary of joining the anti-Hebrew alliance. They decided to avoid a war with the Hebrews at any cost. They secretly sent their ambassadors to Israel with gifts and an offer of a peace treaty. The ambassadors met Joshua and giving him all the presents that they had brought as a token of their sincerity, expressed their willingness to enter into a non-aggression pact.[35] So the Hebrew Congregation went to the Gibeonite cities – Gibeon, Chephirah, Beeroth and Kirjathjearim – but did not attack them because the rulers had agreed to a deal. However, the freemen in general, particularly the Chauvinists, were not happy with the treaty. So they put forward the condition that the Gibeonites accept the suzerainty of Israel and the Gibeonites were forced to agree to be a tributary state.[36] The Chauvinists were happy and the Hebrews assured the Gibeonites of their protection in case of any external aggression.

As Adonizedek, the king of Jerusalem, heard of the bilateral pact between the Hebrews and the Gibeonites, he felt let down by a natural ally. He regarded this as a blatant betrayal by such a mighty tribe like the Gibeonites, "one of the royal cities" greater than Ai. At once, he called a meeting of the kings of Hebron, Jarmuth, Lachish and Eglon at his place and formed a coalition. They decided to take punitive action against Gibeon to punish them for their betrayal[37] and they declared war against Gibeon. The Gibeonites immediately invoked the defence pact with Israel and called upon them to help fight the aggressors, to which Joshua responded with alacrity. Encouraged and supported by the Chauvinists who chalked out the strategy, Joshua with his men arrived after a long and tortuous journey in the night and attacked the invading coalition forces. Their plan of a blitzkrieg worked.[38] The enemy had not expected it. The suddenness of the attack threw the enemy troops into disarray and the Hebrews could slay them without any difficulty. The five kings who led the coalition army fled from the battlefield and hid in a cave but they were caught and killed. The Hebrews occupied the cities that these kings ruled, thus completing the conquest of the southern Canaan.

In this episode, the Bible states, as they fled god dropped huge stones from heaven upon them and many died.[39] Most biblical commentators take it literally and assert that it showed Yahweh always came to Israel's help. If a hailstorm had really occurred as the Bible states, it was indeed a strange coincidence. However, presuming that it had occurred then, the hail could not have fallen on the enemy lines alone as stated in the Bible; the hail would have fallen on the heads of all, not excepting the men of Israel including Joshua. Moreover, it is said that during this war, Joshua prayed to god and ordered: "Sun, stand thou still over Gibeon; and you Moon, in the valley of Ajalon." And lo and behold, "the sun stood still and so did the moon."[40] So, according to the Bible, obeying Joshua's command, both the sun and the moon stood still until the enemy was routed! Biblical scholars have tried to rationalise this miracle also. To give one example, some scholars have suggested that probably the sky must have been overcast, creating an illusion that the sun was standing still. This again is a vain attempt at rationalisation, similar to the one about Israel crossing the Jordan.

The Bible refers us to the book of Jasher to prove the veracity of the statement. It can be inferred from this that the legend of the sun and the moon staying put when Joshua commanded them was borrowed from the book of Jasher, which unfortunately is not extant today. There is no doubt that many Hebrew rhapsodists must have written ballads and songs to commemorate the tribal heroes, real or imaginary, which had been passed on orally from generation to generation. The book of Jasher, which, it is said, was a collection of old Jewish legends, must have incorporated in it the ballads and songs about this real or imaginary war also. The bards who composed the ballads, in order to bring home to the audience the prowess of the Israelite warriors, might have described the war poetically in hyperbolic terms, saying even the two celestial bodies were enthralled and stupefied at the heroism of the Israelites. The biblical scribe who obviously borrowed this episode cleverly twisted the hyperbole and, taking it literally, presented it as a fact to show that Joshua too like Moses liaised with god in favour of the Israelites. This undoubtedly is done to mythicise the character of Joshua and to portray him also as a prophet.

Now that the southern region had been conquered, the kings of the cities of the northern Palestine expected the expansionist Hebrew tribe to turn its covetous eyes to their region. The king Jabin of Hazor rightly guessed that Hazor would be the next target of the Hebrews. Although the city of Hazor was strongly fortified and was the most powerful of all the kingdoms in the region, the king of Hazor did not want to take any risk. He decided to face the enemy together with his three confederates, the kingdoms of Madon, Shimron and Achshaph, as well as all the other powers in the region. They all knew that they would not be able to face the onslaught of the huge Hebrew tribe severally and they readily agreed to the suggestion of Jabin to form a coalition to defend their kingdoms. So a coalition of more than fifteen kingdoms was forged. It included armies of all the kings from the hill regions in the north and those of the kings from the plains in the south of Chinneroth as well as of those in the valley and in the borders of Dor in the West.[41] This grand alliance comprised six tribes – the Canaanites, the Amorites, the Hittites, the Perizzites, the Jebusites, and the Hivites. It was a formidable army, equipped with light chariots, which the Hebrews did not have. They assembled at the waters of Merom, planning to intercept the Hebrews there.

From the point of view of commerce, Hazor was the most important of all the northern kingdoms in those times. As authenticated by archaeological and ancient non-biblical literary evidence, the city lay on the trade route between Mesopotamia and Egypt and hence its importance.[42] So it is but natural that as king Jabin had anticipated, Israel decided to conquer it. Joshua had learnt from experience that it was the suddenness of the attack that helped them win the war against the coalition that attacked Gibeon. So he used the same tactics now and as expected the blitzkrieg succeeded, for the grand alliance was routed in the war. The victorious Israelites exterminated the people of all those cities. Hazor, the king of which was the "head of all those kingdoms," was sacked and ravaged with a vengeance leaving all the other cities intact. But the whole story of the Hebrew invasion and destruction of Hazor is historically not true and is meant to project the fictitious character of Joshua as a great commander and conqueror. According to the biblical chronology itself nearly two centuries later, during the period of Deborah, Israel waged a war with king Jabin of Hazor, the same king whom Joshua is said to have killed. Had Jabin not died then, he should have been over two hundred years old when Deborah attacked Hazor, which story we shall deal with when we discuss the exploits of Deborah.

With the victory over the five kings in the southern region, it may not be wrong to say Israel had succeeded in breaking the backbone of the Canaanite power. According to the Bible the mountainous region, the foothills and Negeb, the three main areas had all come under the control of the Hebrews. Now that the grand alliance of the kings of the northern Canaan too had been defeated, the conquest of Canaan, the land flowing with milk and honey that Moses had promised to give the Hebrews could be deemed to have been completed by Joshua. But historians reject the biblical story that Israel had conquered the southern parts of Canaan, when Joshua is believed to have flourished.[43] They are unanimous in their opinion that contrary to what the book of Joshua states Israel did not conquer the whole of Canaan and distribute the land among all the Hebrew tribes. Had they conquered the south as claimed in the Bible, the Hebrews would have occupied the cities and stayed back there after the war, but it is said that they returned to their camp at Gilgal. Militarily, the Hebrews were comparatively weak and their ill-equipped army was incapable of confronting the powerful and well-trained Canaanite army, the strength of which lay in their chariot brigade. The Hebrews "did not have the strength or technological knowledge to defeat the chariot brigade of the Canaanite cities. That the Hebrew tribes carried out so extensive a program (as described in the Bible) is unlikely."[44]

It is supposed "the editor-author responsible for shaping the major part of (The Book of) Joshua essentially in the form in which it has come down to us probably lived in the last quarter of the seventh century or the first half of the sixth century. He was a man of consuming religious passion, whose concern was not to preserve old traditions in an academic manner but to present the conquest in such a way that it would have clear theological significance for his readers. Here, in speeches attributed to Yahweh and to Joshua, he expresses the concept that Yahweh has unfailingly carried out all the promises to the chosen people. It is this conviction which led the editor to portray the conquest of Palestine under Joshua as more extensive than what the older traditions indicate."[45] Robertson also questions the biblical story of Israel's invasion and conquest of Palestine. He states that there is no mention of the conquest of Palestine by Joshua in any of the contemporary Egyptian records.[46]

Obviously, this falsification of history by the biblical scribes or editors was deliberately done to boost the image of Joshua by holding him up as no less a military commander than the other fictitious character Moses. It also helped project the Hebrews as the pre-eminent tribe of the period. All the defeats that the Hebrews suffered at the hands of its enemies, according to the Bible, were not because the other tribes were superior or because Yahweh who triumphed over the Pharaoh and helped liberate them from slavery was not powerful enough; those defeats were attributed to the failure of the Hebrews to live by Yahweh's commandments, thus keeping the myth of the superiority of the Hebrews and the Hebrews' faith in Yahweh. In fact, it has been pointed out by historians that there is no mention of the conquest of Palestine by someone called Joshua in any of the contemporary Egyptian records. The composer or composers of this biblical story attributed these achievements to Joshua, only to "save the face" so to speak, of Yahweh and thus to preclude the possibility of the tribe's faith in him being shaken. The writers of the source book, from which the book of Joshua is believed to have been compiled, must have thought that a little chronological jugglery was not unjustified if it would achieve those purposes. The claim that the conquest of Canaan and the apportionment of the land to the various tribes of Israel were achieved under Joshua's chieftainship, apart from the historicity of Joshua itself, has thus been rejected by historians. Joshua is as much a fictitious character as Moses is.

The colonisation of Canaan by the Hebrews was achieved by infiltrating little by little, after the period when the biblical character Joshua is supposed to have lived. So possibly during those biblical times when Joshua is believed to have flourished, the barbaric tribes of Israel, based at Gilgal, now and then had suddenly descended upon the neighbouring cities, looted them and returned to the base with all the plunder. The marauding Hebrew tribes, no doubt, would have been led by a bandit, whom the composer calling by the name Joshua, mythicised and lionised, like the romanticised legendary outlaw Robin Hood of Sherwood Forest. There is one difference, though. The fictitious story of Joshua is intended to bolster faith in Yahweh while the folklore of Robin Hood reflects not only the righteous indignation of the poor serfs against landed gentry who, in those days, illegally appropriated land and persecuted the poor but also the hypocrisy and depravity of the clergy.

We are, however, concerned not with history but with the Bible, which states, Joshua conquered the land of the Canaanites. Let us accept the fact that the Bible is not a book of history; its purpose is to instil in the minds of the Hebrews faith in Yahweh. Hence, although we know that it is not historically true to say that Joshua conquered the land of Canaan we shall accept the biblical version because we are analysing the Bible to see what it reveals about the then prevailing social conditions and the evolution of society in general. The Bible states, Joshua, "now old and stricken," distributed the conquered land as instructed by the clergy.[47] This enhanced the prestige and power of the clergy because the chief occupation of the Hebrew tribes was agriculture and being land-hungry they were naturally beholden to the clergy for the land that they got. After completing this task (the conquest of Canaan and the redistribution of land) to the satisfaction of the tribesmen, in the twilight of his life Joshua gathered all the tribes of Israel at Shechem and gave a long sermon to the people. This homily shows Joshua as a staunch religio-purist. In his long talk he eulogised the clergy, enumerating all that it had done to help the Hebrew freemen.[48]

He enjoined the freemen of all tribes not to lose faith in the leadership of the clergy and be carried away by what the clerics of other religions preached.[49] He warned, the clergy would not tolerate any defiance of its commandment to adhere to religio-purism and the transgressors, those who waver in their faith in Yahweh, would be mercilessly punished.[50] His peroration and the pledge that the tribe took confirm the fact that the religio-purism had become stronger than it was in the days of Moses. His entire speech boiled down to calling upon the people not to forsake religio-purism. Religio-liberalism resulting from allotheism, he said, could spell ruin and the society would disintegrate.[51] The freemen, high and low, of all the tribes of Israel pledged in one voice, their allegiance to the clergy and adherence to religio-purism, saying "the Lord our God we will serve, and his voice we will obey."[52] At the end, Joshua made a covenant between the entire Congregation and the clergy and he wrote it down in a book, leaving no room for misinterpretation, equivocation or prevarication in the future.[53] He did not live long after that to see the unforeseen turn the Hebrew society had taken.

Joshua's sermon indicates that as in the days of Moses, religio-purism was the most potent force among the Hebrew tribes during the period of Joshua too. It was undeniably a necessity during the periods of Moses and Joshua to hold together the loose assemblage of fissiparous Hebrew tribes. But it was inapplicable in the post-Joshua period when several tribes espousing different religions and worshipping a variety of gods lived side by side in the territory under the Hebrew rule. It, no doubt, helped strengthen the hands of the Chauvinists but the need of the post-Joshua period was a liberal religious outlook, which alone would have kept the society free from internal tensions. But the religio-purists were unable to change their attitude and tenaciously clung to their ideology. Hence, religio-purism, which was once a progressive ideology had become a retrogressive force and a drag on the society, and its dominance resulted in social stagnation retarding the progress of the Congregation into a monarchy. Ignoring history and based solely on the biblical account of the events, let us assume that Joshua had conquered Canaan. And at the time of Joshua's death, all the tribes of Israel that constituted the Congregation had occupied contiguous territories and had formed a sort of Confederacy of the Hebrew tribes. This was held together by an unwritten multilateral defence pact, a common language and a common Code of Laws rooted in Yahwism with a judge to ensure that there was no breach of law or peace. Yet, each tribe was autonomous and occasional conflicts between the tribes were, metaphorically speaking, open invitations to the neighbouring tribes to invade.

The Confederacy, unlike the Congregation, was a comparatively more well-knit organization, notwithstanding an undercurrent of inter-tribal rivalries. Joshua, by establishing the Confederacy, had unconsciously ushered in a pluralist society, which was unknown to the Hebrews who had been nomadic till then. Various other tribes that were polytheistic and idolatrous inhabited neighbouring territories. There were also several pockets or enclaves occupied by other tribesmen even within the territorial limits of the Hebrew Confederacy and naturally, inter-tribal marriages among all these tribes including the Hebrews had become quite common. This new society with a considerably strong population of persons with mixed ethnic blood inevitably resulted in the dilution of religio-purism and gave rise to the religio-liberal ideology. Consequently, the influence of the forces of religio-liberalism was so strong that the Hebrew clergy was afraid that many lay freemen might stray away from the flock. Joshua had failed to see this reality and his exhortation to abjure religio-liberalism was the result of his lack of understanding of the necessity of the times. This new force, religio-liberalism, was bound to thrive and strengthen further, as it was the inevitable product of the then prevailing social conditions.

The demise of Joshua rang down the curtain on the period of chieftainship and created a political vacuum, ushering in a period of uncertainty. He did not nominate a successor as Moses did; nor did he make any other arrangement to install a person to oversee or lead the Confederacy and the Hebrews were left without a chieftain or a monarch. The infrastructure – a contiguous territory as well as social, economic and cultural prerequisites – that is required to transform a barbaric tribe into monarchy was in place. Yet Israel had shied away from taking the forward step and continued to be a Confederacy of tribes. The progress of Israel, thus, went awry and a queer political set up held together by religion came up. It was not a full-fledged political state. Instead of a polity presided over by a secular monarch that should have sprung up on its own steam generated by the socio-economic forces, the impact of religio-purism gave rise to a polity that was a far cry from monarchy that Moses wanted the Hebrew tribes to have. This was not what Moses had dreamt of; he envisioned a secular monarch to be chosen by the clergy but a regime free from clerical interference.

Instead, the Hebrews had a dispensation based on religion and headed by an individual designated "judge" who was only a glorified tribal chieftain. "The judge in ancient Canaanite and Israelite usage was not so much a legal expert as one who upheld the customs of the people."[54] Asimov states, "the word 'judge' is used in the Bible in the sense of a ruler, since in early cultures, the chief function of a tribal ruler in peacetime was that of judging disputes and reaching, it was to be hoped, some just decision."[55] The judge, as used in this context in the Bible, was the ruler of the Confederacy of the Hebrew tribes and he was expected to maintain law and order, which consisted basically in holding down the slaves. Being the judge, he acted as mediator in disputes among the Hebrew tribes and even disputes between two individuals. In times of aggression by a foreign power, as the ruler of the Confederacy he assumed the role of the Supreme Commander of the Hebrew army. However, the Confederacy did not have a standing army but only a militia for guarding the judge's palace. So in times of wars contingents of it could be sent to the front along with able-bodied, young men who would be called up then to defend the territory of the Confederacy.

The person who was the judge as well as the ruler had no legislative powers. He had no power to make a law or to amend a law; nor had he the power to declare null and void any of the Mosaic laws. He was only an executive authority and so he had to ensure that Israel observed the Mosaic laws strictly and the people faithfully adhered to the tenets of Yahwism as codified by these laws. As such he was expected to be the custodian of these laws. Hence, the judges of Israel of the post-

Joshua period had to be fully conversant with this law. Nevertheless, some of the judges had been compelled to adopt a liberal religious policy, which palpably contradicted the Mosaic Laws by force of circumstances, inviting the displeasure of the clergy and the Chauvinists in general.

However, this was a critical period in the history of the Hebrews. It was a period of transition from a semi-nomadic tribal existence to a city-based settled life and was an uneasy interlude so to say, between a gentile society and a political society. This unconventional and bizarre socio-economic organisation was the result of the stranglehold of religio-purism on the society. In short, instead of an absolute monarchy, this institution of judgeship, which was peculiar to the Hebrews, came into existence and the judges who ruled over and judged the stratified Hebrew society embracing twelve different tribes, were nominated by the clergy. This form of socio-political organisation that the Hebrews were in at that time was neither a commune-based barbaric society nor a monarchical civilised society.

In order to differentiate this socio-political organisation from barbaric tribal communes, which stage it was in the process of leaving behind and absolute monarchy towards which it was groping, let us call it *nascent monarchy*. It may be so called because with a ruler common to all tribes of the Confederacy, this dispensation was similar to and seemed to be paving the way for, absolute monarchy. The institution of private property, the social stratification, the lack of democracy and the disintegration of collectivism, were the features of the Hebrew society at this stage which made it more akin to monarchy than to a tribal commune. Yet it was different from a monarchy. The judge who was the ruler did not have the authority of a monarch. Unlike in an absolute monarchy, in the nascent monarchy there was no state and as such there was no permanent council of ministers to advise and help the judge in the governance as a king would have had. He might seek the advice of anyone in whom he had confidence and his adviser was usually the chief priest or any priest. The territories occupied by all tribes of the Confederacy constituted the jurisdiction of the judge.

The territory that the Hebrew Confederacy occupied and over which the judges ruled, was organised in cities and villages. The archaeologists have unearthed many Hebrew settlements of this period in and around Jerusalem. These settlements, of which the latest to be discovered was Giloh, bear witness to the fact that the tribe had abandoned nomadism altogether and had adopted a sedentary mode of life[56] as a result of which several Hebrew city-states had sprung up in the region during this period. These city-states were to some extent comparable to the city-states of ancient Greece. However, the Hebrew city-states were believed to have been ordained by god but the Greek ones had no such pretensions. Unlike the Greek city-states, which grew up with monarchy, the Hebrew city-states were ruled by governors who had no army under them because the defence of all the city-states was the responsibility of the judge. For example, when Gaal, son of Ebed, raised the banner of revolt in Shechem, Zebul, the governor of Shechem, had to send a messenger to Abimelech, the then judge, requesting him to send the army to suppress it.[57] The same system continued even during the period of Hebrew monarchy. For example, Rehoboam appointed his sons as governors in all the city-states in his kingdom as we shall see in Chapter 7, "The Rise of Imperialism." The Hebrew city-states were a socio-political organisation, midway between local self-government and a full-fledged monarchical state. However, the judge may station a contingent of the army in any city-state.

Interestingly, we find a pattern in the biblical narrative of the period of judges. The clergy anoints the judge and when he dies, allotheism raises its head; the Hebrews forsake their god Yahweh, and turn to other gods, chiefly the gods of the Canaanites. This apostasy angers Yahweh, who is a jealous god, and in retaliation he sends invaders to harass and oppress the Hebrews. The oppressed Hebrews realise their mistake and repent. Going back to Yahweh they cry and appeal to him for help and to deliver them from oppression. Yahweh reminds them how he has been liberating them whenever an alien tribe oppresses them. He tells them to go to those gods whom they have been worshipping and ask for their help. The repentant Hebrews understand that Yahweh is hinting at their apostasy. They confess their sin of being apostates and ask for clemency. They disown the other gods and reiterating their faith in Yahweh, swear to serve him forever. They request him to do whatever he thinks is good for them.

Now Yahweh, his ego satisfied, relents and grieves for the plight of the Hebrews. He selects a judge from among the freemen of the Confederacy and helps him deliver the Hebrews from oppression. This sequence of events repeats itself. These episodes are meant to bring home to the faithful that absolute faith in Yahweh is a requisite for social and personal well-being.

What does this paradigm connote in socio-political terms? When a judge dies and unless and until a successor is nominated, there is no law-enforcing agency and there is a breakdown of law and order. Presumably, the slaves become restive; they rebel. This disrupts cultivation and production suffers. Consequently, there is shortage of food and the people suffer and the wealthy farmers' income is reduced. These wealthy freemen, the landowners, take law into their hands and with the help of mercenaries that each of them maintains, suppress the disaffected slaves.[58] The rivalry among the tribes makes it difficult for the various tribes to reach a consensus on a person who can be elevated to the office of the judge. Each tribe tries to get one of its members chosen for the office. Thus the deadlock continues. The threat of social turmoil looms large. The confederacy is in an anarchic condition when an alien tribe or country attacks and occupies parts of its territory. The Hebrews, both the freemen and the slaves, in that part of the territory are oppressed. The freemen then, approach the clergy that selects a judge who gathers an army and liberates the territory occupied by the intruders. These episodes – the historicity of the protagonists involved or the events themselves is not authenticated and probing it is beyond the scope of this study – show that Israel is still not a unified political society and this disunity is being exploited by the clergy to keep the tribes under their control.

In the period between the death of Joshua and the establishment of the institution of Judgeship, religion was the only organised institution that stood above and controlled all tribes constituting the Confederacy, which was now rudderless without a chieftain or ruler. Naturally, therefore, the freemen of the Confederacy approached the clergy, the administrative body of the religious institution that had become the virtual ruler, to find a solution to the problem.[59] They wanted a commander to attack the Canaanites and the Perizzites and annex the adjoining land still occupied by them. The clergy decided that the Judaists would mobilise able-bodied men and invade the Canaanite cities but stopped short of appointing any individual as chieftain of the Confederacy permanently. As directed by the clergy, the tribe of Judah had to organise an expedition against the Canaanite and the Perizzite tribes.[60]

Although Judah was the most prominent and the most powerful of all the tribes of Israel, it struck an alliance with Simeon, representing a small tribe of not much significance, whose territory was within that of the Judah. And together they attacked the Canaanites, who, being the oldest existing inhabitants of the land at that time, had entrenched themselves in the region. Although the Judah-Simeon coalition forces destroyed the Canaanite city of Zephath and succeeded in subduing the Canaanites, the invaders failed to dislodge the Canaanites from their territory.[61] This was the beginning of the Israelite campaigns and was followed by a series of expeditions on Canaanite territories by various tribes of Israel, to conquer the entire land of Canaan to which they had migrated. However, they did not succeed in conquering the territories of the Canaanites, including also those of the two clans of Canaanites, like the Jebusites and the Amorites, who inhabited there.

The Hebrew tribes that subsequently crossed swords with the Canaanites were those of Manasseh, Ephraim, Zebulun, Asher, and Naphtali, but not one of them could claim a decisive and total victory over the Canaanites, with the result Israel was forced to coexist with all those tribes. However, all of them – the Canaanites, the Jebusites, the Amorites, the inhabitants of Kitron, Beth Shemesh and Beth Anath – became tributaries of the Confederacy.[62] Nevertheless, "Israel dwelt among the Canaanites, the Hittites, the Amorites, the Perizzites, the Hivites and the Jebusite" and inevitably inter-tribal marriages were common,[63] with the result religio-purism of the Hebrews got diluted. This is an important factor that helped the growth of liberalism among the Hebrews.

The prospect of getting a strong leader seemed a far cry after the Judah-Simeon expedition against the Canaanites and Perizzites, and this was because of an unhealthy intra-tribal competition among the various tribes comprising Israel; each tribe was pressing the claim of one of its members for chieftainship. So they were not able to reach an understanding on a compromise candidate that would be acceptable to all the tribes of Israel. However, the problem was solved when Caleb,[64] a very senior member of the Hebrew tribes and a peer of Joshua, threw a challenge, saying "whoever attacks Kirjathsepher (now called Debir) and takes it, to him will I give Achsah, my daughter as wife."[65] Othniel took up the challenge, led the attack and conquered Debir, consequently winning the hand of Caleb's daughter. His conquest of Debir shot him into the limelight and he proved himself capable of leading the Hebrews. This could be just a fictitious story to portray Othneil as a capable leader. He was a member of the Judah tribe, being the son of Caleb's younger brother, Kenaz. So he was doubly qualified, so to speak, for the chieftainship. Still the clergy did not endorse his claim for the office of the chieftain.

The Hebrew Confederacy was in a state of social unrest. So the king of Mesopotamia, Cushan-rishathaim, subjugated Israel without any difficulty and oppressed both the rich and the poor alike for almost a decade.[66] The freemen of all the twelve tribes approached the clergy lamenting their plight. They requested the clergy to select a chieftain from among them to lead the Hebrews against the aggressor and free them from the oppressive rule of the foreigners.[67] The clergy, complying with the tribesmen, formally appointed Othniel, designating him as the "judge."[68] That they did not call him "king" was a clear message to the freemen that it was not a monarchy but the rule of the religio-purists represented by the judge. In other words, the judge was subordinate to and supported by the clergy.[69] Othniel successfully repelled the Cushan, a desert tribe that intruded into the territory of the Confederacy under Cushan-rishathaim, and till the death of Othniel there was peace in the land.[70] Soon after, probably hearing of the death of Othniel and knowing that the Hebrews were again without a leader, the Moabites along with the Ammonites and Amalekites attacked and conquered the "city of palm trees"[71] and ruled over the Israelites for a long time.[72]

Seeing the Hebrews in distress and complying with their request, the clergy chose a new judge and that was Ehud, son of Gera, a Benjaminite, who was left-handed.[73] Interestingly the left-handedness of Ehud helped him defeat the Moabites. As the story goes, "the children of Israel sent a present to Eglon the king of Moab," to deliver which Ehud himself went. The "present" denotes the "tribute" that usually a vanquished tribe (in this case, the Hebrews or Confederacy and in later years, king or nation) paid in cash or kind to the conqueror in acknowledgement of submission. Thanks to his sinistrality, neither Eglon nor his guards suspected him of carrying a dagger because usually, most men being right-handed, weapons are carried on the left side of the person. But as Ehud was left-handed, he was carrying the dagger on his right side, as a result of which the guards did not notice it. After handing over the customary gifts, Ehud said he had a secret message to deliver to the king. Believing him, Eglon sent out all his soldiers when Ehud taking the dagger with his left hand, stabbed Eglon to death and went out unnoticed through the porch. By the time the soldiers came to know of the death of Eglon it was too late. Taking advantage of the consequent panic and confusion in the Moabite camp, Ehud led the army of the Confederacy[74] and massacred the Moabites. He, thus, liberated the Hebrew tribes and they lived peacefully for many years.

After the death of Ehud, there arose another judge, Shamgar, who was the son of Anath. Some biblical scholars are inclined to think he was a Canaanite, judging by his as well as his father's name, which was not Semitic while his father's name was that of a Canaanite goddess.[75] Most probably, he was born of a Hebrew woman married to a Canaanite, for his father's name resembles that of a Canaanite goddess of war. Inter-tribal marriages between the Hebrews and other tribes as pointed out earlier were quite common during that period. The Bible does not say that he was chosen by the clergy, and that reinforces the suspicion that he was not a pure Hebrew. He took over as the judge of the Hebrews on his own and so it may be assumed that the religio-purists had a temporary setback during this period. Nonetheless, he is portrayed here as the deliverer of the Hebrews but the Bible does not give any details about his rule. Being a man of mixed blood, presumably he adopted a liberal religious policy that helped strengthen liberalism and no wonder, the Bible glosses over his period. Curiously, even the duration of his reign also is not mentioned. That he slew six-hundred Philistine warriors "with an ox goad" is a palpably fictitious story and an anachronism. Historically the Hebrew-Philistine conflict happened much later and this episode is believed to be a later interpolation. In the Bible the rule of Shamgar is dealt with in just one verse or one sentence, to state that Shamgar "also delivered Israel" from the Philistines.[76] It is beyond one's comprehension why this is squeezed in here. Maybe, this is intended to let the readers know that religio-purism had a setback as a result of inter-tribal marriages and allotheism among the Hebrews during the period between the death of Ehud and the assumption of judgeship by Deborah.

However, stories, whether fictitious or not, about such characters indicate that the Hebrews were slowly expanding the territory of the Confederacy and had been penetrating deeper and deeper into the land of Canaan. The death of Shamgar was followed by a brief period when the Confederacy was without a judge. Consequently, as the biblical statement "the children of Israel again did evil in the sight of the Lord" indicates. there were fratricidal conflicts among the Hebrews and breakdown of law and order giving rise to a situation congenial for the slaves to rebel.[77] The freemen were panic-stricken. Taking advantage of the anarchy that prevailed in the Confederacy, Jabin, king of Hazor, marched on Israel.[78] Jabin, the Canaanite king, had found a good commander in Sisera who controlled a city on the Mediterranean coast, not very far from Hazor. He was supposed to be a descendant of the Philistines. Hazor was a powerful Canaanite city-state in northern Palestine and Jabin had a strong army equipped with chariots of iron.[79] The Canaanites under him had been plundering the crops of the Hebrews since the death of Shamgar and the Confederacy, with no judge to lead them, had been unable to resist the Canaanites, let alone drive them away from the land. At the same time, tribes like the Kenites, related to the Hebrews, were inching towards Hazor, not militarily though. They were feigning friendship and slyly encroaching slowly upon the arable land around the city of Hazor, which King Jabin looked at with suspicion.

In spite of repeated requests by the people to appoint a judge, strangely the clergy did not take any action.[80] Perhaps because the clergy knew that there was a prophetess, already judging and being a prophetess she did not need the endorsement of the priesthood. Deborah, wife of Lepidoth, not a Levite but presumably an Ephraimite, was the prophetess who had been judging "under the palm tree of

Deborah between Ramah and Bethel in mount Ephraim" at that time.[81] She was the first and the only female judge that the Hebrews ever had. Seeing the plight of Israel, Deborah decided to deliver the tribe from the Canaanite scourge once and for all and decided to mobilise an army. She summoned Barak and commanded him to call for volunteers to form an army of ten thousand men and to lead an expedition against the Canaanites.

Seeing her confidence, the clerics, who had been lying low during the judgeship of Shamgar, were happy and came forward on their own to back her.[82] Barak, however, said that he would go for war only if Deborah would accompany him up to the river Kishon. So she went with him. The Hebrew army, though relatively ill-equipped, met the army of the Canaanites on a ground that had become swampy due to a storm that ravaged the country at that time.[83] It was raining heavily and streams of water flowed down the mountains, bringing down slush and inundating the plains. Deborah, who was obviously good at logistics, had deliberately chosen the monsoon season for launching the attack.[84]

She knew that their heavy vehicles, the iron chariots, would be ineffective under such conditions. Her tactics did help the Hebrews. And as planned, she confronted the enemy in the marshy land, on the banks of the river Kishon that was bound to overflow in the rainy season.[85] So the two armies joined battle on the banks of the river Kishon. The army of the Canaanites was thus greatly handicapped, for their heavy chariots, having got stuck in the quagmire, were practically immobile rendering them useless. No wonder the river Kishon swept them away,[86] for the river was in spate as a result of the torrential rains and the water flowing down the mountains. Deborah's decision to attack the Canaanites at this time was vindicated, for the weather gave the Hebrew army, which was composed mainly of foot soldiers who were miserably ill-equipped as they did not even have sufficient light arms, a definite advantage over the mighty army of the enemy. Deborah highlighted the lack of equipment when she lamented, "...then was war in the gates; was there a shield or spear seen among forty thousand in Israel?"[88]

Nonetheless, the Canaanite army was routed and Sisera, who led the Canaanite army, fled and took refuge in the tent of Jael, the wife of Heber who belonged to the Kenite tribe[89] that had migrated with the Hebrews and had inhabited in the south of Palestine. He hid there, trusting that the Kenites being a tribe that had been friendly with Jabin, the king of Canaan, he would be safe there.[90] But his trust was misplaced, for Jael treacherously murdered him when he was asleep.[91] And that ended the war.

So Deborah succeeded in driving out the Canaanites from the territory of the Confederacy and the Hebrews occupied the land from which the Canaanites had been evicted and started cultivation there. But this was not the victory of Deborah alone. Deborah, no doubt, planned the strategy, but it was Barak who successfully executed it despite the lack of a properly trained army and adequate arms. And no less important was Jael's role, though treacherous, but all is well in love and war. So the credit for the victory has to go to Deborah-Barak duo as well as Jael. Deborah in her victory song expressed her gratitude to the Chauvinists that extended full support to the war effort and willingly offered their services at this crucial moment.[92] She also paid rich tribute to the men who valiantly and selflessly fought the Canaanites as well as to Jael, for the role she played in the victorious war.[93]

But there were some powerful tribes among the Hebrews that refused to cooperate with Deborah. Those who did not join the army led by Deborah and Barak were the Reubenites, the people of Gilead, the Danites, Asher and the inhabitants of Meroz[94] whom Deborah had approached for help. Interestingly, all the tribes who stayed away were connected with the Reubenites, including Asher who was also the son of Jacob in Zilpah and hence Reuben's stepbrother. Deborah's complaint about these people in her victory song exposed the chink in the Hebrew armour.[95] Nevertheless till Deborah died, there was peace in the land.

The exit of Deborah from the world's stage plunged Israel into another period of oppression. The fertile land that the Hebrews had occupied, displacing the Canaanites, was coveted by the Midianites, the Amalekites and a few other eastern tribes and naturally it led to a struggle for the control of that piece of land. The Hebrews were far outnumbered and the invaders swept across the land like a swarm of grasshoppers, taking away their crops and livestock and destroying everything that came their way. They drove the Hebrews out of the land, forcing them to take shelter in the nearby jungles with practically nothing to eat, for they were dispossessed and had no land to till.[96] So they approached the clergy to find a judge for them.[97] The clergy had learnt a lesson from the non-cooperation of the Reubenites with Deborah who was a prophetess and a sworn religio-purist. They thought that the Reubenites' opposition to the direct rule by the religio-purists was the reason for the non-cooperation.

So this time the clergy decided to choose a candidate from among the lay tribesmen and selected Gideon of the Manasseh tribe who was neither a Levite nor a prophet. This was a surprise choice. He and his family were apostates but the clergy advised him to repudiate Baal, the Canaanite god that he worshipped by desecrating the altar of that god,[98] which he did. Incidentally, that earned him the title "Jerubbaal"[99] and made him a hero in the eyes of the Yahwists. However, the clergy selected him because he came from a poor family and he was the poorest of all the family members.[100] Being a reconverted apostate and a man of low class, the clergy calculated, he would not be able to assert himself and they could easily keep him under their control. When the news of Gideon's daring sacrilegious act – daring because it was defiance of a god that the Canaanites considered "king and judge" of the universe – reached the Midianites, they were frightened. Expecting the Hebrews to launch an attack led by him, the Midianites along with the Alkamites and other allies pitched their camp in the valley of Jazreel, ready to meet any eventuality.

The clergy approved his judgeship and he was assured of the support of the clergy as well as the Chauvinists.[101] Now Gideon called upon the Hebrews to join him to fight the Midianites, and young men from the various Hebrew tribes came forward in large numbers in response to the call. The story of wool and dew is a figurative way of saying that he reassured the gathering that they would undoubtedly triumph over the enemy.[102] Gideon wanted only the committed and the courageous, few though they might be. So he told them that those who were sceptical about success and were scared could go back home. About two-thirds of the volunteers withdrew. But of the rest, Gideon wanted only those who were disciplined and would not question his authority. So he gave them a test[103] and he selected only those who were prepared to follow him and obey him implicitly. That was only a third of the existing number of men. Those who failed his test were asked to leave. Obviously, he was not thinking of a direct confrontation with the Midianites because he knew Israel was far outnumbered by them and that the enemy had a well-oiled military machine with superior arms and properly trained soldiers. He, therefore, planned a blitzkrieg, for he was sure that in a pitched, face to face battle the Confederate army would be pulverised.

In preparation, Gideon decided to scout the enemy camp and ascertain their strength and weaknesses, for which he decided to go himself in the night when those in the enemy camp would be fast asleep. But wary of going alone, he took Phurah,[104] one of his trusted soldiers, with him and together they went, when they heard a discussion between two soldiers that betrayed the nervousness of the enemy and their low morale.[105] Sharing that information with his men, he concluded saying "arise, the victory is ours."[106] Thus exuding full confidence, he assured them that he found the enemy quite nervous and could be defeated without doubt. Those words helped boost the morale of the Hebrew army.

He divided them into three groups and gave each man a trumpet and a jar with a torch in it and he instructed them on what they should do. Leading one of the groups he went down under cover of darkness and surrounded the enemy camp. Gideon blew his trumpet followed by the others and at the same time all of them broke their jars exposing the light. Seeing hundreds of lights around, they thought they had been surrounded by a large army of Israel and were panic-stricken. Pandemonium prevailed; the Midianite soldiers ran helter-skelter in total disarray and the Hebrew army drowned them in blood. Those who managed to escape the sword of the Hebrews, fled beyond the river Jordan but the pursuing men of Ephraim who were called up at the last moment captured two Midian princes and beheaded them.[107]

The whole story seems fictitious. The relevant verse does not speak of Gideon giving them swords, but it is preposterous to think that Gideon would be foolish enough to attack a formidable enemy without any kind of weapon whatsoever. However it is said later, when the enemy panicked the Israelites attacked them with swords. So obviously they had carried their swords too. There are various theories put forward to explain how a soldier could have been holding three things – a trumpet, a jar and a sword – at the same time. One theory is that the soldiers did not carry swords. By creating the impression of a huge army encircling the camp Gideon expected the Midianites to be panic-stricken and run away. That explains why he took only a small band of committed men equipped with only trumpets and torches hidden in the jars. This is rather a naïve explanation because the Midianite army was huge and the soldiers were battle wise. They would not be duped like that but would not flee without crossing swords. Another theory put forward to explain this is to suppose that two traditions got interwoven here, "one of which spoke of horns and swords, the other of which knew only of jars, torches and shouts."[108] This makes sense only if it is dovetailed with a tradition which said that it was so planned that the fleeing enemy was intercepted and annihilated by the reservists that Gideon had arranged a little away from the camp. But there is no proof to say that there was a tradition like that.

However, this problem can be solved by applying the principle of *lex parsimoniae*, or "the Ockham's razor," which advises to refrain from multiplying entities beyond what is absolutely necessary when there is more than one conflicting theory. Applying this tenet, it may be presumed that they had their swords in scabbards on their sides, for no sensible army commander would have ventured to attack enemy forces, that too a superior army, without at least a sword; and no soldier but a suicidal maniac would go to the battlefield without a weapon. The original author of this episode did not think it necessary to mention it just as it was not necessary to say that they were wearing clothes.

Whatever it was, this victory created a problem. The Ephraimites were a proud tribe and they took umbrage at Gideon for not initially associating them in the war against the Midianites.[109] When they complained about it, Gideon said that it was the Ephraimites who had captured Oreb and Zeeb, the generals of the Midian army. He added, what they had done at the end of the battle was more significant than what he did at the beginning.[110] That flattery satisfied their ego; they were pacified and did not press their complaint further. Gideon did not want to provoke Ephraim and create a schism in the Hebrew ranks when the tribe was in the midst of a war with the Midianites, for Zebah and Zalmunna, the two kings of Midian, were still at large. Contrary to his approach to Ephraim, he threatened retributive action against Succoth and Penuel when the people there refused to provide food to his war weary men. And he did punish them after he captured the two kings whom he executed, thus also avenging the slaying of his brothers by them in an earlier encounter.[111]

Recognising his achievements and the invaluable service he rendered to the tribe, the freemen of Israel offered him the office of hereditary king, saying "Rule over us, both you, and your son, and your son's son also."[112] This was a very significant development, for it shows that the Hebrews favouring monarchy were gaining strength and they were looking forward to changing their political structure. This was what the clergy had been trying to prevent all these years. Gideon, however, declined the offer.

A period of suspense followed Gideon's death as there was no judge then. Mosaic laws were broken with impunity and there was lawlessness in the land. So here and there the slaves had been revolting and production was in jeopardy; rivalry among the various Hebrew tribes had reached an explosive stage.[113] In spite of all that, significantly, this time the people did not approach the clergy to select a judge for them. They seemed to have turned their back on the priesthood and did not even want the clerics to have a hand in the selection. Most probably, they were thinking of having a king instead of a judge and they knew the clergy had not been in favour of monarchy. The priests must have thought that when the condition worsened, the freemen would go to them and at that time, they could anoint a religio-purist as judge. Sensing the mood of the people, Abimelech, whom Gideon begot through his concubine in Shechem, decided to claim the right to be the king before the people crowned one of his stepbrothers. Ambitious as he was, he acted with promptness and met the rich and influential lay freemen of Shechem, staking his claim to the highest office. Abimelech was, however, conscious of the fact that he was a usurper but that did not deter him from trying.

He planned his moves well and went to Shechem. He spoke to the freemen and convinced them of his ability to be the king. The absence of any other claimant and the indifference of the clergy forced the freemen to support him unconditionally because they were eager to have a king or at least a judge to maintain law and order. They were happy when Abimelech expressed a desire to be the king, for that was what they wanted. Nonetheless, Abimelech did not rule out Gideon's legitimate sons challenging his claim when they hear about his attempts, in which case, he knew, there was little chance of his getting the support of the freemen. The royalist freemen in general would naturally tend to favour them and he might be imprisoned or even executed. In order to obviate that danger, he thought of getting them out of the way for good. So he planned to liquidate Gideon's legitimate sons. He conspired with the affluent freemen in the city who provided him with the funds required for hiring mercenaries[114] to help him slay his stepbrothers. Immediately, he, along with the mercenaries, proceeded to Oprah, where his stepbrothers were and publicly beheaded all of them. It was a bloody *coup d'état*.

Returning to Shechem, in the assembly of the lay freemen of the city, "by the plain of the pillar that was in Shechem," he got himself invested as the king of Israel.[115] Significantly, he was not a nominee of the clergy; he had ignored the clergy altogether and did not seek its advice or support. He took over as king without being anointed by the clergy and the priesthood lost its hold on the government. Abimelech was not a religio-purist; he was a secular king. Meanwhile, Jotham, the youngest of Gideon's sons, who had escaped Abimelech's sword, heard of the news of his brothers' execution. Helpless as he was, Jotham who was in hiding went to Shechem and reminded the royalist freemen of how his father had fought for them and liberated them from the Midianite oppression, risking his life. He told them that by abetting the assassinations of Gideon's sons and elevating the son of Gideon's maidservant to the office of the king, they had done a great injustice to the house of Gideon.[116] But he did not stay there and challenge Abimelech, perhaps because he was not able to convince the freemen. He fled to Beer, lest Abimelech slew him too.

Abimelech, however, could not rule for long. The Chauvinists relentlessly carried out anti-Abimelech propaganda and succeeded in turning the royalists of Shechem against Abimelech.[117] The cause of the disenchantment of the freemen of Shechem with him is not mentioned but it may be surmised that they expected the king to be beholden to them and to help them enrich themselves further. They must also have expected to have a voice in the government but Abimelech seems to have ignored them after he became the king. Jotham's admonition also must have made them realise their mistake, though belatedly, in supporting Abimelech and helping him kill the legitimate successors. Three years elapsed without any problem. They hatched a plot to ambush and kill Abimelech and sent some professional killers to lie in wait at the top of the mountain. But Abimelech came to know of the conspiracy through his spies and he avoided going that way. Meanwhile, aware of the disenchantment of the freemen of Shechem, Gaal, son of Ebed, hoping he could get the support of the people moved into the city and raised the banner of revolt against the king. As expected, the royalists of Shechem threw their lot behind him. On being informed of the revolt by Zebul who was the governor of Shechem, Abimelech came up with his army and suppressed the rebellion.[118]

In vengeance, he set fire to the tower of Shechem, killing all the men and women who had supported Gaal and had taken shelter there, destroyed the city, and scattered salt all over the fields to make the land unfit for cultivation, thus making the city uninhabitable for good.[119] Archaeological evidence, however, does not corroborate the story that the city was destroyed and made uninhabitable. Excavations conducted in the early twentieth century have exposed the remains of a massive wall, surrounding the city and a building with a few rooms around a square courtyard dating back to *circa* the nineteenth century BCE. The period of the judges was supposed to be from *circa* 1220 to 1050 BCE and had Abimelech or any one destroyed Shechem to the extent described here, the ruins of an earlier period would not have existed.[120] However, the biblical story says, after slaughtering all the inhabitants of Shechem, he proceeded to Thebez and overran the city but in the process died of an accident.

After Abimelech, two others, Tola of the clan of Issachar and Jair, a Gileadite, ruled Israel. Both these judges tended to be secular because they were chosen by the lay freemen and held the office of the judge at the pleasure of those freemen. During this period, which according to the Bible lasted for forty-five years, no external aggression or internal disturbances had been recorded.[121] Presumably, there was peace in the land.

Soon after Jair's death, disturbances started, for there was no one to maintain law and order. As a result of sporadic revolts by the slaves and the lawlessness that followed, production went down. In spite of the people approaching the clergy,[122] the priests refused to help find a person to judge. They were angry because for the past several years the priesthood was marginalised. So they decided to teach the freemen a lesson.[123] This anarchic situation was taken advantage of by the Philistines and the Ammonites. They overran the territories "on the other side of the Jordan in the land of the Amorites, which is in Gilead." And laying claim to the territories occupied by the Judaists, Benjaminites and Ephraimites, the invaders harassed them. So the Hebrews requested the clergy to appoint a judge who would be able to liberate them.[124] When they continued to plead for help, the clergy asked the freemen of Gilead to find a suitable person from among them to be anointed as judge.

They could not come to an agreement till the Ammonites attacked them, when they went to invite Jephthath. They did not want him to be the judge but only to be the commander of their army to fight the Ammonites.[125] Jephthah was a Gileadite. He was the son of Gilead,[126] born to a harlot but was reputed to be "a mighty man of valour." His stepbrothers had disowned him, saying, "You shall not inherit in our father's house for you are the son of a strange woman."[127] He was expelled from the house, but not because he was born to a prostitute. The only reason for disowning him was to avoid giving him a share of the property and that he was born of a "strange woman" was a lame excuse to deprive him of the legitimate share of his father's property. The Hebrews were now standing on the doorsteps of civilisation as it were, when property had become an obsession. As Morgan states, "its dominance as a passion over all other passions marks the commencement of civilisation."[128] It was that strong attachment to property that prompted Gilead's sons to drive away Jephthah from their house.

Jephthah's antecedents were anything but praiseworthy. Since leaving his home and hometown he had been a vagrant, idling away his time in the company of anti-social elements.[129] Nevertheless, no one had any objection to accepting him as commander of the Confederate army and the freemen of Gilead went and persuaded him to help defend them against the Ammonites. He agreed to do it on condition that he was made the judge. The royalists had no choice now, for they were eager to free themselves from oppression. They, therefore, decided to cooperate with Jephthah. At his formal investiture at Mizpeh, the Bible states, he "...uttered all his words before the Lord...,"[130] which may be taken to mean that he agreed to accept the supremacy of the clergy and so the clergy was happy. After being anointed by the clergy as judge, he set to work.

Hoping to settle the dispute without bloodshed, his first act was to send messages to the Ammonites explaining to them the historical circumstances that led to the Hebrews coming in possession of the land of the Ammonites.[131] And he asked them why they coveted what had legitimately been the Hebrews' instead of being satisfied with what had been their territory so far.[132] But his diplomatic overtures were in vain; the king of the Ammonites rejected his offer of peacefully settling the issue and Jephthah was compelled to declare war against the Ammonites. Before declaring war against the Ammonites, he requested the clergy to persuade the Chauvinists to cooperate with him and obviously urged by the clergy, the Chauvinists provided him with men and money.[133] That helped him gather and equip a strong army. In the war that ensued Jephthah defeated the Ammonites, and the Hebrews were free again.

This victory, however, seems to have raised hackles in the Ephraimites. It may be recalled that after Gideon's victory over the Midianites, when Gideon who was of humble birth was questioned by the Ephraimites why he did not invite them at the beginning itself to join him in waging the war, he was apologetic. A similar situation had arisen now, for they perhaps thought that this victory would give the Gileadites, whom Ephraim considered a clan inferior to them, a feeling of superiority. So they asked Jephthah the same question that they had asked Gideon and went a step further. They wounded his self-respect, saying, "You Gileadites are fugitives of Ephraim among the Manassites."[134] Although infuriated by this insult Jephthah, the good diplomat that he was, patiently argued with them justifying himself but when he found that the Ephraimites did not accept his explanation he, who was of a different mettle from Gideon, challenged them and drew the sword. In the battle that followed thousands of Ephraimites were killed and were thus humbled.

A period of lull followed the death of Jephthah when three judges, Ibzan, Elon and Abdon, all of whom had many sons, succeeded one after the other within a span of a few years – twenty-five years according to the biblical chronology.[135] All these three judges were not religio-purists, for they were not appointed by the clergy and they did not seek the advice or aid of the clergy. Probably that was the reason why the Bible did not elaborate on the history of that period. After Abdon, the Bible presents a character called Samson as judge. He is a palpably fictitious character whose entire life from birth to death has been mythicised. Born of a barren woman by the grace of god who said, "he shall be a Nazirite[136]...and he shall begin to deliver Israel out of the hand of the Philistines,"[137] Samson is said to have judged when the Philistines were trying to push themselves into the Confederate territory. God's prophecy was not fulfilled, for Samson did not succeed in liberating the Hebrews.

Most biblical scholars themselves regard him as just a legendary folk hero. His strength, it is said, lay in his hair and that is evidently a myth. Comparing his long hair to the sun's rays, some scholars tend to consider Samson a mythical figure, etymologically related to the Canaanite sun-god, Shemesh, whose shrine was in the Danites's original territory.[138]He may be considered a mythical personification of the Hebrews, not because the Hebrews were a very powerful tribe at that time. His dogged but unsuccessful resistance to the Philistine incursions symbolises the ferocity of the losing war that the Hebrews waged against the Philistines. In short, the story of Samson is an allegorical presentation of the Hebrew-Philistine conflict and the capitulation of the Hebrews. As pointed out in Chapter 1, "The Book of Books," the intention of the composers of the Bible was the glorification of the Hebrew tribe. The presentation of Samson, a Hebrew and that too a Nazirite, as a kind of superman with Herculean strength and his exploits were evidently meant to cover up the ignominy of the Hebrews' defeat and humiliation at the hands of the Philistines while, at the same time, giving the readers an exaggerated picture of the Hebrews' power and prowess. And the story of Delilah is intended to give the readers the impression that the Philistines defeated the Hebrews only by guile. Incidentally, it may be pointed out that the story of Delilah reveals that even in those days, sex had been used as a means of espionage and to find out the enemy's military secrets.

It was a difficult period for the Hebrew tribes, which with all its exaggerated power symbolised by Samson, failed to stop the Philistine incursions into the Confederate territory. The Philistines had even carved out for themselves an enclave within the territory occupied by the Confederacy but the Hebrews could only look on and grit their teeth. They could not find another judge to lead them in a war with the Philistines and that had left the Hebrews hopeless and helpless. This was the opportunity for the clergy to capture power for which they had been waiting on the sidelines. And they did not miss it. Ever since the period of Abimelech, power had been slipping off their hands, off and on, as the forces that were opposed to religio-purism had made much headway among the people and had been ignoring the clergy.

At this critical juncture in the history of the Hebrews, when the tribe seemed to be drifting away from religio-purism, there arose a Nazirite. His birth itself has been mythicised[139] like those of John the Baptist and Jesus, for he is said to have been born to Hannah, a barren woman, who became pregnant by the grace of god and gave birth to a son. That child was Samuel. His ancestry has been traced to Aaron and even as a child he "did minister to the Lord before Eli the priest" at Shiloh. In the person of Samuel, the Chauvinists found an opportunity to assert themselves and expand their shrunken base.

Basically a priest, his oracles, it was claimed, conveyed god's will and as a spokesman of god he was believed to have the power to liaise with god to help man. This made him a prophet in the eyes of the people "and the child Samuel grew on, and was in favour both with the Lord and also with men."[140] As he grew up, he became popular with all sections of the people. That kindled his ambition and he planned to cash in on his popularity to declare himself the judge. The priesthood also was waiting for an opportunity like this for one of the priestly class to take cver the judgeship of the tribe. The political situation too was favourable because no one had come forward to lead the Hebrews against the Philistines and the priesthood encouraged Samuel to take over as the judge.[141] Assuming on his own the leadership of the Confederacy, he sent word to the freemen of all tribes to be prepared to wage a war against the Philistines.[142] Although he was not formally anointed as the judge, he had been judging all these years and was quite popular too and the Hebrews had accepted him as its judge. So no one raised any objection when he came forward to lead them in a war against the Philistines. They responded to his call happily and a large army was formed. As per his instructions, the Confederate army pitched its camp at Ebenezer while the Philistines encamped at Aphek. In the battle that followed the Confederate army suffered heavy casualties and its defeat became a rout.

The Confederacy was plunged in a state of anarchy. It is said "Also the Ark of the Lord was captured..."[143] This is significant, for it has a social implication. The "ark" in the synagogues and temples of the Hebrews is a cabinet for keeping holy scrolls of the Pentateuch. The Book of the Covenant in which Moses had written down the laws, is in these scrolls.[144] The Ark of the Covenant was a wooden chest in which the Hebrews kept the two stone tablets on which the Ten Commandments were engraved. It was a symbol that reminded the Hebrews of the necessity to adhere to the Mosaic laws, which ensured the stability of the society, cohesion of the tribes and the peaceful life of the people. The absence of the ark indicates that these laws were being flouted and law and order had broken down totally. So the Ark is the symbol of law and order. In short, the situation in the Confederacy had deteriorated so much that lawlessness had touched the nadir and there was utter chaos threatening the social structure itself. This implies fratricidal conflicts among the Hebrews and uprisings by the slaves.

Samuel, therefore, decided to put down the revolt, broker inter-tribal amity among the Hebrews and restore normalcy of life in general. That he succeeded in suppressing the slaves, negotiating an end to fratricidal clashes among the Hebrews and establishing peace in the Confederacy is implicit in the return of the Ark of the Covenant.[145] He spoke to all Hebrew tribes constituting the Confederacy and impressed upon them the imperative for adherence to Mosaic laws, discipline and unity. That alone, he said, would help emancipate them from Philistine oppression.[146] The freemen of the Confederacy, realising their mistake, promised to abide by the Mosaic Code of Laws and peace was restored.[147] Samuel, now, regrouped the Israelite forces at Mizpeh, planning to mount an attack on the Philistines. On getting intelligence that the Confederate troops had gathered at Mizpeh, the Philistines launched a pre-emptive attack but the Hebrews fought back valiantly and defeated the Philistines. They pursued the fleeing Philistines and inflicted heavy casualties on them. Occupying the cities that the Philistines had captured from them earlier, they entered into a peace treaty with the Amorites.[148] Samuel now confirmed himself as the judge and the freemen who were happy to have got their city back, gladly accepted him, as it was he who had helped them get the Philistines off their back.

Samuel, then, went back to Ramah and resumed his work as the judge. When he was too old to work, he appointed his sons as judges but they "turned after lucre, and took bribes, and perverted judgment."[149] The freemen were unhappy and they came to Samuel and complained to him about the unbecoming behavior of his sons. The royalists said, "...now make us a king to judge us like all the nations."[149] They wanted him to name a king for the Hebrews similar to the monarchs of the other contemporary tribes. Samuel being a prophet and a member of the clergy was a religio-purist and naturally, did not want the reins of government to go out of the hands of the priestly class. In the minds of the religio-purists, monarchy was associated with religio-liberalism – maybe because all the monarchs they had seen were those "who served other gods." So if the Confederacy were to be transformed into a monarchy, in their minds, it amounted to handing over the Confederacy to the forces of religio-liberalism.

Samuel knew it could not be guaranteed that the king would remain a religio-purist. He would be independent and all-powerful and the clergy would be a helpless witness if the king turned out to be a religio-liberal. So it was the fear that the religio-purists would lose their hold on the government that prompted Samuel to discourage the Hebrew freemen from turning the Confederacy into a kingdom. It was for the same reason that after the death of Joshua, the clergy refrained from establishing a monarchy and designated the successor "judge," thus restricting his powers to maintenance of law and order and defence of the Confederacy. But the institution of private property and slavery called for a political state presided over by an absolute monarch. It could not be wished away, for the prevailing social condition of the Hebrews cried for monarchy.

Samuel expostulated with those who wanted to establish a monarchy the foolishness of installing a king. He said the king who would have absolute power might take away all their possessions and hand them over to his favourites and he might even take their kith and kin to serve him as slaves. Undoubtedly what he said was true, for all kings were despotic. However much Samuel tried to persuade the freemen to give up the idea, they were adamant. They insisted that they wanted a king who they said would be able to defend them against their enemies and maintain law and order. Above all, the freemen perhaps felt that an absolute monarch would be the best guarantee against disintegration of the slave system.

In conclusion, it must be emphasised again that the Book of Judges like all other Books in the Bible is not a true history of the period. The story of the judges should not be misconstrued as a chronicle of the events of those times, although it seemingly is. These are episodes composed like all other biblical episodes, by mixing perhaps a little of history with a heavy dose of myths and legends intended to enhance faith in a particular god, that is, Yahweh. There are anachronisms, exaggerations, mythifications of protagonists, whose historicity has not been confirmed and even falsification of history; yet we get a faint picture of the societal structure of the biblical period from these episodes.

NOTES

1. Josh. 1:1, 2. "...the Lord spoke to Joshua, the son of Nun, Moses' minister, saying, Moses my servant is dead; now, therefore arise, go over this Jordan..." (Italics added). "The Lord," the pronoun "I" or "my" referring to god in this episode denotes chief priest.
2. Josh. 1:7. "...that you may observe to do according to all the law, which Moses my servant commanded you; do not turn to the right hand or to the left..." (Italics added)

3. Josh. 1:5. "...as I was with Moses, so I will be with you: I will not fail you, nor forsake you."
4. Josh. 1:8. The book of the law shall not depart from your mouth; but you shall meditate on it day and night that you may observe to do according to all that is written in it; for then you shall make your way prosperous..."
5. Josh. 1:16.
6. Josh. 1:18.
7. Josh. 2:1.
8. Josh. 2:9-11. "I know that the Lord has given you the land and your terror is fallen on us and that all the inhabitants of the land fainthearted because of you"..."And as soon as we had heard these things, our hearts did melt, neither did there remain any more courage in any man because of you..."
9. Josh. 3:5-6.
10. Josh. 3:7. "and the Lord said to Joshua, this day will I begin to exalt you in the eyes of all Israel, that they may know that, as I was with Moses, so I will be with you."
11. Josh. 3:9-10. "...Hereby you shall know that the living God is among you, and that he will without fail drive out from before you, the Canaanites, and the Hittites, and the Perizzites, and the Girgashites, and the Amorites and the Jebusites."
12. Josh. 3:13.
13. Josh. 3:15, 16. "And as they that bore the ark come to see Jordan, and the feet of the priests who bore the ark dipped in the edge of the water..." "That the waters which came down from above stood and rose up upon a heap very far from the city Adam...and those that came down toward the sea of the plain...were cut off and the people passed over."
14. J.M. Haynes, et al. Evidence for ground rupturing earthquakes on the northern Wadi Arab fault at the archaeological site of Qasr Tilah, Dead Sea transform fault system, Jordan. In *Journal of Seismology*, Netherlands, V. 10, No. 4, October 2006, pp. 415-430. (e-version in English).
15. Tina M. Niemi, and Zvi Ben-Avraham, Evidence for Jericho earthquakes from slumped sediments of the Jordan River delta in the Dead Sea. In *Geology* (Journal of the Geological Society of America), V. 22, No. 5, May 1994, p. 395.
16. Josh. 3:13-17/4:19.
17. Josh. 6:20.
18. I. Wilson, *The Bible is History*, Washington DC, 1999, p. 72.

19. Josh. 6:24-25.
20. W. Keller, *The Bible as History*, London, 1957, p. 159.
21. D.A. Carson, et al., Eds., New Bible Commentary, Secunderabad, 2003, p. 22.
22. Josh. 6:19/9:24. "...the silver and the gold and the vessels of brass and of iron, they put into the treasury of the house of the Lord."
23. Num. 31:50-51.
24. Josh. 7:21.
25. Josh. 7:19. "My son, give, I beg you, glory to the Lord God of Israel and make confession to him..."
26. Josh. 7:10-15.
27. Josh. 7:25.
28. Josh. 6:27.
29. Josh. 8:1. "...Fear not...take all the people of war with you...I have given into your hand the king of Ai and his people and his city and his land."
30. Josh. 8:2. "And you shall do to Ai...as you did to Jericho...lay thee an ambush for the city behind it."
31. Josh. 8:18. :"...stretch out the spear that is in your hand toward Ai..."
32. Josh. 8:26-29.
33. Josh. 9:1.
34. Please note that these people were also referred to as Hivites (vide Josh. 9:7) and as "the remnant of the Amorites." (vide II Sam.21:2.)
35. Josh. 9:4-15. "And Joshua made peace with them, and let them live... and the princes of the congregation swore to them..."
36. Josh. 9:21. "And the princes said to them; we will even let them live...let them be hewers of wood and carriers of water for the congregation..." Josh. 9:23. "...for the house of my God."
37. Josh. 10:2-4.
38. Josh. 10:8. "And the Lord said to Joshua, fear them not, for I have delivered them into your hand..."
39. Josh. 10:11. "And it came to pass, as they fled from before Israel...the Lord cast down great stones from heaven upon them...they were more which died with hailstones than they whom the children of Israel slew with the sword."
40. Josh. 10:12, 13. "And the sun stood still and the Moon stayed until the people had avenged themselves upon their enemies. Is not this written in the book of Jasher?"
41. Josh. 11:1-2.
42. I. Wilson, *The Bible is History*, Washington DC, 1999, pp. 66, 68, 82-83.

43. R.H. Smith, The Book of Joshua, In Old Testament History, ed. by C.M. Laymon, Nashville,1983, p. 23. It must be borne in mind that Joshua is a mythological character.
44. R.H. Smith, ibid., pp. 25-26.
45. R.H. Smith, ibid., pp. 3-4.
46. A. Robertson, The Origins of Christianity, London, 1953, p. 21. The interested readers are referred to *The Literature of the Old Testament* by G.F. Moore and *The Historical Background of the Bible* by J.N. Schofield for detailed examination of the problem.
47. Josh. 13:1, 7. "...the Lord said to him...divide this land for an inheritance to the nine tribes, and the half tribe of Mannasseh..."
48. Josh. 24:2-13.
49. Josh. 24:14 "Now therefore fear the Lord, and serve him in sincerity...and out away the gods which your fathers served on the other side of the flood, and in Egypt..."
50. Josh. 24:19. "...You cannot serve the Lord; for he is a holy God; he is a jealous God; he will not forgive your transgressions nor your sins."
51. Josh. 24:20. "If you forsake the Lord, and serve strange gods, then he will turn and punish you, and consume you after he has done you good."
52. Josh. 24:24.
53. Josh. 24:25-26.
54. R.H. Smith, The Book of Judges. In *Old Testament History*, Nashville, 1983, p. 43.
55. I. Asimov, *Guide to the Bible*, New York, 1981, p. 230.
56. M. Grant, *The History of Ancient Israel*, Charles Scribner's Sons, New York, 1984, p. 56.
57. Judg. 9:31. "And he sent messengers to Abimalech secretly, saying, take note! Gal the son of Ebad, and his brothers have come to Shechem, and here they are, fortifying the city against you."
58. In those days there were mercenaries who were prepared even to kill for money just as there are "professional" assassins or murderers even today. Those who helped Abimalech to kill his stepbrothers were such mercenaries (vide Judg. 9:4). The Belials who repudiated Saul, for example, were also a class of thugs like that (vide I Sam. 10:27).
59. Judg. 1:1. "...the children of Israel asked the Lord, saying, Who shall go up for us against Canaanites first..."
60. Judg. 1:2. "...the Lord said, Judah shall go up..."
61. Judg. 1:17, 28, 30.
62. Judg. 1:21-36.
63. Judg. 3:5-8.

64. It may be recalled that Caleb, son of Jephunneh, along with Joshua was one of the twelve spies that Moses sent to Canaan.
65. Judg. 1:12.
66. Judg. 3:7, 8. "And the children of Israel did evil in the sight of the Lord...and served Baalim...Therefore the anger of the Lord was hot against Israel and he sold them into the hand of Chishan-rishathaim, King of Mesopotamia...and served Chushan-rishathaim eight years.
67. Judg. 3:9. "...when the children of Israel cried out to the Lord, the Lord raised up a deliverer to the children of Israel, who delivered them, Othniel (and)...And the sprit of the Lord came upon him..." (Italics added)
68. Judg. 3:10. These words indicate that the clergy approved of his choice as the judge. There is a mix-up of two traditions in this story but it is not discussed here as it is beside the point. After all, these stories are not to be taken as true history although there could be some historical facts in them.
69. Judg. 3:18. "And when the Lord raised them up judges, then the Lord was with the judge..." The Lord in this context denotes "the clergy" and this means the clergy supports the judge.
70. Judg. 3:11. The Bible specifies that he judged for forty years. Please note that the historicity of the judge as well as the number of years each judge is said to have ruled, are questionable.
71. There is a controversy regarding the city. Some scholars think it was Jericho because that was the city nearest to Moab. But this view is disputed on the ground that there is no archaeological evidence that Jericho was inhabited then; in fact, it is doubtful if it even existed at that time. So let us repeat what is given in the Bible, and leave it to research scholars to determine which was the "city of palm trees" referred to here.
72. Judg. 3:12-14.
73. Judg. 3:15. "...when the children of Israel cried out to the Lord, the Lord raised them up a deliverer..."
74. Judg. 3:27-30.
75. R.H. Smith, Interpreters' Concise Commentary, V.2., *Old Testament History*, Nashville, 1983, p. 52.
76. Judg. 3:31.
77. Judg. 4:1-2. "...the children of Israel again did evil in the sight of the Lord...And the Lord sold them into the hand of Jabin..." Joshua was supposed to have defeated Jabin and destroyed Hazor (vide Josh. 1:1-11).
78. It was pointed out when dealing with Joshua that the story of Jabin

was anachronistically included there to boost the image of Joshua. Needless to repeat that there is no evidence about the historicity of the biblical character called Joshua. This is discussed elsewhere in the text.

79. Judg. 4:2, 3.
80. Judg. 4:3. "...the children of Israel cried out to the Lord..."
81. Judg. 4:4.
82. Judg. 4:6. "...Hath not the Lord God of Israel commanded, saying Go and draw toward mount Tabor and take with thee ten thousand men...?"
83. Judg. 5:4-5. "...the heavens dropped, the clouds also dropped water. The mountains melted..."
84. Judg. 5:20. "They fought from heaven; the stars in their courses fought against Sisera."
85. Judg. 4:7. "...I will send the army of Sisera, the captain of Jabin's army with his chariots to confront you at the River Kishon; and I will deliver them into your hand."
86. Judg. 5:21.
87. Judg. 5:8.
88. Kenite was the tribe to which Moses' father belonged.
89. Judg. 5:24-25.
90. Judg. 5:26-27.
91. Judg. 5:3, 9. "...I will sing to the Lord, I will sing praise to the Lord God of Israel...My heart is towards the governors of Israel, that offered themselves willingly..."
92. Judg. 5:18-30.
93. Meroz refers to the inhabitants of a plain in the north of Palestine. Meroz is mentioned in the Bible in many contexts.
94. Judg. 5:15-17.
95. Judg. 6:1-5. "...because of the Midianites the children of Israel made them the dens which are in the mountains, and caves, and strongholds."
96. Judg. 6:7. "...the children of Israel cried out to the Lord."
97. Judg. 6:25-28.
98. Judg. 6:32. The meaning of the word, Jerboa, given in the Bible dictionary is "he that strive with Baal" or "he who defies Baal," implying he is equal to the god, Baal.
99. Judg. 6:15. "...Oh my Lord, how can I save Israel? Behold my family is poor in Manasseh and I am the poorest in my father's house."
100. Judg. 6:34. "The spirit of the Lord came upon Gideon..."
101. Judg. 6:36-40.
102. Judg. 7:4. "And the Lord said to Gideon, The people are yet too many; bring them down to the waters, and I shall try them..."

103. Judg. 7:9-11. "...the Lord said to him...you go down with Phurah your servant...And you shall hear what they say..."
104. Judg. 7:13-14.
105. Judg. 7:15. "Arise; for this Lord has delivered into your hand the host of Midian."
106. Judg. 7:10-25.
107. R.H. Smith, The Book of the Judges. In *Old Testament History*, ed. by C.M.Laymon, Nashville1983, p. 61.
108. Judg. 8:1.
109. Judg. 8:3.
110. Judg. 8:14-19.
111. Judg. 8:22.
112. Judg. 8:33, 34. "The children of Israel turned to other Gods...and remembered not the Lord, their God..."
113. Judg. 9:1-4. "...with which Abimalech hired worthless and reckless men..."
114. Judg. 9:5-6.
115. Judg. 9:16-20.
116. Judg. 9:23. "...God sent an evil spirit between Abimalech and the men of Shechem..."
117. Judg. 9:39-41.
118. Judg. 9:45-49.
119. W. Keller, *The Bible as History*, London, 1957, p. 81. The excavations were conducted by a German archaeologist Ernst Sellin.
120. Judg. 10:1-5.
121. Judg. 10:6. "...the children of Israel cried out to the Lord, saying we have sinned..."
122. Judg. 10:7-8. "...the anger of the Lord was hot against Israel and he sold them into the hands of the Philistines and into the hands of the children of Ammon."
123. Judg. 10:10. "And the children of Israel cried out to the Lord, saying...we have forsaken our God and also served Balaam..."
124. Judg. 11:5.
125. Gilead is the eponym of the Gileadites and the grandson of Manasseh.
126. Judg. 11:2.
127. L.H. Morgan, *Ancient Society*, Palo Alto, 1978, p. 6.
128. Judg. 11:2-3.
129. Judg. 11:8-11.
130. Judg. 11:112-23.
131. Judg. 11:24. "Wilt not thou possess that which Chemosh thy God giveth thee to possess?"

132. Judg. 11:29. "Then the spirit of the Lord came upon Jephthah..."
133. Judg. 12:4.
134. Judg. 12:8-15.
135. Num. 6:2-21. It was, so to say, a Yahwist religious order, Nazorite, Nazirite or Nazarite means "consecrated" – a Jew who had consecrated himself/herself and vowed abstinence for the purpose of some special service. A Nazirite was expected to abstain from alcohol, avoid touching a dead body and using a razor. (See also fn.40 in Chapter 8, 'Anti-Imperialist Movements')
136. Judg. 13:3, 5.
137. M. Grant, *The History of Ancient Israel*, New York, 1984, p. 69.
138. I Sam. 1:17-20.
139. I Sam. 2:26.
140. I Sam. 3:21. "...for the Lord revealed himself to Samuel in Shiloh by the word of the Lord."
141. I Sam. 4:1.
142. I Sam. 4:11.
143. The canonicity of the five books that these scrolls comprise has never been called into question by the Hebrews. The Christians, both the Catholics and the Protestants, also have never disputed the canonicity of the Pentateuch.
144. I Sam. 6:8, 14. "...take the ark of the Lord, and lay it upon the cart...and send it away...and the cart came into the field of Joshua, a Bethshemite..."
145. I Sam. 7:3. "...if you do return to the Lord with all your hearts...he will deliver you out of the hand of the Philistines."
146. I Sam. 7:1, 4. "And the men of Kirjathjearim came and fetched up the ark of the Lord...Then the children of Israel did put away Baalim and Ashtaroth and served the Lord only."
147. I Sam. 7:5-14.
148. I Sam. 8:1-3.
149. I Sam. 8:5.

Part Three

THE ERA OF KINGDOMS AND EMPIRES

6

Factitious Monarchy

Though Samuel felt apprehensive about the consequences of establishing monarchy, in a way he was happy the elders had entrusted him with the task of looking for a suitable person to be the king of Israel. He thought of a clever plan and that was to find a man from among the non-Levites who would be dependent on the clergy. That would satisfy the people at large while ensuring the control of the priesthood on the government. And to make sure that *he* had a voice in the government, he would bring in a person whom he would be able to influence and who would carry out his orders. So his intention was to install his "puppet" on the throne! In that way, he thought, he could rule through proxy and thus the real power would remain in the hands of the clergy, while the people would be under the impression that the king, free from the influence of the clergy, was ruling Israel. So the best solution to the problem was to choose a naïve young man from an insignificant tribe and of a humble birth.

If a member of a noble family of one of the powerful tribes were selected, the clergy would not be able to control him and the power that it wielded now would be lost for good. As he was trying to think of a suitable person, suddenly one name came to his mind. Saul! Yes, son of Kish[1] of the Benjaminite clan![2] He would be the right person who would fill the bill perfectly; he could be anointed as the king of Israel. There was no reason for considering this person for the office of the king except that he was *not* of a noble family and as such would be beholden to the clergy. Obviously, Samuel knew the Benjaminite clan of Kish and perhaps, had even known Kish personally, for otherwise, Saul's name would not have occurred to him.

But he did not want the people to know that Kish and his clan had been known to him. The success of this plan, Samuel knew, depended on duplicity – secrecy but pretense of transparency – as a matter of policy in the selection of the king. He would say it was god's choice and that he had no voice in the matter. He knew that as he was considered a prophet, the lay freemen, not only the religio-purist Chauvinists but also the Liberals would believe him. He also did not want them to think that he was being autocratic by thrusting on them a person of his choice without consulting them. So he would pretend that he was consulting them and make them believe that it was their choice and not his. He would, therefore, present Saul for ratification by the tribe.

Sometimes facts seem stranger than fiction, for the circumstances under which Samuel and Saul met had a dramatic touch. Kish had lost a few donkeys, for which Saul along with their servant had been searching. They roamed all over the place – in the hill country of Ephraim, the land of Shalisha, and the land of Shalim – looking for the lost animals, in vain. Continuing their search, they passed through the territory of the Benjaminites and reached the land of Zuph on the northern border of Benjamin but did not find the asses anywhere. Losing all hopes of finding the animals, Saul decided to go back home, when his servant said he had heard of "a man of God...all that he says comes surely to pass."[3] He added that this 'man of god' lived in the city of Ramah and he would be able to divine where the donkeys were. At his insistence Saul decided to meet that seer and both of them were heading to Ramah.

Samuel was, then, walking towards the hill, obviously, on his way to the land of the Benjaminites to meet Kish and speak to him about his decision to anoint Saul as the king of the Hebrews. But when he reached the city gate, to his surprise, he saw a man resembling Saul coming towards him. Samuel would have seen the boy before when he had been to meet Kish for some reason or other, for otherwise he would not have recognised him. It was Saul himself, no doubt, he thought.[4] What a surprise! Well, he was saved of the trouble of making a journey all the way to Kish's house. Anyway, on seeing Saul walking towards the city, Samuel waited at the city gate.

But neither Saul nor his servant had seen Samuel earlier; Saul had not even heard of him. Saul had had no opportunity to go out of his native city, let alone to Ramah where Samuel was based. Possibly Saul, who was perhaps only a boy then, might have been playing or grazing Kish's asses when Samuel called on them and would not have noticed the visitor. Saul and his servant did not know where "the man of God" stayed in the city. When they saw Samuel standing at the gate of the city, not knowing that this was the person that they were looking for, they went up to him and inquired of him where Samuel the seer was. "I am the seer,"[5] said Samuel and when they said they had come to meet him, he invited them to stay with him that day.

Saul told Samuel the purpose of his visit. Samuel just shrugged it off saying that the animals would be found and told him not to be bothered about such small matters now. There was more important news, he said. And as he was walking back to his house with Saul and his servant, he said that all Hebrew tribes were looking forward to seeing Saul and were thinking of his family.[6] Saul was flabbergasted. He thought Samuel had mistaken him for some other person, for he was not such a celebrity or an important personality for the whole of Confederacy to be waiting to see him. He mumbled that he was a Benjaminite, the smallest of the Hebrew tribes and his family "the least of all the families of the tribe of Benjamin."[7] And he wondered how he and his family had become so important that the entire Israel was thinking of them. Samuel did not reply but walked on, lost in thought. On reaching home Samuel asked his servant to serve dinner and after dinner "Samuel conferred with Saul on the top of the house,"[8] when presumably he told Saul that the elders of the Confederacy had delegated to him the task of finding a man to be their king. He added he could not think of a more suitable person than Saul for ruling the Confederacy and told him to keep this matter strictly confidential until it was announced and approved by the entire tribe.

The next day early in the morning when Saul was returning home with his servant Samuel walked with them up to the city gate to see them off. Asking the servant to walk ahead, for he did not want the servant to see what he was doing, Samuel "took a vial of oil and poured it on his (Saul's) head and kissed him," thus anointing him as the king of Israel.[9] Samuel, then, bade him farewell. After anointing him, Samuel made him understand that it was the clergy that had given him the crown and that he would have the support of the clergy.[10] This was necessary because all these years Israel had been ruled by judges, most of whom were appointed by the clergy. Now when a member of the non-Levite tribe was being made the king, he should know that he was being appointed by the clergy and that he was subordinate to the clergy. On reaching home, when Saul's uncle asked him about his visit to Samuel, Saul told him everything "but not the matter of the kingdom, about which Samuel spoke" because Samuel had sworn him to secrecy.[11]

Although in Ramah, Samuel had anointed Saul as king, he wanted to make the tribes of Israel feel that the choice was theirs. So he called a convention of the tribes of Israel at Mizpah and presented Saul as god's choice, which was approved by the people shouting in unison "God save the king."[12] As could be expected, some dissenting voices were heard, for "the children of Belial said, how shall this man save us?" The "children of Belial"[13] as the Bible refers to them, were a class of criminals, rapists and such other anti-social elements, in one word, the outlaws who did not want a strong ruler. They feared that a strong ruler would be an impediment to their anti-social activities. Naturally, "they despised him, and brought him no presents. But he held his peace."[14] Their refusal to pay tributes to the king was tantamount to rejecting the king and refusing to endorse the establishment of a strong ruler. The tribesmen in general and Saul too understood the reason for their opposition. The vast majority of the tribesmen endorsed Saul, who then went back to Gibeah.

Socially and politically, this was a turning point in the history of the Hebrews. The tribe had now established monarchy and laid the foundation of a full-fledged political state. The Hebrews had thus entered the stage of civilisation in all its aspects. In this form of social organisation, the tribe became irrelevant and the people identified themselves with the territory that is, the kingdom. It was ruled by a king with the help of a council of ministers, a bureaucracy, a police force, a standing army and such other instruments of governance, all of which constituted what came to be called the state. All these paraphernalia of a state were maintained by taxes collected from the people. But the Hebrews continued to identify themselves with their tribes, which, therefore, did not integrate themselves into a cohesive unit, with the result the monarchic state never struck deep roots in the Hebrew society.

The immediate problem that Saul, the new king, faced was external aggression. Saul had to prove himself equal to the task and he soon got an opportunity for it when "Nahash the Ammonite came up and encamped against Jabesh-gilead," a city east of the river Jordan, within the territory of Manasseh. Jabesh-gileadites were not hopeful of getting Israel's help because Israel itself was burdened with the Philistines on its back. Samuel the judge was too old and had failed to push out the Philistines and the insistence of the tribe to find a king was an open expression of lack of confidence in Samuel's leadership. And to cap it all, Samuel had chosen an unknown person, a petty farmer as king who had no experience of governance and had never seen a war front. So they thought that seeking the king's help would be of no use and decided to enter into a pact with the enemy. Nahash's condition for the pact was not just harsh but inhuman; he demanded of the Jabesh-gileadites the right eye of everyone in the city or face invasion. It was to be gouged out as a warning to the Hebrews.

The Jabesh-gileadites agreed but asked Nahesh to give them seven days to think it over, hoping that in the meantime they could try to get King Saul's help – like a drowning man clutching at a straw – and they sent a messenger to Saul in Gibeah. Saul immediately sent messengers to all tribes of Israel to send young men to follow him and Samuel to fight the Ammonites who had threatened the Jabesh-gileadites. The messengers carried with them a yoke of oxen cut in pieces. This broken yoke indicated a stern warning that the land of those refusing to come would be expropriated.[15] The yoke of oxen symbolises farming and a broken yoke indicates preventing tilling of the soil or cultivation, which can be done only by taking away the land from them, thereby depriving them of their means of livelihood. Agriculture was the main occupation of the Hebrews at that time and so this threat had its effect. All able-bodied men volunteered and an army of thousands of men was ready within twenty-four hours. The very next day the Hebrews attacked the Ammonites "and it came to pass, that those who remained were scattered so that two of them were not left together."[16] The people hailed Saul and were happy they had found the right person to lead them against the Philistines.

As suggested by Samuel they all went to Gilgal[17] where Saul was formally crowned in a solemn ceremony, at a large convention of freemen of all tribes of Israel. At the end of the ceremony, Samuel gave a long speech that turned out to be a recapitulation of his period of judgment and a prescription for the king and the tribesmen to follow thereafter. He expatiated on his integrity and honesty,[18] all the hardships that the Hebrews had overcome with the help of the priestly class and the imperative to adhere strictly to the laws of Moses in the future. He made the people understand that although Saul was the king, the clergy was supreme. He made it clear that if the king and the tribesmen refused to heed the voice of the clergy and forsaking the path of religio-purism tilted towards liberalism, the clergy reserved the right to dismantle the institution of kingship.[19]

Obviously, he had not reconciled with the establishment of monarchy yet, as he said that it was wicked of them to have asked for a king.[20] So he could not conceal his anger; he flew into a rage and burst out into a vituperative attack on the tribe.[21] When it is said, "the Lord sent thunder and rain" it does not mean that there was actually a thunderstorm at that time. The bard is metaphorically expressing that Samuel was wild with anger. At the end of his homily Samuel reminded Saul that the clergy had done great things for him by choosing him to be the king and so he should be grateful to the clergy and be guided by it.[22] And turning to the assembly, he said, if they strayed from the path of religio-purism and if the king tried to assert his independence, both the renegade purists and the king would be killed and that would be the end of monarchy.[23] This admonition was an unmistakable warning not only to the freemen but also to Saul. He, thus, made it clear to Saul that the clergy was superior to the king. Perhaps he was afraid that Saul's victory over the Ammonites and Israel's enthusiasm for him might go to his head and the clergy would be sidelined both by the king and the freemen of Israel.

Soon after, Saul planned to drive out the Philistines. He formed a standing army of three thousand men and deployed two thousand of them in Michmash and Bethel under his direct command and the rest under his son Jonathan's command in Gibeah. The Bible says, "Saul reigned for one year; and when he had reigned for two years over Israel," he put his son Jonathan in command of an army contingent. Saul, the youngest of Kish's offspring, is not said to have had a grown-up son when he ascended the throne of Israel. How he could have a son, who was capable of leading an army two years after he was crowned, is beyond one's comprehension. The scribes who documented the oral tradition seem to have overlooked this anomaly. Asimov clarifies it: "To suppose, however, that two years after his anointing he is the father of a grown man capable of conducting men in war, is difficult. The problem here rests with (the English version), which is not actually a translation of the Hebrew but an attempt to make some sense out of the original words. Literally translated, the Hebrew clause that begins the verse reads: *Saul was one year old when he began to reign.* It seems that something has been lost and the Revised Standard Version has the words read, *Saul was...years old when he began to reign; and he reigned...and two years over Israel.* It explains in a footnote that the gaps represent missing material. It may well be that (the lines in the KJV of the Bible[24]) is actually a summarising chronological verse that might say, *Saul was twenty-five years old when he began to reign; and he reigned for twenty-two years over Israel.*"[25] Anyway, since we are not concerned with the historicity of Saul or the point in time when the incident concerned occurred, let us assume that Saul was married and had grown-up offspring because later we find Saul had altogether four grown-up sons including Jonathan. We shall accept the story that Saul made his son, Jonathan, commander of an army contingent.

Coming back to the story, Jonathan successfully launched an attack on the garrison of the Philistines in Geba, which enhanced Saul's prestige. Anticipating a counter-attack Saul mobilised a huge army and as expected, the Philistines reacted by marching into and encamping in Michmash, planning to attack Geba. The sight of the Philistine forces unnerved the Hebrews; many of the soldiers deserted the army and hid themselves wherever they thought they would not be found while some fled to far away places and the few that remained with Saul "followed him trembling."[26] Finding that any more delay would further deplete his army, Saul decided to act without waiting for Samuel, who did not arrive on the day he said he would.

That angered Samuel. Saul explained the situation to him. He said, had he not attacked then, many more from his army would have deserted and the Philistines would have mounted an attack wiping out the entire Hebrew army including himself. But Samuel was not mollified. He said Saul had ignored the clergy. He had thought of making Saul's son heir-apparent, but now that Saul had ignored him he had changed his mind and added that Saul's dynasty would end with him.[27] He was so exasperated that he withdrew his support to the defending army and went to Gibeah. This incident is not only indicative of the growing struggle between the temporal and spiritual leaders for supremacy but also proves that he nominated Saul hoping that he that is, the clergy, would be able to dominate Saul and continue to virtually rule Israel.

The problem of Israel was that they were short of arms, for the Philistines had been refusing to supply them iron,[28] of which they had a monopoly, fearing that the Hebrews would equip themselves with weapons of iron. With Samuel and the clergy non-cooperating, the people panic-stricken and a small army inadequately equipped, Israel was in a hopeless situation. Nevertheless, a day or two later, without even informing Saul, Jonathan with a small contingent of troops crossed the narrow valley and attacked a Philistine garrison. Taken by surprise, for the Philistines never expected the Hebrew army to come through such a difficult terrain, the Philistine army fled in all directions and was easily overpowered. When those on the watchtower informed Saul that the Philistine army was on the run, he ordered his six-hundred-strong army to rush to the aid of Jonathan and chase the Philistines out of the land of the Hebrew kingdom.

When Saul's men reached there, the Hebrews who had earlier enrolled themselves in the Philistine army defected[29] and joined with Saul and Jonathan to fight the Philistines. It was a great victory; Israel was now free from the menace of the Philistines. Nonetheless, although Jonathan was the hero of the day, Saul disapproved of Jonathan acting without his orders, for he was the supreme commander. So he wanted to punish Jonathan with death for having acted on his own. But the freemen of Israel strongly objected to it: "Shall Jonathan die, who has achieved this great victory emancipating Israel?...not one hair on his head should fall to the ground...."[30] Saul relented in deference to their wishes – maybe, his paternal feelings too played a part in his decision to rescind his order. His apparent decision to execute his son for acting on his own was to show that he was impartial in his dealings. It was also meant as a warning to both the freemen and particularly to the slaves that he would not spare anyone who took law into his own hands. At the same time, by relenting in deference to the people's wishes, he showed that he listened to and valued the voice of ordinary lay freemen. Following this victory, he attacked and subjugated the Moabites, the Ammonites, the Edomites and the king of Zobah, after which urged by the clergy, Saul turned against the Amalekites.

The Amalekites had been the Hebrew's traditional enemy since the days of Moses. Samuel reminded him of the dastardly attack of the Amalekites at Rephidim on the Hebrew Congregation being led by Moses and told him to annihilate the Amalekites and exterminate the entire tribe as well as all their livestock.[31] Saul attacked the Amalekites as Samuel had wanted him to, but brought back "the best of the sheep, and of the oxen, and of the fatlings, and the lambs and all that was good" as booty. Samuel naturally, was enraged at what he considered impudent defiance of the clergy. He expressed his disapproval of Saul ignoring the clergy's instructions and doing exactly the opposite of what he specially instructed Saul to carry out. He said, he had made a mistake in choosing Saul as king.[32] Giving vent to his wrath, he reminded Saul of his low social status. Samuel said he was from an ordinary family of a minor tribe and was unheard of till then and yet the clergy selected him for the office of kingship. The clergy had commanded Saul to exterminate the Amalekite tribe and not to take anything belonging to them as booty but he did not pay heed to the clergy's words.[33]

Saul agreed that he did not carry out the wishes of Samuel fully and he pleaded guilty but appealed to Samuel to pardon him. He said to Samuel that he extirpated the entire tribe, taking Agag, the Amalekite king, alive as prisoner of war[34] and that he had brought the booty to be given to Samuel as a tribute.[35] Probably, Saul must have thought that Samuel could be bribed thus and that would pacify him. But he should have known of Samuel's impeccable integrity from the speech that Samuel gave to the assembly of the Hebrews at the time of Saul's second anointing at Gilgal. At that assembly, Samuel had said he would never accept tributes, which in fact was nothing but bribe in a glorified form. Saul explained to Samuel that he did not take any booty but his soldiers did and he also did not take for himself anything from the spoils brought by the soldiers.[36] He did not object to his soldiers taking the booty, and that was what he was faulted for because that, he accepted, amounted to disobedience to the clergy and to Samuel in particular.

This episode makes it clear beyond doubt that Samuel had selected an unknown man from a minor tribe of the Hebrews as king thinking that he would be able to dominate and continue to wield real power. But Saul was a strong and independent-minded person and he did not allow himself to be dominated by the clergy that Samuel represented. He agreed that what he had done was wrong, but justified himself saying, he "feared the people and obeyed their voice."[37] Saul, obviously, wished to be a benevolent king to the extent possible and attached more value to the wishes of the soldiers who were mostly drawn from the lower strata of society (freemen but indigent) than to those of the clergy and the affluent Chauvinists. Finding that Samuel was displeased with him and not wanting to antagonise the clergy (that represented the Chauvinists), Saul entreated Samuel to pardon him and cooperate with him. But Samuel would not accept any of his explanations, for he considered what Saul did, defiance of his authority and said obedience was a better tribute than livestock or other valuables. He suspected Saul of collaborating with the religio-liberals and saying that he would not cooperate with Saul any more, he turned to go. But Saul tried to hold him back when Samuel's robe that he held, tore. That tear was symbolic of the rift between Saul and the clergy.

Pointing at the tear, Samuel said that it portended danger to Saul's position and there would appear a claimant to the throne, whom the people would find a better ruler than Saul. This was an open threat to Saul and it alarmed him to some extent. So Saul again owned up his mistake. He promised he would not in future deviate from the path shown by the clergy and would always abide by the wishes of the clergy.[38] Samuel seemed to have accepted his apology and went with him, after which Samuel asked Saul to bring Agag to him. Agag came happily, thinking that the worst was over and his life would be spared. But when Agag went near Samuel, he could not control his pent-up anger. He drew his sword and "hewed Agag in pieces."[39] So he was only pretending to have condoned Saul. Immediately after cutting Agag, he left and never again did he come to see Saul. Samuel was angry because Saul chose to carry out the wishes of his soldiers, ignoring the clergy's orders. Personally, it hurt his ego but it has a social significance. It shows that Saul tended to support the interest of the lower-middle-class freemen more than that of the upper stratum of society that constituted the Chauvinists, which the clergy represented. That, Samuel thought, portends danger to the society. Although Samuel had threatened Saul of dire consequences, he continued to be a religio-purist as he had been so far but he was suspicious of the priesthood in general. And the clergy too did not trust him.

The kingmaker that he was, Samuel, immediately on his arrival at Ramah, conferred with the other priests to find another person as the king of the Hebrews, who would uphold the interest of the Chauvinists more than that of the lower middle class. His intention seems to be to sow the seeds of dissension in the kingdom by projecting before the freemen a better alternative to Saul and to create in Saul a sense of insecurity. Again, as he did in choosing Saul, Samuel took care not to choose a person from among the powerful religio-purists because the clergy would have no control over him. He had someone in mind, a young man by name David whose great-grandparents were Ruth, a Moabite, and Boaz, a Hebrew in whose house Ruth worked as a servant. The boy's father Jesse, grandson of Boaz, was in Bethlehem and his eighth and the youngest son David was engaged in taking care of his father's flock of sheep. It was a poor farming family that had nothing much to boast.

So when Samuel suggested the name of David, the other priests agreed and asked him to go to Bethlehem and anoint him. There was, however, a problem. Samuel was afraid that if Saul came to know of it, he would be killed without any hesitation. So he did not want to go and anoint David. The rest of the clergy advised him to take a heifer with him and pretend that he was going there to make a sacrifice to the Lord.[40] That was a good idea, thought Samuel, and as planned he went with a heifer to the house of Jesse of the Judah tribe, called Jesse to the sacrifice and sent for David who was out in the fields grazing the sheep. As soon as the lad came, Samuel anointed him as king, a rival to Saul, and returned to Ramah.

Meanwhile, the Philistines had regrouped and marched on the Hebrews. When the news reached Saul, he mustered an army to defend the Hebrews and the two armies met at Shocoh but did not join battle at once; they stood on two mountains with the valley separating them, poised to strike but hesitant to make the first move. Maybe, each side was surreptitiously scouting to gauge the strength of the other before launching an attack. Or perhaps, strategically it was disadvantageous to the army that made the first move because they would be an easy target for the enemy standing on top. But, as the legend goes, there came forward from among the Philistine lines, Goliath, a gigantic figure armed to the teeth. He carried in his hand a bronze javelin and protected himself with a coat of mail and bronze helmet; a long sword in its scabbard hung from his belt and a shield bearer went before him. He bellowed: "Why have you come out to set yourselves in battle array?" Defying the Hebrews to send a man to cross swords with him, he roared, "if he is able to fight with me and kill me then will we be your servants; but if I prevail against him and kill him and you shall be our servants and serve us."[41] No one from among the Hebrew lines dared take up Goliath's challenge.

Three of Jesse's sons were soldiers in Saul's army and Jesse had sent David with food for them and gifts for the commander. When David arrived, he found the two armies arrayed on the battlefield, ready to join battle, and Goliath was walking to and fro between the two armies, defiantly roaring and contemptuously looking at the Hebrew army as none of the Hebrew soldiers took up his challenge. No one from among the Hebrew army was prepared to risk a one-on-one combat with a giant like Goliath. David's pride was piqued. He volunteered to go and fight with Goliath but the Hebrew soldiers scoffed at him. He was a Lilliputian compared to Brobdingnagian Goliath, but the youngster would not be dissuaded. The men, who heard David accept the challenge, conveyed the news to Saul who sent for him. David said to Saul, "Your servant will go and fight with this Philistine." Seeing that this puny little boy was not a match for that giant of a man, Saul refused permission. But David was adamant. Saul tried his best to discourage him, saying that "you are but a youth and he a man of war from his youth;" but David insisted on being allowed to fight with Goliath. Finding that David was firm in his decision, Saul reluctantly consented.[42]

Refusing the coat of mail, brass helmet and sword and arming himself with only a sling and a few stones in a shepherd's bag, David took his staff in his hand and went to fight the Philistine. When Goliath came forward to fight, David taking a stone from the bag, "slung it and struck the Philistine in his forehead, so that the stone sank into his forehead and Goliath fell upon his face to the earth." Immediately, David ran and climbing up on his body, drew the Philistine's sword from its sheath, and cut off his head.[43] Seeing this, the entire Philistine army fled in disarray, when the Hebrew forces pursued and killed every one of them and plundered the deserted Philistine camp. Pleased with David, Saul married off his daughter Michal to him.

The story is dramatic and interesting indeed, but it is palpably fictitious. No two hostile armies could be foolish enough to agree to decide the victor on the basis of a combat between two individuals. However, this story of the diminutive David fighting the gigantic Goliath and winning seems to be an allegory. David's request to the king to fight Goliath is to be understood as David's request to permit him to lead the Hebrew army against the Philistines, presuming that he was trained in the use of arms. The king must have denied permission initially because he must have thought of David's lack of experience in warfare, let alone in commanding an army. The gargantuan Goliath and the diminutive David symbolise the comparative sizes of the two armies. So this is the story of a small and ill-equipped army of the Hebrews defeating a comparatively very large and well-equipped army of the Philistines. David was the commander whom the king newly appointed as he lost confidence in the incumbent commander who, the king found, was wavering and refusing to strike when the Philistine army was menacingly poised at the doorstep of the kingdom. This legend of David and Goliath was obviously intended to portray David as a great hero and to glorify the Hebrews.

David who knew that he had the support of the clergy and had even been anointed as king by Samuel himself, the respected priest and the erstwhile judge, had grabbed this opportunity to show Israel that he would make a better king than Saul. And he did succeed. He was victorious in whatever expedition he led since, with the result his fame soared sky-high. "Saul hath slain his thousands and David hath slain his ten-thousands" had become a household saying in the kingdom. The people began to shower praise on his prowess and naturally the priests who were unhappy with Saul, also praised him and this inevitably aroused Saul's suspicion. He could not have forgotten Samuel's resentment at his ignoring the clergy's instructions and the ominous words that the kingdom was in danger and there would appear a man better than Saul to claim the throne still echoed in his ears. He knew that as Samuel had accused him of insubordination, the clergy was not favourably disposed towards him and now the people in general seemed to be leaning towards David. David had caught the imagination of all classes of the people of the kingdom after his successful operations against the Philistines. So Saul decided to liquidate him, not because he was jealous of David as it seemed, but he suspected that the clergy would rally behind David and overthrow or even assassinate him.

However, what worried Saul the most was the close friendship between David and Jonathan, the heir-apparent. Added to it, David was Saul's son-in-law too and both Saul and Jonathan were closely associated with the army. Saul was not happy particularly with Jonathan's friendship with David. He thought it was too dangerous to be overlooked, for they could join hands to plot a putsch and overthrow him. The best way to avert it was to persuade Jonathan to kill David so that if the attempt succeeded his position would be safe and if it were to fail the friendship between Jonathan and David would turn into enmity and they would never unite to conspire against him. Sensing Saul's aversion towards him and the consequent danger to his life, David decided to go into self-exile and remain underground. Michal Saul's daughter David's wife helped him escape from the house without being noticed.[44] Saul, however, hunted him even in his exile and made several attempts on his life, but David escaped all attempts on his life with the help of the clergy.[45] Jonathan stood solidly by his friend David and even helped foil[46] Saul's assassination bid with the result David's friendship with Jonathan grew stronger by the day, which, incidentally, became proverbial.

Leaving the palace, David fled to Nob and met Ahimelech, the priest. Ahimelech evidently did not know that David was fleeing from Saul but must have known about Samuel's threat to Saul and he must have heard that Saul was suspicious of the clergy. So he, perhaps, thought that David had come to spy on them and was scared. He asked David why he had come alone. David lied saying the king had sent him on a secret mission[47] and explained his being alone, saying his men were expected to meet him later. The priest, believing him, gave him whatever little food there was in the monastery and when David left, finding him unarmed the priest gave him Goliath's sword that was there. After halting a while in two or three places, on the advice of the prophet Gad, he finally went to Judah. When Saul came to know of it he accused his soldiers of keeping him in the dark about David's movements. Doeg, the herdsman of Saul, who was in Ahimelech's monastery, told the king that during his stay there, he had seen David there and Ahimelech had given him food and a sword. So Saul suspected that the priests were plotting to overthrow him with David's help and Ahimelech, along with eighty-four other priests of Nob, had to face the ire of Saul. They as well as their families were executed, accusing Ahimelech of conspiracy against the king. However, Abiathar, one of the sons of Ahimelech, escaped and fled to David. On hearing of the tragedy that had befallen his family, David expressed regret for causing it, though inadvertently, and said: "Stay with me, fear not; for he who seeks my life, seeks your life: but with me you shall be safe."[48]

Even when he was underground, several times David had to encounter the Philistines, in all of which he triumphed and his fame increased all the more. The people of Keilah would have been massacred by the Philistines when the Philistines raided the city but for the timely intervention of David, who with his army of six hundred men fought the Philistines and saved them. And David and his men were staying there. However, suspecting foul play by the people of Keilah, David sought the advice of the clergy. The priests cautioned him against trusting the people of Keilah and as suspected the people of Keilah, the very people whom David had saved, informed the king of David's whereabouts. When the clergy expressed doubt about his safety in Keilah, David and his men had fled to Ziph and hid in the caves in the wilderness.[49]

On his way to Ziph, at Hachilah, Jonathan met David and reassured him of his continued support and said that his father would never be able to lay his hands on David. And he added, "...you shall be king over Israel and I shall be next to you," which assured David that he had a sincere friend in Jonathan whom he could trust. Jonathan also assured David that he had the unconditional backing of the clergy.[50] In the meantime, some people of Ziph went to Gibeah where Saul was camping and informed him of David's hideout. Immediately, Saul, with a strong posse of the army, proceeded to Ziph in search of the fugitive and asked the people to find out where exactly he was hiding. He told them, as soon as they reported back he would go with them to catch him. But when David heard that Saul was coming with a strong contingent of the army, he and his men went into the wilderness, in Maon. But Saul followed him there and they were on opposite sides of a mountain. Saul with his army was slowly closing in on David, blocking all escape routes and practically trapping him when fortunately for David Saul got a message that the Philistines had descended upon his land. So he was constrained to abandon the hunt for David and hasten back to fight the Philistines. David along with his men took this opportunity to go to Engedi to hide in the caves over there.

Saul came to know of it as soon as he returned after driving out the Philistines. So with three thousand men he proceeded to Engedi, where David had an opportunity to kill Saul but, probably considering that it would hurt Jonathan, he spared him.[51] Saul and his soldiers searched all over the place but went back home after failing to find the fugitive. Meanwhile Samuel died. Emboldened by the death of Samuel, Saul, thinking that now David would not have the support of the clergy and that it was a good opportunity to kill David, made another vain attempt to capture David, who was then hiding in the caves of Hachilah.[52] At that time also David is said to have spared the life of Saul although he could have killed the king without any difficulty. Both these stories seem manifestly fictitious, meant only to portray David as a noble person.

Although Saul had told him, "I have sinned. Come back home, my son David. I will not harm you any more because my life was precious in your eyes this day. Indeed, I have played the fool and have erred exceedingly," David did not trust him. He was sure that Saul was bent upon getting rid of him for good and the only way to escape from Saul's wrath was to keep himself away from the king and go to a place where he would never expect to see David. The one such place was the land of the Philistines and ironically, David with his two wives along with his men and their families moved in there and stayed with the Philistine king Achish. David stayed there practically incognito. Saul, through his spies, came to know that David had fled to Gath and was relieved to have got his adversary out of his way for the time being. At David's request, Achish settled David and his men in Ziklag, where David and his men lived like dacoits by raiding neighbouring territories of the Geshurites, the Girzites and the Amalekites, not to speak of the south of Judah, south of Jerahmaelites and south of the Kenites. In all the villages that they hit no one was left alive and they lifted the sheep, oxen, donkeys, camels and even clothing that they found there. Achish was happy because now there was none to forage into his territory from that side.

That was the time when Achish was planning a war against Saul and he asked David and his men to help fight the Hebrews, promising to make David his personal bodyguard for life. David gladly agreed and said, "Surely you shall know what help your servant can do."[53] It is naïve to think that David wanted to be the bodyguard of Achish, the king of Philistines, the sworn enemy of the Hebrews. Moreover, already anointed by Samuel as the king of Israel and although he was forced to go into exile, he still had his eye on the throne of Israel. David's intention, obviously, must have been to attack the Philistines from the rear when the two armies joined battle so that the Philistines could be taught a lesson and he could ingratiate himself with Saul.

The Philistines set up their base at Aphek while the Hebrews under Saul pitched their camp at Jezreel. The Philistine commanders now happened to see David and his men marching at the rear with Achish and they recognised the Hebrews. They would not trust the Hebrews, their traditional enemy, in their midst. They thought that at any moment during the battle this contingent would join forces with their kinsmen and the Philistines would be in a vise as it were, caught between the enemy in front and at the back. So the princes did not want to take a risk and insisted on sending David and his men away. Achish, therefore, had no choice but to tell David and his men to go back. The next day the Philistines marched on the Hebrews.

The two armies met at Gilboa and in the battle that ensued, the Hebrews licked the dust and many of them were slaughtered.

Saul and his sons along with the rest of the army fled, but the Philistines pursued them, and Jonathan, Abinadab and Malchishua, the sons of Saul, were all killed. The battle became fierce and an arrow from the enemy lines hit and badly wounded Saul. So, perhaps to escape being captured and taken as a captive, he committed suicide.[54] The Philistines even went to the other side of the valley and crossing the Jordan, occupied the cities from where the panic-stricken people of Israel, hearing of the death of Saul and his three sons had fled. Ishbosheth, Saul's fourth son somehow escaped being killed. After defeating the Hebrews, when the Philistines returned, Abner, the commander of Saul's army, brought Ishbosheth to Mahanaim and proclaimed him king of the Hebrews that included Gilead, Ashuri, Jezreel, Ephraim and Benjamin and all the rest of the Hebrew territory.[55]

David and his men, who were expelled from the Philistine army, went back to Ziklag. On reaching the city, they found that the Amalekites had sacked and razed to the ground the entire city where they had been camping and had carried away all their women and children. David was in a fix. On one side, the sorrow at the loss of his wives and children had been weighing heavily on him and on the other the threat of his men to kill him for his failure to protect their families was hanging like the Democles' Sword over his head. He did not know what to do. So David consulted Abiather, the priest, who advised him to go after the Amalekites.[56] Encouraged by these words David with his band of six hundred set out after the plunderers and pounced upon them when they were reveling in celebration of the loot they had got from Ziklag and their next victim, the Judah. Taken by surprise they could not offer any resistance and Israel could easily defeat them. David and his men recovered all that had been theirs and those that the Amalekites had plundered from the Judah. However, on arrival at Ziklag, David sent to the freemen of Judah what belonged to them. It was a calculated generosity, for he had been waiting for Saul's death to claim the throne of the Hebrew kingdom and knew that he would need the help of Judah to achieve it.

The Hebrews were yet to learn the art of bow-and-arrow warfare, and now David decided to teach them the use of that weapon, the ultimate weapon in those days. At that time, the news of the death of Saul and his sons reached David. He at once asked the clergy if it would be wise for him to claim the throne of Judah and on getting an affirmative reply, wanted to know where he should go. As advised by the clergy, he moved with his men and their families into Hebron where he was "anointed king over the house of Judah"[57] and he reigned there for over seven years, as a vassal state of Philistine. And all the time his mind was set on consolidating the kingdom of Israel by bringing the northern tribes too under his rule and freeing himself of the Philistine yoke. The tribes of the north continued to owe allegiance to the son of Saul, Ishbosheth who, as stated above, had established himself at Mahanaim[58] supported by Abner, commander-in-chief of the army under Saul. David could have attacked and annexed the northern territory but he did not want to do that as the northern tribes were loyal to Ishbosheth and it might turn out to be counterproductive.

His commander Joab almost provoked a war with Israel[59] when Abner killed Joab's brother at Gibeon, but a showdown was avoided. Meanwhile, Abner had fallen out with Ishbosheth and was secretly negotiating with David[60] who did not miss this opportunity. He sent word to Abner to bring Michal, whom he had married earlier. After David escaped from the palace, Saul had given her in marriage to someone else, obviously to preclude David making any claim to the kingdom as his son-in-law, which was exactly what David thought of doing. He sent a messenger to Ishbosheth too with the same demand and Michal was brought to him. Abner now clandestinely approached the freemen of Israel and convinced them of the need to unite the kingdom under one strong sovereign. And who else but David could do that? When these developments had been taking place, Joab, without the knowledge of David, cleverly maneuvered to bring Abner to Hebron and avenged his brother's death by killing him.[61] David hastened to dissociate himself from the crime, putting the responsibility for the murder of Abner solely on Joab and avoided an armed clash with the northern tribes and Ishbosheth. The news of Abner's murder created a stir among the northern tribes but Ishbosheth was too weak to wage a war against David. The people of the North were not happy with a weak king like him and decided to assassinate him. And they did. The assassins went with his head to David, who promptly executed them lest, he thought, he would be blamed and the northern tribes would revolt against him. It was a masterstroke that endeared him to Israel. The freemen of Israel, now without a king, felt that their security lay in the hands of David.

They anointed him king of Israel saying that long back the clergy had approved of him as king of the Hebrew kingdom[62]. Thus all the tribes of Israel came under David's rule forming the first ever Hebrew kingdom bringing Israel and Judah under one king. David now decided to shift his capital to a centrally located city, Jerusalem, in order that he was identified with both Judah and Israel. But the Jebusites had entrenched themselves strongly there and no power could so far dislodge them. However, David conquered Jerusalem and occupied the fort, after which he also captured the stronghold of Zion where with the help of the king of Tyre who sent "cedar trees and carpenters and masons" David built a palace where he stayed.[63] Since then, Jerusalem came to be known as the City of David.

He succeeded in winning the support of the clergy to his kingship and declared that he was ruling for the people at large.[64] The word "people," however, did not include the slaves; it meant the freemen only. His prestige now was very high and he knew that he was strong enough to take on the Philistines while the Philistines were aware that they could not expect him to remain a vassal any longer. So they thought of attacking Judah.

David got the information about their plan to mount a pre-emptive attack through his spies and he decided to intercept them. He consulted the Chauvinists, who approved his plan and assured him of their cooperation.[65] So he marched against the Philistines and the two armies met at Baalperazim, where David defeated the Philistine army. But they regrouped and spread out across the valley of Rephaim, thus opening a broad battlefront. David was now diffident despite the boost that the victory at Baalperazim gave to the morale of the Israelite army. He again conferred with the clergy for advice and help and they told him that it would be foolish to confront the Philistine forces as the Philistine army was far stronger and battle-wise. On their advice David avoided a frontal attack. Instead, as advised by them the Israelite army hid among the mulberry bushes and when they heard the sound of marching steps of the Philistine army, they allowed it to pass and forming a semicircle suddenly pounced on the Philistines from behind at Geba.[66] In the battle that followed, the Philistines had been decisively defeated and were driven to Gazer.

After that he turned his attention to the internal situation. He brought the Ark of the Lord into the city and placed it in the midst of the tabernacle that he had pitched for it,[67] which connotes, as explained in the previous chapter, that David strengthened law and order and ensured that the slaves were strictly under control. His dancing before the Ark[68] shows that he was prepared to abide by whatever the clergy wanted and to conform to it or that he was prepared to dance to the tune of the clergy, which though a hackneyed expression explains his action graphically. And to confirm it, he chose as his adviser the chief priest, Nathan the prophet. David was planning to construct a temple for the Ark but gave up the idea as advised by Nathan who told him to keep it in abeyance. He said, there was no hurry for it, as it had been in tents all these years.

So he thought of expanding his kingdom. He conquered Gath, the largest Philistine city. He then turned to Moab, which he conquered and established his suzerainty over it. His next target was the Edomites, whom he defeated, and placing garrisons all over Edom forced them to pay tribute to Israel. Evidently, there were internal disturbances and so he thought of reforming the administration by appointing officials to take care of different aspects of governance. He appointed Zadok and Ahimelech, the two priests, as his advisers; Jehoshaphat held the portfolios of finance and home. Seraiah, who would be assisted by the princes, was appointed his private secretary, and the commander-in-chief of the army was Joab.

David now wanted to find out if any member of Saul's family was living, for that might pose a danger to his throne. And to preclude any of Saul's kin claiming the throne, David sought all the remaining male members of the House of Saul and under some pretext or other he executed every one of those that he found.[69] Meanwhile, David heard of Ziba, an old servant of Saul's house, and he summoned him and on questioning him David learnt that Jonathan's son and Saul's grandson, Mephibosheth who was the only legitimate successor, was surviving. He was lame and would not be a threat to David. However,

David brought him to the palace and kept him under close vigil so that no ambitious army officer or any discontented person propped him up as the true successor to the throne to foment a revolt. That this was his intention in keeping Mephibosheth in his palace is evident because David had planned to liquidate all possible claimants to the throne. He, however, made it known that it was out of his love for his old friend that this unfortunate man Mephibosheth, his late friend's son who was physically challenged, was brought to the palace and was being taken care of.[70] It was indeed a clever move that helped him show himself as a loyal friend and a compassionate ruler.

Not long after, the Ammonite king died and his son Hanun succeeded him. When David heard of it, out of courtesy and wishing to maintain friendly relations with that neighbouring kingdom, he sent his ambassadors with a message of condolence to Hanun, whose courtiers, however, thought they were spies in the guise of messengers. It was not without reason that they suspected this. Israel had been hostile to the Ammonites in the past and during Saul's reign the two tribes had fought and Saul had defeated them. So the courtiers told the king that obviously the condolence message was a ploy and actually David had sent these men to scout the land with the intention of invading the country later. Believing the courtiers, the messengers were treated scornfully; they were sent back with half the beard of each of them shaven and their garments ripped in the middle exposing their backs.

This naturally angered David and gave him a good excuse to go to war with the Ammonites. Probably, he had been waiting for some such excuse. On receiving reports about David's preparations for war, Hanun forged an alliance with the Syrians, who too had been viewing with alarm the rise of a powerful kingdom and the expansionism of David and were willing to form a coalition to defend themselves. The coalition was, however, defeated by the Israelite forces commanded by David and Joab at the battle of Helam. And David placed several garrisons of his army in Damascus. Now the kingdoms of the Ammonites, the Syrians, the Moabites, the Philistines the Amalekites and the Edomites were all reduced to tributary nations. The news of the defeat of the Syrians at the hands of David was received with joy by Toi, king of Hamath, who had been at loggerheads with the Syrians.

So in appreciation of the victory and also as a token of his friendship with the kingdom of Israel, he sent to David vessels of gold, silver and brass. David gave all these and the war booties that he had collected from the various defeated nations to the clergy, keeping for himself only less valuable items. The clergy was immensely pleased and urged the Chauvinists to extend their unreserved support to him in all his expeditions.[71] David now brought under his rule not only the twelve tribes of Israel but expanded his kingdom by conquering several neighbouring tribes as well. It may not, therefore, be wrong to say that David paved the way for the rise of imperialism in West Asia in ancient times.

In addition to his many wives, David had taken over all the concubines of Saul, and like any monarch, he had a large harem. His adulterous relationship with Bathsheba, wife of Uriah, a soldier in the army of Israel, who refused to have the comforts of family life when his master, Joab, was on the battlefield, was indeed an act that shows David as a loathsome lecher. And worse still was his most despicable and unscrupulous act of sending her unsuspecting husband, a loyal soldier, to the battlefront with a confidential letter to Joab "saying Set Uriah in the forefront of the hottest battle, and retreat from him, that he may be struck down and die."[72] He did it when he came to know that Bathsheba was pregnant for which he was responsible and could be accused of adultery and culpable homicide amounting to murder.

He sent Uriah into the jaws of death only to avoid the calumny of adultery, which under Mosaic Law would have invited death penalty and as the king he would have had to impose that punishment upon himself.[73] And to cover his illicit relation with Uriah's wife, after the period of mourning David brought her to his house and made her his wife. So to the world outside that was not aware of Bathsheba's pre-marital sex with the king, David did not commit adultery and so Bathsheba's pregnancy did not become a scandal. The death of Uriah in the battle saved David from the difficult situation of punishing himself. Of course, he would have exonerated himself and he perhaps expected the priests to whom he had presented the spoils of war to turn a blind eye to these crimes.[74] However, somehow the secret of David's dastardly role in the death, which was in fact premeditated murder of his loyal soldier Uriah and Joab's connivance in the death leaked out.[75]

The news reached the ears of the priests, who were outraged at this cold-blooded murder, which was what it amounted to, committed by the king himself. The priests did not want to be seen as conniving at these crimes. So Nathan, the senior-most priest, was sent to David to reprimand him for his crime. He, however, said the clergy had condoned it – as David expected – and did not apply the Mosaic Law of "eye for eye and tooth for a tooth" and punish him with death. Instead, applying the same law, the clergy killed the baby born of adultery, although there was no such provision in the Mosaic Code of Law. This actually infringed the Mosaic Law, which states in unequivocal terms that children should not be put to death for the fathers' crimes.[76] This betrays not only David's but also the priests' lack of integrity. Soon, however, Bathsheba conceived again and was delivered of a baby boy who was named Solomon.

The clergy was happy that Bathsheba gave birth to a baby boy. Nathan personally went to convey to David a message expressing the pleasure of the clergy on the birth of a boy and called the boy Jedidiah, meaning "Beloved of Yahweh."[77] This is significant because David had many sons, on the births of none of whom had the clergy expressed its pleasure, and the fact that Nathan named him Jedidiah shows that for some reason, the clergy wanted him to succeed David in spite of his mother being a Hittite. In other words, the composer is giving a hint about the possible political developments in Israel. At this time, David got a message from Joab saying that the besieged Rabbah, the capital of Ammon, that had been holding out all these days had capitulated and urged him to go there immediately. At once David went there with a posse of the army and occupied the city. He plundered all the wealth including the Ammonite king's crown of gold studded with precious stones, which he placed on his head, thus proclaiming himself the ruler of the Ammonites.[78] The people of the city were captured and made slaves.

David had now consolidated his kingdom that extended from the Red Sea to the River Euphrates-Tigris and had been ruling without any problem. A period of peace followed. There was no sign of revolt from any part of the kingdom and no vassal state had dared challenge his suzerainty; none of the neighbouring kingdoms too made any attempt to invade or encroach upon his territory. "Throughout the Fertile Crescent David's name was renowned. The city of Jerusalem, whose royal buildings were designed and constructed by the best artisans of Phoenicia, was a monument to the skill of the Near East. As a result social life underwent profound changes, and Israel's faith was exposed to a more cosmopolitan atmosphere. New conceptions of property were introduced as commercial entrepreneurs, protected by the military power of the king exploited the opportunities of trade."[79] David was a great conqueror who was feared and respected and the Hebrew kingdom was at the zenith of its power during his reign. It was a period of peace that helped boost commerce. The slaves were, no doubt, mercilessly suppressed and put to hard labour while the freemen had a luxurious and comfortable life. That, naturally, is the reason for the bard who must have been beholden to the affluent class, to praise David and his reign.

But trouble was brewing in the royal family. Absalom was David's third son. He had a beautiful sister Tamar whom Amnon, David's eldest son and Absalom's stepbrother, raped. This was a crime, the punishment for which under the Mosaic Law was social ostracisation.[80] Distraught, Tamar went to Absalom and told him what Amnon had done. David heard about this lecherous act of Amnon and was furious but he preferred to ignore it and did not take any action This betrayed not only his partiality for his eldest son who was the natural heir apparent though not formally declared, but above all his contempt for justice. The indifference of David towards the atrocity committed on Tamar's modesty understandably made Absalom hate his father. He simmered with indignation but it took him two years to avenge this outrageous act for which he carefully laid out a plan. He arranged a feast and invited his father and all his brothers to it but David declined. As Absalom insisted, he sent all his sons, Absalom's step-brothers, including Amnon to the feast at which, it was planned, when Amnon got inebriated with wine Absalom's soldiers should kill him. Had David attended the feast, perhaps he too would have been assassinated and the crown would have adorned Absalom's head. Possibly, David had suspected danger to his life but obviously not to Amnon's, for in that case he would not have allowed Amnon to go for the feast. Both father and son must have thought that Absalom had forgotten the unpleasant incident.

Immediately after Amnon's murder, fearing his father's ire, Absalom fled to Geshur, his mother's place. Now the eldest son who, according to the patrilineal system of descent (which had now replaced the old tribal custom of descent in the female line followed by the Hebrews) should have legitimately succeeded to the throne had been eliminated. Being the eldest of all the surviving sons of David, Absalom was eyeing the throne. Joab had been thinking of ways to bring back Absalom, for he feared that if David were to die when Absalom was absent in Geshur, the kingdom would plunge into anarchy and political crisis, leaving the kingdom vulnerable to external aggression. So Joab had been trying to persuade David to absolve Absalom of his crime but David seemed to be adamant although gradually, Joab sensed, he was thawing. So he thought of a ruse,[81] which helped succeed getting David's consent to call back Absalom to Israel. But David consented with the proviso that he could stay in Jerusalem in his own house and would not be restored to his position at court.[82] David was obviously wary of Absalom, for, he must have reasoned, if Absalom could murder Amnon, the rightful heir to the throne, he would not hesitate to kill him to grab the throne. So his life would be in constant threat if Absalom stayed in the palace.

The decision of David to keep Absalom out of the palace, naturally, kindled his suspicion of David's intentions. Was David planning to deny him the right to the throne? That strengthened his determination to make a bid for the throne, which, although he had been lying low, was his ambition for a long time. And after the death of Amnon, he knew that he was the undeclared heir apparent and if he did not strike now, one of the other sons of David or someone else claiming ancestry to Saul might suddenly come up and complicate the problem of succession. So after settling in his house in Jerusalem he persuaded Joab to try and get him an audience with the king. His intention was to make David feel that it was not with any ulterior motive that he desired to come back but it was only his love for his father that prompted him. He said to Joab that he could very well have remained in Geshur if it were to stay without seeing his father and he urged him to intercede on his behalf, saying "let me see the king's face and if there be any iniquity in me, let him execute me."[83] David was won over when Joab gave this message, but he had a lurking suspicion and so he agreed to see Absalom but did not permit him to return to the palace for good. When Absalom came before the king he respectfully bowed to the king and the king kissed him.

During his stay in Jerusalem Absalom took upon himself the duty of pronouncing judgments on behalf of the king, pretending to be empathetic to the sufferings of the have-nots and made veiled criticism of the king. By his calculated politeness he succeeded in endearing himself to the masses, the lower middle class.[84] It is surprising how the spies failed to report Absalom's gimmicks to the king, especially his acting as judge without the authority of the king, and why Joab too did not inform the king. Was Joab's hand behind the communication gap? It is a pertinent question for which the Bible does not provide any answer. However, Joab's anxiety to bring back Absalom to Jerusalem and his behaviour ever since his return had been rather enigmatic and his loyalty to the king was suspect. But Absalom too did not seem to have faith in Joab's loyalty to him, for he did not take Joab into confidence. There seems to have been wheels within wheels in the political drama being played out in and around the palace.

After four years' stay in Jerusalem when he made sure that he had prepared the ground for usurping the throne, Absalom got David's permission to go to Hebron. He said to the king that he was going "to sacrifice to the Lord in fulfilment of a vow I made to him while I was at Geshur – that if he would bring me back to Jerusalem, I would sacrifice to him."[85] Absalom had actually hatched a plot to overthrow David and capture power. Accordingly, before leaving Jerusalem, he despatched his confidants to different parts of the kingdom with instructions to his supporters to be prepared and when they got a signal from him, to rise in revolt simultaneously, announcing that "Absalom reigns in Hebron."[86] His "offering the sacrifice to the Lord" was actually his secret meeting with the priesthood, to which he invited Ahithophel, one of David's counsellors, who at the meeting declared his allegiance to Absalom.

David got the news of the conspiracy through his spies who informed him that Absalom had succeeded in securing the support of the entire Israel and Ahithophel too was among the conspirators.[87] David knew that now his throne as well as his life was in danger and if he remained in Jerusalem, the rebels would besiege the city and the city would be destroyed. Hence, he fled the city with his household accompanied by his battle-wise, elite guards consisting of the Cherethites commanded by Benaiah, the Pelethites and the Gittites, and Ittai, a Gathite. He did not ask Joab to accompany him, maybe because he suspected Joab of conspiring with Absalom, for whose return to Jerusalem he was pleading with David; nor did Joab volunteer to go with him. It may be presumed that Joab and a section of the elite forces took a neutral position in this struggle for power and they stayed back in Jerusalem. Obviously, Joab was sitting on the fence waiting to see who would get the upper hand and to throw in his lot with that camp. Or, was he waiting to strike when the winner got weakened after the clash with his rival? Was he planning to stage an army coup? Neither David nor Absalom was sure. Anyway, neither of the contending parties wished to antagonise him, as his support would be crucial when the chips are down. Hence, both the parties did not contact him, effectively neutralising him for the time being thinking that his support could be obtained later if necessary.

The split in the clergy reflected the split in the Chauvinist camp. The local priests and the Chauvinists at Jerusalem were with David and solidly stood by him during this crisis. Two of the priests, Ahiathar and Zadok, even accompanied him till the city border. When they turned back from there, David told Zadok that he intended to go and hide in the wilderness beyond the river Jordan but would wait at the ford of the river until he got a message from Zadok regarding the situation in Jerusalem. As the fugitive party reached the top of the Mount of Olives, they found Hushai, David's friend and counsellor, who was not a Judean, waiting for them. David told him to go to Absalom and pretending to be supporting him, give him wrong advice to frustrate and counter Ahithophel's counsels. Just past the top of the hill, David saw Ziba hurrying to catch up with them with donkeys and food, and he told David that Mephibosheth who was still in Jerusalem had sent all these for them. As he was nearing Bahurim, Shimei who was of the House of Saul threw stones at the party, cursing David for murdering Saul's descendants and treacherously usurping the throne. All those who accompanied David wanted to kill him but David counselled patience, for if they killed Shimei, he thought, he would be alienating the Northern tribes and that would only help push them into the Absalom camp.

Meanwhile, Absalom and his men arrived in Jerusalem along with Ahithophel, when Hushai too arrived and met Absalom. He pretended to be on Absalom's side as David wanted him to do. Absalom was, however, suspicious of him and asked him why he had deserted his old friend. He replied that the clergy and the people of Israel had chosen to support Absalom and so he too decided to be with Absalom and as he advised David then, he would advise David's son now. Absalom and all the others who were there found no reason to suspect his apparent sincerity. Anyway, now that he had taken control of the palace, a symbol of kingship in the eyes of the people, Absalom was wondering what to do next. Ahithophel advised Absalom to keep up the pressure on David and to pursue him immediately. But to his peril he decided to consult Hushai, who had been planted there to thwart Ahithophel's plans. Hushai, as could be expected, advised against an immediate expedition, saying that it was advisable to mobilize the entire Israel before taking any military action against David. He logically argued out his case, detailing his plan of action, which theoretically was unassailable and could convince Absalom and his supporters who in one voice declared that 'the counsel of Hushai the Archite, is better...' Ahithophel felt insulted that his advice was not accepted. So he left for his hometown and committed suicide, perhaps because he was certain that David would be victorious and be back on the throne and he would have to pay with his life for his betrayal. Hushai immediately informed Zadok and Abiathar, the pro-David priests in Jerusalem, all that had transpired in Absalom's camp and told them to urge David to cross the river Jordan without any delay and go into the wilderness.[88]

The delay foredoomed Absalom's chances of winning the throne, as it gave David enough time to escape and muster the support of the people, which was what Hushai had aimed at. Absalom appointed Amasa as commander-in-chief and with a huge and well-equipped army, crossed the river Jordan in pursuit of David. Meanwhile, Joab had thrown in his lot with David. Being an astute military tactician, he must have foreseen that Absalom's delay had given sufficient time for David to organise a strong army. Absalom's defeat was now beyond doubt. David reaching Mahanaim, where he was warmly received by the Ammonites, reorganised his army, dividing it into three companies with Joab, his brother Abishai and Ittai the Gittite as commanders. The armies of David and Absalom met "in the woods of Ephraim."[89] Both the armies fought fiercely but despite all the handicaps David's army prevailed and Joab made sure that Absalom was killed,[90] notwithstanding David's orders to the contrary. That was the end of the rebellion and David was back on the throne.

Joab's motive for killing Absalom against the orders of the king is incomprehensible. Was it because of his loyalty to the king? He must have thought that if left alive, Absalom would again hatch a conspiracy to capture the throne. Or, could it be because he was toying with the idea of staging an army coup to capture power? Absalom was the legitimate successor to the throne, and if he were alive it would pose a problem because the people would support him only.

David faced a difficult problem now. There were three forces at play – the first was his supporters, which comprised primarily his army, the second was the northern tribesmen who supported Absalom and the third, those freemen of the Judah who supported Absalom. David could have settled it by force but he decided to try to solve the problem diplomatically without any bloodletting if possible. He told Zadok and Abiathar, the priests who were David's staunch supporters, to go over to the northern supporters of Absalom and tell them that after all 'you are my bones and my flesh.' And he offered to Amasa who was Absalom's general, the post of commander-in-chief of his army in place of Joab. That clinched the issue, for the people of Israel now swore their allegiance to David and incidentally, it served as a punishment to Joab for killing Absalom against his orders. Thus a split in the kingdom had been averted without bloodshed. Joab seemed to have understood the reason for relieving him of the top military post and did not take it as an affront or a reflection on his efficiency as commander-in-chief. However, in his heart of hearts he did feel resentment, which he did not show openly; he waited for an opportunity to regain his position or/and take revenge on the king. David placated the Northerners by pardoning Shimei, who had abused and hurled stones at him, and by taking back Maphibosheth who stayed back when the king's entire household went into exile.

Nevertheless, the embers of Absalom's revolt continued to burn. A section of the northern tribe that supported Absalom was hesitant to accept David, fearing reprisal by the king. That was taken advantage of by Sheba, a Benjaminite, who organised a resistance movement. He repudiated David and called upon the former rebels to non-cooperate with the Davidian government.[91] So the bloodbath that David tried to avoid became inevitable. He ordered Amasa to mobilise the army of Judah within three days and put down the insurgency, but Amasa failed to meet the deadline.[92] So David called Abishai and told him to pursue Sheba before he could get into a fortified city where it would be difficult to catch him and he might turn out to be more dangerous than Absalom. At once Joab and Abishai, with a detachment of the king's elite guards, pursued Sheba and the insurgents. On the way they met Amasa, who came forward to greet Joab. At once Joab took his dagger and stabbed him to death. By that time, Sheba had retreated to the city of Abel in Beth-maacah, to which Joab laid siege. The citizens of Abel, finding that this might lead to the sacking of the city and all the misery that it entailed, killed Sheba and threw his head out to Joab. With his death the rebellion collapsed. Joab returned victorious and was reinstated as commander-in-chief.

However, David's troubles were not over yet. Now he heard that the Gibeonites, a non-Israelite people, who had been slave labourers, had been striking work every year for the last three years at the commencement of the season for cultivation. That hampered agricultural activity, resulting in famine.[93] David had so far kept slaves under his thumb. If this was not dealt with immediately, David knew, the other slaves too would emulate the example and it would go out of hand. But he wished to settle it amicably without resorting to force. He consulted the Chauvinists who informed him that the Gibeonite slaves had been demanding punishment to those who committed genocide against them. He then called the ringleaders of the Gibeonites and asked them what their grievances were and how he could redress them. They told him of the gross injustice that Saul had perpetrated against them by trying to exterminate the tribe and demanded that Saul's sons be handed over to the Gibeonites so that they could be punished for the crime that their ancestor had committed against the tribe. This, thought David, was a good opportunity that he had got to get rid of the possible contenders for the throne without being accused of killing them. He presumed, a vast majority of the freemen including the Chauvinists, would have no objection to the idea of handing over Saul's descendants to the Gibeonites because it was being done to avert the strike by slaves jeopardising agricultural activity that affected their income besides causing famine in the country, the cause for which, in their perception, was Saul.

So David conceded their demand. Barring Jonathan's son Mephibosheth, David handed over seven other descendants (two grandsons of Saul and five adopted sons of Michal) to the Gibeonites to be punished as they deemed fit.[94] The king himself was infringing the Mosaic Law, which states that children should not be punished for the crime of their fathers.[95] This shows David's utter contempt for law and justice and reflects badly on his character. The Gibeonites hanged all of them before they started the harvest of barley. Aiah was one of those who were hanged, and Rizpah, his daughter, in protest lay down at the site throughout the harvest season that lasted for six months.[96] David must have been informed of it by his spies. He was afraid that this might spark an insurrection by Saul's supporters of whom there was still a large number. It would provoke his supporters and that would lead to a civil war. In order, therefore, to placate Saul's supporters and to show them that he had no animosity towards the House of Saul, David arranged to bury the bones of those whom the Gibeonites hanged, in the grave of Kish, Saul's father. At the same time, to convince them that he revered Saul's memory, he brought the bones of Saul and Jonathan and interred them too in the sepulchre of Kish. This pleased Saul's supporters and prevented a possible internecine conflict. Now the Philistines began to harass Israel, but David's army defeated them in battles both at Gob and Gath.

The strike by Gibeonite slaves was an eye-opener. An extensive kingdom encompassing a plurality of tribes and vassal states besides a burgeoning slave population, David realised, demanded a strong and large army. So he decided to introduce conscription and, ignoring the advice of the officers of the army including Joab, he ordered a census to be taken of the people of Israel.[97] It was a stupendous task that took nearly ten months to complete! The purpose of the census was primarily to keep a watch on the slave population and to ascertain the manpower, other than the slaves, available for forced labour. It also formed the basis for taxation and military conscription. The people of all classes saw through the game and reacted violently. As Anderson succinctly puts it, "Evidently the census findings were to be the basis for military conscription, taxation and forced labour. By this action, every man was reminded that he owed his primary allegiance not to his tribal unit but to the king. The plan backfired, however."[98] The idea of hiking taxes was not taken kindly to by the affluent class also, conscription was opposed by all sections of the population, and the possibility of introducing forced labour enraged the lower middle class and the poor. So there was a spontaneous uprising, and in the bloody rebellion that followed thousands of men lost their lives. Realising his mistake, before the uprising spread to Jerusalem, David withdrew his order and the revolt came to an end.[99]

Age and the strain of governing a vast country had been telling upon the king's health and he was bedridden but he had not declared anyone as his heir apparent. So Adonijah, Absalom's younger brother, who on being assured of the support of Joab and Abiather, the priest, decided to declare himself the king. He invited all the other sons of David except Solomon for the ceremony. And in the presence of Joab, the commander-in-chief, and Abiathar, the priest, which ensured the support of a section of the army and some of the Chauvinists who had their own grievances against David, he got himself anointed as king, after sacrificing "sheep and oxen and fat cattle by the stone of Zoheleth."[100] But the majority of the Chauvinists, the king's elite bodyguard and other powerful officials were not in favour of Adonijah.[101] When Adonijah and his supporters were feasting and making merry in celebration of the coronation, the rival party with the concurrence of David went to the Tabernacle at Gihon[102] and Zodak, the priest, anointed Solomon as king. And shouting "Long live King Solomon!" the party led by Zodak, Nathan, Benaiah, the captain of David's elite bodyguard, and other dignitaries returned to the palace in a huge procession escorted by the elite bodyguard. When Solomon took his seat on the throne, King David came and blessed him.[103]

In the midst of the revelry, when Adonijah and the guests got the news of Solomon's formal coronation with the king's blessing, the guests melted away in fear while Adonijah fled to the Tabernacle and pleaded for clemency, which Solomon graciously granted on condition that he behaved himself.[104] Before his death David had warned[105] Solomon about Joab and Shimei, and soon after David's death Solomon found that Adonijah still had his mind set on the throne. So he was executed, lest he instigated the people to rebel and again made a bid for the throne. After that Solomon summoned Abiathar and forced him to give up his priesthood, saying that he truly deserved death but was being spared because of his services to David. In fact, Abiathar was not executed because Solomon was wary of offending the priesthood and the section of the Chauvinists that were behind Abiathar. The news of Adonijah's execution scared Joab and he took refuge inside the Tabernacle, but on the orders of Solomon, he was executed there when he refused to come out. And Benaiah, till then the captain of the king's elite bodyguard, was promoted to the post of commander-in-chief.[106] The king, then, sent for Shimei, who was one of those that continued to lament the fall of the dynasty of Saul, and told him that he could leave Jerusalem only on pain of death. But three years later when Shimei left the city for some reason, Solomon got an excuse to execute him. He was summoned to the court and killed.[107] With that the three possible sources of trouble were eliminated and all was quiet on the domestic front.

The one foreign power that was likely to pose a threat to his kingdom was Egypt. So Solomon made an alliance with the Pharaoh and cemented it by marrying his daughter, for which the Pharaoh gave him the city of Gezer as dowry.[108] Solomon, unlike his father, did not extend his kingdom, which was what he inherited from David, but for the addition of Gezer that he got now as dowry. This enhanced the prestige of Solomon, especially because the Hebrews were once slaves in Egypt and now with this marriage they stood on equal footing with the Egyptians. The Chauvinists would not have approved of the inter-tribal marriage but they shut their eyes to this breach of law, maybe because it was basically a political move. Solomon was, however, conscious of it and to please the priesthood, he went to Gibeon and made a thousand burnt offerings at the altar. Solomon, thus, took care to seek and act according to the advice of the priesthood in everything that he did and the Chauvinists were happy. So they affirmed their unstinting support to Solomon. However, it was a conditional offer of help and the conditionality was that he would not stray from the path of religio-purism.[109]

Solomon now turned his attention to reconstituting the administrative setup and appointed his advisers and governors[110] in order to consolidate and strengthen the kingdom that included the whole of Canaan. He was just in his dealings with the middle-class freemen but ruthless with his detractors and mercilessly exploited the lower-middle-class freemen and the slaves. The affluent class was generally happy during his reign, as each family had its own home and garden.[111] There were no external aggressions too. This was made possible because he maintained a huge armed force, which among other things had "forty thousand stalls of horses for his chariots and twelve thousand horsemen."[112] Imagine the capital expenditure on the construction of these chariots and stalls as well as the recurring expenditure on the maintenance of horses and horsemen! In order to meet these expenses, the freemen were taxed heavily, which of course, did not go down well with the affluent Chauvinists. But they tolerated it because the slaves were held down as never before, with the result there were no internal disturbances.

A major part of his reign was devoted to constructing a palatial "house for the Lord"[113] and a sprawling palace for himself. Informing Hiram, the king of Tyre, of his intention to construct these buildings, he sought Hiram's help for the project. He wanted Hiram to send workmen from Tyre to Lebanon to help his own workmen cut cedar timber and said he would pay the wages of Hiram's workmen too. Hiram happily agreed to help and went a step further saying that he would supply cypress too and deliver the logs wherever Solomon wanted them, for he saw this as a good opportunity to make money as Solomon was known for his wealth. And Solomon paid him in kind, twenty thousand measures of wheat and twenty measures of oil every year.[114] The construction of the Temple, a remarkable achievement, took seven years, beginning in the fourth year and ending in the eleventh year of his rule, and the construction of a magnificent palace took another thirteen years. After that, he fortified Jerusalem and apart from cities meant for storage of grain, to keep chariots and accommodate charioteers, he built many others too.

The priests were quite happy and they praised these achievements of Solomon[115] because the Temple brought in good income and gave them an unprecedented importance in society. They told Solomon that as long as he kept the interests of the Chauvinists at heart he would have their unflinching support. The clergy wanted him to strictly go by the Mosaic Code of Law as his father David did and strictly follow the Chauvinists' advice.[116] They warned him that if he failed to heed their advice they would withdraw their support to him and that would be his downfall, for they would split the kingdom and the northern region, Israel, would be declared a separate kingdom.[117] The construction of the Temple and the palace required a large labour force. Solomon conscripted the surviving Amorites, Hittites, Perizzites, Hivites and Jebusites for all the construction work. These non-Israelite tribes could not be exterminated by Israel when their kingdoms were annexed by Israel and the survivors of those tribes had been kept as slaves. He appointed administers, supervisors of the labour forces, military officers, chariot commanders and soldiers,[118] all of whom were drawn from among the Chauvinists.

As stated above, Hiram had helped him in all his construction activities, which cost Solomon a large sum of money and this practically drained Solomon's exchequer empty. So he had to cede to Tyre twenty cities in the land of Galilee to make good the debt due to Hiram for the materials and the labour that he had supplied.[119] But Hiram was not satisfied, as could be inferred from his comment when he came to see the cities that were given to him, for he asked: "What cities are these, which thou hast given me, my brother?"[120] In spite of his construction mania, Solomon's wealth increased as a result of the expanding overseas trade that he carried on with countries in Africa and Asia. Even the Queen of Sheba who was reputed to be fabulously wealthy was astonished to see Solomon's wealth, when she visited Israel. His rule stretched from the Euphrates, where he controlled the great trade-crossing Tipshah, to Gaza and he had a harbour at Eziongeber on the Red Sea, from which he sent vessels to Ophir. The biblical scholars have not been able to connect Ophir with any of the modern ports.

The Bible does not say where Ophir is, although it is mentioned in several episodes.[121] However, we are told that the voyage to and fro Ophir takes three years and so presumably it was a place far away from the Mediterranean. As peacocks and elephants were said to have been brought to the kingdom, it could be a port in Asia or Africa. Most probably, Ophir must be a place in India, the Far East or Congo, to which both these creatures are endemic. There are three species of peacock (a common name for three members of a pheasant family), *Pavo cristatus* (Blue peacock of India), *Pavo muticus* (Green peacock of Myanmar and the Far East) and *Afropavo congensis.* The last one is a colorful pheasant found in Congo, commonly called peacock but not of the genera *Pavo* and so, strictly speaking, it is not peacock but a different bird altogether and is not as beautiful as the peacocks of Asia, especially the Indian species. So Ophir could not have been in Congo but Milman thinks otherwise. He writes, "Hence a fleet, manned by Tyrians, sailed for Ophir, their East Indies, as Tarshish was their West. They coasted along the eastern shore of Africa, in some part of which the real Ophir was probably situated."[122] This, of course, was his conjecture, the evidence to substantiate which he did not provide.

The possibility is that Ophir refers to a port in India. There is ample evidence of trade between the people of the Indus Valley and the West Asian riverine civilisations as for example, Mesopotamia. Pusalkar writes, "At any rate there is an overwhelming mass of evidence showing that a flourishing trade existed between the Indus and Sumer in ancient times. Numerous seals of Indian design and workmanship have been found at various Sumerian and Elamite sites."[123] And that was long before the period of Solomon. So trade between India and West Asia must have continued even during Solomon's time also.

William Logan, an Englishman who was the District Collector of Malabar (now part of Kerala State, India) during the British period in the latter half of the nineteenth century identifies Ophir with Beypore (in Kerala), a port on the West Coast of the peninsular India. That had been the gateway of Indian maritime trade with ancient civilisations in West Asia since ancient times. During the excavations carried out in Kerala in 2008, the Kerala Council of Historical Research had recovered parts of a wooden canoe and bollards. "As determined through analysis using Accelerator Mass Spectrometry radiocarbon, the date range of the canoe sample is 1300 BCE to 100 BCE (that is, 700 plus or minus 600 BCE with 95 per cent probability)," which indicates maritime contacts of Kerala with distant lands as far back in time.[124] Beypore and Kodungallur were the two main ports at that time on the West Coast of the peninsular India. So Logan's theory deserves serious consideration and has to be quoted here fully.

Logan writes, "Some of the more remarkable of the vegetable and animal productions of the Malabar Coast have been known to Western nations from times antecedent to the Christian era and have been the objects of maritime enterprise and commerce through all the succeeding centuries. Perhaps as early as the time of Moses, the great Jewish law-giver, this commerce existed, for cinnamon and cassia played a part in the temple services of the Jews[125] and at any rate the Bible narrative records that silver 'was nothing accounted of in the days of Solomon'—everything was of gold. 'For the king had at sea a navy of Tharshish with the navy of Hiram; once in three years[126] came the navy of Tharshish bringing gold and silver, ivory, and apes and peacocks.'[127] With the exception perhaps of silver, these are all productions of the Malabar Coast, and the Biblical name for the peacock – tuki – is evidently the *Tam. / Mal*[128]. *tokai*, the bird of the tail.

Again, Solomon obtained his gold from *Ophir*. It is hazardous after all that has been written about this place to contribute anything more to the controversy, for as Master Purchas quaintly wrote about it: 'this Golden Country is like Gold, hard to find, and much quarreled, and needs a wise Myner to bring it out of the Labyrinths of darkness, and to try and purifie (sic) the Myners themselves and their reports.' But it may as well be pointed out that Beypore lies at the mouth of the river of the same name, which still brings down gold from the auriferous quartz region of South-East Wainad, the mines of which were well worked in pre-historic times; that *Tundis*, the 'village of great note situated near the sea' mentioned in the early centuries AD (CE) by the author of the Periplus Mar, Eryth lies close to Beypore on the southern bank of the same river; and that the country lying inland from these places is still called Ernad – the bullock, that is grazing, country. If *Ophir*, as is generally now supposed, meant the country of the *Abhira* or cowherds (Kurumbar?), then the name of *Ophir* fits the locality indicated as well as, or better, perhaps than, any of the numerous other places with which it has been identified. There has also been much learned disquisition on the word *Tharshish*, and the name perhaps survived on the coast till the ninth century AD in the word *Tarisa-palli* or church of the Tarisa (Tharshish ?) people...."[129]

All these views about Ophir are doubtless conjectures or hypotheses, for there is no direct and incontrovertible documentary or archaeological evidence to connect Ophir with India, Far East or Africa. In fact, no biblical scholar has ventured to associate Ophir with any of the places known to us today.

However, it is immaterial from where Solomon imported the gold and other valuables; the important point is that Israel's maritime trade with countries far from Tharshish flourished in Solomon's time. Tyre being a staunch ally of Solomon the commercial activities of the Hebrew kingdom in general was at its zenith during Solomon's period. As a result, this period witnessed an unprecedented expansion of trade and the consequent prosperity made the people of all classes happy. Unlike David who expanded the Hebrew kingdom by invading the neighbouring kingdoms and annexing them or reducing them to tributaries, Solomon was not a conqueror. He believed in diplomacy and concentrated on the economic development of the kingdom, which made his reign a magnificent era of peace and prosperity. In short, Solomon's "reign witnessed a great development in Hebrew trade, wealth and culture."[130]

Solomon's achievements were, therefore, primarily in the area of commerce, both inland and overseas, that enhanced the prestige and power of the Hebrew kingdom. The most important factor that helped the commercial activities of the kingdom had been the treaty with Hiram, the king of Tyre. "Tyre furnished the ship builders and mariners; the fruitful plains of Palestine victualed the fleets and supplied the manufacturers and merchants of the Phoenician league with all the necessaries of life."[131] The conquests of David had given the Hebrews an opening to the eastern coast of the gulf. Solomon, who was intent on expanding maritime trade, developed the ports of Elath and Ezion-gerber, which enabled trade with countries in the East and a fleet manned by Tyrians established regular trade with

Ophir. "The whole maritime traffic with eastern Asia, the southern shores of the Arabian peninsula, the coasts of the Persian Gulf, and *without doubt some parts of India*, entered in the same manner, the Red Sea, and was brought to Elath and Ezion-gerber."[132] So the state treasury, which had become practically empty as a result of his building mania, began overflowing again, a part of which naturally flowed down to the nobles or the upper-class freemen constituting the Chauvinists and the priestly class, but not much percolated further down. Let alone the slaves, even the petty traders, the artisans, the agricultural workers that constituted the lower middle class and the unskilled labourers were not benefitted much. Added to it, as a result of the heavy taxes he levied and the imposition of forced labour, this section of the society continued to be discontented.

We had seen that the struggle for supremacy had been going on between the spiritual and temporal powers since the days of Moses and this escalated, resulting in total estrangement between them during the reign of Saul, who began to ignore the clergy totally, although he professed to be a religio-purist. It reached its climax when Samuel swore to see the end of Saul's dynasty and walked out of the palace in a huff. David, who succeeded Saul, was totally subservient to the priesthood, with the result the relationship between the temporals and the spirituals was free from friction and was altogether quite smooth. It was during the period of Solomon the power struggle between the king and the clergy intensified and the rupture between the state and the clergy was complete when the clergy warned Solomon that the kingdom would be split and one part would be given "to your servant."[133]

The reason for the clergy backing him earlier was that he was after all the son of a Hittite woman who was formerly the wife of a soldier in David's army. So, they thought, he must be aware of his lack of legitimacy to the throne and would be indebted to the clergy for their support and that he would not deviate from the path of religio-purism. But for the clergy's intervention at the right time, David would have forsaken him in favour of Absalom, whom the people at large looked up to as David's successor and for whom David had a soft corner even after he revolted. David had instructed Joab, Abishai and Ittai not to harm Absalom under any circumstances despite the fact that he engineered a revolt in a bid to overthrow David. David cried his eyes out when he was told that Absalom was killed[134] and what should have been a day of rejoicing, thus, turned into a day of mourning. Solomon undoubtedly had been placating the clergy[135] and he remained loyal to them because he knew, it was the clergy's support that helped rally the Chauvinists and the king's elite bodyguard behind him. The clergy naturally thought that he would remain a religio-purist and that it would not be difficult for them to influence him and to have their voice heard in the king's palace. Of course, Solomon never displeased the priests and the construction of the Temple was the symbol of his homage and the greatest tribute that he paid to the clergy.

However, Solomon, wise as he was, followed a liberal religious policy that a pluralist society like the one that prevailed then, demanded. But neither the conservative Chauvinists nor the Hebrews in general were ready to accept it. The Judaists had always been religious fanatics and Solomon's religious policy that gave freedom of worship to all the tribes that constituted his kingdom was not appreciated by them. Solomon constructed temples for the Phoenician god Ashtoreth and for the Ammonite goddess Molech, which the Hebrews considered abominable. And "on the hill that is before Jerusalem" he constructed a temple for the god Chemosh of the Moabites. He also built several temples for the various gods and goddesses of the many non-Hebrew wives of his. The Chauvinists regarded this as blasphemy and thought that it encouraged allotheism and idolatry.[136]

The fanatic Judaists, that is the religio-purists, were outraged. Solomon, perhaps, thought it imperative to adopt liberal religious policy to bring about cohesiveness in a pluralist society but on the contrary it polarised the society. The jingoistic powerful Hebrew upper class that constituted the Chauvinists, who were fanatically monotheistic and intolerant of other religions – especially the polytheistic and idolatrous religions – rallied behind their clergy to oppose the king. The non-Hebrew section of the population with their liberal religious outlook, which was inherent to polytheistic religions and a minority of the Hebrews who were inclined to religio-liberalism in consequence of their marriage with non-Hebrews, constituted the Liberals. They were happy with the religious freedom that had been denied to them all these years. They comprised mostly the lower middle class like petty traders, artisans, and unskilled wage labourers who were not politically significant and were, naturally, looked down upon by the elite Hebrews.

Solomon had married, apart from the Pharaoh's daughter, women of various non-Hebrew tribes, like the Moabites, Ammonites, Edomites, Zidonians and Hittites. The priests had cautioned him against marrying women of other tribes, saying that it would diminish his commitment to the cause of religio-purism. And it did. Ignoring all the advice and warnings, he initiated and became the first Hebrew king to implement a liberal religious policy. He gave financial aid to the non-Hebrews generously to construct temples for their gods.[137] The Chauvinists were not happy with what they thought was Solomon's misplaced generosity that helped construction of temples for those alien gods. They feared that it would strengthen the Liberals, correspondingly weakening them and would turn out to be a threat to Judaism. The Chauvinists found to their consternation that Solomon had begun to ignore them. The clergy expressed their indignation to the king for forsaking religio-purism and said they had promised to support him on condition that he would not help the Liberals, but he seemed to have forgotten that.[138] They thought that such a vast kingdom with its coffers overflowing with money had given the king too much power in his hands and made him arrogant.

So they decided to give Solomon pinpricks that would make him seek their help to get rid of those responsible for it. And with that intention the clergy, prompted by the Chauvinists "stirred up" Hadad, who was a member of the royal family of Edom.[139] Long back when David's army had conquered Edom, a few royalist officials fled carrying him, who was a child then, to Egypt where the Pharaoh gave them political asylum. Subsequently, he married the Pharaoh's sister-in-law. When David and Joab died, he returned to Edom and now with the tacit support of the Chauvinists he began to harass Solomon. At about the same time, Rezon, a former official of the king of Zobah, who fled the city when David attacked the city and subdued it, had re-established himself as king in Damascus. Instigated by the Chauvinists, he gathered a few guerillas and occasionally made forays on the kingdom, giving Solomon some sleepless nights.[140] Solomon, however, did not seem to have taken these very seriously and was able to deal with these troublemakers without much difficulty.

Having failed to bring Solomon to his knees, the Chauvinists felt that something more drastic had to be done. There was a suggestion from lay Chauvinists to deprive Solomon's sons of the right to succession. But the clergy overruled it because the clergy had as much sentimental attachment to the Davidic dynasty, as they were proud of the Davidian legacy of strong commitment to religio-purism. As an alternative, it was decided to split the kingdom – separate Israel and Judah – and anoint Solomon's son as the king of Judah while enthroning one from among one of the northern tribes in Israel. And the chief priest was asked to warn Solomon, which he did.[141] But Solomon did not change his religious policy or for that matter any of his policies.

So they decided to go ahead with the plan of splitting the kingdom. The wily priests calculated that if the present kingdom was to be divided and one part given to Israel, the mutual rivalry between Israel and Judah would keep them fighting with each other. And that would act as a check on both of them and the kings of both kingdoms, Judah and Israel, would naturally turn to them for help to meet the threat from the neighbouring Hebrew kingdom.

They were aware of an undercurrent of disaffection among the northern tribes as the kingship had been with the southern tribes ever since monarchy was introduced in the Hebrew world. All the three kings, Saul, David and Solomon, who ruled the Hebrew kingdom so far, were from the two southern tribes – Saul, a Benjaminite and the other two Judahites. That discontent, they thought, could be taken advantage of to drive a wedge between the North and the South. So they conferred with the Chauvinists and together they carried on a whispering campaign about the domination of the North by the South, subtly suggesting to the chieftains of the northern tribes to revolt against Solomon's successor and demand secession from the southern region. The kings of both kingdoms would then woo the Chauvinists, lest they sided with the other king, tilting the balance of power to that side. The clergy could thus be in a strong position as that would give them enough leverage to influence policy decisions.

The Chauvinists decided to foment a rebellion to cause a schism in the united monarchic state, and they entrusted Ahijah, a prophet, with the task of engineering a rebellion. They had also suggested the name of Jeroboam, "a mighty man of valour," who, they thought, would be the right person to lead the rebellion and wanted Ahijah to talk to him confidentially. So Ahijah went incognito – for he had put on a new robe – to avoid being recognised by anyone and had a secret meeting with Jeroboam who was a supervisor of public works under Solomon, in a lonely spot on the outskirts of Jerusalem.[142] Ahijah said to Jeroboam that the Chauvinists had decided to split the kingdom and enthrone him as king of the northern kingdom to be called Israel while a descendant of David will be made the king of the southern one, Judah.

He assured Jeroboam of the full support of the Chauvinists, but on one condition. He wanted him to rule strictly in accordance with the Mosaic Code of Law, which in practice was total subservience to the clergy and by extension, the lay Chauvinists.[143] At the end of the meeting, Ahijah removed the new robe and tore it into twelve pieces, and wore his usual old clothes, lest his new garment aroused the suspicion of the king's spies.[144] *En resume,* although Solomon's period was an era of peace and prosperity, all sections of the population were discontented for various reasons and at the time of his death the kingdom was on the verge of a split. The taxation policy of Solomon had antagonised the economically weaker sections of all tribes because it impoverished them further and his labour policy of conscription of labour disrupted the family life of the labourers who were sent to work in places far off from their homes. His liberal religious policy was resented by the affluent upper middle class, the Chauvinists, particularly the clergy. Their resentment was not because it encouraged allotheism; the clergy objected to this policy primarily because a large sum of money was going into the hands of the non-Hebrew religious establishments which, otherwise, they would have got. The Chauvinists in general felt that this religious policy was strengthening the Liberals and at this rate, they would soon become the dominant force in the country.

All these factors helped Jeroboam to instigate the people against the King. So as advised by Ahijah, Jeroboam, hoping to be the king of Israel and assured of the tacit support of the powerful Chauvinists and the people at large, raised the banner of revolt. But Solomon put down the insurgency and would have killed Jeroboam had he not fled to Egypt where he found sanctuary. However, consequent upon this general discontent and the propaganda carried out by Jeroboam, secessionist forces had become vociferous and dark clouds of rebellion that could plunge the kingdom into a civil war were gathering over the kingdom.

NOTES

1. Also spelt Cis, vide Acts 13:21.
2. I Sam. 9:15-16. "now the Lord had told Samuel in his ear the day before Saul came...Tomorrow about this time I will send you a man but of the land of Benjamin and you shall anoint him to be king over the people of Israel." "—the Lord had told" does not mean that a mysterious person called god told him; it simply means he just thought of Saul whom he had known already.
3. I Sam. 9:6.
4. I Sam. 9:17. "...the Lord said to him, look, the man whom I spoke to you of!" This indicates that Samuel recognised Saul whom he had seen years ago.
5. I Sam. 9:19.
6. I Sam. 9:20. "And on whom is all the desire of Israel? Is it not on you, and on all your father's house?"
7. I Sam. 9:21.
8. I Sam. 9:25.
9. I Sam. 10:1.
10. I Sam. 10:2-8.
11. I Sam. 10:16.
12. I Sam. 10:20-24.
13. Belial is not a proper noun. The meaning of the word is, "wickedness," "lawlessness." Vide Deut. 13:13; Judg. 19:22; I Sam. 25:25.
14. I Sam. 10:27. Belial, an abstract noun, is personified here and used as a proper noun.
15. I Sam. 11:7. "And he took a yoke of oxen, and hewed them in pieces, and sent them throughout all the coasts of Israel by the hands of messengers, saying, Whosoever comes not after Saul and after Samuel so shall be done to his oxen."
16. I Sam. 11:11.
17. Please note they went to Gilgal for crowning Saul. So their base is still at Gilgal which confirms the fact that Israel had not occupied all the

territories that the Bible says Joshua had conquered and distributed among the Hebrew tribes.

18. I Sam. 12:3-4.
19. I Sam. 12:13, 14, 15. "Now, therefore, here is the king that you have chosen, and whom you have desired! And, take note, the Lord has set a king over you. If you fear the Lord, and serve him, and obey his voice and not rebel against the commandment of the Lord, then shall both you and the king that reigns over you will continue following the Lord, your God. But if you will not obey the voice of the Lord, then the hand of the Lord will be against you......." The "Lord" and "God" in this quote denote the priesthood.
20. I Sam. 12:17. "...you may perceive and see that your wickedness is great, which you have done in the sight of the Lord, in asking for a king."
21. I Sam. 12:18. ""...Samuel called up the Lord: and the Lord sent thunder and rain that day. And all the people greatly feared the Lord and Samuel." This connotes wrathful Samuel.
22. I Sam. 12:24. "Only fear the Lord, and serve him in truth with all your heart, for he has done great things for you."
23. I Sam. 12:25. "But if you still do wickedly, you shall be consumed, both you and your king."
24. I Sam. 13:1.
25. I. Asimov, *Guide to the Bible*, New York,1981, pp. 279-280.
26. I Sam. 13:6-7.
27. I Sam. 13:13, 14. "And Samuel said to Saul...You have not kept the commandment of the Lord your god...but now your kingdom shall not continue..."
28. I Sam. 13:19-22.
29. I Sam. 14:21.
30. I Sam. 14:45.
31. I Sam. 15:3.
32. I Sam. 15:11. "I repent that I have set up Saul to be king; for he has turned back from following me, and has not performed my commandments..."
33. I Sam. 15:17-19. "...When you were little in your own sight, were you not made the head of the tribes of Israel, and the Lord anointed you king over Israel? And the Lord sent you on a journey, and said, Go and utterly destroy the sinners the Amalekites, and fight against them until they be consumed. Why then did you not obey the voice of the Lord but did grab the spoil...?" Again, "the Lord" in the quote denotes the clergy.

34. I Sam. 15:7-9.
35. I Sam. 15:15. The phrase "to sacrifice to the Lord your God" means to present to the clergy, that is Samuel who represents the clergy.
36. I Sam. 15:21.
37. I Sam. 15:24.
38. I Sam. 15:30. "...honour me now, I beseech you, before the elders of my people and before Israel and turn again with me that I may worship the Lord your God."
39. I Sam. 15:33.
40. I Sam. 16:2.
41. I Sam. 17:4-9.
42. There is another story of equally doubtful authenticity about David's introduction to Saul's court. Saul's misunderstanding with Samuel and Samuel's warning that he would split the kingdom had made Saul uneasy and on the advice of his courtiers, he got a man to play harp for him to soothe his mind. The harp player happened to be David. Saul was pleased with him and so he made David his armour bearer.
43. I Saam. 17:31-51.
44. I Sam. 19:11-17.
45. I Sam. 18:14. "...David behaved himself wisely in all his ways; and the Lord was with him." In this context also, "the Lord" denotes clergy.
46. I Sam. 20:16-24.
47. I Sam. 21:2. "The king hath commanded me on a business. Let no man know anything of the business whereabout I send thee..."
48. I Sam. 22:23.
49. I Sam. 23:11-12. "Will the men of Keilah deliver me and my men into the hand of Saul? And the Lord said, They will deliver you." "the Lord" denotes the clergy.
50. I Sam. 23:16-17. "...and encouraged him in his faith in God" denotes the full backing of the clergy.
51. I Sam. 24:9-22.
52. I Sam. 26:1-25.
53. I Sam. 28:2.
54. I Chr. 10:4.
55. II Sam. 2:8-9.
56. I Sam. 30:8. "...David enquired at the Lord, saying shall I pursue after this troop? Shall I overtake them? And He answered him, Pursue, for you shall surely overtake them, and without fail recover all." This means David consulted the priesthood and the priests advised him to pursue.
57. II Sam. 2:1. "...enquired of the Lord, saying, Shall I go up into any of the cities of Judah?... And the Lord said to him, Go up...to Hebron."

58. II Sam. 2:8.
59. II Sam. 2:14-23.
60. II Sam. 3:8-12.
61. II Sam. 3:27.
62. II Sam. 5:2. "Also in time past...the Lord said to you, you shall feed my people and you shall be captain over Israel."
63. II Sam. 5:6-11. The Bible says, "Then Hiram, king of Tyre..." This is a mix-up of the two episodes which are just fiction or anachronism, presuming that the characters involved are historical personalities because Hiram is mentioned as the king of Tyre when Solomon who succeeded David was on the throne of Israel.
64. Sam. 5:12. "And David perceived that the Lord had established him king over Israel and he had exalted his kingdom for the sake of this people of Israel."
65. II Sam. 5:19. "And David enquired of the Lord, saying, Shall I go up to the Philistines?...and the Lord said to David Go up..."
66. II Sam. 5:23-24. "And when David enquired of the Lord, he said you shall not go; but encircle behind them and come upon them in front of the mulberry trees. And let it be when you hear the sound of marching in the tops of the mulberry trees, that then you shall advance..."
67. II Sam. 6:17.
68. II Sam. 6:14-16.
69. We come to know of this from Shimel of the House of Saul when he accused David of killing those persons. Vide II Sam.16:5-8. We shall return to it presently.
70. II Sam. 9:6-13. "...Fear not; for I will surely show you kindness for Jonathan's sake, and will restore you all the land of Saul; and you shall eat bread at my table continually...And Mephibosheth dwelt in Jerusalem...:
71. II Sam. 8:14. "...and the Lord preserved David wherever he went."
72. II Sam. 11:2-15.
73. Lev. 20:10.
74. II Sam. 8:10-11. "Which also king David did dedicate to the Lord, with the silver and gold..."
75. II Sam. 12:1, 7, 9. "And the Lord sent Nathan to David...and Nathan said to David...Thus says the Lord god of Israel...you have killed Uriah the Hittite with the sword, and has taken the wife of Uriah the Hittite to be your wife."
76. II Kgs. 14:6.
77. II Sam. 12:24-25. "...and the Lord loved him. And he sent by the

hand of Nathan, the prophet; and he called his name Jedidiah..."

78. II Sam. 12:30.
79. B.W. Anderson, *Understanding the Old Testament*, Englewood Cliffs, 1975, pp. 183-184.
80. Lev. 20:17.
81. II Sam. 14:2-21.
82. II Sam. 14:24.
83. II Sam. 14:32.
84. II Sam. 15:1-6.
85. II Sam. 15:8.
86. II Sam. 15:10.
87. II Sam. 15:13, 31.
88. II Sam. 17:16.
89. II Sam. 18:6.
90. II Sam. 18:14,
91. II Sam. 20:1.
92. II Sam. 20:4-5.
93. II Sam. 21:1. "Then there was a famine in the days of David for three years, year after year and David enquired for the Lord. And the Lord answered, It is for Saul and, for his bloody house, because he slew the Gibeonites."
94. II Sam. 21:2-9.
95. II Kgs. 14:6.
96. II Sam. 21:10. "And Rizpah the daughter of Aiah, tore sackcloth and spread it for her on the rock, from the beginning of harvest until water dropped on them out of heaven..." [Rizpah was a concubine of Saul and Ishbosheth, son of Saul, had accused Saul's cousin, Abner, of sex with her, vide II Sam. 3:7.]
97. II Sam. 24:1-2.
98. B.W. Anderson, *Understanding the Old Testament,* Englewood Cliffs, 1975, p. 183.
99. II Sam. 24:15, 16. "...THE Lord sent a pestilence upon Israel...and there died of people from Dan even to Beersheba seventy thousand men. And when the angel stretched out his hand to destroy Jerusalem, the Lord...said to the angel...It is enough..."
100. It may be noted that he was not anointed even though Abiathar, the priest, was with him.
101. I Kgs. 1:8, 38 ff.
102. It is the name of a mythical river in Eden, vide Gen2:13. (See also Chapter 3, "A Virtual Tower of Babel.")
103. I Kgs. 1:38-40, 48.

104. I Kgs. 1:50-53.
105. I Kgs. 2:5, 8.
106. I Kgs. 2:22-35.
107. I Kgs. 2:46.
108. I Kgs. 3:1/9:6.
109. I Kgs. 3:5, 11, 12, 14. "In Gibeon the Lord appeared to Solomon in a dream by night; and God said, Ask what I shall give you...And God said to him...Behold, I have done according to your words." "And if you will walk in my ways, to keep my statutes and my commandments as your father David did walk, then I will lengthen your days."
110. I Kgs. 4:2-19.
111. I Kgs. 4:25.
112. I Kgs. 4:26.
113. I Kgs. 6:1-38.
114. I Kgs. 5:5-11.
115. I Kgs. 9:2-8.
116. I Kgs. 9:5.
117. I Kgs. 9:7. "Then will I cut off Israel out of the land which I have given them..."
118. I Kgs. 9:20-23.
119. I Kgs. 9:11.
120. I Kgs. 9:13.
121. I Kgs. 9:28/10:22; I Chr.29:4; Job 22:24/28:16; Isa.13:12.
122. H.H. Milman, *The History of the Jews*, V.1, New York, 1870, p. 368.
123. R.C. Majumdar, et al. Eds., *The History and Culture of the Indian People, The Prehistoric Age*, Bk.2, by A. D. Pusalkar, Bombay, 1965, p. 200. "Indus" refers to the ancient civilisation of the Indus Valley in India, which was contemporaneous with other riparian civilisations
124. *The Hindu* of January 9, 2008.
125. Ex. 30:23-24.
126. Please note the Bible says "the voyage to and from Ophir takes three years."
127. I Kgs. 9:28/10:11, 22.
128. Tam is the abbreviation for Tamil, the language of Tamil Nadu, a state in peninsular India and Mal, the abbreviation for Malayalam, the language of the people of Kerala, the neighbouring state on the west coast, in which Beypore is.
129. W. Logan, *Malabar Manual*, V. 1., Madras, 1887, p. 246.
130. A.W.F. Blunt, *Israel in World History*, London, 1927, p. 37.
131. H. H. Milman, op. cit., pp. 367-368.
132. Ibid., p. 369. Italics added.

133. I Kgs. 11:11.
134. II Sam. 18:33.
135. I Kgs. 3:3. "and Solomon loved the Lord...only he sacrificed and burnt incense in high places."
136. I Kgs. 11:4-10.
137. I Kgs. 11:1-8. "...the Lord said to the children of Israel...they will turn away your heart after their gods: Solomon clung to those in love...and his wives turned away his heart after other gods...Then Solomon built an high place for Chemosh, the abomination of Moab in the hill that is before Jerusalem and for Molech, the abomination of the children of Ammon."
138. I Kgs. 11:9-10. "And the Lord was angry with Solomon, because his heart was turned from the Lord God of Israel, which had appeared to him twice. And he commanded him concerning this thing..."
139. I Kgs. 11:14. "...the Lord stirred up an adversary to Solomon, Hadad the Edomite..."
140. I Kgs. 11:23. "...God stirred up another adversary, Rezon..."
141. I Kgs. 11:11-13. "...I will surely rend the kingdom from you, and will give it to your servant...I will rend it out of the hands of your son. However I will not rend away the kingdom; but will give one tribe to your son for David my servant's sake..."
142. I Kgs. 11:29. "And it came to pass at that time when Jeroboam went out of Jerusalem, that the prophet Ahijah the Shilonite found him in the way; and he had clad himself with a new garment; and they two were alone in the field.
143. I Kgs. 11:38. "...And it shall be, if you will listen to all that I command you and walk in my ways and do tht is right in my sight, to keep my statutes and my commandments, as David my servant did; that I will be with you...and will give Israel to you."
144. I Kgs. 11:30.

7

The Rise of Imperialism

With the death of Solomon the throne was naturally claimed by Rehoboam, who was the legitimate successor. It may be recalled that Ahijah, a prophet from the ranks of Yahwist clergy, had a secret meeting with Jeroboam when he said to Jeroboam that the kingdom would be split and he would be to put on the throne of Israel if he would overthrow Solomon. So Jeroboam had raised the banner of revolt that failed and he fled to Egypt. The religious and the anti-people economic and labour policies of the king were the main issues that helped fuel the revolt, bringing all strata of freemen of the northern tribes of Israel together. The domination of the North by the South was a problem that was brought in by the Chauvinists to buttress the seething anger of the people against the government of Judah. The inherent fissiparous tendency of the Hebrew tribes of the northern and southern regions, which remained dormant during the reigns of David and Solomon, began to assert itself. The rivalry between the Judaists and the Ephraimites was a significant factor in the history of the Hebrew kingdom and the apparent unity displayed by the Hebrews during the period of David did not last for more than a couple of generations. The haughty Ephraimites "had never fully acquiesced in the supremacy of the Judah, or in the removal of the Ark and of the divine worship from their cities, Gilgal or Schechem, to the new capital."[1] Added to this was the structural weakness of the Hebrew kingdom which may be attributed primarily to the manner in which the monarchic state was established in the Hebrew society. Had it come into existence naturally as a result of the evolving socio-economic forces, the tribal mindset of the Hebrews too would have got transformed in the process.

The political machinery of the kingdom had always been in the hands of the Judah and the money through taxes and trade was flowing into their pockets. Consequently, they were flourishing and becoming quite powerful economically and politically, thus upsetting the balance of power among the tribes. And this imbalance was creating problems in inter-tribal relations among the Hebrews. To this were added racial and religious prejudices. The Judah was looked down upon by the northern tribes. It "was strongly mixed with Arab and Edomite stocks; Othniel the Menizzite was one of its tribal heroes and Kenaz was an Edomite clan; and we find Judah connected with the Arabian clans of the Kenites and the Jerahmeelites."[2] Moreover, the differences in the religious practices of the northern and southern tribes were one of the causes of their mutual animosity. The southern tribes that were dogmatically anthropomorphic monotheists could not tolerate the theriomorphic polytheism of their brethren in the north.

It was against this background but not aware of it, that Rehoboam decided to hold his coronation at Schechem as the third king of the Davidic dynasty.[3] The freemen of all the ten tribes of the northern region were unhappy with the continued domination by Judah, for which, to a great extent, the Chauvinists were responsible. They deliberately whipped up anti-Judah sentiment among the northern tribes to meet their selfish end. The Chauvinists thought this was an opportune moment to act on their plan of splitting the kingdom. They conveyed the news of the death of Solomon and the proposed coronation of Rehoboam at Shechem to Jeroboam, who was in self-exile in Egypt, with a request to return to Shechem without any delay.[4] On receipt of the message, Jeroboam hurried to Judah and proceeded straight to Shechem to be there at the coronation. When the Chauvinists heard that Jeroboam had come and was there at the coronation, which was attended by all the twelve tribes of Hebrews, they were happy. They welcomed him and urged him to lead a delegation to the king to elicit from him a promise that he would revise Solomon's religious, fiscal and labour policies.

The delegation led by Jeroboam met Rehoboam and wanted him to spell out his policies on religion, taxation and labour. They wanted to know specially if he would continue the religious liberalism, heavy taxation and forced labour that his father Solomon had put into practice. They pointed out that liberal religious policy had resulted in apostasy and allotheism, the heavy taxes had drained the people white and forced labour had completely disrupted the family life of the lower middle class and the wage labourers. Hence, they demanded, he should scrap those policies and strictly adhere to Yahwism, reduce the tax burden and abolish forced labour.[5]

Rehoboam wanted some time to think over the demands before taking any decision on such an important matter and he told the delegation to meet him after three days. The experienced elder freemen, the royalists who supported Rehoboam, advised the king to consider the people's request favourably, but the king relied on the advice of his coterie, a group of inexperienced youth. On the fourth day when the delegation met the king, he said brusquely, he would not give up religious liberalism; he would collect much higher taxes; and he would continue forced labour more rigorously than his father did.[6] He explained saying, under no circumstances would he abandon those wise policies that proved correct as they helped improve the economy of the country and the integration of society comprising different religious groups. This was the answer the secessionists wanted. The king, thus, played into the hands of the secessionists by his tactlessness in dealing with the opposition and impudently refusing any reconsideration of those policies. He totally estranged the freemen rich and poor, making the task easy for Jeroboam and the Chauvinists of Israel who had been scheming to split the kingdom. Taking advantage of the anger of the northern tribes at the king's refusal to comply with their request Jeroboam backed by the Chauvinists, gave a call to the northern tribes to fight for secession from the southern region and to form an independent kingdom of Israel comprising the ten tribes of the North.

So the northerners led by Jeroboam repudiated Rehoboam saying, "Now see to your own house, David" and they went back to their territory. Rehoboam, in keeping with what he said, detailed his officer, Adoram, to draft men from the northern tribes for forced labour camps, but the tribesmen of the North resisted and they stoned Adoram to death.[7] Rehoboam now realised that the northern tribes were violently opposed to his accession to the throne and so it was too dangerous for him to be in Shechem, in the midst of hostile tribes. Perhaps he must have also feared that if he did not reach Jerusalem before the news of the rebellion of the northern tribes and the secession of the North reached the city, a pretender to the throne might turn up, leaving him in the lurch. So he left the city post-haste and on reaching Jerusalem, mobilised the army to be sent to the North to put down the rebellion and save the kingdom from disintegration.

The chief priest of the Judaean clergy, Shemaiah, was informed of the king's intention to send the army to quell the rebellion in the North. Shemaiah, being a priest, was privy to the conspiracy and was more interested in splitting than in the unity of the Hebrew kingdom, for the clergy stood to gain if the kingdom split. And Shemaiah did what the Chauvinists and of course he and the clergy too, wanted. Making use of his position as adviser, Shemaiah told Rehoboam to restrain himself from using force against his brethren to prevent secession.[8] Rehoboam too must have felt that there was little chance of unity now and it was better that he saved his throne. He feared that if he tried to suppress the rebellion, he could possibly be overthrown and one from among the northern tribes would be made the king over Judah too.

Besides, having seen the situation himself, Rehoboam must have realised the futility of risking his throne by trying to put down the rebellion that was so broad-based, widespread and highly motivated. Hence he thought it was better to pretend that he was going by the clergy's advice, for two reasons. First of all it would help cover up his weakness. More importantly, the notion that he acted as per the advice of the clergy, he must have thought, would help him get the support of the Chauvinists of the South if any opposition to his kingship were to be voiced by any pretender or if the North were to invade the South. In a crisis like this when a majority of the Hebrew tribes had revolted and the threat of secession of the northern region was imminent, he rightly thought, the cooperation of the Chauvinists was of utmost importance; rather it would prove to be crucial.

Although Jeroboam was identified with religio-purism, the freemen, including the religio-liberals of all the Hebrew tribes of the northern region, wanted Jeroboam himself who led the rebellion and helped secede from the South, to be their king.[9] With the assured support of the Chauvinists as well as the masses, both religio-purists and Liberals, he was crowned the king of Israel with Shechem as its capital (later shifted to Tirzah[10]) and that ended forever the domination of Judah over Israel and the united kingdom of the Hebrews. They thought that all their troubles had come to an end, but their share of woes was not over. The cold war between the twin kingdoms continued, now and then flaring up into armed conflicts that weakened both the kingdoms. Blunt states, "The cleavage between Judah and Ephraim is one of the most remarkable features in the history of the early monarchy. David brought them together into one polity, but their mutual rivalry was a constant trouble to him and to his son, and it broke out in fatal dissension on Rehoboam's accession."[11]

Jeroboam was unsure of the people's loyalty to his regime and to himself, although the people, rich and poor, were unanimous in choosing him to be the king of the new kingdom of Israel. Besides, it was at the behest of the clergy that he took the lead in stirring the people to revolt against the South, when Rehoboam vowed to continue Solomon's oppressive policies and so he presumed he had the wholehearted support of the Chauvinists too. But Judah had a powerful weapon in its hand – the Temple – that could be used against Israel and that thought was worrying him. He was afraid that if and when the people of the North go to offer sacrifice in the Temple at Jerusalem, they might develop an emotional attachment to Judah and switch their loyalty to Rehoboam, the king of Judah.[12] They would be the fifth column of Judah and would make it easy for Judah to conquer and annex the northern region. A victim of paranoia, Jeroboam decided to prevent the Hebrew population going all the way to Judah to offer sacrifice. He, therefore, set up shrines in the hilly regions and installed idols of two calves of gold, one at Bethel near the southern limit of his kingdom and the other at Dan in the north bordering Judah. He then proclaimed that his subjects could offer sacrifices at these altars instead of going all the way to Jerusalem for the purpose. So he thought he could now rest assured that the people would not go to Judah territory and be brainwashed against him by Rehoboam's henchmen.

This, no doubt, pleased the Liberals but angered the Charuvinists. Contrary to his calculations, they, the very section of society that helped him to the throne, turned against him. They did not naturally approve of his policy and openly accused the king of encouraging idolatry, referring to the installation of golden idols of calves, which contravened the tenets of Mosaic religion. They were upset because it not only legitimised but encouraged idolatry and liberalism. In order to meet the challenge of the Chauvinists, Jerobaom reckoned that dilution of the priestly class, the ideologues of the Chauvinists, with non-Levites would weaken the clergy and they would not be able to poke their nose in matters connected with the state. So he expelled many priests of the Levite tribe and ordained as priests "the lowest of the people" – from tribes other than the Levite. Jeroboam's religious policy not only helped project himself as a committed religio-liberal and get the support of the Liberals but also all the non-Hebrew tribes.

But the priests were, naturally, furious. The appointment of non-Levites to priesthood deprived the traditional priestly class of their income and influence and considerably weakened their political clout. In spite of the warnings of the clergy, he appointed many more priests, all of whom were non-Levites. This forced many Levites to leave Israel and migrate to Jerusalem and this was followed by the migration of many devout Yahwists from all other tribes in Israel to Jerusalem.[13] Jeroboam thought he had broken the backbone of the Chauvinists, particularly the clergy, and he continued to implement his radically liberal religious policy. So he appointed more and more priests from among the non-Levites.[14] But contrary to his expectation, this spelt his doom. Those Levites who remained in Israel turned against him and his liberal religious policy that in effect, was threatening to strike at the root of Yahwism estranged the Chauvinists completely.

He, however, did not foresee any danger from the Chauvinists in general or the clergy in particular, thinking that he had clipped their wings, but he was mistaken. They struck back. They decided to put an end to the dynasty of Jeroboam and hatched a conspiracy to murder Jeroboam's son, the heir to the throne of Israel. It was obviously being planned with the knowledge of Ahijah, who was now superannuated and living in Shiloh. They decided to carry it out at an opportune moment. Jeroboam got intelligence through his spies that a conspiracy was afoot to kill his son. But the cold war between Judah and Israel kept the king tied up with the problem of keeping the southern neighbour at bay and ensuring the security of his kingdom. He, therefore, sent his wife secretly to Shiloh to plead with Ahijah to use his good offices to dissuade the clergy from carrying out the plot. He asked his wife to disguise herself because he did not want the local priests and the lay Chauvinists to know that he was trying to influence Ahijah,[15] lest they pre-empt him and brainwash Ahijah against him. He thought Ahijah, who had tremendous influence with the clergy as well as the lay Chauvinists, was favorably disposed towards him. He told his wife that it was Ahijah who met him secretly and urged him to organise a rebellion against Solomon promising to make him the king of Israel. He was, therefore, sure that Ahijah would be sympathetic and so he hoped that his wife's mission would not fail. In the absence of his wife whenever the king was occupied with affairs of the state, the child was left with his trusted servants, in whose loyalty he had full faith.

His wife was a little too late. The conspirators had come to know through their moles in the palace that Jeroboam was sending his wife to Ahijah, disguising herself to avoid being recognised by the people. The priests immediately went to Shiloh to meet Ahijah before Jeroboam's wife reached there. They told Ahijah that the queen would be coming incognito and even told him what he should say to her.[16] Hence when Ahijah heard the sound of her footsteps, blind though he was, he said, "Come in, you wife of Jeroboam; why feign yourself to be another?"[17] When she told him the purpose of her visit Ahijah expressed his inability to help her out and as the conspirators wanted him to say, he said that it was too late. He added that the lad would be killed even before she got back to the palace.

For the conspirators, this was the best time to act, as the mother was away and the king was busy with the affairs of the state. The child was left in the care of the servants. Presumably with the connivance of the guards only, the conspirators must have murdered the boy and the Chauvinists were happy that they had exterminated Jeroboam's dynasty.

In the meantime, Rehoboam was busy strengthening the defenses by fortifying all the cities and stationing companies of soldiers in them. All these forts were stocked with sufficient provisions and in each of them he appointed one of his sons as governor. He made his favourite son, Abijah, the heir apparent. Although he did not meddle with the Temple and was a religio-purist, he followed a liberal religious policy,[18] which understandably estranged the Chauvinists. To add insult to injury, he ruled the country, taking the Chauvinists for granted and did not consult them or take their advice, which further angered them. But he simply ignored them and ruled with gay abandon with disastrous consequences. The statement that "there were sodomites in the land," is not to be taken literally to mean that the people of the country were indulging in homosexuality. Sodomy, which, incidentally, was forbidden by Mosaic Law as the people in general considered it unnatural and detestable, is used here as a metaphor to indicate that the people were indulging in unlawful activities. The words 'there were sodomites' read with the statement that 'they did according to the abominations of the nations[19] which the Lord cast out before the children of Israel' points to the complete breakdown of law and order in general and a state of anarchy.[20] Obviously, the general deterioration of law and order must have emboldened some slaves also to defy their masters or even escape to freedom, creating a shortage of labour.

The internal disturbances and the rift between the Chauvinists and the Liberals in both Judah and Israel coupled with the cold war punctuated by hostilities between the two fraternal Hebrew kingdoms had weakened both the kingdoms. So much so the spirit of conquest that characterised the Davidian period had been lost completely. On the contrary, they had become easy prey to predatory kingdoms in the neighbourhood whose spies were in both countries. Shishak of Egypt would have got information about the conditions in the kingdom of Judah and in the fifth year of Rehoboam's reign, he invaded the country. Rehoboam and his courtiers were taken unawares; they had been indulging in luxuries neglecting the defenses of the kingdom. Besides, the bulk of the army was deployed on the northern border to ward off incursions from Israel, with which there had been frequent border skirmishes, which at times reached the dimensions of a full-fledged battle. Hence the Egyptian army marched into Judah without any resistance whatsoever; The governors of all the cities had fled to Jerusalem for safety and the invading army easily overran all the fortified cities on the way and reached Jerusalem,

So the Egyptians attacked Jerusalem and Rehoboam surrendered. The news from the palace reaching Shemaiah indicated the capitulation of Rehoboam. He at once rushed to meet the king and the princes who had gathered in Jerusalem. He told them that Rehoboam lost the war because the Chauvinists who could have gathered a strong army did not co-operate and kept themselves aloof as they were offended by his liberal religious policy.[21] So if he consented to change his religious policy, he would speak to Shishak and request him to sign a peace treaty. The king agreed. So Shemaiah met Shishak and a treaty was signed. Shishak said, since Rehoboam had surrendered, he would not destroy the city or massacre the people; nor would he kill the king and annex the kingdom. But he ransacked the Temple, carrying away all the valuables that were there and reduced Judah into a tributary nation.[22]

Rehoboam died and was succeeded by Abijah, who being a religio-purist, reversed the liberal religious policy of his father and implemented a purist religious policy. Consequently, he was very popular with the Chauvinists. During his brief reign, he too, like his father, was constantly at war with Israel. He contended that as the descendant of David, he had the right to the throne of Israel also. Complaining that Israel took advantage of Rehoboam's inexperience, he ridiculed those that rebelled and seceded from Judah led by Jeroboam. Camping on the Mount Zemaraim, Abijah sent a message to Jeroboam stating that the Davidian dynasty had an inalienable right to rule over Israel, for it was David who consolidated the kingdom and even expanded it. He, therefore, called upon Jeroboam and the people of Israel to refrain from fighting and appealed to them not to resist but return to the fold of the Hebrews.[23] In short, he wanted Israel to accede to Judah. But, as could be expected, Israel rejected his claim to the throne and his appeal for the unification of the kingdom. So Abijah attacked and captured Bethel, Jeshanah, Ephrain and the territories adjoining them.[24] However, Abijah did not live long and on his death, his son Asa came to the throne of Judah when Jeroboam was still ruling Israel.

He too was a strong religio-purist who went a step further and persecuted the non-Hebrews and even disowned his mother who was an idolater.[25] This pleased the Chauvinists. He fortified the cities of Judah and maintained a strong army with a strong regiment of lancers and a regiment of archers. After a short stint of peace, the Judah had to face an aggression by Zerah, the king of Ethiopia with a strong army of chariots. He was marching towards Mareshah, an important city of Judah, but Asa intercepted him in the valley of Zephathah. In the battle that followed, Judah defeated the Ethiopians, who fled, but Asa and his men pursued them to Gerar and annihilated them. The Judah then pillaged all the surrounding cities and carried back to Jerusalem a large quantity of booty including livestock. Since then, there was peace in the land of Judah.

Meanwhile, the death of his son and his defeat in the war with Judah must have had their effect on Jeroboam, for not long after the loss of territory to Judah, he died. The Liberals had become a force to be reckoned with, in Israel. The Chauvinists who conspired and killed Jeroboam's child did not know that Jeroboam had another son by name Nadab, and the death of Jeroboam brought him on the throne of Israel,[26] with the support of the Liberals. The Chauvinists, taken by surprise, could only look on helplessly. He continued the liberal religious policy of his father and was quite unpopular with the Chauvinists. So this time they decided to wipe out the dynasty and conspired with Baasha, a general in the army of Jeroboam, to stage a putsch. And when Nadab was leading the Israelite army, which was besieging the Philistine city of Gibbethon, Baasha, son of Ahijah of the tribe of Issachar, plotted with his colleagues and assassinated Nadab. He also killed, as desired by the Chauvinists, all surviving members of the house of Jeroboam, leaving no one in the line of descent in that dynasty.

So with the support of the Chauvinists, Baasha ascended the throne of Israel when Asa was already at the helm of Judah after the death of his father, Abijah. There were frequent hostilities between the South and the North, with the northern kingdom having the upper hand now. So Asa conscripted all able-bodied men and sent an emissary to Syria to forge an alliance with King Benhadad against Israel. Alarmed at the rising power of Israel, Benhadad jumped at the opportunity and attacked and destroyed some of the cities of Israel. On receiving the news of Benhadad's aggression, Baasha evacuated Ramah which was under construction and went to Tirzah, when Asa attacked Ramah. He looted the stones and timber that were in Ramah and used them to build Geba and Mizpah.[27] Asa lived for some more years when, but for occasional border skirmishes with Israel, peace prevailed.

To the dismay of the Chauvinists, Baasha turned out to be a religio-liberal and refused to carry out the diktat of the priests or the lay Chauvinists. So Jehu, a priest, as a representative of the Chauvinists spoke to him. He said it was the Chauvinists that prepared the ground for him to wear the crown but he was disregarding their advice and acting against their interests. He warned him that if he continued his liberal religious policy he could not expect the Chauvinists to sit back with folded hands and just watch him do whatever he liked. He would have to face serious consequences.[28] Baasha did take the warning seriously but instead of changing his religious policy to please them, he tightened his and his family's security. Being an army officer and a conspirator himself, he also knew how to counteract the conspirators. He had spies all over the country and the Chauvinists failed to depose or assassinate him. He reigned over Israel until he died a natural death. His death was followed by a period of instability as a result of the intrigues of the Chauvinists, trying in vain to put on the throne a pliant king. Meanwhile, however, Baasha's son, Elah, succeeded to the throne of Israel. Asa was still ruling Judah, then.

Elah was not aware of the Chauvinist's plot against his father and Elijah had no suspicion of any plot against him. No one warned him as they did Baasha, which, through hindsight the Chauvinists realised, was a mistake. The warning helped Baasha, for after that he tightened his security so much that the conspirators failed to break through his thick security wall. However, the clergy was not able to find a religio-purist to be crowned as king of Israel now. The army too was not happy with Elah, a very weak king who was almost an alcoholic. Aware of the Chauvinists' opposition to Elah, Zimri, the captain of half the division of the royal chariot troops, decided to capture power and he hatched a conspiracy with Arza, the palace steward. Hardly a year after Elah was crowned, knowing his weakness for alcohol he was inveigled to the house of Arza and made to drink. When he was almost inebriated, Zimri went into the house and assassinated Elah and declared himself the king of Israel. This murder took both the Chauvinists and the Liberals by surprise and so also the army.

Zimri wiped out all members of the House of Baasha. The Chauvinists had been seething with anger against Baasha and Elah, both of whom were liberals and had given freedom of worship to the followers of all religions. They were, therefore, happy that by Zimri's hands, they revenged themselves on the House of Baasha but at the same time they were wary of supporting him. Not knowing whether Zimri was a liberal or a religio-purist, they decided on a watch-and-wait policy and they neither supported nor opposed him. But the army was not prepared to wait; the commander-in-chief as well as the entire armed forces found it difficult to recognise Zimri as king because they would have to obey the orders of the former captain of half the division of the Royal Chariot troops now.

The army, which was then laying siege of the Philistine city of Gibbethon, on hearing of the news of the assassination, proclaimed Omri, the commander-in-chief, as the king of Israel. Omri and his men at once abandoned the siege and marched on the capital, Tirzah, where Zimri was, and besieged the city. The Chauvinists on the advice of the clergy announced their support to Omri who, being an army officer, they hoped, would be a religio-purist and would adopt a purist religious policy. With no chance of victory and driven to a corner, Zimri committed suicide, and Omri became the king of Israel. But the Liberals, thinking that Omri was a religio-purist because he was supported by the Chauvinists, opposed him and rallied behind Tibni, son of Ginath, pretender to the throne.[29] This struggle for the throne, according to the Bible, went on for about four long years, ending with the defeat and death of Tibni.

Firmly in the saddle now, Omri decided to shift the capital and he built a city on the hill Samaria and named the new capital of Israel, Samaria which was about ten kilometres (six miles) west of Tirzah. Strategically situated on a hill, he fortified it and built his palace there. The Bible does not say much about him perhaps because he was not a religio-purist, but the Mesha Stele popularly known as the Moabite Stone[30] of the ninth century BCE has recorded his conquest and oppression of Moab. The Moabite Stone of the ninth century acclaim him as "an able statesman and a fairly successful soldier. In Assyrian records, the northern kingdom is called by his name, and years later, when his whole house was destroyed by Jehu, the regicide is called 'son of Omri,' a rare tribute to Omri's reputation."[31] He continued the liberal religious policy of his predecessors, thus alienating the Chauvinists.[32] However, all those motley group of Liberals who mistakenly supported Tibni rallied behind Omri now. The Chauvinists could not find a servile political or military leader who was prepared to organise a rebellion against Omri, for they found Omri was loved and respected by the men in uniform. And he was a strong ruler too, for there was peace in the kingdom and he reigned without any problem. Asa was still the king of Judah when Omri died about twelve years after he overthrew Zimri and his son Ahab ascended the throne of Israel.

Ahab also was anathema to the Chauvinists. In fact, he completely shunned the religio-purists and he married a Zidonian (Phoenician) princess, Jezebel, who was a strong personality and an equally strong liberal. Ahab, following the liberal religious policy of his predecessors, allowed her the freedom to worship her god, Baal. She persuaded Ahab to build a temple for Baal and other deities, which he did, offending the religious sensibilities of the Chauvinists. They were furious and decided to warn Ahab. So they sent Elijah, the priest.

He told the king in unambiguous terms that unless he reversed his policy, the Chauvinists would be forced to strike back by blockading the city. He warned the king that if the liberal religious policy was not reversed, they would not allow food grains and vegetables, including fodder, to be brought into the city, which would result in famine. Unlike the modern cities, which grew around an industrial complex, these Hebrew cities were surrounded by farms and were sustained by agriculture. But the king refused to comply with their demand. As threatened, the mercenaries of the Chauvinists lay in ambush in different places along the route and attacked the caravans bringing agricultural produce from the surrounding villages. It was impossible for the king's men to ensure the security of the entire long route and the soldiers failed to stop those mercenaries carrying out such guerilla type of operations. Possibly there was a nexus between the guerillas and the soldiers who were, however, allowed to carry provisions to the palace, lest they be suspected of conniving with the blockaders. After a few caravans were thus attacked, the villagers, finding that the king's soldiers could not provide protection, stopped bringing supplies to the city. So the blockade was very successful. Consequently, there was acute food shortage in the city.[33] Ahab was enraged and so was Jezebel, who had become very powerful now. As Elijah was the person who told them that if they did not change their policy the city would be blockaded, they presumed that he was the brain behind this blockade. So Jezebel persuaded Ahab to capture and kill Elijah.

Immediately, the pro-Chauvinists who were in the palace secretly passed on the information to the clergy about the king's intention to kill Elijah. So he went underground. The king's men who were sent to arrest him could not trace the fugitive prophet. The Chauvinists arranged a place for him to stay and couriers to supply him with food secretly.[34] As days passed the blockade began to show its effect on the city and the famine became very severe in the capital, causing the death of many children, not to speak of an equal number or more of men and women. The affluent Chauvinists got their supplies with the help of the mercenaries. So Ahab persecuted the religio-purists in retaliation at the instance of Jezebel, when Obadiah, the governor of the palace, a crypto-purist,[35] helped all the priests go into hiding in two caves and secretly provided them food from the palace to which supplies were brought by soldiers. There were a hundred priests hiding in two caves.[36] But when many innocent purists fell to the retributive sword of the king, the Chauvinists were forced to lift the blockade unconditionally. Elijah in retaliation, called upon the Chauvinists to capture and bring all the prophets of Baal, "down to the brook Kishon" and kill them. So the Chauvinists engaged the mercenaries to take them to the banks of Kishon and slay them.[37] And it was done.

On hearing of the mass execution of Baal's prophets by Elijah, Jezebel vowed to kill Elijah within twenty-four hours. When Elijah was informed of Jezebel's vow to slay him, he fled to Beersheba in Judah's territory, which was beyond Jezebel's reach. Leaving behind his servant to keep the line of communication with the Chauvinists in Israel, he proceeded to the desert and hid in a cave. Elijah knew that the Chauvinists in Israel were not strong enough to fight Ahab, who had the support of the Liberals. He, therefore, chalked out a strategy for a prolonged struggle to overthrow Ahab and thought of a person to be crowned as king when Ahab was ousted from power and/or killed. He meticulously planned his moves but he thought he might not live long enough to execute it. He thought, being old as he was he might die a natural death any time, even if he were to escape being killed by the king's men. So he detailed his plan to Elisha, whom he anointed as his successor[38] and told Elisha to guide the Chauvinists in their fight against Ahab.

Around this time, Benhadad II of Syria formed a coalition with thirty-two nations and besieged Samaria. He sent an ultimatum to Ahab asking him to part with his wealth as well as his wives and children[39] or face invasion. Ahab agreed. Then came another message with more demands to which Ahab was reluctant to give in. So he consulted the Liberals, who told him not to yield, and when Benhadad got Ahab's reply, he threatened to reduce the city to a handful of dust. The Chauvinists now thought that this was an opportunity for them to prove that they were the king's true loyal supporters. So they sent a priest as their representative to the king to inform the king that the Chauvinists had offered to cooperate unconditionally and he should now know that they were more loyal than the Liberals. He advised the king to mount an offensive without waiting for the Syrians to attack and assured the king of Chauvinists' loyalty and support.[40] Meanwhile, the Chauvinists called up the provincial leaders and mustered an army of seven thousand men. They launched an offensive against the Syrians who were camping outside the city and defeated them. Ahab and his men pursued the fleeing enemy and slew them but the Syrian king managed to escape.

Trouble was brewing again. The priest came again and gave Ahab the secret intelligence that the Chauvinists got from their network of spies. He informed the king about Syria's plans to attack Israel at the turn of the year.[41] He also told the king that they were planning to invade via Aphek thinking that the soldiers of Israel were not trained to fight in the plains. And he assured the king that with the help of the Chauvinists the army of Israel would be able to defeat the Syrians in the plains too as they did in the mountains.[42] As expected, the end of the year saw the Syrians marching on Aphek, a city in the plains. Benhadad chose to draw the Hebrews down to the plains because his strategists advised him to do so. They thought that the Israelite army was good at mountain warfare but it would be at a disadvantage in the plains, where, they pesumed, the Syrian soldiers were better trained to fight.[43]

Thanks to this early intelligence, the Israelite army intercepted the Syrians outside the city of Aphek and the two armies joined battle. This time too, the Chauvinists cooperated with Ahab to prove their loyalty and hoped that the king would see the light and turn to religio-purism. Israel fought fiercely and the Syrian army fled. Benhadad surrendered. He was forced to return the territories of Israel that his father had annexed and to allow commercial privileges in Damascus. As *quid pro quo*, Benhadad's life was spared but the Chauvinists were not happy with the treaty, for they evidently wanted to do away with Benhadad and annex Syria or at least reduce it to a tributary nation. They expressed their displeasure to the king. They said, they co-operated with the objective of getting rid of Benhadad and they warned Ahab of dire consequences because he spared Benhadad's life.[44]

These victories had made Jezebel all the more proud and arrogant and she virtually took over the reins of government. Her high-handedness knew no bounds. If she fancied a property, she would send messages to the servile nobles and elder freemen of the town, under the king's seal, to frame the owner accusing him of blasphemy and treason and to execute him; she would then appropriate his property. The case of Naboth illustrates this proclivity.[45] The Chauvinists found this intolerable and they condemned the king, for this was against the Mosaic Law. Meanwhile Elijah had come out of hiding and was in Gilgal with his anointed successor Elisha,[46] but owing to the threat to his life from Jezebel, Elijah was given security by mercenaries hired by the Chauvinists. And they sent Elijah to the king to tell him that the appropriation of Naboth's estate was illegal under Mosaic laws and to inform him that the Chauvinists had vowed to exterminate Ahab's dynasty.[47]

At that time, Asa died, leaving the throne of Judah to his son Jehoshaphat, who pursued the religious policy of his father and maintained a powerful army. He also fortified his kingdom. He revamped the judicial system and telling the judges to be fair he warned them against taking bribes.[48] The peace in the kingdom was shattered by the invasion of the Moabites and the Ammonites, when Jehoshaphat appealed to the Chauvinists for help. In response, Zechariah, a Levite, exhorted the people to take up arms and face the invading army without fear. So the people of Judah fought and massacred the enemy forces.[49] Now Jehoshaphat decided to make peace and establish friendly ties with his northern neighbour and he went on a visit to Israel, when Ahab brought up the problem of Ramoth-gilead. Once under the Hebrews, this territory had changed hands several times in the wars between Israel and Syria and was in Syrian hands at that time.[50] Ahab now proposed that Israel and Judah send a joint expedition to recover that city. Jehoshaphat agreed but he wanted to consult the priest. While the Phoenician priests supported the war the Chauvinists opposed it. Anyway, a political decision was taken by the two kings, ignoring the opposition of the Chauvinists, and the joint expeditionary force led by both Ahab and Jehoshaphat attacked Syria. It was a bloody war and the Hebrews were in a good position when an arrow struck Ahab by accident, which proved fatal, and that decided the outcome of the battle. The Hebrews withdrew. Ahab was succeeded by his son Ahaziah to the throne of Israel and Jehoshaphat continued to rule Judah.

It was perhaps Jezebel's ruthlessness coupled with political acumen that prevented foreign aggression and helped keep the domestic front free from any disturbances in Ahab's time. With the death of Ahab, Jezebel lost her position and power, for Ahaziah kept her at arm's length. Now that she was out of the way, those who had been lying low began to raise their heads, beginning with the Moabite rebellion. Ahaziah was helpless, for after he had a fall seriously injuring himself, he had been laid up and was unable to take any punitive military action against the Moabites. He did not have the support of the powerful Chauvinists because of his continuance of his father's liberal religious policy and the liberals comprising the lower middle class and the wage labourers, did not have the resources that the Chauvinists had, to support a war. Ahaziah knew that but he thought he could at least call up the Liberals to join the army.

So he sent messengers to the leaders of Liberals for advice and to help him suppress the Moabite rebellion. Elijah was, then, in Jericho.[51] The exit of Jezebel from the corridors of power had emboldened the Chauvinists and at their behest, Elijah with his mercenaries stopped them from meeting the liberal leaders and told them to go back. The Chauvinists, thus, successfully cut off the line of communication between the king and the Liberal leaders.[52] When the soldiers gave the king a description of the man who dared prevent the king's soldiers from executing his orders, Ahaziah recognised the person: it was unmistakably Elijah, he said.

So Ahaziah sent a contingent of fifty soldiers to arrest Elijah but the mercenaries of the Chauvinists guarding Elijah attacked and killed them. The second time also the soldiers sent by the king to capture Elijah were killed by the mercenaries. However, the captain of the contingent that went for the third time pleaded with Elijah not to kill them but to be kind enough to go with them and meet the king. So Elijah consulted the Chauvinists who advised him to go and meet the king taking the mercenaries with him for his security.[53] Ahaziah was on the verge of death when Elijah met him and he died before he could reply to Elijah's accusation that the king had ignored the Chauvinists in favour of the Liberals.

As Ahaziah was childless, his brother Joram ascended the throne of Israel at his capital Samaria, and soon after that Elijah died,[54] leaving the leadership of the clergy to Elisha and as prophet in his place.[55] Joram's first concern was the Moabite insurgency. The strategic relations that Ahab had established with Judah were intact, and Joram decided to attack Moab in alliance with Jehoshaphat, who was in his eighteenth year as the king of Judah. His plan was to go through the wilderness of Edom and enter Moab from the south to take the Moabites by surprise because they would not be expecting any invader to come through the dry, unfriendly sandy terrain in the south. He, therefore, forged an alliance with the king of Edom too. The idea was good but the desert through which the army had to go was the problem. Yet Jehoshaphat agreed, but being a religio-purist, he wanted to seek the advice of the clergy in order to ensure the support of the powerful Chauvinists for the war and at his insistence the three kings went down to Elisha for a four-party conference.

When Jehoshaphat told him that they had come to seek his advice, Elisha gave vent to his ire at Joram for sticking to the liberal religious policy of his predecessor and told him to seek the advice of Liberal leaders whom his father and mother had been consulting. But when

Joram apologised, saying that he had realised his mistake[56] he cooled down. Yet he said that "were it not that I regarded the presence of Jehoshaphat the king of Judah, I would not have looked at you...." He warned them that the desert through which the army would be going was arid land and in the entire region no water would be found. So he told them to arrange camps[57] at intervals all along the route and stock sufficient water which could be taken from Edom by camels laden with barrels of water before they marched on Moab. He also predicted that they would win the war.[58]

The allies did as advised by Elisha. The governments of Israel, Judah and Edom joined together and taking care that the Moabites did not come to know of it, they pitched camps at intervals on their route to Moab with a few soldiers in each camp and stocked sufficient water in every camp. So when the army marched to Moab, they did not face any shortage of water. The Moabites did not expect any of the neighbouring countries to venture an invasion from the south and they did not even have any border security force on that side. So they did not have intelligence about the activities going on in the wilderness in the south and were taken by surprise when the allies attacked them. Nevertheless, led by the eldest son of Mesha, the king of Moab, the Moabite army fought desperately but they suffered heavy casualties including Mesha's son and heir to the throne, who commanded the army.[59]

The Bible says, Mesha had sacrificed his son. In reality, Mesha must have been a war casualty. So figuratively speaking the king "sacrificed" his son in the war. The allies, no doubt, won the battle but they lost the war. They were unable to convert the victory in the battle to their advantage, for they had been forced to beat a retreat. This is rather strange, for no conqueror ever withdraws after being victorious in the battle without occupying the invaded country or making it a tributary state. What could be the reason for the invaders to have decided to withdraw from Moab unilaterally? The Bible gives a hint, when it says "And there was great indignation against Israel." This is a clear indication that the entire population rose as one man against the enemy. Refusing to surrender, they organised underground resistance movement and continued guerilla warfare, with the result the invaders found it difficult to occupy the land and enslave the

Moabites. They were compelled to leave Moab and go back to their countries.[60]

Obviously, the triple alliance actually had made a logistical blunder by attacking via the southern wilderness and that caused their defeat. The supply line being through the wilderness, the base was practically cut off from the battle front and reinforcements and food from the base could not easily reach the invading forces. Incidentally, Elisha's advice betrayed his ignorance of logistics and his prophecy that they would easily win the war did not come true. All that a prophet says does not happen, as pointed out in Chapter 2, "The Universe, and God," and whatever does come true, happens fortuitously.

Jehoshaphat did not live long after this, and with his death his son Jehoram became the king of Judah.[61] It was in the fifth year of Joram of Israel. There were no pretenders to the throne and so the succession was smooth. He had married Athaliah, one of the daughters of Ahab and Jezebel, and so Judah witnessed a reversal of the religious policy of his father. Athaliah was as domineering a wife as her mother Jezebel had been and so she pressured her husband Jehoram to adopt the liberal religious policy of her father, which antagonised the powerful Chauvinists. Thus in Judah, liberalism found a foothold again. But the clergy supported him because he was of the lineage of David and the Chauvinists were reluctant to go against the wishes of the clergy and overthrow him.[62] He was an indifferent ruler. He neglected the army and also failed to keep an eye on the vassal states. Making use of this opportunity, Edom rose in revolt and liberated itself from the suzerainty of Judah. King Jehoram, who went to suppress the revolt, was captured and executed. On his death Ahaziah inherited a truncated kingdom of Judah.

It may be recalled that Elijah had thought of a plan to bring about change of regimes in Syria and Israel and before his death he had confided to Elisha the plan in detail. He had also told Elisha that he had spoken to the army officers who promised to co-operate and there would be no problem whatsoever. Elisha now decided to carry out, one by one, the task that Elijah had entrusted him with and he did it punctiliously and ruthlessly. Aware of the spadework done by Elijah and the soured relations between Syria and Israel, he went to

Damascus to carry out Elijah's plan. There was no other reason for Elisha to go to Damascus at that time, when the Syrian king was ailing. He must have thought that the king's illness was a good opportunity for him to get access to the palace and meet Hazael, who was Benhadad's confidant. Obviously, Benhadad did not know of a medicine man like Elisha, and Elisha did not want anyone to suspect that he had gone to Damascus to get an audience with the king. He was sure that if he made his presence in Damascus known to the public and propagated his power in "casting away devils from people who were afflicted with them" the news would somehow reach the ears of the bed-ridden king who would then call him for consultation. He would thus get an opportunity to meet Hazael. So he discreetly gave publicity of his healing power and as expected, the news of the presence in Damascus of a witch doctor, who had cured Nathan of his leprosy, reached the king.

The plan worked well although not exactly as he hoped it would. As soon as the king heard of the presence of a witch doctor in Damascus, he sent Hazael to call on Elisha with gifts and to ask what the prognosis was in his case. On hearing of the king's symptoms and condition, Elisha forecast that there was no chance of recovery and Benhadad would die. However, he did not want Hazael to say so to the king but to tell him instead that he would certainly recover. During the conversation, Elisha slyly suggested to Hazael to murder Benhadad and proclaim himself the king. The hint to attack Israel that he dropped feigning sorrow was also not lost on Hazael.[63]

The simple political meaning of this fictitious story is that Elisha hatched a conspiracy with Hazael to murder Benhadad and also overthrow the king of Israel. Hazael naturally acquiesced in the plan. The next day, early in the morning Hazael smothered the king to death with a thick wet cloth, and when the city woke up, the people heard the startling news that Benhadad had died and Hazael had acceded to the throne. The secrecy, the thoroughness and the lightning speed with which the coup was accomplished did not give anyone the time to stake a claim to the throne of Syria. Hazael had already been occupying a key position in the palace and he had the army under his control; hence no one dared oppose him when he occupied the throne.[64] He now waited for an opportunity to attack Israel.

Presuming that the people of Syria would not have accepted Hazael because of the manner in which he became the king, Ahaziah of Judah together with king Joram of Israel declared war on Syria and attacked Ramoth-gilead. King Joram was wounded in the battle and he left for Jezreel for treatment and recuperation. When the news reached Elisha, he conferred with the Chauvinists and they decided to make use of this opportunity to get rid of Joram and enthrone a servile religio-purist in Israel. The people could be made to understand that an invalid king would be a liability in times of crises and that the country needed an able-bodied young man of prowess on the throne. So on the suggestion of Elisha, the clergy sent one of the young priests to Ramoth-gilead with a vial of oil. He was instructed to call Jehu, the son of Jehoshaphat, away from his colleagues and anoint him as king of Israel *in camera* to avoid premature publicity. And the priest did what he was told to. The conspiratorial nature of this is obvious from the instructions that Elisha had given to the priest whom he sent to Ramoth-gilead.[65]

When the young priest arrived, Jehu was sitting in the courtyard, in the company of his comrades-in-arms. He said to Jehu that he had brought a confidential message for him. So Jehu went into the house, when the priest took the box of oil and poured it on his head, saying he was anointing him king of Israel as desired by the clergy and rushed out of the premises as he was told to.[66] But there was a condition. Jehu should wipe out the house of Ahab, leaving no trace of the dynasty to avenge the injustice he had been doing to the religio-purists.[67] Jehu vowed to do it. After being anointed when Jehu went back to his colleagues, they asked him from where that "mad fellow" had come. Evidently, they did not know the man, the young priest, whom they would not have seen at all. However, thinking that they knew the priest, Jehu replied, "You know the man and his message."[68]

When Jehu told them that the "mad fellow" anointed him king as ordained by the priesthood,[69] the alacritous reaction of his comrades was as if they had been eagerly waiting for the announcement. All the army officers immediately rose from their seats and "blew the trumpets, shouting, Jehu is king."[70] This reply shows that they were expecting Elisha, presuming that they had known of Elijah's death, to come and anoint Jehu. The whole sequence of events beginning with the arrival of the young priest at the army camp confirms that Elijah, long before his death, had prepared the ground for anointing Jehu as king of Israel. As he told Elisha, he had also spoken to the army officers and had ensured the backing of the army. That Jehu too was a party to this plot is confirmed, as the Bible says, "So Jehu son of Jehoshaphet, the son of Nimshi, conspired against Joram...."[71] The other army officers seemed to have been eagerly waiting for a signal to strike.

Once anointed and the kingship of Jehu becoming a *fait accompli*, no one would dare question his authority because Jehu had the social and political sanction, above all the support of the army, to take any action he deemed fit against dissidents. He was assured of the support of the Chauvinists on condition that he extirpated the dynasty of Ahab and avenged the murder of the many prophets by Jezebel, which he promised to do. Jehu, being prudent, commanded that no one from Ramoth-gilead would leave the city lest someone informed Joram of the news of his being anointed as king of Israel. And Jehu called up his men in Ramoth-gilead and rushed to Jezreel where Joram was convalescing. Ahaziah who had gone to visit the sick king was also there when Jehu with his army entered Jezreel. On seeing Jehu coming with the army, the two kings seemed to have suspected foul play, for they came out in full strength and met Jehu in the vineyard that Joram had unlawfully taken over, framing its owner, Naboth, on false charges.

When Joram enquired if Jehu had come with peaceful intentions, he replied, "What peace as long as the evil deeds of your mother Jezebel and her witchcrafts are many?" Immediately, both Joram and Ahaziah turned round their chariots and fled. But Jehu pursued them and shot Joram with arrows to death, thus removing the only possible impediment that was in his way to the throne.[72] Back at the capital Samaria, he killed Jezebel and as promised he eliminated all surviving members of the House of Ahab. After that, he ordered all non-Hebrews to gather in one place. Not knowing why they were summoned, all of them assembled in Samaria and Jehu killed every one of them, after which he pulled down the sacred pillar of the temple of Baal[73] but he did not strictly adhere to religio-purism. During his period Hazael invaded and annexed some territories of Israel as Elisha had wanted him to do.

Meanwhile Ahaziah fled to Samaria, from where he was caught and brought to Jehu, who killed him. As soon as the news of the death of Ahaziah reached his palace in Judah, Athalia, the Queen Mother, killed all his children who were heirs to the throne.[74] But one of his sons, Joash, an infant then, was rescued from the jaws of death as it were, by his aunt Jehosheba, who was married to Jehoiada, the priest. Perhaps this boy was one of the legitimate children of Ahaziah. Realizing that Athalia, a ruthlessly ambitious woman would have killed him too, Jehosheba managed to sneak out with the baby. She carried him away to the safety of the Temple and with the help of her husband hid the child in one of its storerooms.[75] This went unnoticed by the Queen Mother; maybe because the king must have begotten a large number of children in the many wives and concubines he had in his harem and she would not have kept count of the number of children she killed.

Oblivious of it, Athalia, the only woman to have occupied the throne of Judah, ruled for six years when the little boy was cared for by a nurse, protected by his aunt and uncle. By the time the little prince attained the age of seven, Jehoida succeeded in winning over a section of the army and one day asked them to assemble in the Temple. Swearing them to secrecy, he divulged the secret presenting the young prince to them and giving them weapons wanted them to ensure the security of the boy, so that no harm came to him.[76] He knew if Athalia were to come to know of this, she would not hesitate to come in with a posse of soldiers that owed allegiance to her and kill the prince. So placing the crown on the boy's head, he anointed him and declared him king of Judah, when those assembled there clapped and the jubilant people shouted "God save the king."

Attracted by the noise and the slogan raised by the people, Athalia asked the palace officials what was causing the commotion. When they found out and reported the matter to the queen, she rushed to the Temple and seeing the king surrounded by armed guards, accused all those present there of treason. But on the orders of Jehoida, the guards dragged her out of the Temple and executed her, and Joash became the king of Judah with Jehoida acting as the regent. So now although Joash was the king, it was Jehoida, supported by the Chauvinists, who ruled the kingdom. They were sure that this arrangement could continue without any hitch until Joash attained majority when the people might force Jehoida to hand over power to the legitimate king or the boy himself would insist on Jehoida handing over the kingdom to him.

As expected Joash, who was now a young man, took the reins of government in his hands. He ordered that all contributions to the Temple would be spent towards the maintenance of the Temple building, which had been in a state of utter neglect. For about sixteen years although nothing was transferred to the state treasury out of the temple revenue, the Temple building continued to be in disrepair. He asked the priests why it was so. He told them not to take for themselves any money donated to the Temple but to use it solely for the maintenance of the building.[77] Obviously, the corrupt priesthood used the entire income of the Temple for their personal comforts. Joash tactfully arranged to keep control of the Temple revenue, thus putting a stop to the corruption of the priests without defaming or offending them and got the building repaired. This, no doubt, pleased the Chauvinists. The money meant for repairs was paid directly to the supervisors of maintenance work for paying the wages of the workers and buying building materials. The supervisors were not asked to account for the money, for they were honest, unlike the priests. The priests were allowed to take only the money contributed for guilt offerings and sin offerings.[78] After completing the repair work, the Temple income was spent for the purchase of gold and silver vessels and such other articles for the Temple.

About this time, Joash came to know from his spies that Hazael, the king of Syria, after conquering the Philistine city of Gath was moving towards Jerusalem. Joash was a weak-kneed king and was not prepared to face a Syrian attack. He, therefore, collected all the silver and gold in the treasuries of the palace and the Temple without consulting either the priests or leaders of the lay Chauvinists and sent it across to Hazael as tribute, thus averting the invasion. The army officers considered it lack of confidence in them; the Chauvinists resented it as they were kept in the dark; the clergy was indignant that the gold and silver belonging to the Temple were removed ignoring their opposition. The Temple was now as good as plundered. So they plotted against the king and won over two of the king's trusted officers who turned assassins. After his death his son Amaziah was crowned the king of Judah.[79]

It was when Joash was the king of Judah, that Jehu died and Jehoahaz, the son of Jehu, ascended the throne of Israel. The Chauvinists were unhappy with his liberal religious policy and giving the Liberals an important place in society, as it weakened the hold the Chauvinists had on the government. But the Liberals were not a strong force among the people. The disaffected Chauvinists who had always been vindictive and jealous of their powers waited for an opportunity to teach the king a lesson and they got it when the country faced an invasion by Hazael's son who had taken the titular name as Benhadad III when he ascended the throne after Hazael's death. Obviously, the Chauvinists played a treacherous role by covertly supporting the invader.[80]

It must be understood that the sentiment of patriotism was not known to the Hebrews in those times. The first loyalty of the Hebrew people continued to be to their religion and the country came only next. Hence the Chauvinists who were known to be religio-purists had a strong hold on the freemen who were swayed by the call of religion more than by the call of their country and even among the Hebrews who were Liberals, there were many who were inclined to join hands with the Chauvinists. With a majority of the freemen non-cooperating with the government, Jehoahaz was helpless and Israel was inevitably defeated. The king of Syria destroyed the once-powerful Israelite Army so much that he "had made them lick the dust at threshing"[81] and having lost its military superiority, Israel was reduced to the status of a vassal state.

Not long after this Jehoahaz died and his son Jehoash succeeded him to the throne of Israel. Joash was still on the throne of Judah. Jehoash, however, refused to change the liberal religious policy that his father had implemented, disregarding the pressure of the Chauvinists. So the Chauvinists were indignant. At this time, Elisha fell ill, and on hearing the news Jehoash rushed to see him and was there at his bedside when he passed away. That was a very clever move. Whether he did it just to placate the Chauvinists or not, it did please them, causing a thaw in their relations with Jehoash. The Chauvinists also had been suffering under the oppression of the Syrians and they somehow wanted to get rid of the aggressor. This, they thought, was a good excuse to mend fences and offered to cooperate with the king to attack Syria. So with a strong army, Jehoash attacked Syria three times and in all the three wars Syria was defeated with the result Jehoash recaptured the cities that Syria had annexed earlier.[82]

It was in the second year of Jehoash that Amaziah came to power in Judah. He neither encouraged the Liberals nor did anything to offend them, thus pleasing both the Liberals and the Chauvinists. As soon as he found his feet, he avenged his father's murder by executing the two servants who carried out the conspirators' orders but spared their offspring. Thus removing what he thought would be a threat to his life, he turned his attention to strengthening and equipping the army. His foreign policy was guided by a desire to regain the past glory of Judah and his first move in this direction was to retake Edom that had defied Judah and had become independent.

This victory boosted his morale and prestige and he decided to challenge Israel and declared Judah's sovereignty over that country. Jehoash responded by mustering an army and marching into Judah. The army of Judah met the Israeli army at Beth-shemesh and in the battle that followed Judah was defeated. Their army fled and Amaziah was taken as a captive to Jerusalem and released. The Israeli army pulled down the walls of Jerusalem, ransacked the city, plundered the Temple and took hostages including Obed-edom, who was in charge of the treasury. However, Amaziah reigned for a few more years even after the death of Jehoash. Amaziah gradually leaned towards liberalism[83] and so the Chauvinists plotted to kill him but coming to know of the plot against his life through his spies, he fled to Lachish. The conspirators, however, sent the assassins to Lachish and got him killed there.

The people now enthroned his son Azariah (also called Uzziah) as the king of Judah. He was a religio-purist and naturally he adopted a religious policy that pleased the Chauvinists.[84] He was a powerful king and had a well-equipped and well-trained standing army. He declared war against the Philistines and conquered Gath and pulled down the walls of two other Philistine cities, Jabneh and Ashdod, and built new cities in those places. He defeated the Arabians of Gurbaal and the Mehunims and the Ammonites were made to pay him tribute. Meanwhile he took care to fortify Jerusalem. Being diplomatic, in order not to hurt the religious sensibilities of the Liberals, Azariah did not prohibit the worship of other deities or idolatry, which, however, the Chauvinists objected to. Although he did everything according to the wishes of the Chauvinists with whose unstinted support he was triumphant in two or three wars against the neighbouring kingdoms, which made him proud and encroaching on the privileges of the clergy, he burnt incense upon the altar. It was a rite that only priests were entitled to perform.[85]

So the Chauvinists goaded by the clergy conspired with his son, Jotham, who with the tacit support of the Chauvinists deposed his father, Azariah, and placing him under house arrest, acted as regent. Azariah was completely isolated as they would a leper in those days, for no one was allowed to meet him, nor was he allowed to meet anyone. Jotham must have got intelligence that the Liberals were conspiring to liberate Azariah and restore him to the throne. He, therefore, took care to keep his father all alone in a house in a secluded area, incommunicado and no one except a few of his trusted officials knew where exactly he was confined.[86] So the Liberals were not able to contact him. They could not, therefore, rescue him from confinement and unleash a rebellion against Jotham by projecting him as the legitimate king. Anyway, till he died, Jotham performed the duties of the king without any problem, thanks to the support of the Chauvinists. We shall return to the history of Judah after we take a peep into Israel, which was in turmoil.

Jehoash of Israel did not live long after his war with Judah. His death brought his son Jeroboam II on the throne of Israel. He antagonised the Chauvinists by his liberal religious policy but they did not want to rub him on the wrong side, for he was a powerful king. On the other hand, on the advice of the prophet Jonah, the Chauvinists adopted a conciliatory attitude and extended its hand of friendship to the king. With no opposition on the home front he turned his attention outward and recovered the territories between Hamath and the Red Sea that Israel had lost to Syria. It was at this time when Israel had become a powerful force in the region that Jeroboam II died. He was survived by his son Zachariah, who succeeded him to the throne of Israel,[87] which plunged into chaos.

Zachariah's reign, thus, marked the beginning of a period of instability in Israel with plots, counter plots and palace revolutions. The Chauvinists of Israel, who were as powerful, sectarian and politically conscious as their counterparts in Judah, were deeply involved in all these machinations. Zachariah did not rule for long. Like several of his liberal predecessors, he followed a liberal religious policy,[88] which helped Shallum, son of one Jabesh, who was quite ambitious. He knew that the Chauvinists resented Zachariah's liberalism and, assured of their support, he assassinated Zachariah and grabbed the throne of Israel.[89] This was even before Azariah (Uzziah) of Judah was incarcerated. The death of Zachariah put an end to the house of Jehu. Shallum had been on the throne for a little over one month when another non-entity, Menahem, son of Gadi, from Tirzah, the former capital of Israel, came to Samaria, assassinated Shallum and declared himself the king of Israel.[90] He was ruthless. When the people of the city of Tiphsah refused to accept his right to the throne, he fiendishly butchered the men, women and children and razed the city to the ground. He too was a liberal who believed in the freedom of worship and allowed idolatry.[91] But the Chauvinists, knowing how ruthless he could be, did not dare oppose him, for they had no doubt that if he suspected them of plotting against him, he would have no mercy and would not hesitate to exterminate them.

At this time, the decline of Egypt, Hittite and Syria had created a political vacuum in West Asia and this was to some extent filled by Assyria. So the Chauvinists seemed to have secretly contacted the Assyrian king Pul (known in historical records as Tiglath-pileser) to help them rid the country of Menahem. But Menahem was informed by his spies of the Assyrian King's intention to attack Israel and of the hand of the Chauvinists in the invasion. It may be recalled that during the reign of Jehoahaz also the Chauvinists acted treacherously to meet their selfish ends. When the Assyrian king marched against Israel he was heavily bribed by Menahem to refrain from invading the country. He paid this to King Pul by extorting huge amounts from the rich freemen who constituted the Chauvinists, in the form of special tax.[92] So it was, in effect, a kind of punitive tax that nearly broke the back of the affluent Chauvinists. So King Pul, who was obviously not interested in annexing Israel, went back home, for he got what he had wanted without spilling a drop of blood.

Menahem, who ruled for about a decade, died a natural death and his son Pekahiah succeeded him to the throne of Israel[93] when Azariah was in the fiftieth year of his reign in the neighbouring Hebrew kingdom. His religious policy was in no way different from that of his father,[94] and that enraged the Chauvinists. The Chauvinists cultivated the army officers and succeeded in turning them against the king. So with the full backing of the Chauvinists, Pekah, the army captain, assassinated Pekahiah and ascended the throne. Pekah too was a liberal and would not make any change in the religious policy as the Chauvinists expected of him when they instigated him to assassinate Pekahiah. But the Chauvinists were helpless.[95] Pekah kept a vigilant eye on the army commanders, for he knew the Chauvinists would try to influence them as they did him. He formed an alliance with King Rezin of Syria and declared war on Judah. We shall go into its details when we deal with Ahaz who was ruling Judah then.

So the Chauvinists who were bent upon getting rid of Pekah, contacted the Assyrian king Tiglath-pileser (Pul) as they did when Maneheim was ruling the country. This time, however, King Pul descended upon Israel, captured several cities – Ijon, Abelbethmaacah, Janoah, Kedesh, Hazor, Gilead, Galilee and all the land of Naphtali – and carried away the people to Assyria as captives.[96] It was a humiliating defeat for Israle. The people of all sections of the population of Israel were naturally disillusioned and indignant because, contrary to their expectation, Pekah, who was an army captain, failed to ensure the security of their life and property. The anger of the freemen, both the Chauvinists and the Liberals, was compounded by their sorrow at the loss of their kith and kin that the Assyrian king took away as prisoners. It naturally reflected on the army in general and their morale plummeted.

At this time, Azariah, who was the nominal king of Judah and had been under house arrest, died and his son Jotham, who had been acting as regent till then, was formally crowned the king of Judah.[97] He tried to please the Chauvinists by building the Upper Gate of the Temple and reinforced the wall of Ophel.[98] Although he did not actively help the Liberals, he refrained from offending them because he did not pull down the shrines of the deities of other religions. He attacked the Ammonites and compelled them to pay heavy tribute, in cash and kind, for three years.

In the seventeenth year of Pekah's rule, Jotham died and his son Ahaz ascended the throne of Judah. Let alone his liberal religious policy, Ahaz was considered an apostate by the Chauvinists because his personal religious practice itself was violative of the Mosaic precepts.[99] As a result, he burned his bridges and there was practically no possibility of a rapprochement with the Chauvinists. The Liberals were now given the pride of place and he took only their advice. At this time, the latent rivalry between Israel and Judah manifested itself and Pekah of Israel in alliance with Rezin, the king of Syria declared war on Judah and besieged Jerusalem[100] but they did not conquer it. Ahaz's leniency towards the Liberals was not to the liking of the Chauvinists and so they presumably collaborated with the invaders during their incursions into Judah. In the war Judah suffered heavy casualties, which included Ahaz's son, the king's administrator and the king's second-in-command. The invaders, however, failed to subdue Jerusalem and King Rezin of Syria, taking advantage of the situation, captured Elath and drove out the Hebrews. The Edomites, making use of this opportunity, went and settled there permanently.[101]

Ahaz sent a messenger with gifts of gold and silver to the Assyrian king Tiglath-pileser appealing to him to help fight back the belligerent Syria-Israel coalition. The Assyrian king equipped the army with the money he got and promptly marched on Damascus, conquered it, slew Rezin and took the people captive.[102] The Israelite army slaughtered a large number of Judahean troops and took myriad men, women and children prisoner to be carried away to Israel.[103] The Chauvinists were rattled by these developments and feared that the entire country might be lost and their family and property too would be in jeopardy. So they sent one of their leaders, Oded, a prophet, to plead with the Israelite army to free the captives. He met the army, which was on its way back, and requested them to release the prisoners who, he said, were after all their kinsfolk. The army officers belonging to the tribe of Ephraim urged the others to release the prisoners saying that they did not want to add to the problems they already had with the Chauvinists in Israel.[104]

Meanwhile, the Edomites from the north and the Philistines from the south and west invaded Judah. The army of Edom captured the people and carried them away as slaves[105] while the Philistines annexed many cities – Beethshemesh, Ajalon, Gederoth and Shocho, Timnah and Gimzo – and the surrounding villages in the lowland and settled there.[106] In response to Ahaz's request for help against the Edomite and the Philistine invaders, Tiglath-pilesar, king of Assyria, went to Judah, but instead of helping Judah to drive out the invaders, he only harassed Ahaz.[107] He extorted heavy tribute from Ahaz, thus leaving the Judahean treasury empty. Ahaz immediately paid a visit to Damascus and entered into a pact that reduced Judah into a tributary state.[108] On his return from there, he suppressed the Chauvinists, possibly to please the king of Assyria, and religio-purism was weakened as never before in the history of the Hebrews.

The situation in Israel at this time was quite explosive and congenial for any conspirator to capture power, and Hoshea did it; he assassinated Pekah and proclaimed himself the king of Israel. There is confusion in the Bible; it is not clear who was ruling Judah at that time.[109] The people, especially the Liberals, were happy with Hoshea, whose liberalism, needless to say, was not to the liking of the Chauvinists,[110] but the Liberals were a strong force numerically and the people in general were inclined to be liberal-minded, thanks to the co-existence of several different religions consequent upon a series of liberal regimes that preceded Hoshea. The Chauvinists, therefore, had not been able to foment a rebellion to overthrow him. So they resorted to treachery by inviting the Assyrian king to help them, and that proved disastrous to the whole kingdom. Assyria was ruled by King Shalmaneser at that time, and unlike King Pul he was a conqueror. He attacked Israel and defeated Hoshea and Israel was constrained to pay tribute to Assyria. Hoshea now revolted. He withheld the payment of tribute to Assyria and secretly sought the help of the Egyptian king to free Israel of Assyrian suzerainty. Shalmeneser got scent of Hoshea's clandestine move through his spies and took pre-emptive action by imprisoning him and putting him in chains before he could pull off an alliance with Egypt.[111] The king of Assyria, then, deployed the troops in the land of Israel and they besieged Samaria until it fell after three years[112] and the people of Israel were taken prisoner and sent to Assyria. They were confined to "Halah, and in Habor by the river Gozan and in the cities of Medes."[113] With the fall of Samaria, the independent kingdom of Israel got wiped off the map of West Asia and it came to be known as Samaria.

However, Judah, one of the twin Hebrew kingdoms, continued its existence. Two years after the dissolution and disappearance of the kingdom of Israel, Ahaz died and his son Hezekiah became the king of Judah.[114] He took a roundabout turn in his religious policy in favour of religio-purism to the delight of the Chauvinists, who had been dreaming of it.[115] A fanatic religio-purist, Hezekiah pulled down all the shrines, obelisks and idols and practically removed the symbols of all religions except that of Yahweh. And the Liberals were persecuted. He renovated and opened the Temple, the symbol of Yahweh supremacy, and proved his commitment to the Mosaic teachings. All this helped further strengthen the Chauvinists.[116]

Hezekiah knew the Chauvinists were itching to cleanse the population by extirpating the non-Hebrews and apostates. He had already started the process by destroying all non-Hebrew shrines. Thus creating a favourable background, he called a conference of the Levites and all the Hebrew tribesmen,[117] at which he announced that he wanted to make a covenant with the Chauvinists.[118] The objective of the covenant, to put it in his own words, was to pacify the indignant clergy and by extension, the Chauvinists who were radical religio-purists. It was intended to rejuvenate religio-purism that had been under attack by the Liberals all these years as several of the kings that occupied the throne of Judah before him had been lenient towards them and had adopted a religious policy that encouraged and strengthened liberalism.

So by this covenant, Hezekiah affirmed his commitment to religio-purism and his determination to unite the Chauvinists of all Hebrew tribes. In keeping with it, he called a general assembly of the Hebrews of Israel, Judah, Ephraim and Manasseh at the Temple in Jerusalem in the month of May to coincide with the Passover celebration. The day was chosen to emphasise the unity of the Hebrew tribes and to whip up an anti-liberal sentiment among the Hebrews. The meeting achieved its objective. After all the celebrations were over, a massive campaign against the minority non-Hebrew people was unleashed.

The Hebrew masses driven by religious frenzy smashed the idols, destroyed the groves, pulled down the altars and damaged everything that the minority non-Hebrews regarded as sacred.[119] The Bible is silent about the human casualties that this campaign caused. It may, however, be surmised that this vandalism of the Hebrews would have enraged the minority communities and they would have tried to prevent it, resulting in violent clashes between the majority religious group and the minorities. Since the Hebrews had the support of the king who was a Hebrew Chauvinist himself, the powerful army too must have been used to help the Chauvinists in the genocide and a large number of the members of minority communities would have been killed. Hezekiah now made it mandatory for the people to donate a part of all their earnings, both in kind and in cash, to the Levites. And the king constructed storerooms to keep safely whatever was received in kind.[120]

After that Hezekiah turned his attention to developing the infrastructure in the kingdom. He constructed dams across the river Gihon to irrigate the land on the western side of the city of David that helped boost agriculture and enrich the Hebrew freemen who owned most of the farms. As a result, the state coffers overflowed with the money collected by way of taxes and the economy of the kingdom was booming.[121] He had the most powerful army in the region, which emboldened him to defy Assyria and he refused to pay tribute. In an attempt to expand the kingdom, he attacked the Philistines and annexed the territory up to Gaza. He had to put a halt to it when Sennacherib, king of Assyria, marched against Judah, attracted by its prosperity. At the same time it was meant to punish Hezekiah for his failure to pay tribute. He laid siege to and captured all the fortified cities of Judah.[122] Hezekiah paid him the tribute due to him for which Hezekiah had to take all the valuables that were in the Temple and even strip the gold from the doors of the Temple. That satisfied Sennacherib and he went away but later he came back planning to besiege Jerusalem. When Hezekiah came to know that the Assyrians were marching towards Jerusalem, he called a war council, at which it was decided to cut off the water supply to the besieging Assyrian army by plugging the springs outside the city and he reinforced the fortifications. The council also recruited and trained a large army and equipped them with new weapons. Hezekiah gave them a talk to pep up their morale. Nonetheless he wished to avoid an armed conflict and he sent three of his high officials on a peace mission in an attempt to avert war and avoid bloodshed.[123] Confident of defeating the Judahean army, the king of Assyria arrogantly refused to compromise. When all his efforts to avert a war failed, Hezekiah was forced to order his army to join battle with the Assyrians. The Assyrian army was annihilated and Sennacherib withdrew in disgrace.[124] Hezekiah reigned happily and till his death there was no foreign aggression. There was quiet on the domestic front also, for the Chauvinists were happy with his religious policy. The Liberals and the slaves were kept under his iron heel.

After his death, his son Manasseh ascended the throne. Unlike his father, Manasseh was a liberal and did not succumb to the pressure of the Chauvinists. He scrapped his father's religious policy and allowed complete freedom of worship indicative of a liberal backlash, much to the chagrin of the Chauvinists. Manasseh renovated all destroyed altars of Baal and reinstated the images that they worshipped.[125] In the process, he had to be tough with the Chauvinists, for they resisted the religious liberalisation, which resulted in the loss of the privileged position that they held under Hezekiah. The liberals who had been mercilessly persecuted and socially marginalised during the reign of Hezekiah now retaliated with the tacit support of the king; several of the Hebrew priests and leaders of the Chauvinists were done to death. Dead bodies lay all over Jerusalem.[126]

The non-Hebrew population had as much freedom as their Hebrew brethren under Manasseh's rule and his period was marked by peace and prosperity except for an Assyrian attack once. The invaders took him to Babylon as a prisoner of war[127] but strangely he was released and allowed to return to Judah. That taught him a lesson. Concentrating on internal problems created by the religio-puristic ideology of his father, he had been neglecting the defenses of the country. Hence soon after his return, he raised the height of and bolstered up with buttresses the fortification of Jerusalem "on the west side of Gihon, in the valley"[128] and deployed his army in all the walled cities of the kingdom. Obviously, the Chauvinists had not cooperated with him when the Assyrians attacked and so he gave the malcontent Chauvinists some sops that pacified them to some extent, thus reversing the polarisation of society that his sectarian liberal religious policy had caused.[129] And he assured the Chauvinists protection from liberal extremists. He, thus, bequeathed to his son Amon a politically stable and economically prosperous kingdom, free from the domination of the Chauvinists.

Amon continued the liberal religious policy.[130] The Chauvinists waited for an opportunity to get rid of him. The officialdom, which was traditionally conservative, had been lying low during the reign of Manasseh. It was dominated by religio-purists and was obviously sympathetic to the Chauvinists' cause but did not dare go against Manasseh. Amon being inexperienced and politically naïve, was a soft target, and barely two years after he donned the royal mantle, he fell to an assassin's sword.

The Liberals, comprising mostly the lower-middle-class freemen like the petty landowners and traders who had become a powerful force, retaliated. They rose against the officers who were behind the conspiracy and put to the sword all those involved in the assassination of Amon and hoping his son too would follow in the footsteps of his father, they elevated his son Josiah to the throne.[131] He was only a boy of eight at that time and naturally, there being no regent, he was guided by the religio-purist bureaucracy as the Liberals had no experience in governance. So virtually, the religio-purist officials were ruling the kingdom. However, when Josiah took up the reins of the government in his hands, he stuck to the middle path, favouring neither the religio-purists nor the religio-liberal as he thought it would please both the Chauvinists and the Liberals.[132] That was just a pretence to hoodwink the Liberals who helped him to the throne. He betrayed his true colours when he personally supervised the demolition of all heathen or non-Hebrew altars in the kingdom and ordered the renovation of the Temple.[133]

In order to preclude a reversal of this trend and to tighten their grip on the government, the Chauvinists with the help of Hilkiah, the priest, copied out the Mosaic Law and sent it to the king through his scribe.[134] The scribe read out to the king what was written in the scroll, which demanded that the king strictly adhered to the Mosaic Law and warned that the Chauvinists would resist violently if he followed the liberal religious policy of his father.[135] When the king heard this he was remorseful and expressed his repentance, in case he had unconsciously strayed from the religio-purist path.[136] He at once sent Hilkiah along with three of the palace officials to Huldah, a prophetess and sorceress who was the ideological mentor of the Chauvinists. She reiterated the threat, saying that if the king dithered she would advise the Chauvinists to take up arms and overthrow him.[137] Her message was carried to the king who immediately called a conference at the Temple, to which he invited the leaders of the Chauvinists in Judah and Jerusalem, the Levites, the lower middle class – in short, the freemen of all Hebrew tribes. At the conference, the king read out the demands mentioned in the scroll and he made a covenant pledging his unconditional acceptance of all the conditions put forward by the Chauvinists.[138] He demanded that all Hebrew tribes stuck to it, and all those who assembled there, on their part, agreed to adhere to the covenant.[139]

Thus the two parties now came to an understanding by which the king would completely scrap whatever remained of the liberalist ideology in the religious policy of the state and the Chauvinists would refrain from violent agitations and conspiratorial activities. In order to assure the Chauvinists of his commitment, the king celebrated the Passover with great pomp and pageantry. At this time, Josiah got the news of Nechoh, the Pharaoh, marching against Assyria and he decided to intervene in favour of Assyria despite Egypt cautioning him against it, for Josiah probably feared that if Assyria fell, Egypt was bound to turn to Judah. As Egypt had a very strong army, Josiah must have calculated that it was better to align with Assyria so that the armies of Assyria and Judah together would be able to defeat Egypt. That would serve two purposes. Firstly, he would not have to face Egypt alone if or when, as he surmised, Egypt turned against Judah after conquering Assyria. Secondly, the war would not be fought on the soil of Judah. In the war, however, Josiah was fatally wounded and his son Jehoahaz was crowned king of Judah.

He ruled for three months, when Egypt attacked Judah. The Pharaoh had warned Judah in unequivocal terms not to align with Assyria and cross swords with him, as the Egyptian army was well equipped and very strong.[140] But Josiah had ignored his warning and fought against Egypt. Anyway, the Pharaoh took Jehoahaz to Babylon in chains putting his elder brother Eliakim, a Liberal, whose name was changed to Jehoiakim by the Pharaoh, on the throne of Judah reducing it to a tributary of Egypt.[141] Jehoiakim was, therefore, forced to levy heavy taxes on the people of Judah, which naturally made him very unpopular. At this time Nebuchadnezzar, king of Babylon, who conquered Egypt, descended upon Judah and established its suzerainty over the country. Judah under Jehoiakim remained a vassal state for three years, when in a clever move to divert the attention of the people from their financial problems caused by the heavy taxes, Jehoiakim rebelled against the Suzerain.[142] Nebuchadnezzar, however, did not directly attack Judah, perhaps because he overestimated the strength of Jehoiakim or thought that Jehokiam had the support of the Pharaoh of Egypt. So he decided to soften the target as much as possible and sent Syrian guerillas into Jerusalem besides helping the Moabites and the Ammonites invade and plunder Judah.[143] After that, the Babylonian army, which he himself commanded, launched a full-scale attack and conquered Jerusalem. The city was sacked and all the valuables in the Temple and the state treasury were looted. He also carried away all good artisans and craftsmen and battlewise warriors to Babylon as captives. The Babylonian Empire now extended from the river Nile to the Euphrates. Jehoiakim too was taken to Babylon in fetters,[144] leaving his son Jehoiachin, who was a Liberal, on the throne.

During his reign, the Babylonian army laid siege to Jerusalem when Nebuchadnezzar again arrived to command the army himself. Jehoiachin surrendered and was taken prisoner. And the Babylonians plundered whatever remained of the treasures in the Temple and the palace besides carrying off thousands of people, including the king, his harem, "the princes and all the mighty men of valour...and all the craftsmen and smiths" as captives. He filled the vacuum on the throne of Judah by making Mattaniah, Jehoiachin's uncle, changing his name to Zedekiah, the king, who followed a liberal religious policy. He ruled for about a decade and rose in revolt.

Nebuchadnezzar mobilised a large army and besieged Jerusalem for two years. The king and his troops tried to escape but were caught in the plains of Jericho. The entire royal family was annihilated, the palaces were destroyed and the Temple was plundered. All princes and the priests were taken prisoner. In short, the upper class comprising the nobility, the intelligentsia and the big landowners as well as some of the lower middle class like the craftsmen, were exiled to Babylon where all of them, including the princes and priests, were kept as slaves. The bulk of the Hebrew population, comprising the poor peasants, the unskilled workers and the slaves who would have been a liability in Babylon, were left behind.

The Judah kingdom now became the Judaea province of Babylon. The hostility between the kingdoms of Judah and Israel as well as the uncompromising struggle between the chauvinistic religio-purists and the Liberals had made it easy for the newly risen imperialist powers to annex the Hebrew kingdoms. Incidentally, the hidden irony in identifying Nebuchadnezzar as the king of the Chaldees[145] by the Chronicler is too obvious to be lost on the readers. Asimov writes, "one wonders if the Chronicler uses the phrase, 'king of the Chaldees' rather than the more natural 'king of Babylon,' does so to deliberately stress the irony. After all, Abraham, to whom Canaan was first promised, reached that land from Ur of the Chaldees and now the Jews are carried out of that land by the king of the Chaldees."[146]

The rise of the Persian Empire under King Cyrus, engulfed the entire Fertile Crescent, particularly Babylon, bringing together under one umbrella a medley of tribes and peoples who spoke different languages and espoused different religions. These included the Hebrews who had been taken to Babylon by Nebuchadnezzar as slaves. This was a turning point in the history of the Hebrew tribes. Cyrus was a Zarathustrian but he did not interfere in the religious beliefs of other people and gave them freedom of worship. He issued a proclamation permitting the Hebrews to leave Babylon, if they so desired, and go back to Judah, where they could rebuild the Temple in Jerusalem that Nebuchadnezzar had destroyed. He gave back to the Hebrews all the valuables that had been looted from the Temple by Nebuchadnezzar. Thousands of Hebrews, the rich and the poor, priests and singers from different cities in Babylon, taking a large number of slaves as well as all the movable property and their livestock, returned to their native land.[147] They were determined to reconstruct the Temple.

Several of the exiles who had married non-Hebrews and had children in those wives and were well-settled, possessing landed property, stayed back. It could also be because they feared they would be treated badly by the Hebrews of "pure blood" that they decided not to go to Judah. However, they gave whatever assistance they could in the form of gold, silver and garments for the priests to finance the construction of the Temple.[148] Evidently those who returned to Jerusalem were mostly the exiles from the kingdom of Judah.[149] Few of those who belonged to the tribes that once constituted the kingdom of Israel and who were brought to Babylon long before the people of Judah had been exiled, moved back into Jerusalem. Maybe over the years they had imbibed the local culture and integrated themselves completely with the local tribes that they had lost their Hebrew identity and were quite at home where they had been for generations. Under the circumstances although their roots were in Jerusalem they must have thought it unwise, if not puerile, to uproot themselves from Babylon and be transplanted in Judah, where they would have no voice.

Moreover, they would have heard from their grandparents and from others that the land which the Hebrews once ruled had been colonised by the invaders who deported the Hebrews from there. And naturally, they were not sure of the reception they would get from the colonists. They were not wrong. The interregnum between the fall of the Hebrew kingdoms and the return of the Hebrews from Babylon witnessed decimation of the Hebrew influence in the region. The Hebrews who were left behind after the Assyrian invaders from Israel and the Babylonian conquerors from Judah had carried away prisoners of war, were mostly the slaves, the unskilled workers, the petty traders and the farm workers, many of whom were illiterate. And naturally, there was an influx of people from the victorious countries and all of them had occupied Samaria, the capital of Israel. They intermarried with the local population and in course of time spread over the entire territory of the erstwhile kingdom of Israel, which now came to be known as Samaria, and the people of this region were called the Samaritans. Subsequently, the Babylonian conquest of Judah and the banishment of the Hebrews from that kingdom by Nebuchadnezzar had created a vacuum there, which was soon filled by the land-hungry Samaritans who migrated from the north and colonised it.

However, thousands of Hebrews in Babylon decided to go back to the country of their ancestors. The most important of those who led the returnees were Zerubbabel, Jeshua and Nehemiah – not that all the others were insignificant. Zerubbabel was the son of Shealtiel (who was the eldest son of Jehoiachin also known by its variant, Jeconiah) and thus the grandson of King Jehoiachin.[150] However, the chronicler describes Zerubbabel as the son of Pedaiah who was one of the brothers of Shealtiel (or Salathiel), in which case he would be a nephew of Shealtiel.[151] One explanation that the biblical scholars give for this apparent discrepancy is that Shealtiel might have died childless and Pedaiah being his brother would have married Sheltiel's widow as per the Mosaic Law of Inheritance and begot Zerubbabel.[152] Hence, he was the biological son of Pedaiah and the legal son of Shealtiel. It is immaterial whose son he was – whether he was the son of Shealtiel or Pedaiah – he could not but be the grandson of Jeconiah and as such was a descendant of King David. Jeshua, the other important leader of the returnees, was the son of Jezodak[153] and was the high priest of the Jews. The next one, Nehemiah, helped organise the Jews to reconstruct the broken-down wall of the Temple. Incidentally, after their return from exile in Babylon, in *circa* the sixth century BCE the Hebrews came to be called the Jews.

When King Cyrus had decreed that the Hebrews could go back to Jerusalem and rebuild the Temple, he instructed his treasurer to hand over the valuables from the Temple to Sheshbazzar, the leader of the exiles returning to Judah. Several biblical scholars surmise that Sheshbazzar was a descendant of David as he was referred to as the prince of Judah and they try to connect him somehow with the Davidic dynasty, only because Cyrus called him the prince of Judah. They have put forward various arguments to justify their contentions.

Asimov identifies him with Shenzar[154] (son of Jeconiah, son of Jehoiakim and grandson of Josiah), born in captivity. This is based on the assumption that being the son of Jeconiah he had a claim to the throne of Judah if his elder brothers were no more or incapacitated because he was in his own right the prince of Judah. Another reason for this could be that the name rhymes with one Sheshbazzar, while some others argue that Sheshbazzar and Zerubbabel are one and the same person. Their argument is that he could have had two names, as for example Daniel, who was also given a Babylonian name Belteshazzar. A few connect them based on the fictitious story of Zacharias' prophecy. However, this misunderstanding is the result of giving undue importance to the story of Zechariah's prophecy, and treating it as a fact: "The hands of Zerubbabel have laid the foundation of this house, his hands shall also finish it...."[155] This misunderstanding is understandable when the prophecy is read with the verse "Then came the same Sheshbazzar and laid the foundation...."[156]

All these arguments are rather contrived and specious. The name Sheshbazzar means "offshoot of Babylon," indicating that he was conceived and born in Babylon. So it is doubtless a Babylonian name and not a Hebrew one. In Zechariah's prophecy, the words "laid the foundation" do not denote the ceremonial laying of the foundation of the Temple by Zerubbabel; nor does it imply that Sheshbazzar was present at the site on the occasion. It only means that he was responsible for starting the work of reconstructing the Temple. It is like saying, for example, Harriet Beecher Stowe, who wrote the anti-slavery novel *Uncle Tom's Cabin* [and of whom Abraham Lincoln said "The little woman who started this big war"], laid the foundation for the abolition of slavery in the US. This does not mean she abolished slavery or piloted a bill in the legislature to abolish slavery.

That these two men were not one and the same is abundantly clear from the letter that Tatnai, a Persian governor, Shetharboznai, a Persian official, and Apharsachites and the people of Samaria, who objected to the construction of the Temple, sent to the Persian king. The letter stated that when questioned as to who permitted the construction of the Temple, those at the site replied that King Cyrus had issued an edict to build it. They added that the vessels of gold and silver "were delivered unto one whose name was Sheshbazzar whom he had made governor...(and) then came the same Sheshbazzar and laid the foundation" of the Temple.[157] Those whom Tattenai and others questioned included Zerubbabel and had Zerubbabel and Sheshbazzar been the same person, they would not have said, "one whose name was Sheshbazzar whom he had made governor" and "then came the same Sheshbazzar." Zerubbabel would have said that King Cyrus had given the vessels to him whom the king had made governor and he only laid the foundation.

There is no reason why Sheshbazzar should be connected to any of the other biblical characters just because Cyrus called him the "prince of Judah" and his name happened to rhyme with one member of the Davidian dynasty. Sheshbazzar was neither Shenazar nor Zerubbabel; these three were three different individuals, and Sheshbazzar was not connected with the Davidian dynasty while the other two were. His name Sheshbazzar, as stated above, means "offshoot of Babylon," which unmistakably indicates that he was a Babylonian. So it is doubtless that he was not a Hebrew and was in no way connected with the House of David.

Why, then, did Cyrus address Sheshbazzar as the "prince of Judah" and why was he entrusted with the Temple property in preference to even Zerubbabel, a prince and Jeshua, the high priest? King Cyrus was a great conqueror and at the same time, a shrewd politician as his liberal religious policy indicates. It was this perspicacity and circumspection that determined his decision to avoid appointing a known scion of the Judah dynasty, Zerubbabel, the governor of Judah. He must have feared that being the true prince of Judah by virtue of his birth, he would proclaim himself the king and declaring independence, he would secede Judah from the empire. The aura of his lineage would naturally help rally the people behind him. Moreover, the loyalty of the Jews staying behind in Babylon would be more to him than to the country that they had adopted. And these Jews in Babylon would turn out to be quislings if at any time the Jews of Judah were to invade Babylon.

Sheshbazzar must have been a trusted official of the king's treasury, second only to Mithredath, the treasurer. So using his prerogative as the imperial power, Cyrus declared Sheshbazzar the "prince of Judah" and appointed him governor of Judah. The title must have been conferred on him specifically for the purpose of giving him the right to carry from Babylon to Jerusalem the gold and silver vessels taken from the Temple and to rule over Jerusalem as the governor. Obviously he did not trust any of the Jews or perhaps he did not want to give prominence to any one of them by entrusting him with the task of carrying the valuables of the Temple.[158] On reaching Jerusalem, Sheshbazzar, by virtue of the power vested in him as the prince of Judah and as the governor who represented the king, laid the foundation of the Temple.

After that he was not heard of. He could not have continued to hold the post of the governor *in absentia*. Zerubbabel[159] and his clan along with Jeshua and his fellow priests rebuilt the altar of the god of Israel and sacrificed burnt offerings on it to ward off any possible attack by enemies and they celebrated the Feast of the Tabernacle. Sheshbazzar was not present when burnt offerings were sacrificed or at the Feast of the Tabernacle, which confirms that he was not a Hebrew but a Babylonian. Had he been of royal lineage, the Bible would have undoubtedly mentioned his connection with the Davidian dynasty as it had done in the case of Joseph, a carpenter and father of Jesus. So it may be assumed that he returned to Babylon and resumed his official duties under King Cyrus even before the altar of the god of Israel was constructed and burnt offerings were sacrificed, for as a non-Hebrew he was not concerned with all that. Or probably he died.

Ever since Sheshbazzar left, the work on the Temple was all but stopped and Darius, the then king of Persia, must have heard of the lackadaisical attitude of those carrying out the renovation of the Temple building. So Darius sent a message to Zerubbabel, who got it after the Feast of the Tabernacle, and he ordered them to resume the work immediately.[160] He expressed his displeasure with Zerubbabel and the priests for neglecting the work[161] on "my house"[162] and being concerned with their personal matters only. That he said "*my* house" shows the personal interest the king, though a Persian, was taking in the construction of the Temple. He was indignant that discontinuing the repair of the temple, they built luxurious houses for themselves and were wasting their time. The message was a strong indictment. He also threatened to stop financial and all other forms of aid for the construction work that he had been giving them so far if the Jews continued to be lethargic.[163] The threat really shook them up and fearing serious consequences, Joshua and the Jewish community as a whole immediately started the work on the Temple under the direction of Zerubbabel.[164] The king, however, made it clear that although he had given back all the valuables of the Temple, the entire property, "...the gold and silver and articles of the House of God..." belonged to him.[165] It was a warning against misusing the property of the Temple. The king was pleased with the alacrity with which they resumed the work and sent a message appreciating their work. He gave a hint that he would relegate more powers to Zerubbabel in the administration of Judah but he made it clear that Zerubbabel would yet owe allegiance to the king of Persia.[166]

But the work of repairing the building had not been taken up so far and it continued to be in ruins. Meanwhile, Nehemiah mobilised the Jewish community and began to rebuild the broken-down wall around the city. Eliashib, the high priest, built as far as the Towers of the Hundred and of Hananel, the sheepgate. The people from Jericho and a group led by Zaccur were also working next to them. The Fish gate was built by Hassenaah's sons, Meremoth, Meshullam, Zadok, and men from Tekoa were also engaged in repairing the wall. In short, the Jews, including the Levites, formed groups and each group under a leader was busy repairing a part of the wall and thus the entire wall was rebuilt; all the gates too were repaired and reinforced. When the Samaritans saw that the exiles who had returned from Babylon were renovating the Temple and the city wall they approached Zerubbabel and offered their help in the construction work. They said to Zerubbabel and the other leaders that they revered and had been offering sacrifice to the Hebrew god since they came into Samaria. But the Hebrew leaders rejected the offer. There was no reason for the Jews to have taken this negative attitude except their inherent suspicion of the non-Hebrews – more so in this case because the Samaritans were descendants of those brought in by the conquerors and were the colonisers who ejected them from their land.

This rebuff only earned them the animosity of the colonists, who, however, did not dare physically obstruct the work, for that would have led to a clash and they knew the king would not tolerate causing breach of peace. They would be on the mat instead of the Jews about whom they were thinking of complaining. So they sent a letter to Darius, the king, cautioning him against permitting the Jews to reconstruct the wall and pointing out that Jerusalem had been a hotbed of rebellions and it was not safe to allow the city wall to be reconstructed. They stated that if the Jews were allowed to rebuild the wall, they would refuse to pay taxes and suggested that the king looked "in the book of the records of your fathers; you will also find in the book of the records, and know that this city in olden times has been the centre of rebellions against kings...for which reason this city was destroyed."[167] So if the construction of the wall was allowed to be completed, they wrote, the king could as well write off this part of his kingdom. The king, in the reply he sent to the chancellor Rehum, the scribe Shamshai and others, wrote, "Inform those men that I command they cease the work on the wall until the command is given by me...." And he ordered that they should ensure that the work is stopped immediately, before the situation got out of control.[168] So the king's letter gave them the authority to force the Hebrews to stop the work on the wall.

To sum up, as a result of a series of invasions by Assyria, the northern kingdom, Israel, passed into oblivion; and the ten Hebrew tribes inhabiting there had been exiled[169] little by little and were replaced by people brought from elsewhere. Since then the territory of the erstwhile kingdom of Israel had been known as Samaria, which was the name of the capital of the kingdom at that time, and the new inhabitants were identified as the Samaritans. The southern Hebrew kingdom, Judah, however, tottered along for about a century and a half after the fall of Israel till it was overrun by the Babylonian king, Nebuchadnezzar. Ever since, it had been a province of Babylon, directly controlled by the king of Babylon, and it is said almost the entire population of the Hebrews in Judah was taken as captives to Babylon. Subsequently, the conquest of Babylon by Persia inevitably brought Judah, the erstwhile Hebrew kingdom, also under the Persian rule and Cyrus, the Persian king, passed a decree allowing the descendants of the Hebrews who had been brought to Babylon as captives by Nebuchadnezzar, to return to their native land, Judah. By then what was once the kingdom of Judah came to be known as Judaea, which King Cyrus maintained as a province[170] of the Persian Empire, administered by a governor.

NOTES

1. H.H. Milman, *The History of the Jews*, V. 1, New York, 1870, p. 379.
2. A.W.F. Blunt, *Israel in World History*, London, 1927, p. 31.
3. I Kgs. 11:43; 12:1. Vide Appendix for a list of the kings of the Hebrew kingdoms, undivided and divided. Saul was not of the House of David.
4. I Kgs. 12:2-3. "...Jeroboam...who was yet in Egypt, heard of it...That

they sent and called him..."

5. 1 Kgs. 12:4. "...Thy father made our yoke heavy, but make thou it lighter unto us...."
6. I Kgs. 12:13-14.
7. I Kgs. 12:18.
8. I Kgs. 12:22-24. "...the word of god came to Sahmaiah, saying, Speak to Rehoboam...Thus says the Lord, You shall not go up, nor fight against your brethren the children of Israel..."
9. I Kgs. 12:20.
10. I Kgs. 14:17.
11. A.W.F. Blunt, *Israel in World History*, London, 1927, p. 31.
12. I Kgs. 12:27.
13. II Chr. 11:14, 16.
14. I Kgs. 13:33. "...returned not from his evil way."
15. I kgs. 14:2, 3. "...Jeroboam said to his wife, Arise, I pray you, and disguise yourself, that you be not known to be the wife of Jeroboam; and get you to Shiloh; behold, there is Ahijah the prophet who told me that I should be king over this people...he shall tell you what shall become of the child."
16. I Ks. 14:5. "And the Lord said to Ahijah, Behold, the wife of Jeroboam comes to ask a thing of you for her son; for he is sick; thus and thus shall you say to her; for it shall be, when she comes in, that she shall feign herself to be another woman."
17. I Kgs. 14:6.
18. I Kgs. 14:22-23.
19. The word 'nations' denotes 'tribes' and the phrase 'to the abominations of the nations' indicates intra-tribal and inter-tribal conflicts.
20. I Kgs. 14:24. "And there were also sodomites in the land; and they did according to all the admonitions of the nations which the Lord cast out before the children of Israel.
21. II Chr. 12:5. "Then came Shemaiah the prophet to Rehoboam and to the princes...and said to them, Thus says the Lord, you have forsaken me, and therefore have I also left you in the hand of Shishak. Whereupon the princes of Israel and the king humbled themselves..."
22. II Chr. 12:7, 8-9. "The word of the Lord came to Shemaiah, saying, they have humbled themselves, therefore I will not destroy them...Nevertheless they shall be his servants..."
23. II Chr. 13:3-7, 12. "And Abijah stood on mount Zemaraim...and said, Hear me, you Jeroboam, and all Israel; should you not know that the Lord God of Israel gave the kingdom over Israel to David for ever and even to him and his sons by a covenant at salt?" " O children of Israel,

do not fight against the Lord God of your fathers."

24. II Chr. 13:19.
25. II Chr. 14:3, 5/15:16.
26. I Kgs. 14:20.
27. I Kgs. 15:16-22; II Chr. 16:5-6.
28. I Kgs. 16:1, 2, 3. "...I exalted you out of the dust and made you prince...and you have walked in the way of Jeroboam...Behold I will take away the prosperity of Baasha and...of his house..."
29. I Kgs. 16:21-22.
30. This stone was discovered by accident in 1868 at Dhiban (now called Dibon in Jordan). The inscription gives a detailed account of the Moabite rebellion.
31. A.L. Sachar, *A History of the Jews*, New York, 1965, p. 47.
32. I Kgs. 16:25-26.
33. I Kgs. 17:1. "As the Lord god of Israel lives, before whom I stand, there shall not be dew or rain these years..."
34. I Kgs. 17:2, 3, 4. "And the word of the Lord came to him saying go away from here...and hide by the brook Cherith...and I have commanded the ravens to feed you there."
35. I Kgs. 18:3, 7.
36. I Kgs. 18:4.
37. I Kgs. 18:40.
38. I Kgs. 19:15, 16. "And the Lord said to him, Go, return on your way to the wilderness of Damascus; and when you reach there , you shall anoint Hazel as king over Syria; and...you shall anoint Jehu the son of Nimshi as King over Israel; and Elisha, the son of Shaphat...you shall anoint as prophet in your place."
39. I Kgs. 20:3. "...your silver and your gold are mine; your wives and your children...are mine."
40. I Kgs. 20:13. "...Thus says the Lord, Have you seen all this multitude? Behold I will deliver it into your hand this day and you will know that I am the Lord."
41. I Kgs, 20:22. "And the prophet came to the king of Israel, and said to him, Go, strengthen yourself; and see what you do; for at the return of the year the king of Syria will come up against you."
42. I Kgs. 20:28. "...the Syrians have said, The Lord is God of the hills, but he is not God of the valleys, therefore I will deliver all this multitude into your hand; and you will know that I am the Lord."
43. I Kgs. 20:23. "Their gods are gods of the hills; therefore they are stronger than we; but let us fight against them in the plain and surely we shall be stronger than they."

44. I Kgs. 20:42. "...Because you have let go out of your hand a man whom I appointed to utter destruction, therefore your life shall go for his life..."
45. I Kgs. 21:1-16.
46. II Kgs. 2:1.
47. I kgs. 21:19. "And you shall speak to him, saying, Thus says the Lord, Have you killed and also taken possession?...In the place where dogs licked the blood of Naboth shall dogs lick your blood..."
48. II Chr. 19:5-11.
49. II Chr. 20:1, 16-24.
50. I Kgs. 22:2-3.
51. II Kgs. 2:4. "Then Elijah said to him, 'Elisha stay here please...:' So they came to Jericho.
52. II Kgs. 1:3-16. "...But the angel of the Lord said to Elijah the Rishbite, Arise, go up to meet the messengers of the king of Samaria and say to them, Is it not because there is not a God in Israel that you go to inquire Baalzebub...?"
53. II Kgs. I:15. "And the angel of the Lord said to Elijah, Go down with him; be not afraid of him..."
54. II Kgs. 2:11.
55. I Kgs. 19:16; II Kgs.2:9-10.
56. II Kgs. 3:13. "And the king of Israel said to him, Nay; for the Lord has called these three kings together, to deliver them into the hand of Moab."
57. II Kgs. 3:16. "...Make the valley full of ditches. For thus says the Lord, You shall not see wind, neither shall you see rain; yet that valley shall be filled with water that you may drink..."
58. II Kgs. 3:18. "And this is but a light thing in the sight of the Lord; he will deliver the Moabites also into your hand."
59. II Kgs. 3:27. "Then he took his eldest son that should have reigned in his stead, and offered him fro a burnt offering upon the wall."
60. II Kgs. 3:27. "...they departed from him, and returned to their own land..."
61. II Kgs. 8:16.
62. II Kgs. 8:19. "Yet the Lord would not destroy Judah for David his servant's sake, as he promised him to give him always a light, and to his children."
63. II Kgs. 8:7-13. "...And Elisha said to him, Go and tell him, he would certainly recover; however the Lord had showed me that he shall surely die. And he set his countenance in stare until he was ashamed: and the man of God wept. And Hazel said, why are you weeping, my lord?

And he answered: Because I know the evil that you will do to the people of Israel...The Lord also showed me that you will be the king over Syria."

64. II Kgs. 8:14-15.
65. II Kgs. 9:2-3."...make him rise up from among his comrades and take him to an inner chamber...Then take the box of oil, and pour on his head and say, So says the Lord, I have anointed you king over Israel. Then open the door, and flee, and do not even look back."
66. II Kgs. 9:6-10.
67. II Kgs. 9:7. "...you shall smite the house of Ahab your master that I may avenge the blood...of all the servants of the Lord, at the hands of Jezebel."
68. II Kgs. 9:11.
69. II Kgs. 9:12. "...Thus saith the Lord, I have anointed thee king of Israel."
70. II Kgs. 9:13.
71. II Kgs. 9:14.
72. II Kgs. 9:15-27.
73. II Kgs. 10:18-28.
74. II Kgs. 11:1. Ahaziah's children were naturally Athaliah's grandchildren, whether they were born of his legitimate wife or concubines. Leaving aside those he begot in his concubines, there could at least be one legitimate grandchild. However, parents and children and siblings killing or imprisoning one another to usurp the throne had been a feature of absolute monarchies in all countries at all times.
75. II Kgs. 11:2-3; II Chr.22:11.
76. II Kgs. 11:4-12.
77. II Kgs. 12:8.
78. II Kgs. 12:16.
79. II Kgs. 12:21.
80. II Kgs. 13:3. "And the anger of the Lord was kindled against Israel, and he delivered them...into the hand of Benhadad, the son of Hazael..."
81. II Kgs. 13:7.
82. II Kgs. 13:23. "And the Lord was gracious to them, had compassion on them, and respected them, because of his covenant with Abraham..."
83. II Chr. 25:27. "...Amaziah did turn away from following the Lord..."
84. II Chr. 26:4. "...he did what was right in the sight of the Lord."
85. II Chr. 26:16-19. "...and had a censer in his hand to burn incense; and while he was wroth with the priests the leprosy even rose up in his forehead..."

86. II Kgs. 15:5, II Chr. 26:21. "And the Lord struck the king, so that he was a leper until the day of his death and he dwelt in different houses. And Jonathan the king's son was over the house, judging the people of the land." Lepers were not allowed to mingle with the people in those days and were totally isolated. So when it said, he contracted leprosy, it means he was imprisoned and was not allowed to meet the people.
87. II Kgs. 15:8.
88. II Kgs. 15:9. "...he did what was evil in the sight of the Lord..."
89. II Kgs. 15:8-10.
90. II Kgs. 15:14.
91. II Kgs. 15:18. "...he did what was evil in the sight of the Lord..."
92. II Kgs. 15:q19-20. "...And Menahem exacted the money from all the wealthy men of Israel, each man fifty shekel of silver, to give to the king of Assyria..."
93. II Kgs. 15:23.
94. II Kgs. 15:24. "...he did what was evil in the sight of the Lord..."
95. II Kgs. 15:28. "...he did what was evil in the sight of the Lord..."
96. II Kgs. 15:29.
97. II Kgs. 15:7.
98. II Kgs. 15:35; II Chr.27:3.
99. II Kgs. 16:2-4; II Chr.28:24-25;
100. II Kgs. 15:37. "In those days, the Lord began to send against Judah Rezim the king of Syria, and Pekah, the son of Remaliah."
101. II Kgs. 16:6.
102. II Kgs. 16:9.
103. II Chr. 28:5-8.
104. II Chr. 28:9-15.
105. II Chr. 28:17.
106. II Chr. 28:18.
107. II Chr, 28:20.
108. II Kgs. 16:10-18: II Chr. 28:23. "...he sacrificed to the gods of Damascus, which had defeated him..."
109. In one place the Bible says this happened "in the twentieth year of Jotham, the son of Uzziah" (II Kgs. 15:30) while in the same book, two chapters later, it is said "in the twelfth year of Ahaz, king of Judah, began Hoshea, the son of Elah to reign in Samaria" (II Kgs. 17:1). Ahaz ascended the throne of Judah only after Jotham's death. Biblical scholars have put forward various theories to explain this discrepancy but none of them has been found satisfactory. Anyway, a probe into this problem is beyond the scope of this study.
110. II Kgs. 17:2. "...he did that which was evil in the sight of the Lord..."

111. II Kgs. 17:4.
112. II Kgs. 18'9-10.
113. II kgs. 18:11.
114. II Chr. 28:27.
115. II Chr. 29:2. "...and he did what was right in the sight of the Lord..."
116. II Kgs. 18:3-6.
117. II Chr. 29:4.
118. II Chr. 129:10. "Now it is my heart to make a covenant with the Lord God of Israel, that his fierce wrath may turn away from us."
119. II Chr. 31:1.
120. II Chr. 31:4-12.
121. II Chr. 32:27, 30.
122. II Kgs. 18:13.
123. II Kgs. 18:18.
124. II Kgs. 19:36.
125. II Chr. 33:3. "...he did that what was evil in the sight of the Lord..."
126. II Kgs. 21:16. "Moreover Manasseh shed innocent blood very much, till he had filled Jerusalem from one end to another; beside his sin with which he made Judah to sin, in doing that which was evil in the sight of the Lord." "Which was evil in the sight of the Lord" connote liberalism.
127. II Chr. 33:11.
128. II Chr. 33:14. Gihon is the mythical river in Eden (See Chapter 3, "A Virtual Tower of Babel"). It is also an important spring in Jerusalem, where Solomon was anointed as king (vide I Kgs. 1:38-39).
129. II Chr. 33:15, 16. "He took away the foreign gods and the idol from the house of the Lord...repaired the altar of the Lord and sacrificed thereon peace offerings and thank offerings..."
130. II Chr. 33:22. "But he did what was evil in the sight of the Lord..."
131. II Chr. 33:25. But the people of the land executed all those who had conspired against king Amon. Then the people of the land made his son Josiah king in his place."
132. II Chr. 34:2. "He did not turn aside to the right hand or to the left."
133. II Chr. 34:8.
134. II Chr. 34:14. "...Hikiah, the priest found a book of the law of the Lord given by Moses."
135. II Chr. 34:21. "...great is the wrath of the Lord that is poured on us, because our fathers have not kept the word of the Lord..."
136. II Chr. 34:19. "...when the king had heard the words of the law, that he tore his clothes."
137. II Chr. 34:23-24. "Tell me the man who sent you, '...Behold, I will

bring disaster on this place, and on the inhabitants there..."

138. II Chr. 34:31. "...made a covenant before the Lord, to follow the Lord, and to keep his commandments, and his testimonies, and his statutes, with all his heart, and with all his soul to perform the words of the covenant..."
139. II Chr. 34:32. "...made all those present in Jerusalem and Benjamin to adhere to it. And the inhabitants of Jerusalem did according to the covenant of God..."
140. II chr. 35:21. "...refrain from meddling with God, who is with me..." This connotes that he had a strong army.
141. II Kgs. 23:34-37; II Chr. 36:4-5. "...and he did evil in the sight of the Lord his God."
142. II Kgs. 24:1.
143. II Kgs. 24:2.
144. II Chr. 36:6.
145. II Chr. 36:17.
146. I. Asimov, *Guide to the Bible*, New York, 1981. p. 428.
147. Ezra 2:1-67.
148. Ezra 2:69.
149. Ezra 1:5. "...then the heads of the fathers' houses of Judah and Benjamin and the priests and the Levites rose up to go and build the house of the Lord that is in Jerusalem."
150. Ezra 3:2/5:2; Hag/1:12, 14; Mt.1:12; Lk.3:27.
151. I Chr. 3:17-19.
152. Deut. 25:5-6.
153. Ezra 2:2/5:2; Neh. 7:7; Hag. 1:12-14.
154. Asimov. op. cit., p. 438.
155. Zech. 4:9.
156. Ezra 5:16.
157. Ezra 5:14, 16.
158. Acts. 7:59
159. Ezra 5:2.
160. Hag. 1:1-8. "In the second year of Darius...came the word of the Lord by Haggai the prophet to Zerubbabel...governor of Judah and to Joshua...the high priest saying,...This people say, The time has not come..." Go up to the mountains, and bring wood, and build the temple."
161. Hag. 1:4. "Is it time for you to dwell in your panelled houses when the temple lie in ruins?"
162. Hag. 1:9. "...Why? Says the Lord if hosts. "Because of My house that

is in ruins, while every one of you runs to his own house" The 'Lord' in this context is the king of Persia. It was his message to Zerubbabel.

163. Hag. 1:10, 11. "Therefore the heavens above you held back the dew..., as I called for a drought..."
164. Hag. 1:14. "...the Lord stirred up the spirit of Zerubbabel...and the spirit of Joshua and the spirit of all the remnant of the people..."
165. Hag. 2:8. "The silver is mine, and the gold is mine says the Lord of hosts." In this context too, 'Lord' stands for the king of Persia. Ezra 6:5. In this passage also "God" stands for the king.
166. Hag. 2:23. "...I will take you, O Zerubbabel my servant, the son of Shealtiel...and will make you a signet ring..." The words, "my servant" indicates that Darius expected Zerubbabel to owe allegiance to the King of Persia.
167. Ezra 4:15.
168. Ezra 4:22-23.
169. Those are said to be the ten "lost tribes" of Jews.
170. Ezra 1:1-6.

8

Anti-imperialist Movements

The onslaught of Alexander the Great tolled the knell of the Persian hegemony and brought Judaea under the Greeks. But Alexander's death a few years later without leaving a male successor, resulted in the division of his empire among his generals, bringing Judaea under the Seleucid kings of the Hellenistic Syrian kingdom. The oppressive rule of Antiochus Epiphanes,[1] the Seleucid king, became more and more intolerable day by day. He pillaged Jerusalem and desecrated the temple. He harassed the elite of society – the influential and the affluent – not as a class but individually almost every day and constantly threatened to raze the city to the ground. He compelled them to abrogate their laws, refrain from circumcising their infants and to sacrifice pig's flesh upon the altar.[2] The king, thus, hurt their religious sensibilities and created a sense of insecurity in them, thereby losing the sympathy of the affluent class, the only section of the population that would have been the support of the imperial power in Judaea. The last straw was his attempt at imposing the Hellenistic culture on the Jews that finally compelled Mattathias, a man of the priestly line of Joarib, to call upon the freemen of Judaea to resist and that inevitably led to an armed revolt against the Hellenistic rule.

Though advanced in years, Mattathias, then living in a village called Modin, gathered an army and together with his five sons spearheaded the resistance to the Hellenistic rule.[3] When many of them refused to fight on the Sabbath day, he told them that "by observing the law so religiously," they would become their own enemies, for on that day if the enemy attacked them they would become easy prey to their swords. He fought the Hellenistic army and defeated Antiochus Epiphanes, driving him out of the country. And he ruled Judaea for a year. That was the beginning of the period of the Maccabees.[4] After his death, one of his sons, Judas Maccabeus, who assumed the leadership, forged an alliance with the Romans and repelled Antiochus when he made a second expedition.[5] Judas finally succeeded in liberating Judaea, which remained an independent political entity ruled by the Maccabees,[6] who were Hasmonaeans or members of a Jewish priestly family.

They may, hence, be considered priest-kings rather than secular kings, indicating the resurgence of religio-purism. Nearly a century later, the Roman Empire engulfed most of Northwest Europe including Britain and in the east Greece, Turkey, as well as all the countries around the Mediterranean Sea, and along with those countries Judaea too was submerged in the *Pax Romana* or the "Peace of Rome." Thus the Maccabeean rule came to an end in the first century BCE. But Judaea was the one restive element that disturbed the peace the powerful Imperial Rome 'clamped' on its tributary kingdoms – yes, it was an eerie peace imposed by the Roman imperialism with the might of its arms.

The Jews were bigoted monotheists and rabid iconoclasts, to whom polytheism and idolatry of the Romans were anathema, and they could not tolerate the polytheistic religion of the Roman rulers. Besides, the imperial power harassed the wealthy farming community only to get hold of the agricultural land that was the main source of income of the Jewish affluent class. Consequently, spontaneous revolts flared up now and then in Judaea, apparently caused by religious sectarianism, but the underlying cause was conflicting economic interests manifested in their struggle for arable land. The Romans, no doubt, succeeded in suppressing all those uprisings with a heavy hand. It was thus a period of turbulence. So Julius Caesar, who was the emperor at that time, appointed Antipater, known in history as Herod the Great I, procurator of Judaea, who was later made king of Judaea by the Roman Senate and was thus the virtual ruler of Judaea. He appointed his son Herod Antipas, governor of Galilee. After the death of Herod Antipater, the kingdom was divided among his surviving three sons. The eldest of them, Antipas, called Herod the tetrarch, who divorced his first wife and married Herodias, his niece and former wife of one of his stepbrothers, ruled Galilee and Parea. The second son, Archaelaus, called Herod the Ethnarch, was made the ruler of Judaea, Samaria and Idumaea but was exiled a few years later by the Emperor and reducing his principality into a province, Coponius, a Roman, was appointed its procurator.[7] Philip, the third son, was appointed the ruler of Gaulanitis, Batanaea, and Trachonitis.

When Philip died, Tiberius Caesar, who was on the throne of Rome then, ordered the principality over which Philip ruled to be attached to the province of Syria. But following the death of Tiberius when "Caligula" Gaius Caesar Augustus Germanicus succeeded as the emperor, he restored *status quo ante.* And he gave his confidant and protégé, Herod Agrippa I, grandson of Herod the Great I, the title "King of the Jews" and put him in charge of Philip's tetrarchy, adding to it the kingdom of Lysanias as well as Abilene, of which Varus was the governor.[8]

The Herodian family claimed to be Jews, but the blue-blooded Hebrew Chauvinists did not accept the claim because the Herodian family had Edomite and Arab blood. However, in order to get the support of the religio-purist Chauvinists, Herod rebuilt the Temple and constructed a compound wall around it, enclosing an additional piece of land that was as wide as the one attached to the Temple till then. The budgeted outlay for the project was humongous, and in addition to it he also laid out a large sum of money to provide the Temple with gold and silver vessels.[9] Although the Chauvinists were a little mollified, the chasm between them and the Herodian rulers remained unbridgeable. Nonetheless, the Chauvinists, in their own interest, supported the Establishment. Agrippa, as said above, was the nephew of Antipas and Philip, but they were contemporaries.[10] When Agrippa was made king of the Jews, Herod Antipas, at the instance of his wife Herodias went to Rome to seek an audience with Caligula and ask for a royal title. But instead of the crown, he got the boot; and he, along with his wife, was banished to Spain.

A brittle peace prevailed in the erstwhile Hebrew kingdom of Judaea. The possibility of a Jewish insurrection leading to a full-scale war with Rome at any time had been looming large in the political horizon of Judaea. In the eyes of the Jews, the Romans were pagans and contemptible, but the Romans, being the rulers, considered themselves superior to the Hebrews. They looked down upon the Jews and they had been trying to impose their culture on the Jews. The circumspect Jewish leaders had realised that a direct, armed confrontation with the imperial Roman power would be disastrous to the Jews. Two prominent leaders that this new situation had thrown up were John, who was later popularly known as John the Baptist and regarded as Precursor to a Messiah, and Jesus of Nazareth, later called the Nazarene, who was regarded as the Christ or Messiah.[11] Their historicity has been a point of debate and several biblical scholars and historians regard them as mythical characters. This is primarily because the Bible has mythified both of them – more so Jesus – to such an extent that even historical facts seem mythology. Anyway, we shall discuss the problem of their historicity in the relevant contexts.

Let us see how the Bible portrays John. The story of John's birth itself is couched in myth, which states, he was bestowed upon his parents in response to their prayers. About his parentage, the Bible says, "There was in the days of Herod,[12] the king of Judaea, a certain priest named Zacharias, of the course of Abia: and his wife was of the daughters of Aaron, and her name was Elisabeth."[13] Both his parents, Zacharias and Elisabeth, were of priestly descent, and Zacharias belonged to the course of Abia.[14] For a long time after their marriage, the couple had no offspring, as Elisabeth was barren. However, when they were quite old, an angel appeared before Zacharias and said to him, "I am Gabriel that stand in the presence of God and am sent to speak to you, and to bring you these glad tidings."[15] The happy news was that Zacharias' prayer was heard and a son would be born to the old couple as a divine gift to them. He added that the baby should be named John. Except that he was born in the time of Herod the Great I, the Bible does not say anything about his childhood or youth; nor does it say anything about his activities during this period. The little information that we have about his childhood is only what can be gleaned from the Gospels, which say eight days after his birth the boy was circumcised[16] and "the child grew, and waxed strong in spirit, and was in the deserts till the day of his showing to Israel."[17] That is all.

Jesus' birth has been mythicised much more than that of John because John was considered the Precursor of the Messiah only, while

Jesus was regarded as the Christ and Son of God. Six months after John's mother Elisabeth became pregnant, a kinswoman[18] of hers, Mary who was at that time betrothed to a man by name Joseph, also got pregnant by the grace of god.[19] When she realised that she had conceived she did not reveal it to anyone in Nazareth, where she lived at that time. But she knew this could not be kept a secret for long; yet, she kept it a secret. Why did she not tell her siblings or her parents that she was pregnant? Normally, the first person to whom a girl in such a predicament would have confided would be her sister or mother. The Bible does not say if she had any sibling or any relative other than Elisabeth.

However, when Jesus was crucified, the Bible says, "Now there stood by the cross of Jesus his mother, and his mother's sister, Mary, the wife of Cleophas and Mary Magdalene."[20] Two sisters having the same name, is rather strange. So she could not be her sibling; maybe her cousin. We never met her before that and the Bible does not say where she and her husband were staying. If Mary had no sisters, she should have confided to her mother, but nowhere is it said that Mary told her mother about her pregnancy. In fact, the Bible does not in any place mention anything about her parents. It is strange that the Bible, which gives the genealogy of even some minor characters, does not give the genealogy or any other particulars about the family, especially the parents of an important protagonist like Mary. The only biographical information that the Bible gives about her is that she was betrothed to Joseph and was the mother of Jesus as well as James and Joses,[21] apart from her relationship with Elisabeth.

Was her mother no more? Was Mary the offspring of an unwed mother? If her mother had a husband and Mary was born to them, could it be that both of them were dead already? And was she the only child of her mother, presuming that the wife of Cleophas was her cousin or a distant relative, for as stated above, sisters or even stepsisters, having the same name is incredible? Was she living alone in the house? No answer to any of these questions is found in the Bible. The only biographical information that the Bible gives about her is that she was married to Joseph and was the mother of Jesus as well as James and Joses,[22] apart from her relationship with Elisabeth. However, biblical (Catholic) scholars, based on a tradition founded upon the report of the Infancy Gospel of James or Protoevangelion, an apocryphal Gospel ascribed to the 2[23] century CE, state that Mary's parents were Joachim and Anna. Joachim was a descendant of David and Anna was that of the tribe of the Levite, Aaron.[24] They were living in Sephoris and Mary is believed to have been born to them in their advanced age. After the child was born, Anne in keeping with her vow, took the baby to the Temple as an offering to god.[25]

Presumably, she had neither parents nor siblings alive when she came to know of her pregnancy. Had they been alive she would not have thought of going to Elisabeth to seek her advice, and even if she wanted to go, her parents would not have allowed her to travel all the way in her present condition. Or at least, one of them would have accompanied her, had she insisted on going. How did Mary, a pregnant woman, go all the way from Nazareth in Galilee[26] where she was when she conceived, to a "city of Judah" where Elisabeth was staying? Did she walk? Did she go riding a donkey, which was the common mode of transport in those times? Did she go alone or did someone accompany her? If so, who was it? All these and many other questions remain unanswered. She did not tell anyone that she was going. And her long absence from home too does not seem to have been noticed by anyone, because after she returned from Elisabeth's house no one is said to have questioned her about her long absence. Was she, then, living alone in the house? Or did she not return to Nazareth? In that case where did she go? We shall try to find answers to all these in the next chapter, "The Son of Man." For the time being as the biblical story says, let us just say she went "with haste" all the way to a "City of Judah" to her kinswoman Elisabeth and confessed to her. But the Bible does not reveal what she confessed.

The Bible circumvents the problem of her pre-marital pregnancy by mythicising it. It says Mary got pregnant by the Holy Ghost. Her pregnancy was, thus, what is described by the Roman Catholic Church as "Immaculate Conception." This is a doctrine fabricated with a motive to explain away the otherwise inexplicable phenomenon of Mary's conception without the involvement of the male element, and the motive was to attribute divinity to the baby in the womb. In biology, this phenomenon of development of eggs in certain female organisms without fertilisation by union with the sperm of the opposite sex is called parthenogenesis. In other words, this is reproduction without copulation, which is common among the class Hexapoda[27] of Phylum Arthropoda but certainly not among higher forms of life, particularly those belonging to the class Mammalia of Phylum Chordata. Man or *Homo sapiens* come under the class Mammalia and parthenogenesis is not a possibility as far as human beings are concerned. So Immaculate Conception or a woman conceiving sans sexual intercourse was impossible in those days, for the technique of artificial insemination was not known then; nor was the technique of *in vitro* fertilisation. Or, to put it differently, Mary should have had sexual intercourse with a man and cannot be considered a virgin. Who was that man?

There is, however, another question that needs to be answered. The Bible says that Joseph came to know of Mary's pregnancy after their betrothal. The question is how he came to know that his fiancée was pregnant. The Bible tells us that when he lay thinking over this problem he fell asleep and had a dream. In his dream an angel appeared and told him that "that which is conceived in her is of the Holy Ghost,"[28] and that his fiancée was a virgin, as she had not had sexual intercourse. The angel also said to him that he need not, therefore, hesitate to marry her. He also enjoined him to refrain from deflowering her until she was delivered of the baby in her womb. No one with common sense would have believed that she got pregnant without having sex with a man. Certainly Joseph was not a simpleton to swallow the cock-and-bull story of the Holy Ghost being responsible for her pregnancy; nor would anyone else have believed it. Naturally, Joseph was in a dilemma and like Hamlet he soliloquised: "To be or not to be: that is the question." His problem was whether it was "nobler in the mind" to condone her immorality or to expose it and get her punished. If he complained and left it for the law to take its course, he knew, she would be condemned to death by stoning.[29]

Joseph thought of the pros and cons of annulling the engagement quietly, without giving any publicity.[30] But he knew, pregnancy could not be kept a secret for long and some day when the society comes to know of it she would not live to deliver the baby, for the Mosaic Law would come into play. He thought of telling the others of his dream in which the angel said that she was conceived of the Holy Ghost. If they believe it, the Mosaic Law about adultery would not be applicable because there was no sex involved and though pregnant, she continued to be a virgin. But would they believe it? Wouldn't they consider him a nincompoop? Despite his dream, he found it difficult to accept it and he was in a daze so to say, ever since he came to know that his fiancée was pregnant before the betrothal. Why did she keep him in the dark about her pregnancy until their betrothal? In short, he spent many sleepless nights, pondering this problem, distraught with suspicion that was gnawing his heart. Finally he thought, suspecting her was tantamount to disbelieving the angel of god who had assured him of her virginity and decided to marry her. And whoever refused to believe what the angel had told him in his dream, he would accuse them of suspecting the word of god.

There is no doubt that Mary's pregnancy was the result of illicit premarital sex and viewing from a materialist angle, an angel, which is a product of imagination, talking to Joseph in his dream is pure myth. Obviously, a person, who knew of Mary's condition and for whom Joseph had great respect, did play a part in influencing Joseph to come to such a decision. It could not have been a dream. It could only have been a man that spoke to him and persuaded him to condone Mary's misdemeanour. Considering the confused state of mind that Joseph was in at that time, whatever happened in those days was like a dream to him. Who was the person who spoke to Joseph on behalf of Mary? It could not be her parents because as stated earlier, nowhere in the Bible are her parents mentioned and presumably they were not alive then. It could not be anyone else but Mary's kinswoman Elisabeth or her husband Zacharias – both or one of them must have spoken to him. Evidently, it was with the intention of requesting them to plead with Joseph on her behalf that Mary had been to their house and stayed there for three months. She must have requested them with tears rolling down her cheeks, to go to Joseph and entreat him to be merciful.

In compliance with her request, most likely Zacharias had come and spoken to Joseph and the entire sequence of events seemed like a dream to Joseph. Being a priest, Zacharias must have said that the life now blossoming in her, even if it were the result of illicit sex, was as sacred as the Holy Ghost itself. If she were to be left to the mercy of the law-enforcing agency to be stoned to death, along with her the baby in her womb, an innocent life, would be nipped in the bud. And that sin, Zacharias must have said, would devolve upon Joseph. The only way to avoid it, Zacharias would have argued, was to excuse the trespass of this simple rustic girl, who was, obviously, seduced and deserted by some unscrupulous man. The advice of Zacharias, who belonged to one of the courses,[31] must have carried much weight with Joseph and had certainly influenced him. So Joseph, who was a simple man, magnanimous and kindhearted, felt pity for the girl and agreed to marry her. Hence, whoever was Jesus' father, he had to be a human being and Jesus certainly was the son of a man. We shall probe into this secret in detail in the next chapter, "The Son of Man."

Not satisfied with portraying Jesus as the son of the Holy Ghost, the author mythicises him further by weaving around his birth and life some more myths. Mary is said to have given birth to Jesus in the town of Bethlehem in Judaea during the reign of King Herod the Great. On his birth, suddenly there appeared a star in the sky, seeing which three wise men came from a distant place in the east to Jerusalem to worship the baby, king of the Jews.[32] When the king heard of the three men who had come to see the baby, he sent a courier to ask them to meet him and he inquired of them when the star was sighted. They told him that the star indicating Jesus' birth first appeared to them two years ago, on seeing which they had started on their journey and guided by that star, they had now reached Jerusalem. They did not know where the baby was and they expected the star to guide them. Herod graciously permitted them to go and see the baby and ordered that on their way back they should come to the palace and tell him where the baby was, ostensibly for him to go and make obeisance to the baby. But the wise men were shrewd enough to see through the king's game. So after paying homage to the baby, they returned home by a different route, and when Herod heard that the wise men had disobeyed him, he was livid with rage.

Needless to say, the story of the three wise men is nothing but fantasy meant to attribute divinity to Jesus. Bethlehem being a small town, it was possible that when Joseph and Mary arrived there the people had asked them who they were and to what family or clan they belonged. When Joseph told them of his parentage, the people would have known that he was of the House of David. So they traced the lineage of the baby to David and they would naturally have said that the baby was a descendant of David and the legitimate successor to his throne. They must have kept it a secret, for they knew the baby's life would be in danger if Herod came to know of it. However, the news of the birth of a baby who, one day would be the "King of the Jews" slowly spread and reached Herod through his spies. They told him that it was rumoured a baby of the lineage of David was born two years back but they did not know where the baby was. Perturbed by this news, Herod called a meeting of the priests and other leaders of the Chauvinists to find out if they knew the whereabouts of the child.[33] No one knew. They could only tell him of Micah's prophecy that the ruler of Israel would rise from the insignificant town of Bethlehem.[34]

He, therefore, ordered his soldiers to "slew all the children that were in Bethlehem and in all the adjoining districts, from two years old and under...."[35] The news spread like wildfire. Joseph and Mary too heard of the king's decision to kill all the babies below the age of two in Bethlehem and its outskirts. Immediately, they took baby Jesus and quietly left for Egypt,[36] a safe haven which they were sure was beyond the jurisdiction of Herod and his soldiers. They returned a few years later when they heard of the death of Herod. But on the way to Bethlehem, they came to know that the new king was Herod's son Archaelaus, and thinking that it would not be safe to go back to Judaea, they went to Galilee and settled in Nazareth, Joseph's hometown. Jesus was, therefore, associated with Nazareth and had been identified as the Nazarene. We meet Jesus next in the Temple in Jerusalem, as a small boy of twelve "sitting in the midst of the doctors, both hearing them and asking them questions,"[37] which, obviously, is an exaggeration intended to portray him as an extraordinary lad.

Coming back to the story of John the Baptist, he is now a grown-up man living in the wilderness of Judaea. Although the Bible portrays him as a religious man and a prophet, he was not leading the life of an ascetic, meditating and praying, in the desert of Judaea. Nonetheless, he was a man of the world and his mind and heart were with the Jewish freemen who once had an independent kingdom, which subsequently split and had now become a province of – or as it would be said today, was colonised by – the Roman imperialists, ruled by representatives loyal to the Emperor Tiberius Caesar (14 – 37 CE). Pontius Pilate was the procurator (26 – 36 CE) of Judaea and Herod the governor of Galilee at that time. John was carrying on a whispering campaign against the Roman imperialists and was clandestinely building up an anti-imperialist movement.

John was known as "the Baptist" because he was baptising all those who had come to listen to his sermons, by making them take a dip in the river Jordan and saying, "Repent, for the Kingdom of Heaven is at hand!"[38] The baptism that John the Baptist ceremonially performed was apparently a religious ritual by which the persons who got themselves baptised were considered to have expiated for and were absolved of their sins. But he did not explicitly state what sin they had committed for which they should repent; nor did he define the Kingdom of Heaven. The sin was ostensibly associating with the pagans; it was a sin for a Jew who was a monotheist to associate himself with the polytheistic and idolatrous pagans. In political terms, those who had been baptised were presumed to have taken a pledge to cut off their anti-national act of cooperating with the Roman imperialists and their representatives in Judaea. So collaborating with imperialists was what he implied by sin and the ritual of taking a dip in the river Jordan was the Baptist's method of enrolling new members in his movement that may be called the 'Baptismal Movement.' It symbolically cleanses the person baptised of the stigma of being a stooge of Roman imperialists.

He highlighted the religious aspect of the Movement because he knew the Hebrew mind well; he knew that the Jews in general were moved more easily by religion than by political ideology. In fact, religion had always played a major role in the social and political life of the Hebrews and had been a decisive factor in their history since the days of Moses, who adopted religio-purism as his ideology to unify the various Hebrew tribes. Religion, as we saw, permeated the Hebrew society from those days, through the periods of Joshua and the judges as well as the period of monarchy till the fall of the two Hebrew kingdoms. Again, religion was the force that spurred the Maccabee revolt and it may be recalled that Mattathias, after driving out Antiochus Epiphanes, destroyed their idol altars and massacred the idolaters, thus establishing a Hebrew theocratic monarchy as it were, under the Maccabee priest-kings. In order to distinguish the Jewish fraternity from the rest and to instil in the Jews a feeling of oneness, he ordered the Hebrews to circumcise the boys who had not been circumcised till then, without fail.[39] It may be recalled that Abraham wanted the monotheists to circumcise to ensure that they did not revert to polytheism and idolatry. Mattathias, however, considered circumcision as a sign of political and religious solidarity of the Hebrews in resisting the political domination and religious persecution by the Hellenistic Syrian kings.

The Baptist, thus, forged a novel and effective weapon, which is religion, to prepare the ground for an anti-imperialist mass movement. It may not be wrong to say that in the history of the world, this was the first time that religion, a potent emotive force, had been consciously used as a political weapon. John the Baptist seems to have astute political acumen. He knew the situation in Judaea then was not conducive to unleash an anti-imperialist mass movement or even to organise a mass-based anti-imperialist organisation. He knew it was impossible for the people of a comparatively tiny province like Judaea, to wage an armed struggle against the behemoth of the mighty Roman Empire. A rebellion against the powerful Roman Empire at this stage could only be a pipe dream, for it would be ruthlessly crushed by the powerful imperialist army and their Jewish cohorts.

The Baptist was, therefore, clandestinely organising the anti-imperialist forces behind the smokescreen of a religious reform movement so that the powers that be would not be able to accuse him of treason. This religious reform movement was aimed at isolating the powerful Chauvinists led by the clergy who swore by Yahweh but in practice were worshippers of Mammon. The dichotomy in the Judaean society of those times was wide and unbridgeable. On one side, there were the Chauvinists comprising mostly the affluent Pharisees[40] and Sadducees.[41] The natural leadership of these Chauvinists who claimed to be religio-purists was the clergy, which of course thrived on the munificence of these rich Chauvinists and was corrupt. And the Chauvinists, taking advantage of the clergy's dependence on them, made use of the synagogue not for worship but for marketing their wares and for pawn-broking and other financial dealings like moneylending. On the other side, there was a restive, resurgent section of the lower middle class and the poor wage labourers; and at the bottom there were the slaves, the bugbear of the affluent slave owners. This oppressed section of the people threatened to explode into revolt at any time.

All these potential rebels had to be held down, and for this the Chauvinists needed the help of the rulers, the Romans as well as Herod[42] who represented the Roman imperialists in Judaea. The security of the Chauvinists and their properties lay in the hands of the armed forces of Herod. Both these, the monotheistic Chauvinists and the clergy, ironically, thrived under the protective umbrella of the Roman pagans and so they stood solidly behind the Roman imperialists. The Chauvinists, therefore, had a vested interest in collaborating with Herod. In the final analysis, therefore, the rich Pharisees, Sadducees and the Hebrew priesthood that constituted the Chauvinists, had been collaborating with Roman imperialism, which in turn relied on the support of the Chauvinists to keep their hold on Judaea.

The problem that John the Baptist faced was this: a large section of the religious-minded oppressed people, the lower middle class and the unskilled manual workers, as well as those patriotic freemen that had no vested interests, were carried away by the apparent religio-purism of the Chauvinists led by the corrupt clergy. Under the circumstances, the immediate task of an anti-imperialist organisation like the one that the Baptist had been building up was to isolate the pro-imperialist forces from the misguided section of the people, the lower middle class and the unskilled workers. The Baptist, therefore, thought that it was imperative to expose the hypocrisy of the Chauvinists and discredit them and so he openly chastised the rabbis and the Chauvinists. He refused to baptise the Chauvinists – the Pharisees and the Sadducees – calling them a brood of vipers and telling them that they would not be able to escape the consequences of their actions. In other words, he was wary of enrolling them as members of the Baptismal Movement and told them that they would not escape the wrath of the people. They should not think that they would be excused if they claimed to be followers of Abraham.[43] This was a warning to them.

Such attacks, he reckoned, would expose their hypocrisy and diminish their influence that would weaken their hold on the lower middle class and that would help shrink the support base of the imperialist power in Judaea. Once that was achieved, this movement would call upon the people to rise in revolt against the imperialists and declare an independent Kingdom of the Jews. The ultimate objective of the Baptismal Movement was, thus, restoration of the erstwhile independent kingdom of the Jews! So the Kingdom of Heaven that he spoke of was the independent kingdom of the Jews. The people generally imagined 'heaven' as a place where peace and prosperity prevailed in perpetuity and where one would be in a state of eternal bliss. That was how the Baptist visualised the kingdom of the Jews that would come into being, once the people of Judaea freed themselves from the Roman domination. The people knew that the heaven of the Jews was not that of the pagans and so the Kingdom of Heaven that John the Baptist had been speaking of could not be the kingdom of the Pagans; it had to be the kingdom of the Jews.

He was aware that the rulers had seen through his game and he was a suspect in the eyes of the authorities. His life was in peril and so he mostly confined himself to the wilderness. Occasionally, however, undaunted by threats to his life, he went to Jerusalem and all around the country on both sides of the River Jordan. Wherever he went, the people came from far and near and crowded around him to listen to him. He spoke to them of the basic principles of the Baptismal Movement, telling them enigmatically about the Kingdom of Heaven, which the people vaguely understood as the Kingdom of the Jews. He exhorted the people to turn away from their sins, which implied that they got rid of the "sinners," the Roman imperialists. By the time the authorities came to know about his presence in a city, he would withdraw into the wilderness. He never went into a synagogue and preached, for he feared that if he went into a synagogue, it would be easy for the long arm of the law to reach him. This threat of persecution considerably enhanced his popularity among the people and he succeeded in creating an impression that an ascetic like him, being a monotheist, was being unjustly persecuted by the representatives of a country of pagans, thus earning him the sympathy and support of all classes of the Jews, except the Pharisees and the Sadducees.

Never in public did he utter a word that could be construed as political. The rulers, therefore, could not arrest him or prevent him from 'preaching' because they found nothing treasonable in his speeches that were manifestly religious. Had he carried out open political propaganda, it would not have had so much impact on the common man and the rulers could have charged him with treason and executed him. Besides, he hid behind the façade of his priestly background and his feigned asceticism did help draw people towards him in large numbers eager to be baptised and to join his reform movement. It was precisely this, his reformist ideas that angered the Chauvinists and particularly the priestly class, for they realised that the movement was aimed at undermining their reputation and respectability and making them a target of ridicule.

So the priests and the Levites went from Jerusalem to ask him if he was the Messiah. He said to them, he was not that prophet whom they believed "...God will raise up for you a Prophet from your midst...."[44] His candour disarmed them, yet the Levites questioned his right to baptise and asked him, "Why do you baptise then, if you be not that Christ, nor Elias, nor that prophet?"[45] He replied there was one among the Jews whom they did not know yet; he was the Christ.[46] He indicated that his successor would "baptise with fire,"[47] which is a metaphorical way of saying his successor would organise a violent revolution, but those who questioned him did not understand the real import of what he said.

John belonged to a priestly family, but Jesus, being of the lineage of David, had royal blood in him. He was the legitimate king of the Jews, for the Jewish freemen considered Jesus the direct descendent of David the Conqueror, whose rule was still cherished by them as the golden era in the history of the Jews. Presumably, John the Baptist thought of cashing in on the Jewish pride in their ethnicity, by making Jesus the leader of his movement. He had the right to the throne of "the kingdom of the Jews," if the imperial power were to be overthrown, and an independent Jewish monarchy established. Joseph had two other sons whom he begot in his first wife and they were older than Jesus, but why they were not thought of as having a right to the throne is incomprehensible.

At last he came. There stood before John the Baptist, a young man of about thirty years of age waiting to be baptised! This was the person that John had in mind when he said that a more virile and indomitable person would come to lead the movement. This was Jesus – the man whom John waited for, to lead the movement.[48] Being of royal blood, the Baptist thought Jesus was the right person to lead an anti-imperialist movement. The last time we saw this young man who had just been baptised was eighteen years ago as a boy of twelve sitting in the Temple. The Gospels are silent about the intervening period in his life. There are various theories about his whereabouts during this period, but they are all in the realm of conjecture.

Wherever he had been all these years, he was presumably watching the situation in the country and was being influenced by the Baptist's propaganda. He saw more and more people going to Jordan to be baptised by John and heard them pay glowing tributes to the Baptist. Presumably, John the Baptist had been in touch with him secretly and pressuring him to take the reins of the movement. This is plausible, for the Baptist had been repeatedly saying with confidence that there was someone else who would take over the leadership of the movement from him. Anyway, finally, Jesus took the plunge, figuratively and literally, for he got himself baptised by taking a dip in the river Jordan and formally joined the movement.[49] The Baptist too was happy because he knew that Jesus' leadership would give the movement a momentum because he was sure, if Jesus took over the leadership, the Jews would rally behind Jesus *en masse.*

So it happened. John was right, for it did help swell the ranks of the movement in a short period. Jews from all walks of life, high and low, rich and poor, came forward in large numbers to get baptised by Jesus and to listen to his speeches, keeping the ruling class guessing and on tenterhooks. Jesus was also baptising from the other side of Jordan while John the Baptist continued to baptise as before. This upsurge of enthusiasm was unprecedented and some of John's disciples "...came to John, and said to him, Rabbi, he who was with you beyond the Jordan, whom you have baptised, behold, the same man is baptising, and all men come to him."[50] The news gladdened John and he said, "You yourselves had heard what I said, I am not the Christ, but that I have been sent before him."[51] And he continued, "...this, my joy therefore is fulfilled."[52] John was delighted that what he foresaw was happening and now the movement that he started was growing stronger and stronger and, he hoped, would soon muster enough strength to achieve its objective. The Romans would be thrown out and his dream of re-establishing the kingdom of the Jews would become a reality.

But his joy was short-lived, for he was arrested and thrown into jail. We understand from the Gospels that John was imprisoned and subsequently beheaded by King Herod. It is said his body was taken by his followers and buried, but the Bible does not mention where he was buried and archaeologists have not so far succeeded in discovering the burial site. His incarceration and execution, according to the Gospels, was due purely to personal reasons. He is said to have told King Herod to his face that the king's marriage with Herodias, the former wife of his stepbrother and his own niece, was illegal.[53] This affront infuriated the king and more so Herodias. So the king, pressured by his wife, put him in prison but stopped short of killing him because the king was aware of his popularity and the hold he had on the people. He, therefore, feared that his execution would cause an upheaval of unforeseen dimensions. However, the Baptist is not known to have met Herod face to face to have reproached the king for his marriage with Herodias. The fictitious story of him reproving Herod to his face was only meant to portray him as a brave leader, although he stayed in the wilderness and seldom came into cities or preached at synagogues as Jesus did.

But the queen bided her time and the opportunity arose when her daughter who was also the king's grandniece, Salome, was asked to dance at the king's birthday party. Pleased with the dance, the king "promised with an oath to give her whatsoever she would ask."[54] As instructed by her mother, whom she consulted, she asked for the Baptist's head on a charger. The king was in a fix. He was, as pointed out above, wary of killing John because he knew that John had a large following and he feared that if John was beheaded it might spark a mass uprising. But he had no choice, for the promise was given under oath that the guests who had gathered there had heard. He could not but comply with the request lest he tarnished his image as a man who kept his word. So on the orders of the king, the Baptist was beheaded in prison and his head was brought on a large plate and given to Salome, who took it to her mother. On hearing of the news of the

Baptist's execution his disciples came for his body and they buried him. Needless to say, as the story of John the Baptist accusing king Herod of incest being a fictitious one, this episode, which is so to say a sequel to that also cannot be anything but fictitious.

Josephus Flavius, however, looks at the execution of John differently. According to him, John was a good man who preached moral rectitude. Inspired by his words people from all over went to listen to his homilies and the spell that John cast over the people frightened Herod. He suspected that John with his immense influence could one day decide to call upon the people, who seemed to follow him blindly, to revolt. That would be calamitous. In order to preclude such an eventuality he decided to liquidate John slyly. So he got John arrested and imprisoned him at the castle of Macherus and later executed him.[55]

Hence the real reason for the arrest was obviously his rising mass appeal, which frightened Herod because he thought that, if no action was taken then, it might encourage the Baptist to incite the people to rebel against the Emperor. That would make his position shaky. On one side he would have to face the rebellion and on the other, he would have to answer to the Emperor at whose pleasure he occupied the throne, for not having taken pre-emptive action and prevented the rebellion. Yet, after putting him behind bars, Herod waited for a few days or perhaps months to see if the people would revolt in protest and ordered his execution only when he found that John's arrest had not caused any violent reaction. Not surprisingly, the uprising that Herod feared would follow John's execution did not happen; there was not even a ripple among his supporters, the reason for which could be John's emphasis on religion rather than on the political objective of the movement. Although the ultimate objective of the movement was the overthrow of Roman imperialism, he emphasised the corruption among the rabbis and reform of the religious establishment, with the result his followers had not had the opportunity to imbibe the anti-imperialist spirit of the movement.

No incontrovertible archaeological evidence has been so far found to confirm John's historicity. Yet it cannot be denied that John the Baptist was a historical personality, which the testimony of Josephus, a historian who flourished in the first century CE (*circa* 37 to 100

CE), proves. Apart from this, an incident related to baby John is described in the Infancy Gospel of James. It states that when Elizabeth heard that all children who were two years old or younger were being killed at the orders of Herod she took John and went into hiding in the nearby hills. Herod seems to have known that baby John could not be found and he ordered his soldiers to search for the lad. Why he was looking for John and not Jesus whom the three wise men had come to pay respects to, is inexplicable. Maybe, he suspected that this was the child whom they had come to see. Anyway, when the soldiers reported that they failed to find the boy, he sent them to the temple to ask Zachariah where he had hidden his son. Zachariah naturally feigned ignorance, saying "I am here as a servant of God and am serving the temple. How should I know where my son is?"[56] Herod was furious. He again sent his soldiers warning him that he would have to pay with his blood if he did not tell where the child was hidden. And when the soldiers came and questioned him, he said, "I am a witness of God. Have my blood."[57] The next day at daybreak, Zachariah was found murdered.[58]

The Infancy Gospel of James, of course, is certainly more reliable than the synoptic Gospels. Even if we ignore all that, the legacy that John had left behind along with Jesus cannot be over emphasised. His life was so intertwined with that of Jesus that it is an important factor that cannot be overlooked in deciding the Baptist's historicity. We shall certainly give him the benefit of the doubt and would not simply dump him into the realm of mythology.

Be that as it may, the immediate task before Jesus who had been planning an armed insurrection was to create awareness among the people. John the Baptist had always been emphasising the religious aspect by baptising his followers and projecting the Baptismal Movement as purely a religious reform movement and he deliberately soft-pedalled the political objective. On the other hand, Jesus, as expected, practically tore off the religious mask and made it clear that the movement was as much political as it was religious; rather, more political than religious. Therefore, being a good organiser, soon after his baptism Jesus set himself to the task of reorienting the movement. In order to rid itself of its religious slant, Jesus did not stress the baptismal aspect and he did not want to be known as baptist. As he was known to have hailed from Nazareth, he came to be called Nazarene[59] and the followers of Jesus were called Nazarenes.[60] Jesus himself wanted him to be called so. It was a very clever ploy that Jesus adopted to hoodwink the government, for the Chauvinists and the ruling class understood the term as "those hailing from Nazareth" while Jesus and his Apostles meant it differently.

The word Nazarene is also spelt Nazoraean and has a different connotation. *Nazoraean* does not denote "one hailing from Nazareth," nor is it a term derived from the word "Nazarite" or "Nazirite,"[61] which John the Baptist was. *Not rim* is a Hebrew word, the root of which is *Natzar*, meaning "to keep safe," and so *Not rim* or Nazoraeans in English "would mean 'keepers' of secrets' or of some special rules or usages,"[62] which in this context connote the Mosaic Law. It is, therefore, apposite to call them Nazoraeans because it was *apparently* a "religious sect" that rigidly adhered to the Mosaic Code of Law and could also be interpreted as an organisation with a secret mission. Hence, it threw a challenge to the Jewish clergy and the Chauvinists, since it portrayed Jesus and his followers as strict followers of the Mosaic Code. But to the Nazoraeans it denoted that being members of a secret organisation, the ideals and aims of the movement had to be kept strictly confidential. Naturally, therefore, the Baptismal Movement, the leadership of which Jesus took over from John the Baptist, may now be called the Nazoraean (covert) Movement. We call it so because it had become an organisation with a secret political agenda and not because it was led by Jesus of Nazareth as the freemen of Judaea and the ruling class were made to believe.

In the case of this organisation, the meaning "keepers of secret" or an organisation with a secret mission is relevant because they did not openly proclaim the real objective of their organisation, which is the overthrow of the Roman rule. It was kept a secret from the government and its supporters. And it cannot, by any stretch of imagination, mean the "true adherents of the Mosaic tenets." The ethic unveiled by Jesus, the Nazoraean, was in many ways different from, rather diametrically opposite of, the Judaistic code of ethics without, however, openly repudiating it as we saw in Chapter 1, "The Book of Books." Jesus, in his maiden speech to the people, proclaimed, "Think not that I have come to destroy the law, or the prophets: I have come not to destroy but to fulfil."[63] As the founder-leader of the Nazoraean Movement, without directly rejecting the tenets or the patriarchs and prophets of the parent religion, he accepted them and ingeniously syncretised those tenets with his own and cleverly related those patriarchs and prophets to himself. In his first speech to the "great multitudes of people" itself, he tactfully made it clear to his followers that he did not accept the principles of John the Baptist, let alone Moses.

This exercise of juxtaposition of the Mosaic tenets with his new principles was tantamount to cutting off the connection with the Baptismal Movement and opening a new chapter in the long story of Jewish resistance. Why, then, did he preface it with the declaration that he had "not come to destroy but to fulfil the Mosaic Law"? It was nothing more than a diplomatic statement. He did not want to antagonise the large majority or perhaps the entire population of the Jews who still regarded the Mosaic Law as given by their god, Yahweh, and hence unalterable. This statement helped throw dust in their eyes. After deluding his audience thus, he proceeded with the task of rejecting the Mosaic laws one by one and replacing each of them with his own principles, which contradicted those of Moses. This was made necessary by the changed historical conditions, for what was suited to the barbaric tribes of Moses was not in keeping with the ethos of a civilised people of the period of Jesus. In short, by subtly contradicting the Mosaic laws, he cleverly demolished the ethical foundation of the moribund barbaric society of the Mosaic period and very effectively replaced it by his own principles that were compatible with a civilised society.

Be that as it may, the Baptismal Movement used religion as the principal and the only political weapon, but to the Nazoraean Movement religion was a thin veil to cover its political face. After weaving the religious veil of the Nazoraean Movement, he turned his attention to build up the infrastructure, which was the organisation. The Baptismal Movement had been a loose-knit conglomeration of individuals around the personality of John the Baptist, whose was the lone voice that carried the message of the movement. The first thing Jesus did was to select twelve men to carry on the propaganda, which the Baptist was doing all by himself. They were expected to propagate the ideology of the movement among the masses and urge them to agitate against the hegemony of imperial Rome. Jesus wanted them to be known as the apostles because he wanted his propaganda machinery to be given a religious mask to avoid raising the suspicion of the rulers. We may, therefore, call it the Apostolic Committee, which was expected to lead the armed insurrection when Jesus gave the call.

The word *apostle* means "messenger" or "one sent forth." They were the ones specially selected and sent with certain powers as the accredited representatives of the sender. In a politically relevant secular term, they may be defined as the 'official propagandists' of the Nazoraean Movement. As Jesus would have the Herodians and the Chauvinists like the Pharisees and Saddeucees believe, they were the messengers of the "good news" that the Kingdom of Heaven would be attained during their lifetime. But as leader of the Nazoraean Movement, Jesus wanted them to be the propagandists who would go around unobtrusively instilling in the minds of the people the idea of overthrowing, by force if necessary, the Roman imperialism and reestablishing the Kingdom of the Jews – code-named "Kingdom of Heaven" – during their lifetime.

All these men who would be the consultants and propagandists were picked from among the lower strata of society, the working class and lower middle class, and so were the early followers. The wealthy Chauvinists, therefore, derisively called the followers of Jesus "Ebionites," a term derived from the Hebrew word *Evionim*, meaning "poor ones."[64] They were, Simon, whom Jesus surnamed, Peter, meaning "rock"[65] and his brother Andrew; James and his brother, John, the sons of Zebedee, both of whom Jesus surnamed Boanerges,[66] that is the "sons of thunder"; Philip; and Bartholomew. The other six were Thomas, identified as "Doubting Thomas";[67] Matthew, the publican;[68] James, the son of Alphaeus; Lebbaeus whose surname was Thaddaeus; Simon, the Canaanite, who was a member of the Zealot, a subversive political party advocating violent overthrow of the Roman government; and Judas Iscariot, who was also a Zealot.[69] Of these, all were Galileans except Judas, who was *Ish Kerioth* that is Hebrew for "a man of Kerioth," which was in the south of Judah.[70] Interestingly, Asimov points out, that lately, a new interpretation has been made to the word 'Iscariot.' According to these interpreters, the scribe inadvertently transposed the first two letters. His surname should have been 'Sicariot,' which would make him too a Galilean. And Sicariot could be a member of the party of *Sicarii*, a word derived from a Greek word that referred to men carrying little knives, *sicae*, under their robes and meaning 'assassins.'[71] In selecting them, Jesus also ensured that all the twelve tribes of Israel were represented and in fact, that was why the number of apostles was twelve, one from each of the tribes. And he, being the Son of God, regarded himself as the representative of the Levites, the tribe of the Hebrew priests. This was a clever move that would help get the support of all the twelve Jewish tribes as well as the Levites.

The choice of these twelve apostles showed Jesus' perspicacity. Simon, he thought, would make a strong leader who would stand like a rock against the onslaught of the enemy. So he nicknamed him Peter, saying, "You are Simon, the son of Jona; you shall be called *Cephas...*,"[72] an Aramaic word, which was translated into Greek as *Petros*, both meaning "rock." The brothers James and John were powerful mass orators who spoke in voices as loud as the sound of a thunderbolt and could electrify and sway the masses; they would, thus, make good propagandists. Matthew being a publican was the lowest category of those engaged in the collection of revenue. The publican was usually a muscleman who if necessary, would be able to tussle singlehandedly with and collect tax from habitual tax evaders. They knew no fear and Jesus wanted brave men like that to lead the violent insurrection that he was planning. Jesus must have taken Simon and Judas into the inner circle knowing their antecedents. Having imbibed the ideology of an organisation that stood for violent overthrow of the Roman imperialists and experienced in leading armed uprisings, both Simon the Canaanite and Judas would be good leaders when he gave the call to rise in revolt.

Although both were *prima facie* religio-political movements, the emphasis of the Nazoraean Movement was fundamentally different from those of the Baptismal Movement. In the first meeting of the Apostolic Committee, which met *in camera*, he gave a long talk in which he laid bare the ideology of the movement. Jesus said to his Apostles that they should not have the illusion that he had come to bring peace in Judaea; he did not come to bring peace but had come to fight with a sword. "Think not that I am come to peace on earth; I came not to send peace, but a sword."[73] In other words, he had not come to compromise with the Romans and to live peacefully as their meek subjects but to lead an armed insurrection against the imperial power of Rome. His statement also indicated that he had not assumed the leadership of the anti-Roman movement to continue the non-violent struggle using religion as weapon as John the Baptist advocated; he wanted the members of the Nazoraean Movement to take up arms and fight for the liberation of Judaea. However, he did not totally reject the role of religion in this struggle for freedom; he intended to use that also.

He, thus, deviated from the Baptismal Movement without completely disclaiming the legacy of John the Baptist, for if he did that, he feared, several members might drop out of the movement. He joined the Baptismal Movement and took over the entire organisation, only to radicalise and convert it into a militant organisation. So he would use sword as his weapon and religion as a camouflage only. The Baptismal Movement, no doubt, did the spadework by conscientising the masses. No doubt, Jesus held the Baptist in great esteem and he showered praises on the Baptist, saying "Truly, I say to you, Among those that are born of women there has not risen one greater than John the Baptist..."[74] But he did not believe that John's method would have helped in liberating the Judaeans from the imperialist yoke. He clarified it further by saying that since the Romans conquered Judaea, the country had been witness to violence. Apart from members of the movement, many innocent people too must have been tortured and put to death on suspicion as imperialist powers invariably do, and the people of Judaea had been subjected to such violence for a long time. This revealed the path that Jesus intended to take. The kingdom of Judaea that had been suffering violence since the time of John the Baptist (not that it was all a bed of roses earlier) would be taken by force through a violent struggle.[75] That was exactly what John the Baptist meant when he said that the one who would come after him would baptise with fire. Jesus thus conceded that his principle of non-resistance to evil and showing the left cheek when someone slaps on the right did not apply in dealing with an imperialist power.

Moreover, he said, it was possible that in this struggle against Roman domination, families might be split. Whoever thought that his family was greater than or more important than the movement and the freedom of the country and whoever did not follow him unquestioningly, even at the risk of being disowned by his father, had no place in the movement.[76] In short, he demanded that the Nazoraeans dedicate themselves to the movement and sacrifice everything that they so far held near and dear. He added, whoever is reluctant to take the cross does not deserve to be a member of his movement – "And he that taketh not the cross, and followeth after me, is not worthy of me."[77] The cross, in those times, was used to put to death by crucifying those who had been sentenced to capital punishment for any crimes committed by them. Jesus here used it as a symbol of death. He, therefore, wanted his followers to be ready to die for the cause for which the movement stood. Besides, he said, he would regard those who were not part of the movement as collaborators of the imperialists and enemies of Judaea.[78] In his scheme of things, there was no room for neutrals. He would not tolerate dissidence and he told his Apostles to bring before him and kill whoever did not accept him as king of the Jews.[79] And he warned them against being tempted by "the leaven of the Pharisees" and the Herodians.[80] Jesus used the word "leaven" metaphorically to mean "bribe." He told them that the rich Pharisees and the governmental authorities would try to bribe them to wean them away from the movement and added, ideology is more important than wealth or power.[81]

However, Jesus knew that these twelve men would not be able to go around the vast country to propagate his ideals and so he selected seventy more propagandists.[82] Again Jesus recruited fifty more and finally there were all together a hundred and twenty[83] propagandists. The Bible does not refer to these one hundred and twenty men as apostles. They were committed members of the movement and judging by the duties given to them, they may be regarded as members of a committee constituted for the purpose of propagating the ideals and objectives of the Nazoraean Movement. They were not expected to lead the struggle. Jesus sent them in pairs to all the towns and villages that he planned to visit and to spread the message that the Kingdom of Heaven was at hand. He told them how they should conduct themselves when they went on tour around the land and repeated what he told the members of the Apostolic Committee and said: "I send you forth as lambs among wolves." Jesus expected that the Chauvinists could be hostile and would possibly even physically attack them – why, they might even kill them. But, he said, they would not be able to kill the ideology of the movement. He specially advised them to be humble and tolerant whatever might be the provocation. He gave them detailed instructions as to what they should wear, where they should board, how they should deport themselves, what they should do if they were to be persecuted in a town and so on. He said that whatever he told them "in the dark" or secretly, they should speak out openly to the people at large.[84]

It was at that time that John was executed. When the news of John's arrest and imprisonment was conveyed to Jesus, fearing that he too would be arrested he went and hid in a deserted place.[85] But the news of his being there spread like wildfire and there was an incessant stream of men, women and children to his hideout. So, feeling insecure there, he went by boat to Tyre and Sidon[86] but when the local people recognised him and began to go to him in large numbers, Jesus left the place and sailed to Galilee and going up a mountain, hid there along with his Apostles.[87] The people, somehow, came to know of his presence there and the multitude flowed out of the surrounding areas to his hiding place. So he moved from there, again by boat, to the region of Magdala,[88] where too the people crowded around him. Not feeling secure there, he proceeded to the region of Judaea beyond the river Jordan.[89] In all these places he spoke to the masses. He noticed that in all these places, there were the Pharisees and Sadducees among the multitude that went to listen to him. He suspected they were spies who had been asked to shadow him and that any day he would be arrested. Finally, he went to Capernaum, where he felt he was secure, for he had many followers there.[90]

This made him think of the future of his movement in case he was killed. He knew that he was the next target of the Chauvinists and the Herodians, for he was aware of their hostility towards him. They were waiting for an opportunity to arrest him and put him to death. He did not want the movement to suffer if he were to be killed before the Roman imperialists had been thrown out. No doubt, he had groomed twelve Apostles as leaders and he expected them to carry forward the torch of freedom that he had lit.

Like John the Baptist, Jesus too neither did nor even said anything publicly to give the impression that he was having any political objectives. Had he said so openly, the authorities would have crushed the movement. Yet it was an open secret because the Apostles and the propagandists had been secretly campaigning and telling the masses Jesus' intention of establishing the kingdom of the Jews. The Chauvinists in general and the priests in particular were virulently hostile to Jesus and his ostensible religious movement. They considered his teachings blasphemous and irreligious because he did not stop his Apostles who were hungry, plucking heads of grain to eat, and he himself tended the sick on the Sabbath, both of which contravened the Mosaic Laws. When the Pharisees questioned him about the propriety of working on the Sabbath day, he argued justifying what they did. So the Chauvinists were conspiring to get his movement suppressed and get him executed, taking advantage of the antipathy of the Romans towards it. The Herodians, however, viewed the movement more as a political movement directed against the Roman rule and they too were waiting for an opportunity to arrest him. Most probably, they would have got scent of its secret political agenda through their spies.

But as stated above, Jesus, like John the Baptist, had always been judicious in his utterances and never said a word that could be construed treasonable. He always targeted the priesthood and said his objective was to establish the *Kingdom of Heaven.*[91] Neither of them had ever explicitly stated what exactly they meant by "the Kingdom of Heaven." Nonetheless, occasionally, in the midst of his preachings, Jesus slyly brought home to those who listened to him that he would liberate them from oppression. For instance, on the Sabbath day, when he preached in the synagogue in Nazareth, he said, "He has anointed Me to preach the Gospel to the poor; He has sent me to heal the broken hearted, to proclaim liberty to the captives and ... to set at liberty those who are oppressed."[92] So the masses understood that the *Kingdom of Heaven* was the code name for the *Kingdom of the Jews.* Many of those who had joined the Baptismal Movement thought that it was a reformist movement and hoped that it would free them from the tyranny of the affluent Chauvinists. They were not aware of its political agenda.

However, thanks to the covert campaigns carried out by Jesus and his propagandists, they now knew that it meant the kingdom of the Jews as is evident from the mythical story of Jesus appearing before the Apostles after his crucifixion and resurrection. The question that the Apostles are said to have asked the apparition of Jesus makes it clear that the people were aware that the movement was aimed at overthrowing the imperial Roman power and establishing an independent kingdom of the Jews. In that myth we hear the Apostles inquiring of the apparition: "Lord, will you at this time (that is, during Jesus' Second Advent) restore again the kingdom of Israel?"[93] The word "Israel" in this context denotes the twelve tribes of the Hebrews, now called the Jews, and so "the kingdom of Israel" denotes "the kingdom of the Jews." For a long time, the imperialists and their Judaean collaborators did not have a clear idea of what exactly Jesus meant by saying "Kingdom of Heaven."

In course of time, however, all those, including the Pharisees and the Herodians, who heard Jesus speak, had a faint idea of what exactly he meant by the kingdom of Heaven. And Herod had been getting intelligence from his spies too. But no one had any concrete proof and so Herod, who wanted to be identified with the Yahwist, could not ban the movement, which was apparently a religious movement, or take any action against Jesus, whom the common people called rabbi. However, since the execution of the Baptist, Jesus was being kept under surveillance by the king's men and was the target of the Chauvinists. Jesus was aware of it and that was why he went on moving from place to place, which incidentally helped widen the mass base of the movement. They joined hands in their conspiracy to do away with Jesus and had been trying to find an excuse. As Jesus' popularity among the freemen had been soaring and the multitudes that crowded around him had been getting increasingly restive, the Herodians and the Chauvinists became more and more jittery.

Jesus, no doubt, was conscious of the risk involved in carrying out a campaign against corruption among the clergy, yet he did not mince words. He also condemned not only the Pharisees but the scribes as well, accusing them of hypocrisy, and told the masses not to follow their example, for they did not practice what they preached. Nor did he spare Herod, the governor, himself. Narrating the abominable behaviour of the Pharisees he said that they loved to wear expensive clothes like those worn by the rich and strut about in the market when they wanted everyone to bow to them; they occupied the best seats in the synagogue and high tables at banquets. Worst of all, they cheated the widows and appropriated their houses while pretending to be pious by reciting long prayers in public. So, warned Jesus, they would not be able to "escape the damnation of hell."[94]

He chastised the Pharisees and Herod, calling the Pharisees hypocrites, and when some Pharisees told him to go out of Jerusalem, for Herod would kill him, he defied Herod. He said he would be there the next three days and so "go tell that fox, Behold, I cast out demons...today and tomorrow, and the third day I shall be perfected."[95] Once when the Chauvinists and the scribes asked Jesus why his Apostles were breaking Mosaic tradition Jesus retorted, reminding them of prophet Isaiah's remarks about their insincerity. Jesus said those who pay lip service to religion by following tradition, neglect the essence of it.[96] He said that they stick to insignificant details while they violate the fundamentals of the Mosaic Code. For example, contrary to the Mosaic Law that anyone who spoke against his parents must die, he said the Pharisees always tended to condone any person who did not help his parents, if he had given to the temple what he should have given to his parents. The Pharisees were trying to accuse Jesus of breaking the Jewish tradition but his response silenced them.

Unlike the Baptist who talked to the people mostly in the wilderness and never in the synagogues, Jesus spoke to the people in towns and villages and he even went into the synagogues and rebuked the priesthood. There, in the synagogue, he often had wordy duels with the rabbis and the religio-purist freemen. As a result, he succeeded in getting the support of the masses for his organisation, which was the vanguard of the anti-Chauvinist and anti-imperialist movement. And wherever he went, the multitudes followed him. Although many a time, as pointed out already, he contradicted Moses he always claimed that he was only "fulfilling" Moses' teachings, as a result of which the clergy or the religio-purists could not accuse him of blasphemy also. Several times the Chauvinists, especially the Pharisees and the

Sadducees, had come to qui Jesus to find an excuse to arrest him, but they never succeeded. He always outwitted them.

Jesus always empathised with the poor, the downtrodden and the marginalised. One day he was in Judaea on the other side of the Jordan and was successfully fielding tricky questions from the Pharisees, when a wealthy young man approached him and asked him what he should do to attain eternal life. He said he had been following the commandments since his youth. In that case, Jesus told him to sell all his possessions and distribute the proceeds among the poor. The young man, however, was reluctant to follow the advice, for he did not wish to give away his possessions. So he went away sulking, when Jesus looked around and said that such people had no place in the Kingdom of Heaven. "It is easier," he added, "for a camel to go through the eye of a needle, than for a rich man to enter into the Kingdom of God!"[97] Jesus then praised the Apostles for the sacrifice they had made by renouncing their home and family and other possessions to fight for the Kingdom of Heaven and exhorted them to be prepared for the supreme sacrifice. He warned them of the possibility of being killed or executed, if they were to be caught, during the armed rebellion which he was planning. However, he said, if they died fighting for the freedom of the country they would be immortalised; in other words, being martyrs they would be remembered for ever by the people.[98]

Jesus now decided to throw down the gauntlet. He started his journey to Jerusalem when he called aside the Apostolic Committee members and told them that the enemies were waiting to capture him on reaching the city.[99] There was a possibility of his being arrested, tortured and executed for treason. It can happen to anyone charged with treason and so it was a warning to the Apostles, for he wanted them to be prepared for the worst in case they were to be caught. But in order to keep up their morale, he told them not to be disheartened, for even if he were to be killed he would rise again the third day to lead them to victory. Although the Apostles did not understand how that was possible,[100] they did not question him, for they thought that being the Christ and the Son of God, such a possibility could not be ruled out. Neither Jesus himself nor anyone else had recorded what Jesus said or did during his lifetime. That he said he would rise on the third day if he were killed could only be a product of editorial imagination in keeping with their portrayal of Jesus as 'son of god.' If, however, he had said so, it could only be to ensure that the Apostles did not lose hope and gave up the struggle if he was arrested and executed. He wanted them to carry on the fight. And they moved on accompanied by the multitude. When he reached the Mount of Olives, he felt too tired to climb the hill and so he sent two of the Apostles to get a foal of a donkey, a colt, from one of the nearby villages and he mounted the colt.

Immediately he dispatched two of his men in advance to Jerusalem to announce that their king was coming to them.[101] Before he began to climb, he said to his Apostles to bring before him and kill anyone who objected to his reigning over them, for they were his enemies.[102] Incidentally, it may not be wrong to say, Jesus was acting as a despotic monarch as all kings were at that time. Jesus proclaimed himself the king and wanted the people of Jerusalem to know that their king was coming to Jerusalem. By that time the multitude accompanying him had grown into a vast ocean of humanity. When he drew near the descent of the Mount of Olives, the people shouted: "Blessed be the king who comes in the name of the Lord: peace in heaven and glory in the highest."[103] The people rejoiced greatly; they were excited and cried out in exultation that at last god had given them a king.

There were also the Pharisees who owed allegiance to Herod and the Roman Emperor in the crowd and they did not want to be seen as supporters of Jesus. So they objected to the slogan and asked Jesus to tell the people to stop shouting treasonable slogans. But Jesus refused. He said that if they did not shout, the stones lying there would.[104] In other words, the people of the erstwhile Hebrew kingdom wanted him as their king and he had accepted it. By saying that "the stones would immediately cry out," he meant that all people of Judaea wanted him to be the king. As he entered Jerusalem, the people who saw him passing poured out on to the streets and followed him, raising the slogan, "Hosannah; Blessed be the kingdom of our father David, that comes in the name of the Lord...."[105] The people had begun to talk boldly and unequivocally about the establishment of the kingdom of David, which was the kingdom of the Jews, and it naturally frightened the Chauvinists and the Herodians.

As Jesus saw the multitude gathered around him he began to speak to them, when the Sadducees who did not accept certain doctrines of Jesus asked him some questions. He answered all their questions without giving them a chance to accuse him of treason; when one of the scribes standing nearby and listening to the discussion came forward and asked Jesus a question on the commandments he answered without giving him a chance to accuse him of sacrilege. The scribes were bookkeepers who, in Jesus' time, had become teachers of religion and had attained great influence and power as a class. Hearing Jesus answer their questions discreetly, the people who had gathered there applauded him. But at every opportunity that he got, he ruthlessly exposed the corruption of the clergy and vehemently and openly criticised them, thus boldly vocalising what the people in general hesitated to talk about, fearing the wrath of the clergy.

When Jesus entered the temple, what he saw made him wild with anger. The temple, which was a sacred place, had been profaned by traders. Accusing them of making it a den of thieves, he physically threw out the merchants and their customers, knocked down the tables of the moneychangers and pushed out those selling doves. He forbade all those bringing in goods for sale. He asked them, "Is it not written, my house shall be called of all nations the house of prayer?"[106] A man of courage and fired by idealism, he stalked the earth like a giant, and confident of the support he had of the masses, he was carrying on a crusade against the powerful rabbis that had come to be hated by the people. When the rabbis and the lay Chauvinists heard of what he had done, they were furious, for they were the actual traders and those who were in the synagogue were their men. They wanted to capture him and kill him but they were afraid that it would lead to widespread riots and bloodbath. The situation was so explosive that a small spark would have flared up into a huge conflagration engulfing the entire country, which they wanted to avoid. The rebellious mood of the people unnerved the authorities and so the clergy was secretly conferring, rather hatching a conspiracy, with the lay Chauvinists to arrest Jesus quietly without attracting the attention of the masses.

The next day, seeing him preach at the temple, the chief priest and the scribes along with the Chauvinists confronted him and asked him on whose authority he was preaching. Instead of answering that, he asked them a question: "The baptism of John, where was it from? Was it from heaven or from men?" They were in a dilemma. If they said, it was "from heaven" he would question why then they refused to believe him; and if they said "of men" the people who regarded him as prophet would stone them to death. So they said they did not know. In that case, he said he too need not tell them on whose authority he was preaching there[107] and he continued his discourses.

After that he came out and sitting at the doorstep watched devotees drop money into the treasury, when he saw the rich tossing large amounts while a poor widow put two copper coins. This elicited from him a caustic comment about the rich. He said that the poor widow had given more than what all those wealthy people put together, because poor as she was she had given all that she had while the filthy rich had given only a very small portion of their savings[108]. His championship of the underdog and his incredible popularity among the masses frightened the wealthy Chauvinists and particularly the rabbis who lived complacently in their shade. These two classes, the affluent upper middle class and the priesthood aligned with the Establishment, the Roman imperialism and its puppet government, the Herodians, to meet the challenge of Jesus and the Nazoraeans. It was late in the afternoon and he was aware of the danger of staying in Jerusalem. So he returned to Bethany to the home of Simon the leper and stayed there overnight.

When Jesus and the Apostles were having dinner, Mary (Magdalene), a poor woman, entered and anointed Jesus with spikenard, an expensive perfume.[109] All those members of the Apostolic Committee who were there were indignant. As one who truly and sincerely practised what Jesus preached, Judas was surprised that Jesus was not objecting to it. He thought Jesus had fallen a prey to sycophancy. Judas had always been trying to live up to the ideals of the movement that Jesus preached, but curiously Jesus justified what the woman did. He could not stomach it. He remembered Jesus telling the young man to sell all that he had, and give the proceeds to the poor and wondered how Jesus could now condone what this woman had done. He was furious. This was double standard, he thought. A militant throughout his life, Judas was straightforward, impetuous and outspoken, and he frequently vociferated whatever he felt even at the risk of displeasing Jesus. He said that the woman was wasting the oil, for it could have been sold for three hundred pence and the money given to the poor.[110] The other apostles too felt the same but they hesitated to speak out. As a Zealot, Judas had always been a champion of the marginalised and the downtrodden, and this incident left a bad taste in his mouth; he, to a great extent, lost his regard for Jesus. Unable to contain himself, Judas immediately got up and went away.

Judas of course, was too naïve. He failed to understand the difference between the situation when Jesus advised that young man to sell all his possessions and give to the poor and the present situation when he condoned Mary's action. First of all this woman was indigent and in doing what she had done, she was making a great sacrifice. Secondly, she suddenly came in and anointed him before he realised what she was doing; and to chastise her after that would have only hurt her feelings. So even though he must have disapproved of what she did, being kind and considerate, Jesus was reluctant to deprecate her. He was a true revolutionary whose militancy was tempered with compassion and empathy. But Judas, who was a militant but not a revolutionary, could not appreciate tender and finer human sentiments.

John, the Evangelist, condemns Judas in his Gospel saying, "...not that he cared for the poor; but because he was a thief, and was in charge of the fund, and used to take what was put in it."[111] It must be understood that Jesus had picked Judas from among the twelve Apostles to be the treasurer of the movement[112] because Jesus trusted him more than he trusted any other member of the Apostolic Committee. Had Jesus not trusted him, he would not have entrusted him with the funds. Jesus was not a fool; he was a shrewd man. Had Judas been pilfering money from the Nazoraean Movement fund as John accuses him of, Jesus or anyone of the Apostolic Committee would have come to know of it. Besides, had he been pilfering money Judas would have been living an ostentatious life, which he was not. His empathy for the poor was as unassailable as that of Jesus. If at all he had taken any money from the Nazoraean fund, he must have taken it with the knowledge of all or at least of Jesus and must have used a major part of it for procuring arms and the rest, given to the poor. Neither Jesus, nor any one of the other Apostles had ever accused or even suspected him of misappropriation of funds so far.

On the day of the Passover, the atmosphere in Jerusalem was surcharged with anti-imperialist sentiments and the expectation of an impending violent outburst. The chief priests, the scribes and leaders of the lay Chauvinists assembled at the palace of Caiaphas, the high priest. They were feverishly plotting to arrest Jesus without attracting the attention of the people and execute him. But they did not want to do it during the feast, lest there be an uproar among the people and that would only help Jesus and the rebels.

There was already a distinct possibility of an uprising against Herod aimed at the overthrow of the Roman imperialists which would have invited retaliation by the Roman army, throwing the whole country into a boiling cauldron of war. The people were prepared for it and were eagerly waiting for a word from Jesus' mouth to take up arms, but in vain. The Nazoraeans were disappointed; more so Judas the Iscariot, who had been a Zealot earlier and was a militant rebel in a hurry. At the secret meeting that Jesus had with the Apostolic committee, when he heard Jesus proclaim that he had not come to preach peace but to cross swords with the Romans, Judas thought he had taken the right decision in joining the movement. But at this critical juncture Jesus failed the people; he seemed to have developed cold feet. He lost his patience with Jesus and was furious at what he thought was the sudden *volte face* of Jesus when the entire nation was ready to rise as one man against the Roman imperialists. So, he thought, Jesus was not equal to the task and if Jesus could be removed from the scene for a few days, he could take over the leadership of the movement and call upon the people to rise in revolt.

The best way to do that was to help the priests to capture Jesus and keep him in their custody so that the Herodians would not be able to lay their hands upon Jesus and kill him. He would be safe and once the rebellion succeeded the clergy could be forced to release him and crown him king of the Jews. He also decided to demand payment for it so that he could use that money for purchasing arms. He was sure that the clergy would not mind paying him. He was certainly aware of the nexus between the clergy and the Herodians but being naïve as militants usually are, he did not think that the rabbis would stoop so low as to get Jesus killed. Anyway, he decided to take a calculated risk. He went to the chief priests and asked them how much he would be paid if he helped them arrest Jesus.[113] They could not believe their ears. What a coincidence! This was what they wanted and they offered thirty pieces of silver. A good amount, thought Judas, and he wanted it to be paid in advance. The deal was struck and the money was paid on the spot.

After the feast of the Passover, Jesus went with his apostles to the garden of Gethsemane on the Mount of Olives. A few days back, sitting on the Mount of Olives, he had spoken to his Apostles, giving them an idea of the struggle ahead. He told them that when they rose in revolt the Roman imperialists would strike back with all their might and possibly all the countries that had been overrun by the Romans could be drawn into the vortex of the struggle, taking this opportunity to free themselves. As a result the people at large would suffer; there would be a food shortage, and epidemic caused by rotting bodies of those who died in the strife.[114] He might be killed, he said, and warned them not to be duped by anyone who might come pretending to be Christ and sympathetic to their cause; he might be a double agent planted by the imperialists.[115] Significantly, he had called himself the "son of man," at that time and again when he spoke to his disciples he repeatedly referred to him as the "son of man" only.[116] As he claimed he was king of the Jews, he wanted the people to regard him as a man, a human being, like any of them.

When Jesus was in the garden of Gethsemane where he was praying after the Passover feast, the chief priests and the elders followed by an armed mob came there. Judas, who was expected to help them identify Jesus, was also with them. He walked up to Jesus and saying, "Greetings, Rabbi," kissed him. At once some from among the mob came forward and caught hold of Jesus, when "one of those who were with Jesus stretched out his hand, drew his sword, and struck a servant of the high priest's and smote off his ear."[117] But finding that the enemy had come fully armed and the Nazoraeans were far outnumbered by them, Jesus thought it would be unwise to resist and told him to put the sword back in the scabbard saying, "Whoever takes the sword will perish by the sword."[118] He had realised the hopelessness of his position and thought that it was foolish to provoke an armed clash, then. It would have ended in the death of himself and the Apostles, leaving the Nazoraean Movement like a rudderless ship in a turbulent ocean.

Jesus had indubitably planned an armed insurrection, for otherwise there was no reason why the Apostles should carry swords with them at the Passover feast. Evidently, Judas was not informed of Jesus' intention of starting the insurrection soon after the Passover feast. Jesus had told the Apostles to be prepared for the planned uprising, probably when Judas was not there. Many a time Judas must have gone away like that because, being in charge of the funds and a former Zealot, he must have been entrusted with the job of secretly collecting and storing arms to be distributed among the partisans when the call for the rebellion was given. And even later, no one thought of informing him of the decision, maybe because, they did not notice his absence when Jesus revealed his plan for the revolt. This communication gap was the cause of the tragedy, for which no one could be faulted.

Jesus did not wish to call upon the people to take up arms on the day of the Passover feast, for he did not want to see bloodshed on a day that the Jews considered sacred and wanted to spend that day peacefully. And of course, he would not have even dreamt that the Chauvinists, particularly the rabbis, would choose the day of the feast to arrest him. If Judas had an inkling of Jesus' intention to give the call to the people to revolt the day after the Passover feast, he would not have helped the priests to arrest Jesus. However, Judas realised his mistake when, the next morning to his utter dismay, he found that the chief priests and the leaders of the Chauvinists "took counsel against Jesus to put him to death."[119] Judas did not expect the rabbis to act with such malice. Remorseful of what he had done, he at once went back to the chief priests and saying that he had committed a blunder in helping them capture an innocent man, "threw down the pieces of silver in the temple and departed."[120] Tormented by a feeling of guilt, he went and hanged himself. If it were just for the sake of money that he had agreed to help the chief priest arrest Jesus, he would not have committed suicide, let alone return the money.

Understandably, Matthew, Mark, Luke and John in their Gospels, have portrayed Judas as a betrayer and his name has become a synonym for it. These Gospels were composed many years before they were reduced to writing and were being orally conveyed from generation to generation as testified by Papias, one of the earliest church officials who flourished at the turn of the first century CE. The original composers were biased against Judas, for they were influenced by the propaganda against Judas carried on by the surviving eleven Apostles. Those Apostles were trying to cover up the infamy of their act of betrayal, for at the critical juncture, all of them had deserted Jesus, including Simon the Canaanite who was once a Zealot. None except Simon the Peter even dared go anywhere near the chief priest's palace when Jesus, who was taken into custody, was being interrogated. But when a servant girl said "you too were with Jesus of Galilee," he disowned Jesus without batting an eyelid.[121] The Evangelists who many years later committed to writing the bardic compositions, which were based on what the surviving Apostles said, merely accepted what came down to them by word of mouth. Hence, it was generally believed that Judas "betrayed" Jesus. Unfortunately Judas did not live to explain why he helped the rabbis to arrest Jesus.

Coming back to the story of Jesus, the next morning Jesus was bound and taken to Pontius Pilate for interrogation. When he was asked, "Art thou the king of the Jews?" without any hesitation, Jesus replied, "You said it!"[122] Yet, Pilate did not find him guilty on any count and wanted to release him. But from among the crowd, the Chauvinists "cried out saying, if you let this man go, you are not Caesar's friend, whosoever makes him a king speaks against Caesar."[123] And a little later, the chief priest representing the clergy was heard saying, "We have no king but Caesar."[124] Prodded by the clergy and the lay Chauvinists, the crowd cried out in chorus, "Away with him, away with him! Crucify him!" Pilate must have thought that he would be in trouble if he acquitted a man who challenged the authority of Rome by claiming that he was the king of the Jews. It was treason. So he had no alternative but to convict him and, succumbing to the pressure of the crowd, he condemned Jesus to death by crucifixion. The stories about his resurrection on the third day[125] and his apostles meeting him on the mountain in Galilee as well as the story of his Ascension[126] are nothing but myths created later by those who converted the Nazoraean Movement into a religious movement.

Jesus, "when he cried again with a loud voice, yielded up the ghost."[127] That he died on the cross is testified by the Bible itself, and this is irrefutable because when his body was taken to be interred, it was lifeless. No sooner did the news of Jesus' execution spread than there was a spontaneous outbreak of violence. All over Judaea widespread riots erupted, the mob damaging the temple, the buildings that housed the government departments as well as the residences of the Roman officials and those of the Jews who had been thriving under their patronage. It is said, "...the graves were opened and many bodies of the saints...came out of the graves,"[128] which actually indicates that Jails were broken into, setting free many partisans of the anti-imperialist movement, who had been condemned to death on charges of treason. The centurion and the Roman soldiers who were standing beneath the cross were frightened at the ferocity of the sudden uprising. Nonplussed by the fury of the mob, they withdrew to the safety of their barracks.[129] But as all the eleven Apostles who were expected to lead the movement had gone into hiding fearing a Roman counterattack, the insurrection ended as abruptly as it started for want of a central leadership to guide the insurgents.

The arrest and execution of Jesus prevented a violent anti-imperialist rebellion for the time being. Dark clouds that had been gathering on the political horizon of Judaea that threatened a destructive cloudburst passed off like a mild storm. But the situation in Judaea continued to be volatile and could any time reach the flash point. This is evident from the speech given a few years later to the freemen by Herod Agrippa II, warning the Judaeans against an armed revolt. Sensing the possibility of a Jewish insurrection leading to a full scale war with Rome, Herod Agrippa II convened a meeting of all the freemen of his principality in a huge hall and gave a long talk emphasising the futility of challenging the Roman Empire. It may not be irrelevant in this context to give a gist of it as it gives us an insight into the explosive situation that prevailed for a long time after Jesus' execution. Agrippa brought home to the people the futility of attempting an armed revolt. In his strongly worded speech he said to the Jews not to utter a word against the procurators or nurture any thought of liberating the Jews. They would be wise to be servile to the procurators and please them; never provoke them, for the might of

Rome is behind the procurators. The writ of the Roman Emperor runs in almost a third of the world and the powers that were greater than Judaea had been brought under the iron heel of Rome. He concluded saying, if the Jews entered into a war with Rome, the entire nation would be completely ravaged and the survivors would have no place to escape to and take refuge. All the kingdoms around Judaea were under the Romans and none of those countries would give them asylum fearing reprisal by the imperial power of Rome.[130]

There is no gainsaying the fact that the Jewish Wars that broke out later were the outburst of nationalism and the anti-imperialist sentiment that the Nazoraean Movement had instilled in the Jewish masses. The execution of Jesus was no doubt hailed by the rabbis and the elite Jewish Chauvinists, but it had a dampening effect on the lower middle class and the poor in general, for they had no leader now. However, the anti-imperialist legacy left by Jesus could not be erased so easily. The pent-up anger of the people against Rome burst forth into an anti-imperialist war under the leadership of a Jew by name Simeon Bar Kosba, who was hailed as the Messiah. The Nazoraean Movement that had once been the vanguard of anti-imperialist struggle, having lost its revolutionary fervour was in disarray. Its weakness lay in the fact that it had been a personality-centered movement, having been built around the personality of Jesus just as the Baptismal Movement was built around the personality of John the Baptist. The exit of Jesus from the stage had created a vacuum that neither any one of the Apostles nor the Apostles collectively could fill.

The Nazoraean Movement was basically a poor man's movement and the core committee that Jesus formed to lead the movement consisted of men from the poorer section of the population. Jesus always condemned the rich and spoke in support of the poor, but he did not utter a word against slavery – not that there were no slaves then or that the slaves were happy and contented. There were slaves; even rabbis had slaves to work for them. For example, when Peter who was arrested and imprisoned, managed to escape from the prison with the help of the guards who were sympathetic to him[131] and went to the house of Mary, mother of John Mark, his knock at the door was answered by a slave, a girl by name Rhoda.[132] Again, we find slaves, both male and female, were employed by the high priest who came to arrest Jesus as well as the one to whom he was taken first, after the arrest.[133] In the eyes of Jesus the poor included the lower middle class and the workers only but not the slaves; nowhere did he express a word in the interest of the slaves. Why was Jesus, who empathised with poor freemen, totally unconcerned with the plight of slaves?

The reason is obvious. Jesus, the great leader that he was, knew by instinct the *sign* of the times. It may be recalled that the Pharisees and the Sadducees "desired Jesus to show them a *sign* from Heaven" to prove that he was the Son of God. Although the Pharisees and the Sadducees meant "miracle" when they said "sign," Jesus cleverly twisted it and used the word *sign* in a different sense as is evident from his reply. By relating *sign* to weather, he took it to mean "indication." For instance when he said a red sky in the evening indicates fair weather or a "red and lowering" sky in the morning portends bad weather, he meant that such conditions of the sky necessarily point to the kind of weather that could be expected. So when he asked them if they could not understand "the signs of the times" he meant the "indications of the times."[134]

So he knew the futility of condemning slavery and that was why he accepted the slave system, which by instinct he recognised was what that period indicated. As pointed out elsewhere earlier, the acquisition of property by individuals and the consequent disintegration of the tribal communes based on collectivism of the barbaric period gave rise to the stratification of society and the system of slavery. The slave system, therefore, was a necessity of the period and was the mainstay of the society and disintegration of the system would have destabilised the society. Morgan writes, "During the Later Period of barbarism a new element that of aristocracy, had a marked development. The individuality of persons and the increase of wealth now possessed by individuals in masses were laying the foundation of personal influence. Slavery also by permanently degrading a portion of the people, tended to establish contrasts of condition unknown in the previous ethnical periods...It soon disturbed the balance of society by introducing unequal privileges and degrees of respect for individuals...and thus became the source of discord and strife."[135]

Paradoxically, as pointed out in Chapter 4, "The Consolidation of Slavery," it was a leap forward from the tribal society, despite the ruthless oppression and exploitation of man by man inherent in the situation.

In Jesus' time, as society had moved up into the stage of civilisation this contrast became wider and irreversible. The historical Jesus had the insight to understand the necessity to maintain the integrity of the society. He realised that any attempt to tinker with slavery would weaken the social system and would lead to chaos in the society. Paradoxically, that he did not denounce or attempt to dismantle slavery speaks volumes for his greatness.[135] It is this, his instinctive ability to understand the societal needs of the period more than anything else that has made him great and immortal.

NOTES

1. Catholic Bible (CB), 1 Maccabeees (Mac), 1:10, 20 et seq. He took the title Epiphanes meaning "Visible God" which he thought he really was and acted accordingly, with the result the people called him Epimanes, meaning "the madman."
2. F. Josephus. The Wars of the Jews, 1, 1, 2. In *Complete Works*, tr. By W. Whiston, Kregel Publications, Grand Rapids, 1977, p. 429.
3. CB, 1 Mac. 2:1-7.
4. F. Josephus, The Antiquities of the Jews, 12, 6, 1. In *Complete Works*, tr. by W. Whiston, Kregel Publications, Grand Rapids, 1977, pp. 258-159.
5. F. Josephus, The Wars of the Jews, 1,1,3. In ibid., p. 429.
6. Vide Appendix 2 for the genealogy. Further details of the Maccabees are given in the Book of the Maccabees included in the Apocrypha, which is a deuteron-canonical book of the Catholic Bible. See Chapter 1, "The Book of Books."
7. F. Josephus, War, 2, 8, 1. In op. cit., p. 476.
8. Lk. 3:1; F. Josephus, Wars, 2, 12, 8. In op. cit., p. 482.
9. F. Josephus, War, 1, 21, 1. In op. cit., p. 452.
10. Herod Antipas died after 39 CE and Herod Agrippa I died in 44 CE.
11. Mt. 3:1; Mk. 1:4., Lk. 1:60; Jn. 1:6. (cf. Yahya and Isa in the Qur'an.)
12. Herod Antipater or Herod the Great I, the founder of the Herodian dynasty.
13. Lk. 1:5.

14. I Chr.24:10. Abia was the eighth of the twenty-four courses into which the priests were divided.
15. Lk. 1:19.
16. Lk. 1:59. A rite among the Jews, believed to have been instituted by Yahweh as the sigh of the covenant between him and Abraham and his descendants. (vide Gen. 17:10.
17. Lk. 1:80. Israel here refers to Judaea.
18. Lk. 1:36. "...And, behold, your cousin Elisabeth...she has also conceived..." A small confusion has been created by Luke when referring to Elisabeth. In one place, he says that she "was of the daughter of Aaron." (Lk. 1:5), in which case, she would be Mary's aunt but shortly later he contradicts himself when he identifies her as the cousin of Mary. A cousin of Mary could not by any stretch of the imagination, be "of the daughter of Aaron." Ignoring the historicity of Aaron, he may be said to have 'flourished' a few centuries back. Considering the difference in their age – Elisabeth was quite old while Mary was only in her teens – Elisabeth could only be her aunt and not cousin. Anyway, as far as this study is concerned their relationship is immaterial. Probably they were distant relatives and so we shall just say Elisabeth was a 'kinswoman' of Mary.
19. Lk. 1:27, 30, 31. "...the angel Gabriel was sent by God to a city of Galilee named Nazareth...To a virgin of the house of David...And the angel came to her, and said, Hail, you who are highly favoured, the Lord is with you...Fear not, Mary; for you have found favour with God. And, behold, you shall conceive in your womb, and bring forth a son, and shall call his name Jesus."
20. Jn. 19:25. This Cleophas should not be confused with the Cleopas who walked with the apparition of Jesus to the village called Emmaus (Lk. 24:18). That they were two different individuals is obvious from the conversation between Cleopas and the phantom of Jesus.
21. Mt. 27:56; Mk. 15:40; Lk. 24:10.
22. Mt. 27:56, Mk. 15:40; Lk. 24:10.
23. *Catholic Encyclopaedia*, New York, 1912, V. 15. There is no mention of these two characters, Joachim and Anna, anywhere in the King James Version of the Bible.
24. IGJ. 4:2.
25. Lk. 1:26.
26. Six-legged creatures, commonly known as 'insects.'
27. Mt. 1:20.
28. Deut. 22:13-14, 20-21. The Mosaic Law states, "If any man take a wife, and go in to her...and say, I took this woman, and when I came

to her, I found her not a maid...(and) if this thing be true, and the token of virginity not found for the damsel; Then they shall bring out the damsel to the door of her father's house , and the men of her city shall stone her with stones until she dies."

29. Mt. 1:19. "...Joseph her husband, being a just man, and not willing to make her a public example, was minded to put her away privily."
30. David divided the priests and the Levites into twenty-four groups, each with its own head. These groups are called 'courses,' each of which officiated a week at a time. Vide Lk 1:8; I Chr. 24:1 ff.
31. Mt. 2:1-2. "Where is he that is born King of the Jews? For we have seen his star in the east, and have come to worship him."
32. Mt. 2:4.
33. Mic. 5:2.
34. Mt. 2:16.
35. Mt. 2:13. "...behold the angel of the Lord appeared to Joseph, in a dream saying, Arise and take the young child and his mother by night and go to Egypt."
36. Lk. 2:46.
37. Mt. 3:2.
38. F. Josephus, The Antiquities, 12, 6, 2. In op. cit., p. 258.
39. Also called chasidim, meaning "loved of god,' they were a very influential class and a strict sect of Jews (Acts. 126:5). Being very clannish, they wore a type of garb to distinguish themselves from others. They played a very significant role in the life of Jesus as mentioned in the Gospels in several places. A few of them, like Nicodemus (Jn. 3:1) and Gamaliel (Acts 5:34) joined the Nazorean Movement of Jesus.
40. Another sect of Jews that differed with the Pharisees in many doctrinal questions. For example, unlike the Pharisees, "...the Sadducees say there is no resurrection, neither angel nor spirit..." (Acts 23:8)
41. Herod Antipas, the tetrarch. All incidents connected with Antipas described here occurred before he and his wife Herodias were exiled.
42. Mt. 3:7-9. "O brood of vipers, who has warned you to flee from the wrath to come? Bear, therefore, fruits worthy of repentance. And think not to say within yourselves, We have Abraham as our father..."
43. Deut. 18:15.
44. Jn. 1:25.
45. Jn. 1:26.
46. Mt. 311; Mk. 1:7-8; Lk. 3:16; Jn. 1:27. "I indeed baptise you with water into repentance; but he who comes after me is mightier than I, whose shoes I am not worthy to bear; he will baptise you with the Holy Ghost and with fire."

47. Mt. 3:13. "Then comes Jesus from Galilee to Jordan to John, to be baptised by him."
48. Lk. 3:21-23.
49. Jn. 3:26.
50. Jn. 3:28.
51. Jn. 8:29.
52. Lk. 3:19.
53. Mt. 14:7.
54. F. Josephus, *The Antiquities*, 18, 5, 2. In op. cit., p. 382.
55. Infancy Gospel of James or Protoevangelion (IGJ), 23:3.
56. Ibid., 23:7.
57. IGJ. 23:1-9.
58. Acts 22:8.
59. Mt. 2:23.
60. See Ch. 5, Fn 131; Ch. 8, Fn 40.
61. A. Robertson, *The Origin of Christianity*, London, 1953, p. 74.
62. Mt. 5:17. The law that Jesus speaks of, is the Mosaic Law.
63. S. Jacobovici and C. Pellegrino, *The Jesus Family Tomb*, New York, 2007, p. 34.
64. Mt. 16:18. Peter means "rock." The original Aramaic word Kepah was translated into the Greek Petros both meaning "rock" became Peter in English.
65. Mk. 3:17. They were called so because they had a powerful voice like the sound of a thunderbolt.
66. He was called Doubting Thomas because he doubted when the other apostles said that Jesus presented himself to then in the evening of his so-called resurrection, to which he was not a witness. Vide Jn. 20:24-25.
67. The 'publican' was a tax collector under the Romans. An official of the lowest rank in the department of revenue, engaged in collecting taxes from the people.
68. Mt. 10:2-4; Mk. 3:14-19; Lk. 6:13-16; Acts 1:13. The political party called the Zealots was stated to resist Roman aggression and they resorted to violence, when Quirinius was the governor. Josephus condemns them for their 'wild and brutish disposition.'
69. Kerioth is in the south of Judah. Vide Josh.15:25. Judas is popularly known as Judas Iscariot. This 'surname' Iscariot is generally said to be derived from the Hebrew Ish Kerioth.
70. I. Asimov, *Guide to the Bible*, New York, p. 841.
71. Jn. 1:42, Mt. 16:17. "You are blessed, Simon Bar-Jona..." Simon Bar-Jona or Shimon bar Jonah in Hebrew, means Simon, son of Jona.

72. Mt. 10:34. "Think not that I am come to send peace on earth; I came not to send peace, but a sword."
73. Mt. 11:11.
74. Mt. 11:12. "And since the days of John the Baptist until now the kingdom of heaven suffers violence, and the violent take it by force."
75. Mt. 10:35-37. "For I have come to set a man against his father...and a man's enemies shall be those of his own household..."
76. Mt. 10:38. "And he that does not take his cross, and follows Me, is not worthy of Me."
77. Mt. 12:30. "He that is not with Me is against Me."
78. Lk. 19:27. "But bring here those enemies of mine, who did not want me to reign over them, and slay them before me."
79. Mt. 16:6; Mk. 8:15. "Take heed, beware of the leaven of the Pharisees and of the leaven of Herod." Leaven is a substance that makes dough rise. It is used figuratively here.
80. Mt. 16:26. "For what is a man profited, if he gains the whole world and loses his own soul?..."
81. Lk. 10:1.
82. Acts 1:15.
83. Mt. 10:16-31; Lk.10:3-16.
84. Mt. 14:13.
85. Mt. 15:21.
86. Mt. 15:29.
87. Mt. 15:39.
88. Mt. 19:1.
89. Lk. 4:31.
90. Mt. 3:1. "Repent, for the Kingdom of Heaven is at hand," said John the Baptist. / Mt.4:17. "...Repent, for the Kingdom of Heaven is at hand," said Jesus.
91. Lk. 4:18.
92. Acts 1:6.
93. Mt. 23:1-33.
94. Lk. 13:32. "And he said to them, Go tell that fox..."
95. Mt. 7:6. "...This people honour me with their lips, but their heart is far from me."
96. Mt. 19:23; Mk.10:25.
97. Mt. 19:27-30. "...and shall inherit everlasting life."
98. Mt. 20:18.
99. Lk. 18:34.
100. Mt. 21:5. "Tell the daughter of Sion, Behold, your king is coming to you, meek and sitting on an ass..." Sion is a mountain near Jerusalem

and so 'the daughter of Sion' refers to Jerusalem.

101. Lk. 19:27. "But those enemies of mine, who did not want me to reign over them, bring them here and slay them before me."
102. Lk. 19:38.
103. Lk. 19:40. "I tell you that, If these should hold their peace, the stones would immediately cry out."
104. Mk. 11:10.
105. Mk. 11:15-17; Lk. 19:45-46.
106. Mt. 21:23-27; Lk. 20:2-8.
107. Lk. 211-4.
108. Spikenard is an aromatic rhizome of the plant, Nardostachys fatamansi DC (grandiflora) belonging to the Valerianaceae family. This is a medicinal plant too and is used in Indian (Ayurvedic), Chinese and Japanese traditional medicines.
109. Mt. 26:6-9; Mk. 14:3-5; Jn. 12:3-5. "And there were some who were angry within themselves, and said, Why was this perfume wasted? For it might have been sold for more than three hundred pence, and have been given to the poor; And they murmured against her." Neither Matthew nor Mark say who those "disciples" or "some" are that murmured but John pinpoints the person who said it. John writes, "Then said one of his disciples, Judas Iscariot...Why was not this fragrant oil sold for three hundred pence, and given to the poor."
110. Jn. 12:6.
111. Jn. 12:6/13:29.
112. Mt. 26:14-16.
113. Mt. 24:7. "For nations will rise against nation, and kingdoms against kingdom..."
114. Mt. 24:23. "Then if any man shall say to you, Lo here is Christ, or there, do not believe it."
115. Mt. 24:27, 37, 44/26:2, 24, 45. (just a few examples).
116. Mt. 26:51.
117. Mt. 26:52.
118. Mt. 27:1-2.
119. Mt. 27:3-5.
120. Mt. 26:69-74.
121. Mt. 27:11.
122. Jn. 19:12.
123. Jn. 19:15.
124. Mt. 28:6; Mk. 16:6; Lk. 24:7.
125. Lk. 24:51; Acts I:9.
126. Mt. 27:50.

127. Mt. 27:52-53. "Behold, the veil of the temple was torn into two; and the earth quaked and the rocks split...And the graves were opened, and many bodies of he saints who had fallen asleep rose, And came out of the graves..."
128. Mt. 27:54. "Now when the centurion and those who were with him watching Jesus, saw the earth quake and the things that happened, they feared greatly..."
129. F. Josephus, *Wars*. In op. cit., pp. 487-490.
130. Acts 12:7-8.
131. Acts 12:13-15.
132. Jn. 18:10, 17-18.
133. Mt. 16:3. "When it is evening, you say, It will be fair weather; for the sky is red. And in the morning, it will be foul whether today; for the sky is red and lowering. O you hypocrites, you can discern the face of the sky; but you cannot discern the signs of the times?"
134. L.H. Morgan, op. cit., p. 551,
135. See Chapter 4, "Consolidation of Slavery."

Part Four

TAILPIECE

9

The Son of Man

After Jesus' death, the Apostles who had survived Jesus co-opted one more member, by name Matthias,[1] into the practically defunct Apostolic Committee to fill the vacancy caused by the death of Judas. The torture and execution of Jesus deterred them from continuing the anti-imperialist struggle, for they thought, if they continued they too would be captured and subjected to such torture and crucifixion. Perhaps, more than the fear of torture and crucifixion, after deserting and disowning their leader – or to put it in proper perspective, after ***betraying*** their leader – they had no face to go back to the people. They decided to wait for his Second Advent which he had promised, and to lead them again in their struggle against Roman imperialism for the establishment of the Kingdom of the Jews. Whether they believed in his Second Advent or not, waiting for it gave them an excuse to keep themselves out of sight of the authorities and the people. Meanwhile, they deified Jesus, keeping in abeyance the political agenda of the Nazoraean Movement and reorient it into a religious movement sans any political objectives whatsoever. This could be a tactical move to keep the organisation intact so that they could revert to political action after the Parousia that they said they expected would happen during their lifetime.

Nonetheless, they were still called the Nazoraens by the people and the government. Rome still looked upon the Nazoraeans as a militant anti-imperialist organisation, and to be identified as "Nazoraean" or Nazarene continued to bear the odium of being a member of the clandestine anti-Roman movement. But the Apostles did not want it to be considered so any more. Hence they highlighted Jesus of Nazarene's claim that he was the *Christ* (the Messiah) and put into cold storage the political agenda of the movement. Jesus of Nazarene, thus, came to be identified as Jesus *the Christ*. Public memory being proverbially short, as a result of the propaganda based on the precepts of Jesus *the Christ*, the revolutionary role that he played was soon erased from social memory and the people began to call the Nazoraean Movement, the Christian Movement or "Christianity." Incidentally, although it had all the prerequisites of a religion, it was after the followers of Jesus had given up the hope of Jesus' Second Advent and a couple of decades after Jesus' death that it actually turned into a religion. Now the Apostles claimed the religious legacy of John the Baptist, which Jesus had practically discarded, turning the religious movement that he took over from John the Baptist into a vanguard of anti-imperialist movement. The Apostles, now, emphasised the role of John the Baptist as the *precursor* to Jesus *the Christ*, mythicising both of them and calling Jesus, the "Son of God" as Jesus had said of himself until he decided to take the plunge and proclaimed himself the king of the Jews and "son of man."[2] Consequently, today the world has practically forgotten the historical role that Jesus played and sees only the mythical Jesus that the Bible portrays with only a hint of the historical Jesus thrown in, thus belittling a great visionary and revolutionary.

Several biblical scholars of Europe influenced by the rationalism of the Enlightenment Era of the eighteenth century had tried to prove the historicity of Jesus. Schweitzer says their motivation for investigating the historicity of Jesus was primarily to counter "the tyranny of dogma" and not to probe the veracity of historical Jesus. "For Bhardt and Venturini He was the tool of a secret order....For Reinhard, Hess, Paulus, and the rest of the rationalistic writers He is the admirable revealer of true virtue, which is coincident with right reason" asserts Schweitzer.[3] Schweitzer's rejection of the rationalists' attempt to establish the historicity of Jesus was the result of his preconceived notion of a mythicised Jesus because he looked at the problem of Jesus' historicity through theological spectacles. Whatever was the motive of rationalists, their demythification of Jesus would have helped many of the credulous Christians who were carried away by the false propaganda of the priesthood, free themselves from the illusion created by the Church. What the rationalists of the eighteenth century had done, therefore, was indubitably an invaluable service that contributed to rational thinking, and incidentally to clearing the mythological smoke screen created by the clergy to hide a historical personality to serve their vested interests.

Many biblical scholars, who look at Jesus through religious eyes, dismiss the historical Jesus, categorically stating that such a person never existed; they regard him, who is believed to have advocated the establishment of the "Kingdom of Heaven," as a creation of theologists who have put him in a historical context. Albert Schweitzer, for example, dismisses the Jesus of history saying, "the Jesus of Nazareth who came forward publicly as the Messiah, who preached the ethic of the Kingdom of God, who founded the Kingdom of Heaven upon earth, and died to give His work its final consecration, never had any existence. He is a figure designed by rationalism, endowed with life by liberalism, and clothed by modern theology in an historical garb."[4] There are also the sceptics who doubt the historicity of Jesus. A distinguished philosopher like Bertrand Russell shrugs off the question of his historicity, saying it is too difficult a problem and it is futile to attempt an investigation of it. He writes, "Historically it is quite doubtful whether Christ ever existed at all, and if he did, we do not know anything about him, so that I am not concerned with the historical question, which is a very difficult one."[5] A prolific writer of science fiction, Isaac Asimov too is a sceptic who doubts the historicity of Jesus. "Josephus who mentions John the Baptist," he writes, "does not mention Jesus. There is one paragraph in his history of the Jews which is devoted to Jesus but is generally believed to be an insertion by some early Christian editor...Nor, in fact is there mention of Jesus in any contemporary or nearly contemporary record we have, outside the New Testament."[6]

To say that Jesus never existed but was only a figure "designed by rationalism and clothed by modern theology in an historical garb" as Schweitzer does and shove him into the realm of mythology is to ignore the plethora of evidence of his historicity. It is beyond one's comprehension why a philosopher and thinker like Russell simply brushes aside the problem of Jesus' historicity as "a very difficult" one. And Asimov is absolutely wrong when he says there are no "contemporary or nearly contemporary" documents extant today outside the New Testament, particularly the synoptic Gospels that mention Jesus. Contrary to these views, Daniel-Rops says, "the Life of Christ is set definitely in historical time, not in some remote legendary period as are the traditions concerning Orpheus, Osiris or Mithra. The Roman Empire of the first century is known to us in remarkable detail. (Jesus was a contemporary of Tiberius.) Great men like Livy or Seneca, whose work has come down to us were writing when Jesus was alive...Plutarch and Tacitus were of the generation that followed him....The man therefore is fixed in a social and political milieu, which has been exhaustively studied." Taking into cognizance the Gospels alone, he continues, "No mythical existence could be related so precisely to its setting, unless the Evangelists and the Apostles were such specialists in historical fiction that they could compose severally a figure which throughout their works always maintains a perfect unity."[7] It may be noted that he does not regard the Gospels as chronicles of Jesus' life and period but only points to the Gospels to bring home the fact that it is impossible to portray a mythical character by four persons writing independently of one another without contradicting on any aspect, including the locale in which he lived and worked.

As pointed out in Chapter 1, "The Book of Books," from the writings of Papias we know that the Gospels had been composed long before they were written down. Those early preachers stressed the supposed divinity of Jesus, giving little importance to the anti-imperialist movement that he led because they were more interested in spreading his religious teachings than in the anti-imperialist message of the Nazoraean Movement led by the historical Jesus. They were missionaries who went around spreading the religio-philosophical message of Jesus among the pagans and other religious groups and proselytising them. They were neither historians nor biographers; nor were the Evangelists who wrote down the Gospels. Yet we discern historical and biographical facts, howsoever little they are, about Jesus in those Gospels. The Evangelists are believed to have collected these facts from different sources and are not known to have conferred with one another before writing them down or collaborated in writing those Gospels. In spite of that, they do not contradict one another; on the other hand they fully concur on the few historical facts that they have documented and this undeniably attests the authenticity of those facts – vague though they may be – contained in them. So whatever little historical and biographical facts that we can glean from them, may be accepted as corroborative proof of Jesus' historicity, of which as already pointed out above, there is abundant non-biblical documentary and archaeological evidence.

It is, therefore, not correct to aver there are no contemporary or nearly contemporary non-biblical documents that mention Jesus. In fact, other than the synoptic Gospels there is a sizable body of non-biblical literature that testifies to Jesus' historicity, a few of which we shall discuss presently. The earliest extant non-biblical work that mentions Jesus, as stated already, is that of Flavius Josephus, who was born four years after Jesus was said to have been executed, and it needs to be quoted in full. Josephus writes, "Now, there was about this time, Jesus, a wise man, if it be lawful to call him a man, for he was a doer of wonderful works – a teacher of such men as receive the truth with pleasure. He drew over to him both many of the Jews, and many of the Gentiles. He was [the] Christ; and when Pilate, at the suggestion of the principal men amongst us, had condemned him to the cross, (CE 33, April 3) those that loved him at the first did not forsake him, for he appeared to them alive again the third day, (April 5) as the divine prophets had foretold these and ten thousand other wonderful things concerning him; and the tribe of Christians, so named from him, are not extinct at this day."[8] This passage as stated above has been controversial. Most of the scholars explain away this paragraph about Jesus in Josephus' book, *The Antiquities of the Jews*, saying that it must be an interpolation and they contend that a Jew like Josephus could not have written about Jesus in such glowing terms. They are correct – not because, as they say a Jew would not have eulogised him like that. What makes it incredible is the statement that three days after he was crucified he appeared to those that loved him! And that incidentally betrays a Christian hand behind it. However, when they say it was possibly interpolated later by a Christian editor, they seem to overlook a passing reference to Jesus in another context in the same book.

A little later, in the same book, there is again a passing reference to Jesus and his stepbrother, James. Josephus writes, Albinus, the then procurator of Judaea, assembled the Sanhedrin and brought before it James, "the brother of Jesus, who was called Christ" and some of his companions, accusing them of breaking the law, and sentenced them to be stoned to death.[9] This cannot be ruled out as interpolation and it is not hard to believe that this was written by Josephus only, because there is no glorification or exultation of Jesus in this statement. So let us accept that the earlier statement extolling Jesus was interpolation but this casual reference to Jesus could only have been from Josephus' own pen. However, it is quite strange that only a passing reference was made to Jesus, who had made such a lasting impact on humanity. It must be borne in mind that Josephus wrote *The Wars of the Jews* in 78/79 CE and *The Antiquities of the Jews* in 93/94 CE, about only five to six decades after Jesus' death.

There could be many, other than Josephus, still living at that time that would have seen or heard of Jesus. That the Nazarenes, as the Christians or the followers of Jesus "the Christ" were called then, had been persecuted by the Roman emperors is itself a proof that the Christians existed then and that proves Jesus, based on whose thoughts grew a religion now known as Christianity, was a historical personality. In fact, there is enough evidence to say that Christianity had reached India hardly *two decades* after Jesus was crucified, which we shall discuss presently. Yet, there is a complete blackout of information not only on Jesus but on Christianity as well in Josephus' books. This is understandable. Josephus was a wealthy rabbi who collaborated with the Roman imperialists against the Jewish insurgents, for which he was rewarded by the imperialists and he was dependent on the Roman generosity. Obviously he did not want to rub them on the wrong side by writing about Jesus, a revolutionary who had defied Roman hegemony and laid the foundation for the anti-imperialist insurgency. At the same time, as a historian, he did not want to write disparagingly about a great man like Jesus who played an important role in conscientising the oppressed masses; nor could he totally ignore a towering personality like Jesus who left an indelible mark on the history of that period. *Ergo* that excessively flattering portrayal of Jesus that we find in the earlier passage could be interpolation but the other one where Jesus' name was mentioned in passing could have been what Josephus himself wrote. And the epithet "the Christ" must have been added to identify the individual as Yeshua (Jesus) was a very common name among the Jews at that time.

Apart from what is said in Josephus' book which many scholars do not accept, there are several other writers of that period who have mentioned the Christians or Jesus in their works. The references to Christians or Christianity indirectly prove the historicity of Jesus who called himself the Christ, because of which the Nazoraeans later came to be called the Christians. Seventy-six years after crucifixion, in 109 CE, Tacitus, wrote: "Nero fastened the guilt and inflicted the most exquisite tortures on a class hated for their abominations, called Christians by the populace. Christus, from whom the name had its origin, suffered the extreme penalty during the reign of Tiberius at the hands of one of our procurators, Pontius Pilatus, and a most mischievous superstition, thus checked for the moment, again broke out not only in Judaea, the first source of the evil, but even in Rome,..."[10] Tacitus must have heard contemporaries of Jesus speaking of the execution of "Christus" (the Christ or the Messiah) which was what Jesus said he was. Suetonius (*circa* CE 69-130), a contemporary of Tacitus, in his book states that Claudius had expelled the Jews from Rome for creating frequent disturbances, which were instigated by Christus or Christ that was then known to be Jesus.[11] We hear an echo of this in The Acts of the Apostles, which states, Paul "...found a certain Jew named Aquila, born in Pontus, recently come from Italy with his wife Priscilla; (because Claudius had commanded all Jews to depart from Rome)...."[12]

There are several other pagan authors of the second century CE whose writings have come down to us that irrefutably confirm the historicity of Jesus. Lucian, of Samosaata, (125-180 CE), in his book *Passing of Peregrinus* for example, writes: "It was then that he learned the wondrous lore of the Christians, by associating with their priests and scribes in Palestine. And – how, how else could it be? – in a trice he made them all look like children, for he was prophet, cult-leader, head of the synagogue, and everything, all by himself. He interpreted and explained some of their books and even composed many,[13] and they revered him as a god, made use of him as a lawgiver, and set him down as a protector, next after that other, to be sure, whom they still worship, the man who was crucified in Palestine because he introduced this new cult into the world."[14] The man who was worshipped, who was crucified in Palestine was unmistakably Jesus; none else.

Celsus, a Platonic philosopher who about 178 CE, wrote against the Christians a work known only from Origen's reply, calls Jesus a ringleader of sedition. Heirocles, an imperial governor who attacked Christianity at the end of the third century in a work quoted by Lactantius, describes Jesus as a bandit leader with nine hundred followers. The celebrated work, *Advernus Christianos* in fifteen books, of which only fragments remain, written in the third century CE, by Prophyrius, a neo-Platonic philosopher and a disciple of Plotinus, shows the author's acquaintance with the Jewish as well as the Christian Bible. There are many more works of the writers of the first and second centuries CE that are extant that refer to Jesus, the Christ. It is, therefore, not correct to assert that Jesus never existed but was only a fictitious figure. Jesus was irrefutably a historical personality who had left indelible 'footprints on the sands of time.'

Interestingly, in 1980, in Talpiot, Jerusalem, the remains of a tomb were accidentally stumbled upon, which proved to be a startling archaeological discovery.[15] Inside this tomb were found ten ossuaries, six of which had inscriptions. The authenticity or legitimacy of the inscriptions is unquestionable because they were found *in situ* by archaeologists who had mapped the tomb, catalogued the ossuaries and verified the inscriptions. One of the inscriptions was "Yeshua bar Yosef" that may be translated as "Jesus, son of Joseph." Adjacent to this, in the same tomb another ossuary was found. The inscription on one side of it read, "Maria," which is the Latinised version of the biblical name "Miriam" or "Mary" in English. Another ossuary found next to Maria's had four Hebrew letters, *Vav, Yud, Samech* and *Hey*, chiselled on it. This is pronounced "Yosa" or "Joses" in English and that was the name of one of the stepbrothers of Jesus.[16] What clinched the issue that this was the tomb of the biblical Jesus' family, was the discovery of two other ossuaries – one of which with the inscription "Mariamme also known as Mara" and the other with the inscription, "Judah, son of Jesus."

The biblical scholars had concluded that the one with the inscription of Mariamne was that of Mary Magdalene, the Greek version of which is "Miriam," (Mariamene or Mariamne). The Acts of Philip,[17] a fifth century text, for example, calls Mary Magdalene "Mariamne" and Jesus' mother "Maria." And Philip portrays Mariamne as "a beloved apostle, a healer, a preacher and a master (Mara) in her own right." Tiny fragments collected from the ossuaries of Jesus and Mariamne were sent to the Palaeo-DNA laboratory at Lakehead University in Ontario for a DNA test. The mitochondrial DNA extracted from both the ossuaries confirmed that those were Middle Eastern people of antiquity (which usually refers to a period between 5000 BCE and 476 CE) and were not related. Never would two unrelated individuals of different sexes be interred in a family tomb in the first century in Jerusalem unless they were husband and wife. The other ossuary on which was inscribed "Judah, son of Jesus" was a problem that puzzled the archaeologists.

Did Jesus have a son? The Gospels, Jacobovici and Pellegrino point out, provide the answer to this question. At the last Passover feast as the legend has it, Jesus expressed a suspicion that one of his Apostles would betray him, when, John writes of one who was "lying on Jesus' breast"[18] asking him who that could be. No adult, be it an Apostle or however closely related he might be, would lean against the chest of another; only a boy or an adolescent would do so. When the soldiers arrested Jesus and all his Apostles had fled, "a certain young man, having a linen cloth cast about his naked body" followed Jesus and as some men from the crowd "laid hold on him ...he left the linen cloth and ran away naked."[19] Neither John nor Mark reveals his identity; they would have named him had he been one of the Apostles. All the four Evangelists, for example, speak of Peter being present at the palace of Caiaphas, the high priest, where Jesus was taken for interrogation. This youngster again appeared after Jesus was crucified – he was with Mary, Jesus' mother, and Mary Magdalene. And Jesus, looking at his mother said, "Woman, behold your son!" and he said to his 'disciple,' "Behold your mother." Usually a man addresses his wife and not his mother as "woman," and so the Mary to whom Jesus spoke from the cross could be Mary Magdalene and not his mother Mary. Since then that 'disciple' and Mary, son and mother, stayed together, which supports the assumption that this young man was Jesus' son.

Incidentally, if the inference is correct, it is significant that Jesus named his son Judah, after his Apostle Judas who was accused by the Evangelists of betraying Jesus. Both these words – Judah and Judas – mean "praised" and Jesus used a variation, probably to avoid confusing one with the other. This shows without doubt that among all his apostles, he loved and had a great regard for Judas. A man like Jesus would certainly not have misjudged Judas with whom he had been moving closely, and it is unbelievable that Judas betrayed Jesus, thus substantiating what is stated in the previous chapter.

Anyway, the reason for dealing with this archaeological discovery of Jesus' family sepulchre is not to prove or disprove the veracity of the claim that Jesus was married and had a son. That is beside the point. If, however, Jesus had fallen in love with Mary Magdalene and married her, no one could fault him for it because he had never deprecated or said a word against the institution of marriage. It is natural for a young man to fall in love and marry. It has to be borne in mind, Jesus actually highlighted the sanctity of marriage when he said, "Have you not read that he who made them at the beginning made them male and female?...for this reason a man shall leave his father and mother and be joined to his wife, and the two shall become one flesh. So then, they are no longer two but one flesh. Therefore what God has joined together, let no man separate."[20] And even if it were a woman of ill repute like Mary Magdalene that he married, it was in keeping with his philosophy: "Those who are healthy need no physician, but those who are sick. But you go and learn what that means, I will have mercy and not sacrifice: for I have not come to call the righteous, but sinners to repentance."[21] And Jesus condemned married men and women committing adultery.[22] Mary Magdalene, though she had been a courtesan, had not been said to have fornicated after marriage. So by marrying a fallen woman Jesus had shown by example how he successfully called a sinner to repentance. He practised what he preached.

It is not surprising that both the Catholic and Protestant churches were indifferent to this discovery, not caring to investigate the veracity of such a significant archaeological finding. The reason is obvious. If it is confirmed, the Church will have to accept that Jesus was married and had a son, a possibility the Church – the Catholic as well as the

Protestant – has been denying all these years. In the case of the Catholic Church, the supposed infallibility of the Pope will be called into question. It is unfortunate that the Church mulishly holds on to the view that Jesus was not married, and is not interested in proving the historicity of a great revolutionary like Jesus. Or, perhaps the church wants to keep up the mythical image of Jesus as "son of god" on which depends the justification for its existence and naturally does not want the flock to see him as "son of man." However, as far as we are concerned, it has a bearing on the problem of the historicity of Jesus. If it is truly Jesus' tomb – in all probability it is, even though the Church for whatever reason has refused to recognise it – his historicity cannot be doubted. The likelihood of another family with all the members bearing the same names is itself improbable. And it is impossible to accept that there existed "two Jesuses in the first-century Jerusalem with a father called Joseph, a close relative called Jos'e, and two Marys in their lives – one called Maria and the other a Greek-speaking woman known as the Master."[23] Incidentally another ossuary with the inscription "Yakov"[24] [James], son of Joseph and stepbrother of Jesus, had also been found in the tomb; in fact it was that which triggered the four-year investigation by Jacobovici and Pellegrino that began in 2002 and ended in 2006.

The Bible says Jesus had twelve apostles of whom we discussed in the previous chapter and naturally they must have closely interacted with Jesus. The historicity of those apostles, who were contemporaneous with him, could be accepted as evidence – though circumstantial or indirect – of the historicity of Jesus. But the historicity of Jesus' Apostles is as much obscured by an overgrowth of myths and legends around them as that of Jesus is, and consequently they too are looked at as legendary rather than historical figures. The legacies that each one of them had left behind speak volumes for their historicity and cannot be simply brushed aside. Further, they lived in historical times and were closely associated with the life and work of a historical person called Jesus *the Christ*, whose teachings they are known to have propagated, which itself, incidentally, is a proof that both they and Jesus were historical persons. "Some day a critical scholar needs to take a good look at the mass of legend which has come to us from early medieval times, and even from the last days of Roman power.

He needs to try to separate the historical germ from the great overgrowth of pure fantasy, which one finds in those stories. In a word, a higher criticism of the medieval legends needs to be made, and that criticism needs to be carried over into early church history."[25] It is not necessary to discuss all the twelve Apostles but we shall as examples, go into the problem of the historicity of Apostle Thomas in detail and take a peep into the historicity of Apostle Simon the Peter.[26]

The oldest written record in support of the tradition regarding Thomas' apostolic work in India is the *Acta Thomae*, an apocryphal book, the original manuscript of which is in the British Museum and specimens of it are in the Bibliotheque Nationale as well as in the Berlin Museum. Shorter redactions of this exist in Ethiopic and Latin. Dated around the end of the first century CE, *Acta Thomae* gives in nine parts the history of the apostolic work of Thomas in India in detail. This document of course, is like the synoptic Gospels and cannot be treated on a par with historical records. However, let us begin the investigation with this. As stated earlier, after the execution of Jesus, the Nazoraean movement, divesting itself of the political agenda, gradually transformed itself into a peace movement with a religious thrust and the followers of the religion that grew out of it came to be known as the 'Nazarene' which eventually changed to Christians, after *Christ*, which Jesus claimed that he was and on whose teachings the religion was based. The Apostles now became preachers of this religion. According to the book *Acta Thomae*, after the death of Jesus, the Apostles met at Jerusalem and decided to go to different parts of the world to spread the message of Jesus – not his political ideology but his religious teachings. To Thomas' lot fell West Asia and India. Christian scholars hold conflicting views on the Indian apostolate of Thomas. There are some who accept the veracity of the South Indian apostolate without denying the North Indian apostolate; some others consider the North Indian apostolate reliable but do not deny South Indian apostolate; a few uphold the North Indian apostolate while denying the South Indian apostolate altogether; a fourth group totally denies any sort of Indian apostolate of Thomas.[27]

That Thomas went to India cannot be denied thanks to the overwhelming evidence testifying it, but where in India he went *first* – the north or to the south – is the problem. Some believe he went first to the north of India, from where he moved to the south, while some others hold that he went to the peninsular India in the south before going to the northern part. Those who say that he went to the north are not sure if he travelled by land taking the Silk Route or by sea. Anyway, it is immaterial how he travelled or to which part of India he went first; both tradition and a sizeable body of documentary evidence concur that he did go to India and preached Christianity. Besides, tradition has it that he introduced Christianity in India and what is believed to be his tomb is in India.[28]

Professor Ninan in his paper presented during the Fermont celebrations in 1997, states that Thomas travelled by ship and landed in a port called Sandruk Mahosa. He went from there to the Kingdom of Gudophoara of the Parthian dynasty from Takshasila, in the Indus Valley. King Gudophoara had been a mysterious character until recent excavations brought out some coins, on one side of which is Gudophoara's face with his name clearly inscribed and on the other side, the figure of Siva, a Hindu god, with the trident and the inscription '"maharaja-rajaraja-samahata-dramia-devavrata-Gundaphorasa" written in Greek.[29] He flourished in the first century CE, succeeding to the throne in 16 CE as the inscription on Takth-I-Bahi stone, measuring 42.5 by 36.25 cm and which is in the Lahore Museum, shows. Thomas converted many people in the region to Christianity and appointed one Xantippus (Xenophon) as deacon to the churches in North India, after which he travelled all over India on a proselytising mission.[30]

Most scholars, however, aver that he first landed in Kodungallur in Kerala on the west coast of peninsular India,[31] where he baptised many people and established seven churches. They are Malayattur, Palayur (near Chavakkad), Koovakkayal near (North Paravur), Kokkamangalam (South Pallippuram), Kollam, Niranam and Nilakkal. Nevertheless, there is no consensus among modern historians about the historical veracity of this tradition, but Sreedhara Menon, a noted Kerala historian, does not dispute its possibility. He writes, "Christianity was introduced in Kerala in the first century AD (CE) that is, three centuries before it gained official recognition in Europe or became the established religion in Rome. (It became the official state religion of the Roman Empire under Constantine, following his conversion to Christianity in 312 CE only.) The belief in the St. Thomas tradition is firm and widespread among the Christians of Kerala, though many modern historians have rejected the evidence on which it rests. In the background of the extensive trade relations between Kerala and the Mediterranean countries before the Christian Era, *there is nothing intrinsically improbable in the St. Thomas tradition.* The traditional account preserved by the Jews who came to Cranganore (Kodungallur) in 68 AD (CE) contains a reference to the existence of a Christian community at the place. The statement of Pantaenus, the head of the Alexandrian School who visited Kerala in the second century AD (CE), that he found a flourishing Christian community here is also cited as evidence in favour of the apostolic origin of the Kerala church."[32] Eusebius, in his book *Ecclesiastical History*, records that Pantaenus, a stoic philosopher who later embraced Christianity and became a Christian missionary, visited South India, when he found the Gospel of Matthew in Hebrew with the Christians there. Basham states "at the time contact between India and the West was close and an enterprising missionary could easily have travelled from Palestine to India."[33]

A small community of Christians, called *Tardaiqual naiquenar*, claiming to be descendants of the Apostle Thomas, Mundadan writes, was found in "Bepur" (Beypore), a port at the mouth of the Beypore river, on the Malabar (Kerala) coast.[34] The possibility of Thomas going to Beypore cannot be ruled out because, Logan in his "Manual of Malabar" associates Ophir with the port of Beypore, at which, he surmises, King Solomon's mercantile marine frequently called even as early as 1000 BCE. So Thomas would have heard of Beypore. All this, however, can certainly be treated as evidence of Jesus' historicity and cannot be rejected or regarded as inconsequential. It may be noted that Jesus died in 33 CE and a Christian community existed in Kerala when the Jews arrived there just about thirty-five years later from the country of the birth of Christianity where it was yet to strike root. Unless one of the apostles had come to India to spread the Gospel, this would not have happened, for by then it had not come to be accepted even in the neighbouring countries of Judaea, where apostles had been preaching since the death of Jesus. It is also significant that those who were converted by Thomas were known in Malayalam as

Nasraanikal, the Malayalam form of "Nazoraeans" or "Nazarenes," as the followers of Jesus were called in those times in the land of its birth itself. The term *Kristianikal*, the Malayalam word for "Christians" came into use much later.

After his apostolic work in Kerala he moved to Chennai in Tamil Nadu, where he converted many people to Christianity. According to tradition, during his apostolic work in Chennai (Madras), he is believed to have stayed in a cave at what is now called Little Mount[35] in Saidapet. A few years later, he seemed to have invited the wrath of the Hindu priesthood and escaped to a mountain, now called St. Thomas Mount, on the outskirts of the city, where he was killed by the Hindu fanatics. His body was taken by his followers and buried at Mylapore, where his tomb still exists, which has not been disputed by anyone so far. "In the four hundred years between 1523 and 1903 the tomb in Mylapore was broken open three times for one reason or other: in 1523 the first Portuguese excavation took place; in 1893-1896 the present Gothic cathedral was built; in 1903 the tomb was widened westward when the present crypt was built in commemoration of the tricentenary of the erection of the Mylapore diocese."[36] In *c.* 200 CE, it is believed his remains had been removed to Edessa. This is testified by an entry in a Syrian ecclesiastical calendar which states that Thomas was pierced with a lance in India and his body is at Urhai (old name of Edessa) where it was brought by a merchant called Khabin. Ephraem who, in the forty-second of his *Carmina Nisibina* writes, the Apostle was killed in India and his remains were subsequently buried in Edessa brought there by a merchant.[37] These remains were later taken from there to Ortona in Italy where they now lie entombed.[38]

It has been found that the bricks used for the tomb said to be of the Apostle Thomas are similar to those used for a Roman settlement of the early first century CE, the remains of which were exhumed by the Archaeological Department of India in 1945 in Arikemedu, a place not far from Mylapore. There is, therefore, no doubt that the tomb was built sometime in the first century CE, when the tradition says Thomas was killed. So it may not be wrong to presume that the tomb was that of Thomas the Apostle and, as the bricks used for the tomb were of the first century CE, he must have died sometime in the first century.

It cannot be, therefore, denied that he died in Tamila Nadu and naturally he would have gone there soon after completing his apostolic work in Kerala. He could not have been foolish enough to go all the way to North India and again come back to Tamil Nadu, which lay adjacent to Kerala. His apostolic work in India obviously ended in Tamil Nadu, where he was murdered, and so there was also no possibility of his going to the north from there. However, that Thomas had been to the north is indisputable. Prof. Ninan's paper on Thomas' apostolic work in the north and the Apostle's association with king Gudaphoara testify that he had been to the north. If that testimony is accepted, after that only he came down to the south, and it is also incontestable that he carried out apostolic work both in the north and the south. And his journey to the south could have been by sea, disembarking at Beypore or Kodungallur in Kerala. Had he come by land from the north, he would have carried out his apostolic work in Tamil Nadu before he moved to Kerala. That he went to Kerala from Tamil Nadu is not possible because as his tomb testifies, he spent his last days in Tamil Nadu where he was killed.

Those who doubt the veracity of Thomas' apostolic work in India and the fact that it spread in India even before it found acceptance in the land of its birth are those who are ignorant of the social condition in India in those times. Hinduism was (and is) a very liberal, non-institutionalised polytheistic religion which gives unbridled freedom of thought and worship to its followers. But the Hindu community was riven by the caste system and inhuman practices like untouchability,[39] the notion that touching persons belonging to a low caste defiles members of higher castes, were widespread in those days. And if a high-caste Hindu by accident touches a low-caste he has to cleanse himself by taking a ritual bath. In those days in Kerala, a state in the west coast of the peninsular India, even seeing a low-caste person was believed to pollute one of the high-caste. Incidentally, this provoked Swami Vivekananda, a Hindu monk and religious reformer of the twentieth century, to call Kerala a "lunatic asylum."

India, and particularly Kerala, was thus a fertile ground for proselytisation, and it was in such a society that Apostle Thomas found himself when he landed at Kodungallur, a port in the erstwhile kingdom of Cochin, which today is a part of Kerala State. Once a person was converted to Christianity, he was not considered an untouchable anymore and he acquired a status in society equal to that of a high-caste Hindu. So the low-caste Hindus naturally found conversion to Christianity an easy way of escape from their demeaning social condition and willingly converted themselves to Christianity in large numbers. The patronage extended to Apostle Thomas by the king of Cochin gave a certain amount of prestige and respect to him as well as to Christianity. This prompted even a few higher caste Hindus also to convert to the new religion. No wonder Christianity caught on in India long before it was accepted even in the country of its birth.

Let us now go into the historicity of Simon whom Jesus named Peter who was another member of the Apostolic Committee constituted by Jesus. Tradition has it that Simon died in Rome and was buried in a cemetery underneath what is now known as St. Peter's Basilica. There is no archaeological evidence to substantiate this claim whatever the traditionalists say, notwithstanding. In fact, the Vatican had been excavating there extensively, hoping to find some evidence of it, in vain. First of all the argument that Simon died in Rome is based on flimsy grounds and cannot be accepted. McBirnie relies on a few verses in "The Revelation of St. John the Divine,"[40] which he himself describes as "a cryptic account of martyrdom of Paul and Peter."[41] It is, no doubt, difficult to connect these verses with the death of Paul and Peter by any stretch of imagination. Besides, the value of McBirnie's testimony from a historian's perspective is questionable as he regards all miracles as historical facts and depends totally on tradition.

It may be noted that in a Judeo-Christian necropolis of Dominus Flevit, an ossuary inscribed with the name "Shimon bar Jonah" (Shimon, son of Jonah) had been found some time in the latter half of the twentieth century. Shimon is the Hebrew form of the name Simon. This was ignored by the Church, probably because it was found in a Judeo-Christian cemetery or because it was not in the Vatican as it had been thought to be. More research needs to be done to verify the authenticity of it, which at present remains ignored in a museum in the back of the Church of the Flagellation.[42] These two tombs of the two apostles, if authenticated – there is no reason to disbelieve it, despite the unwillingness of the Church to take notice of and probe into the genuineness of Peter's ossuary – prove their historicity beyond doubt and by extension, the historicity of Jesus too.

In short, the twelve Apostles – two of which were Thomas with the surname Didymus, who was called "Doubting Thomas and Simon the Peter – are all said to have been selected by Jesus himself and as such were contemporaries of Jesus. There is no doubt that Thomas, one of these Apostles, flourished in the first century CE and was actively carrying out apostolic work. And an ossuary said to be of Peter, though ignored by the Church, proves that such a person did exist. That these two Apostles were historical persons indirectly proves the historicity of Jesus, whose life was intermingled with the Apostles. As a historical personality, Jesus was not the "Son of God" and could not have been fathered by the Holy Ghost but only by a human being and was a son of a man, whoever it was.

That brings us to the problem of Jesus' paternity. When his mother, Mary, was pregnant, the angel, one of the mythical characters in the Bible says, "that which is conceived in her" was of the Holy Ghost.[43] In other words, Jesus was not fathered by man, which in ordinary language means that she conceived without having sex with a man. Biologically, the doctrine of Immaculate Conception in an impossibility as explained in Chapter 8 and as such is nothing but an absurdity. The doctrine is a motivated *suggestio falsi* as it were, which had been concocted by an imaginative brain with the intention of covering with a religious cloak the fact that Mary had illicit premarital sex; and to give Jesus an aura of divinity by portraying him as the embodiment of the Holy Ghost and as Son of God.

She must have had a sexual relationship with a man but for which she would not have conceived. Who that was, is a question that has to be addressed. Let us, therefore, investigate Jesus' paternity looking at all three of them, Joseph, Mary and Jesus, as ordinary human beings – man, woman and child – in flesh and blood, accepting the fact that Mary had become pregnant before her betrothal as a result of premarital sex.

Apart from Joseph and Mary, the two people who knew of Mary's pregnancy were Elisabeth and Zacharias, to whom she is said to have confessed it. But did she confide to them who the person responsible for the pregnancy was? From what followed, it may be assumed that she did. Anyway, it cannot be denied that someone, a human being, had seduced her or raped her; or she had consensual sex with someone before her betrothal. Judging by the ethic of the Hebrew society of those times, having premarital sex and getting pregnant was not a serious crime; nor would it be a stigma on the woman or her family. Under the Mosaic Law "if a man finds a damsel that is a virgin, who is not betrothed, and he seizes her, and sleeps with her, and they be found," the man would give fifty shekels to her father. The law further stipulates that he was bound to marry her as he had outraged her modesty and he would have no right at all to divorce her under any circumstances.[44]

But the secrecy surrounding Mary's pregnancy is intriguing and raises a few questions. Who could that be with whom she had slept? Did Mary confidentially tell Joseph about her pregnancy after their betrothal? How else could *he* have known of her pregnancy before the consummation of their marriage? We understand from the Bible that Mary got pregnant in Nazareth, from which it can be inferred that at the time she got pregnant she was staying in Nazareth.[45] The Bible does not disclose who Mary's parents were and with whom and in which city or village Mary was living as a child before her betrothal and where the betrothal took place; nor does it say anything about her marriage. However, the Infancy Gospel of James (IGJ) or the Protoevangelion (an apocryphal Gospel ascribed to the second century CE) states that Mary's parents were Joachim and Anne. This may be accepted considering the date of its composition which was only a few years after the crucifixion of Jesus and the fact that the Gospel was authored by James who was the stepbrother of Jesus. The earliest known manuscript of this Gospel, a papyrus dating back to c. 3th century, is preserved in the Bodmer Library of Geneva and it was Origen of Alexandria who first mentioned this work.

According to that Gospel, an elderly couple without children, Joachim and Anne, stood condemned by the society, to which a barren woman like Anne was unacceptable. They were socially ostracized and the priests even refused to accept Joachim's offerings as he was childless. Joachim finds to his dismay that "in the history of the twelve tribes of his people" he is the only one who is childless and he withdraws into the wilderness to lead a life of asceticism until god tells him why Anne is not conceiving. Anne is now in a worse situation. Shunned by the society and deserted by her husband also, she suffers alone the ignominy of her barrenness. So she has been lamenting and praying to god to give her a child and in her old age, when her husband has been away in the wilderness, Anne gets pregnant. The story of Anne's pregnancy is not different from those of the pregnancies of Elisabeth, the mother of John the Baptist, and Mary, the mother of Jesus.

One day a messenger of god appears before her and informs her that god has heard her prayer and she will soon conceive. The same angel goes to Joachim also to tell him that his wife Anne is now pregnant.[46] And Joachim returns home. It is questionable how she conceived when Joachim was away and also if at such an old age, past the period of menopause, a woman can conceive. So Anne's pregnancy, like the pregnancies of Elisabeth and Mary, is a myth. However, since she had a husband, forgetting the fact that she got pregnant when he had retreated into the wilderness to fast and pray, we may presume that she got pregnant as any faithful married woman would.

Mary, who was born to Anne at an advanced age, was the first and the last child of that couple and needless to say, she had no siblings. Being too old to take care of the child, the parents left her at the age of three at the temple of which Zacharias, husband of Mary's cousin, Elisabeth, was the high priest.[47] This temple, as can be deduced from the Gospel of Luke, was in "a city of Judah,"[48] which, probably, was Jerusalem, and so it can be inferred that Mary was born and brought up in Jerusalem and her ancestral house was in that city. And for the next ten years she had been living in the temple. Now that she was thirteen, in order to avoid the temple being polluted when the girl attained puberty, the priests in whose care her parents had left her, decided to marry her off to Joseph, an old carpenter, who was a widower with two grown-up sons. Obviously her parents had passed away by that time, for had they been alive, Mary would have been sent back home to her parents. Or, at least her parents would have been informed of the intention to get her married and they would have come to the temple when the child was being handed over to Joseph. Joseph, however, refused to marry her, saying he would be ridiculed by the people if he, a man in an advanced age, married such a young girl.[49] However, when the priests said that it was god's command that the girl had to be left in his care and insisted on his taking care of her, Joseph agreed and said he would be her guardian *in loco parentis*.

Who was Joseph? Both Matthew and Luke trace his ancestry to Abraham and Luke goes back further, tracing it to Adam and god. There are glaring discrepancies in the two genealogical trees, both of which, of course are manifestly fictitious, intended to mythify Joseph. The Evangelists Matthew and Luke or whoever were the scribes, must have drawn the material for their Gospels obviously from two different traditions or sources. Luke explicitly states that he derived his facts from "eyewitnesses and ministers of the word"[50] while Matthew does not reveal his source; hence the differences in the genealogy of Joseph that these two Gospels give are understandable. Anyway, as both the genealogical trees show, he was a descendant of David.

Coming back to the story of Mary, after agreeing to be her guardian Joseph took her to his house in Nazareth where he stayed[51] with his two sons that he fathered in his late wife, and no sooner he arrived home than he left her in his house and went to work. It was during her stay there, when she was perhaps going on to fifteen or sixteen, that she attained puberty, after which Joseph either raped her or slept with her. As Joseph was reputed to be a just man, he would not have raped her and even if he had such an intention, the presence of his two sons in the house must have deterred him from that heinous action. Possibly, Mary had consented to have sex with him, for which she could not be found fault with. That Joseph was the man to whom the priests had thought fit to marry her off must have been at the back of her mind when she agreed to sleep with him. The same thought must have encouraged Joseph also to make advances to her. As they had been living together for over two to three years now, they must have fallen in love; and probably, they must have had sex many times since Mary attained puberty. He was, however, hesitating to propose to her, thinking of the disparity in their ages. Meanwhile, Mary realised that she had become pregnant. She had completed sixteen[52] when she came to know that she was pregnant, but reticent as she was and feeling shy, she did not tell Joseph.

It may be surmised that one day, back at home in the evening after work, Joseph proposed to her. She was naturally delighted. She too was in love with him and perhaps waiting for him to propose as she knew the baby growing in her womb was his. So she gladly consented but still, being a teenager she was too timid and shy to tell him that she was pregnant. Why did Joseph who thought he was too old to marry so young a girl suddenly decide to take the plunge? Of course he had begun to love her and had also slept with her and from her behaviour he must have guessed that she too was in love with him. But his main objection to marrying her was the possibility of the people of Jerusalem deriding him. So either he had consulted the people or the elders in the city must have questioned him about his relationship with Mary. They must have asked why an old widower like him was co-habiting with a young unmarried girl. They would have said he could as well marry her if he wanted a wife and that remarriage of a widower was not forbidden by the Mosaic Law. In case he wanted one of them to speak to the girl, they must have said, they could. They would convince her that it was improper for a young, unmarried girl to co-habit with a widower and that it would be better for them to get married. That, perhaps, made Joseph reconsider his earlier decision not to marry her because of the difference in age and he now thought that the elders in the community would not ridicule him for marrying a young girl.

And he betrothed her. The Bible does not say where they had their betrothal. Joseph did not want to have it in Nazareth because although he knew that the elders would not mock him, he was not sure how the youngsters would view it. So the betrothal must have been at the temple in Jerusalem where Zacharias was the priest. Even after the formal engagement, Mary hesitated to tell him that she was pregnant. Perhaps, she did not know how to put it across to him and how he would take it. There was no other woman, a close relative, to whom she could confide and who in turn would have conveyed the news to Joseph. As no one in Nazareth knew of their betrothal – in the eyes of the people of Nazareth, she was not even his fiancée – he feared the gossips of Nazareth would scandalise her if she stayed with him. Worse still, he would fall foul of the elders of Nazareth who had hinted it was unacceptable that he co-habited with an unmarried girl.

So he left her in her ancestral home in Jerusalem. Since Mary was alone in her house Joseph visited her occasionally and, as can be expected, he often slept with her.

Mary now decided to go to her cousin Elisabeth whose husband was Zacharias who was the high priest of the temple where she had stayed as a girl till she was taken under the wing of Joseph. So she told Joseph that she was going to stay with her cousin for a few days and went to Elisabeth's house. She had gone there with the idea of confiding to her and seeking her advice or asking her to tell Joseph about her pregnancy. They knew how miserable it had been for Mary's parents because they were childless, as her mother, Anne, was barren and so both Elisabeth and Zacharias were very happy to know that Mary was pregnant. Elisabeth was six months pregnant then. Nevertheless, Mary stayed with them and when "Elisabeth's full time came that she should be delivered"[53] Mary had to go back to her ancestral home. She was three months pregnant then and had begun to show and being shy by nature, she did not want anyone to see her.[54] So she seldom stirred out of the house.

Three months had elapsed and Joseph decided to go to Jerusalem to find out if Mary was back at home. So that evening after his work, he went to Jerusalem and on entering her house, he was shocked to see her pregnant. He was furious and castigated her for making a cuckold of him and wanted to know who was responsible for her pregnancy. He wept bitterly, for he had loved her so much and could not bear to think that she had cheated on him. He asked her how she could do this to him when she knew that he loved her like the apple of the eye. And he said he did not know how he could face the people of Nazareth now, for they would all laugh at him with contempt.[55] Mary cried her eyes out and swore she did not cheat on him. She said the baby in her womb was his and she had conceived even before their betrothal. But naturally he would not believe it because she had not even hinted that she was pregnant. Meanwhile Annas, a scribe, happened to go there and seeing Mary pregnant, he ran to the high priest that was Zacharias and told him that Joseph had broken the law by defiling the girl whom he had not married yet.[56] Maybe, he also told him that Joseph was in a very bad temper and Mary was crying.

Zacharias guessed what was happening there and thought he must clear Joseph's suspicion. However, to satisfy the scribe and the society, he sent his servant to Mary's house with the message that both of them should present themselves at the court. So Joseph and Mary went and Zacharias was waiting for them. He spoke at length to Joseph about Mary's unblemished character. He told him that she had not been unfaithful to him and convinced him of her innocence.[57] It was not as the Bible says an angel that spoke to Joseph in his dream but Zacharias who spoke to him when Joseph was fully awake. The news of Mary's pregnancy, to explain it figuratively, had dazed him as it were, as he suspected her of infidelity, and the conversation he had with Zacharias seemed like a dream and he considered Zacharias an angel as he cleared his suspicion about Mary's fidelity. Anyway Zacharias did not have much difficulty in convincing Joseph of Mary's faithfulness to him, for Joseph had great respect for Zacharias as all laymen had for priests in those days. He did not think that being a priest Zacharias would lie, especially in a case that was probably related to adultery. He was relieved, for he truly loved Mary and loved her passionately and now he was happy that Mary was pregnant. So it is not surprising that he decided to marry her even after knowing that she was pregnant before they were betrothed, for he was certain that he himself had fathered the baby in her womb.

But Joseph faced another problem. He had not married her so far (although in one place Matthew refers to him as Mary's husband,[58] nowhere in the Bible it is said that they got married). If she had her delivery in Nazareth or Jerusalem, the people would know that she conceived before her marriage. Even if he were to marry her now and when Mary was delivered of a fully developed baby in about three to four months, it would be scandalous. How could he avoid such a situation? Zacharias understood his predicament and told him not to go to Nazareth or to stay in Jerusalem. He advised Joseph to take Mary from Jerusalem and go to Bethlehem in Judah, a city far from Nazareth but not very far (a little over nine kilometres or five miles) from Jerusalem for Mary's delivery that was expected in about three months.[59] The Bible connects their moving out of Nazareth with the census ordered by Tiberius[60] and thus avoids the problem of explaining the reason for the two of them going to an unknown place, Bethlehem, when Mary was in the sixth month of pregnancy. So Mary was delivered of the baby in Bethlehem.

It is to avoid answering many embarrassing questions that the Bible is silent about their marriage; it does not say when they got married or where they got married. The editors of the Bible did not want any blemish on the characters of Joseph and Mary; nor did they want Jesus to have a stigma as a child born out of wedlock. As it is, by stating that she was conceived of the Holy Ghost or describing Mary's pregnancy as Immaculate Conception, Mary cannot be blamed of immorality and Joseph who consented to marry her knowing that she was pregnant before their betrothal, is seen as "a just man." Above all, Jesus cannot be regarded as a child of an unwed mother. He is now considered the "Son of God" and that helped composers of the Gospels to portray him as a Messiah.

There is, therefore, no gainsaying the fact that Mary had conceived only after having sex with a man before their marriage and that person who was the biological father of Jesus was none other than Joseph himself. And Joseph's suspicion was baseless. Now that we know without an iota of doubt that the only person she had sex with was Joseph, it can be said that her character was irreproachable and her chastity was impeccable but she was deflowered before her marriage and was no more a virgin. Her virginity is as much a myth as her Immaculate Conception .

So Jesus' biological parents were Joseph and Mary and Jesus was the *son of a man* like any other human being on this earth. He was not a creation of the Christologists or god in human form, as some religious scholars tend to assert deliberately downplaying his historicity. Unfortunately, the historical Jesus has been eclipsed by the Jesus of Christology, the reason for which is the undue importance given to the religious movement that his Apostles led after his death over the revolutionary movement that he spearheaded and shoving him into the realm of mythology, thereby diminishing his stature. So it can be said with certainty that he was a true son of man who fought and sacrificed his life on the altar of freedom from hegemonistic imperial Rome. The torch of freedom that he lit then had been ablaze and could not be put out. No wonder, a few years later the fire of anti-imperialism engulfed the land of Judaea and shook the mighty Roman

Empire to its very foundation. Looking at his life and teachings from a materialist perspective, it has to be conceded that the Jesus of history is far greater and more important than the Jesus of Christology.

NOTES

1. Acts 1:23-26.
2. Mt. 24:27, 37, 44/26:2, 24, 45 to give a few instances when he said he was son of man.
3. A. Schweitzer, *The Quest of the Historical Jesus*, New York, 1961, p. 4. The secret order that Schweitzer refers to is the Illuminati, the objective of which was the furtherance of rational religion.
4. A. Schweitzer, ibid., p. 398.
5. Russell, B., *Why I am Not a Christian*, G. Allen and Unwin, London, 1964, p. 11.
6. I. Asimov, *Guide to the Bible*, New York, 1981, p. 809.
7. H. Daniel-Rops, *Jesus and His Times*, tr. by Ruby Millar, New York, 1954, p. 14.
8. F. Josephus, The Antiquities of the Jews, 18,3,3. In *Complete Works*, tr. By W. Whiston, Grand Rapids, 1977, p. 379.
9. Ibid, 20,9,1. In *Complete Works*, p. 423.
10. Tacitus, *The Annals*, xv (CE 62-65), tr. by A.J.Church and W.J. Bodribb. The Internet Classics Archive by Daniel C. Stevenson.
11. Suetonius, Lives of the Caesars, Section xxv.
12. Acts 18:2.
13. All those books must have been indubitably destroyed by the Jews who have always been religious bigots and intolerant of other religions.
14. Lucian, *Passing of Peregrinus*, tr. by A.M.Harman, 1936 and extract transcribed by Roger Pearson, 2001. (On-line) [Note by Roger Pearson: "...this version is now in the public domain pursuant to the 1978 version of the US Copyright Code, since the copyright on the earlier volumes has lapsed and that on the later volumes was not renewed in the appropriate years."]
15. S. Jacobovici and C Pellegrino, *Jesus Family Tomb*, Foreword, New York, 2007, p.vii. The details of this discovery and the particulars of the ossuaries given in this and the following two paragraphs are solely based on this book.
16. Mt. 13:55.
17. This is probably a copy or a redaction of an earlier manuscript. It has not so far been translated into English but a French translation of it

appeared in 1996. The book deals with the evangelical mission of Philip, Mary Magdalene's brother.

18. Jn. 13:25. "Then, leaning back on Jesus' breast, he said to Him, 'Lord, who is it?'"
19. Mk. 14:51-52.
20. Mt. 19:4-6. We do not know if Jesus had actually uttered these words. But it is attributed to Jesus and it reveals his idea of marriage.
21. Mt. 9:12-13.
22. Mt. 19:9.
23. S. Jacobovici and C Pellegrino, op. cit., p. 206.
24. The inscription on James' ossuary states, "Yakov bar Iosef, achuid' Yeshua" which means "Jacob, son of Joseph, brother of Jesus." 'James' was introduced as a translation for the Hebrew 'yakov' or 'Jacob" quite recently. Jacob passing through Latin, Italian, Spanish became James by the time it reached England when in 1611, King James Version of the Bible was under preparation. Prior to that in all Gospels, the names of Jesus' four brothers were given as Jacob, Simon, Joseph and Judah. Vide S. Jacobovici and C Pellegrino, ibid., p. 29.
25. W.S. McBirnie, *The Search for the Twelve Apostles* (Introduction), Wheaton, 1976, p. 12.
26. The reason for choosing these two apostles as examples is given in the Preface.
27. A.M. Mundadan, *Traditions of St. Thomas Christians*, Bangalore, 1970, p. 3.
28. This author had seen this tomb some time in the late 1940s. There was, however, no epitaph on it to identify whose tomb it was.
29. "Maharaja-rajaraja-samahata-dramia-devavrata." This is a title of honour similar to "His Excellency the King and the Emperor."
30. M.M. Ninan, *Story of St. Thomas the Apostle and the St. Thomas Church of India*. Paper presented as a part of the exhibition during the Fermont Celebrations connected with the 50th year of Indian independence (On-line).
31. A.M. Medlycott, St. Thomas Christians. In *Catholic Encyclopaedia*, V. 14, New York, 1912.
32. M.S.Menon, *A Survey of Kerala History*, Kottayam, 1967, p. 99. (Brackets and Italics added).
33. A.L. Basham, *The Wonder that was India*, London, 1954, p. 345.
34. A.M. Mundadan, op. cit., pp. 110-111.
35. This author had visited that site. There is no inscription or any other proof of Thomas' stay there but there are many myths about his stay and the miracles he performed. For example, one of the myths says

that one day, he was thirsty. But being a rocky hillock, there was no water for him to drink and so with his hand he made a pit in the rock and water gushed from it.

36. A.M. Mundadan, op. cit., p. 11.
37. A. Medlycott, St. Thomas Christians. In *Catholic Encyclopaedia*, V.14, New York, 1924.
38. W.S. McBirnie, op. cit., p. 154.
39. This is forbidden under the Constitution of India. Article 17 of the Constitution states, "the enforcement of any disability arising out of untouchability shall be an offence punishable in accordance with law." In spite of this and the laws making untouchability a criminal act, even today this despicable practice has not been totally wiped out.
40. Rev. 11:3-13.
41. W.S. McBirnie, *The Search for the Twelve Apostles*, Wheaton, 1976, p. 64.
42. S. Jacobovici and C. Pellegrino, op. cit., p. 201.
43. Mt. 1:18, Lk. 1:26-35. Holy Ghost or Holy Spirit is the 'Supernatural Power' (Acts 1:8), the 'Absolute' or as the common man says, 'God'. According to the Bible, (New Testament), the Holy Ghost has many attributes. There is no need to go into the details, as it is not relevant to our study. However, here are a few examples of its supposed attributes: the Holy Spirit is god like Father and Son (Mt. 28:19), is mind (Rom 8:27), thought, knowledge and words (I cor. 2:10-13), could be a person lied to and tempted (Acts 5:3, 4,9).
44. Deut. 22:28-29.
45. Lk. 1:26,27,31. "And in the sixth month the angel Gabriel was sent from God unto a city of Galilee, named Nazareth, [26] To a virgin espoused to a man whose name was Joseph of the house of David and the virgin's name was Mary. [27] And behold thou shalt conceive in thy womb and bring forth a son..." [31]
46. IGJ. 4:1-4.
47. Ibid 8:6.
48. Lk. 1:39. "And Mary arose in those days, and went into the hill country with haste, into a city of Judah,..."
49. IGJ. 9:8.
50. Lk. 1:2.
51. Lk. 1:26; 2:4. It can be inferred from these verses that he was living in Nazareth.
52. IGJ. 12:9.
53. Lk. 1:56.
54. IGJ. 12:7-8.

55. Ibid., 13:1-10.
56. Ibid., 15:3-6.
57. Ibid., 16:3-8.
58. Mt. 1:19.
59. Lk. 2:4-5.
60. Lk. 2:1-4

APPENDIX

Genealogical Tables, Lists of Hebrew Kings and Tribes

GENEALOGY OF JESUS CHRIST
(From Adam to Jesus)

According to Matthew

Adam to Abraham

Adam → Seth Enos → Cainan → Mahalaleel → Jared → Enoch → Methuselah → Lamech → Noah[1].........Noah → Shem → Arphaxad → Salah → Eber → Peleg → Reu → Serug → Nahor → Terah → [Abraham (earlier called, Abram)].[2]

Abraham to Jesus

Abraham → Isaac Jacob → Judah → Perez → Hezron → Ram → Amminadab → Nahshon → Salmon → Boaz → Obed → Jesse → **David** [the king][3] → Solomon [the king] → Rehoboam → Abia → Asa →Josaphat → Joram → Ozias → Joatham → Achaz → Ezekias → Manasses→ Amon → Josias → Jechonias (Deportation to Babylon).[4] → Salathiel → Zorobabel → Abiud → Eliakim → Azor → Sadok → Achim → Eliud → Eleazar → Matthan → Jacob → Joseph → Jesus.[5]

According to Luke

God to Jesus

(God →) **Adam** → Seth → Enos → Cainan → Maleleel → Jared → Enoch → Mathusala → Lamech → Noe → Sem →Arphaxad →

Cainan → Sala → Heber → Phalec → Ragau → Saruch → Nachor → Thara → **Abraham** (earlier called, Abram) → Isaac → Jacob → Juda → Phares → Esrom → Aram → Aminadab → Naason → Salmon → Boaz → Obed → Jesse → **David** → Nathan → Mattatha → Menan → Melea → Eliakim → Jonan → Joseph → Juda → Simeon → Levi → Matthat → Jorim → Eliezer → Jose → Er → Elmodam → Cosam → Addi → Melchi → Neri → Salathiel → Zorobabel → Rhesa → Joanna → Juda → Joseph → Semei → Mattathias → Maath → Nagge → Esli → Naum → Amos → Mattathias → Joseph → Janna → Melchi → Levi → Matthat → Heli → Joseph → **Jesus.**[6]

Note: Matthew (New Testament) gives the genealogy of Jesus beginning with Abraham and ending, "...Joseph, the husband of Mary, to whom was born Jesus who is called Christ."[7] And it adds, "So all the generations from Abraham to David are fourteen generations, and from David until the carrying away into Babylon are fourteen generations, and from the carrying away into Babylon unto Christ are fourteen generations."[8] So according to that, there are forty-two generations. However, when you actually count it adds up to only forty-one generations. There are fourteen generations from Abraham to David, the King and another fourteen from Solomon to deportation to Babylon, the fourteenth being Jechonias. But after reaching Babylon till Jesus, as pointed out above, there are only thirteen generations.[9]

Luke, on the other hand gives the genealogy of Jesus in which there are seventy-six generations from Adam to Jesus. He adds "god" also, when it becomes seventy-seven generations.

HEBREW MONARCHS
(Succession of Kings)
(BCE)

Saul 1020-1004
David (c. 1020 to 928)
Solomon 965-928

ISRAEL (Northern Kingdom)

[First Period] Jeroboam, Nadah, Baasha, Elah, Zimri, Omri, Ahab, Ahaziah, **Jehoram,**

[Second Period] Jehu, Jehoahaz, Jehoash, Jeroboam II, [Interrugnum] Zachariah, Shallum, Menahem, Pekahiah, Pekah, Hoshea. (Samaria fell).

JUDAH (Southern Kingdom)

[First Period] (David → Solomon), Rehoboam, Abijah, Asa, Jehoshaphat, Jehoram, Ahaziah,

[Second period] Athalia, Joash, Amaziah, Azariah alias Uzziah, Jotham, Ahaz, Hezekiah, Manasseh, Amon, Josiah, Jehoahaz, Jehoiakim, Jehoiachin, Zedekiah. (Jereusalem destroyed; Judah fell.)

TRIBES OF ISRAEL

Traditional Division

Reuben, Simeon, Levi, Judah, Dan, Naphtali, Gad, Asher, Issachar, Zebulun, Joseph, Benjamin.

Division according to Appointment of Land in Israel

Reuben, Simeon, Judah, Dan, Naphtali, Gad, Asher, Issachar, Zebulun, Joseph, Benjamin, Ephraim, Manasseh.

MACCABEES FAMILY

(Mattathias) → Judas → Jonathan → Simeon → John Hyrcanus → Aristobulus I → Alexander Jannaeus → Salome Alexandra → Aristobulus II →...[The Romans took over]...(Hyrcanus II Matthias Antigonus).

HERODIAN FAMILY

Herod (Antipater) the Great I [First Procurator of Judaea and later, King of Judaea] → (Archelaus; Herod Antipas; Philip) → Herod Agrippa I (Grandson of Herod the Great) [King of the Jews] → Herod Agrippa II [King of territory East of Galilee]

NOTES

1. Gen.5:1-32.
2. Gen.11:10-27. (From Adam to Terah there are nineteen generations.)
3. Mt.1:2-6.

4. Mt.1:7-11.
5. Mt.1:12-16. (From Abraham to Jesus there are only forty-one generatios.)
6. LK.3:23-38. (There are fifty-six generations from Abraham to Jesus)
7. Mt. 1.16.
8. Mt. 1.17.
9. None of the Christian priests and Christian friends of this writer, who were consulted could explain this glaring discrepancy. However, Easau Joseph.John, a teacher who is a friend of the author, wrote back quoting from a commentary on the Bible, which was, perhaps, the only way to explain it. He wrote: True the three fourteens in Mathew Chapter 1 do not arithmetically add up to 42 unless, of course, as you said, you count David and Jechonias twice. Yet, that would make conceptual sense because Abraham, David and Jechonias signalised the start of three remarkable periods, i.e. and I quote, 'In the first fourteen, we have the family of David rising, and looking forth as the morning, in the second, we have it flourishing in its meridian lustre, in the third, we have it declining and growing less and less, dwindling into the family of a poor carpenter, and the Christ shines forth out of it, the glory of his people of Israel.' So by resorting to a sort of what may be described as 'poetic jugglery' the loose ends can be tied up clumsily but it is not quite convincing. For 1+2 can never be 4!

Bibliography

Selected List of Books Suggested for Collateral Reading
(Non-fiction, Novels and Plays)
N.B. The historical veracity of what is stated in some of the books given in this list is questionable.

Anderson, B.W., *Understanding the Old Testament,* Englewood Cliffs, 1975.

Armstrong, K., *A Short History of Myth,* Penguin Books, New Delhi, 2005.

Arnold, Mathew, *Literature and Dogma, An Essay Towards a Better Understanding of the Bible,* New York, 1924.

Asimov, I., Guide to the Bible, Wings Books, New York, 1981.

Baigent, Michael, et al., *The Holy Bible and the Holy Grail,* Dell, London, 1982.

Basham, A.L., *The Wonder that was India,* London, 1954.

Begin, Z.B., et al, "A 40,000 year unchanging seismic regime in the Dead Sea rift," In *Geology, Journal of the Geological Society of America,* April, 2005, V.33, No. 4.

Bevan, E.R. and C. Singer, Eds., *Legacy of Israel,* Clarendon Press, Oxford, 1928.

Blunt, A.W.F., *Israel in World History,* OUP, London, 1927.

Boccaccio, G., *Decameron,* tr. by J.M. Rigg, 1903. (Fiction)

Bojowald, M., "Follow the Bouncing Universe," In *Scientific American,* October, 2008, V.298, No, 4.

Brown, Dan, *DaVinci Code,* 2003. (Fiction)

Buber, M., *On the Bible,* ed .N.Glatzer, New York, 1982.

Campbell, J., *The Masks of God, Primitive Mythology,* Hammondsworth, 1969

Carson, D.A., et al., Eds., *New Bible Commentary,* Secunderabad, 2003.

Catholic Encyclopaedia, The, V.XIV, New York, 1912.

Caudwell, C., *Further Studies in a Dying Culture*, Calcutta, 1990.

Caudwell, C., *Illusion and Reality*, Seven Seas Publishers, Berlin, 1977.

Chardin, T. de, *The Phenomenon of Man*, Harper Colophon Books, New York, 1959.

Chattopadhyaya, D., *Indian Atheism*, Calcutta, 1960.

Childe, G., *What Happened in History*, Hammondsworth, 1975.

Cross, F.M., *Canaanite Myth and Hebrew Epic*, Harvard University Press, Cambridge, 1973.

Daiches, D., *Moses*, Praeger Publishers, New York, 1975.

Daniel-Rops, H., *Daily Life in the Time of Jesus*, tr. by P. O'Brien, Hawthorn Books, New York, 1963.

Daniken, von, *Chariots of the Gods*. (Fiction)

Daniel-Rops, H., *Jesus and his Times*, tr. by Ruby Millar, Dutton, New York, 1954.

Darwin, C., *The Descent of Man*, The Werner Co., Akron, 1874.

Dawkins, Richard, *The God Delusion*, Houghton Mifflin, Boston, 2006.

Dowling, Levi H., *The Life and Work of Jesus in India*, Mosaic Books, New Delhi, 2004.

Ehman, Y., and Gershoni, I., Eds., *Transmitting Jewish Traditions: Orality, Textuality and Cultural Diffusion*, Yale University Press, New Haven, 2000.

Engels, F., *The Family, Private Property and the State*, Moscow, 1948.

Engels, F., *Herr Eugen Duhring's Revolution in Science*, Martin Lawrence, London, 1934.

Erskine, J., *The Human Life of Jesus*, New York, 1946.

Every, George, *Christian Mythology*, Hamlyn, London, 1970.

Faber-Kaiser, A., *Jesus Died in Kashmir*, Gordon & Cremonesi, London, 1977.

Fast, Howard, *Thirty Pieces of Silver*, 1954. (Play)

Fox, Ralph, *The Novel and the People*, Moscow, 1956.

Frazer, J.G., *The Golden Bough*, V.1, Macmillan, New York, 1963.

Friedman, R.E., *Bible with Sources Revealed*, Harper-Collins, New York, 2003.

Friedman, R.E., *Who Wrote the Bible*? New York, 1987.

Fromm, Eric, *You shall be as Gods*, Fawcett, Greenwich, 1969.

Garder, Jostein, *The Christmas Mystery*, tr. by Elizabeth Rokkan (Novel)

Gardner, Laurence, *Bloodlline of the Holy Grail*, Element Books, Shaftesbury, 1996.

Gibbon, E., *Decline and Fall of the Roman Empire*, Frederick Warne, London, 1895, Chapters 15 and 16.

Gibson, S., *Cave of John the Baptist*, The, Doubleday, New York, 2004.

Ginsburgh, Irwin, *First, Man. Then, Adam*, Simon and Schuster, New York, 1977.

Grant, M., *History of Ancient Israel*, The, Charles Scribner, 1984.

Graves, R., *The Greek Myths*, Baltimore, 1955.

Graves, R., *King Jesus*, 1946. (Novel)

Greenberg, Gary, *101 Myths of the Bible*, Naperville, 2000.

Hammer, Meredith, *The Ancient Ecclesiastical Histories of the First Six Hundred Years after Christ* written in the Greek Tongue by Three Learned Historiographers Eufebius, Socrates and Eugarius, Thomas Vautrollier, London, 1585. [English translation]

Haskins, J., *Religions*, Philadelphia, 1973.

Hawkes, J., *The First Great Civilisations*, Random House, New York, 1973.

Hawkings, S., *A Brief History of Science*, London, 1989, p.50.

Hawkings, S., *A Brief History of Time*, Bantam Books, London, 1989.

Haynes, J.M., et al., "Evidence for Ground Rupturing Earthquakes on the Northern Wadi Arab Fault at the Archaeological site of Qasr Tilah, Dead Sea Transform Fault System, Jordan," In *Journal of Seismology*, Netherlands., October. 2006, V.10, No.4, (English version, on-line).

Hoffmeier, J.K., *Israel in Egypt*, New York, 1997.

Hogarth, D.G., *The Ancient East*, New York, (Year ?),

Infancy Gospel of James, tr. by M.R.James, (On-line).

Ingersoll, R.G., *Great Speeches Complete*, Rhodes and McClure, Chicago, 1896.

Jacobovici, S. and Pellegrino, C., *Jesus Family Tomb*, Harper San Francisco, New York, 2007.

Jacobsen, T., "The Eridu Genesis," In *Journal of Biblical Literature*, 100/4, 1981.

John, Erskine, *The Human Life of Jesus*, William Morrow, New York, 1946.

Josephus, Flavius, *Complete Works*, tr. by William Whiston, Kregel Publications, Grand Rapids, 1977.

Kagan, E.J., et al, "Dating Large Infrequent Earthquakes by Damaged Cave Deposits," In *Geology, Journal of the Geological Society of America*, April, 2005, V.33, No. 4.

Kazantsaki, Nikos, *The Last Temptation of Christ*. (Novel)

Keller, Werner, *The Bible as History*, Hodder & Stoughton, London, 1957.

Kempis, Thomas A., *Imitation of Christ*, tr. by B.I. Knott, Fontana, 1967.

Kersten, Holger, *Jesus Lived in India*, Element, Melbourne, 1998.

Koestler, Arthur, *The Thirteenth Tribe*, Random House, New York, 1976.

Krauses, L.M. and Scherrer, R.J., "The End of Cosmology?" *Scientific American*, March 2008, V.298, No.3.

Krosney, Herbert, The Lost Gospel, The Quest for the Gospel of Judas Iscariot, *National Geographic*, Washington, 2006.

Lawrence, Jerome and Lee, Robert E., *Inherit the Wind.* (Play)

Levy, H., *Social Thinking*, Cobbett Press, London, 1945.

Lin, D.N.C., "The Genesis of Planets," In *Scientific American*, May 2008, V.298, No.5.

Linklater, Eric, *Judas.* (Novel)

Logan, W., *Malabar Manual*, V.1., Madras, 1887

Lucian, *Passing of Peregrinus*, tr. by A.M.Harman, 1936 and extract transcribed by Roger Pearson, 2001. (On-line)

Malinowski, B., *Magic, Science, and Religion*, New York, 1954

Marx, K., *A Contribution to the Critique of Hegel's Philosophy of Law*, Progress Publishers, Moscow,1976.

Matthews, J., *The Grail*, Thomas and Hudson, London, 1981.

McBirnie, William S., *The Search for the Twelve Apostles*, Tyndale House Publishers, Wheaton, 1976.

Medlycott, A.M., St. Thomas Christians. In *Catholic Encyclopaedia*, V.14, New York, 1912.

Menon, M.S., *A Survey of Kerala History*, Kottayam, 1967,

Milman, H.H., *The History of the Jews*, V.1, New York, 1870.

Milton, J., *Paradise Lost.* (Poetry)

Morris, D., *The Naked Ape*, Dell Publishing Co., New York, 1967.

Mundadan, A.M., *Traditions of St. Thomas Christians*, Dhrmaram College, Bangalore, 1970.

Newby, G.D., *A Concise Encyclopaedia of Islam*, Oxford, 2002.

Niemi, Tina M. and Ben-Avraham, Zvi, "Evidence for Jericho Earthquakes from Slumped Sediments of the Jordan River Delta in the Dead Sea." In *Geology, Journal of the Geological Society of America*, May 1994, V.22, No.5.

Ninan, M.M., *Story of St. Thomas the Apostle and the St. Thomas Church of India*, (On-line).

Noble *Qur'an, The*, tr., by M.T.Hilali and M.M.Khan, Madinah Al-Munawwarah, Madinah.

Oparin, A.I., *The Origin of Life*, Moscow, 1955.

Osborne, J., *Luther.* (Play)

Pagels, E., *Beyond Belief – The Secret Gospel of Thomas*, New York, 2004.

Parfitt, T., *The Thirteenth Gate*, Adler and Adler, 1987.

Pritchard, J.B., *Gibeon: Where the Sun Stood Still*, Princeton, New Jersey, 1962.

Pusalkar, A.D., The Prehistoric Age. In *The History and Culture of the Indian People*, ed by R.C. Majumdar, et al. Bk.2, Bombay, 1965,

Redford, D.B., *Egypt, Canaan and Israel in Ancient Times*, Princeton University Press, Princeton, 1992.
Richardson, A., *The Origins of Christianity*, Lawrence and Wishart, London, 1953.
Robinson, J.A., *Honest to God*, London, 1976.
Russell, Bertrand, *Why I am Not a Christian*, Watts & Co, London, 1927.
Sachar, A.L., *A History of the Jews*, New York, 1965,
Schniedewind, W.M., *How the Bible Became a Book*, Cambridge University, Cambridge, 2004.
Schniedewind, W.M., *When Was the Bible Written*? CUP, Cambridge, 2004.
Schweitzer, Albert, *The Quest of the Historical Jesus*, The Macmillan, New York, 1961.
Service, E.R., *The Hunters*, Englewood Cliffs, 1966.
Suetonius, T. Gaius, *Lives of the Caesars*, (On-line)
Smith, R.H., *The Book of Joshua*, In 'Old Testament History,' ed. by C.M.Laymon, Nashville,1983
Smith, R.H., *The Book of Judges*. In 'Old Testament History,' Nashville, 1983.
Sora, Stevens, *The Lost Treasure of the Knights Templar*, Rochester, 1999.
Sora, Stevens, *Treasures from the Heaven*, John Wiley, New Jersey, 2005.
Steve, M. J., *The Living World of the Bible*, London, 1961.
Stix, G., "Traces of a Distant Past," In *Scientific American*, July, 2008, V.298, No.1.
Swain, J.W., *The Ancient World*, V.1., Harper Brothers, New York, 1950.
Tacitus, Cornelius, *The Annals*, xv (CE 62-65), tr. by A.J.Church and W.J.Bodribb, The Internet Classics Archive.
Tawney, R.H., *Religion and the Rise of Capitalism*, Penguin, Hammondsworth, 1975.
Thiering, B., *Jesus the Man*, Atria Books, New York, 2006.
Thiessen, H.C., *Introduction to the New Testament*, Grand Rapids, 1962.
Thompson, G.D., *Aeschylus and Aathens*, Berlin, 1977
Toynbee, A., *An Historian's Approach to Religion*, OUP, London, 1956.
Tuckett, C., *Reading the New Testament*, Fortress Press, Philadelphia, 1987.
Wallace, A.R., *Contributions to the Theory of Natural Selection*, London, 1870.
Walter, P., *Christianity: The Origins of a Pagan Religion*, tr, by J.E.Graham, Inner Traditions, Rochester, Vermont, 2006.
Whiston, William, *New Theory of the Earth*, London, 1708.
Whitehouse, Thomas, *Lingerings of Light in a Dark Land; Syrian Church of Malabar*, W. Brown, London, 1873.
Wilson, I., *The Bible is History*, Washington DC, 1999.
Wilson, Ian, *The Blood and the Shroud*, Orion, London, 1999.
Wilson, Ian, *Jesus: The Evidence*, HarperCollins, New York, 1996.
Wilson, Ian, *The Turin Shroud*, London, 1978.

Index